Methods for Teaching Foreign Languages

Creating a Community of Learners in the Classroom

Joan Kelly Hall

University of Georgia

Merrill
Prentice Hall

Upper Saddle River, New Jersey
Columbus, Ohio

Library of Congress Cataloging-in-Publication Data

Hall, Joan Kelly.

Methods for teaching foreign lanuages : creating a community of learners in the classroom / Joan Kelly Hall.

p.cm.

Includes Bibliographical references and index.

ISBN 0-13-087910-X

1. Lanuage and lanuages–Study and teaching. I. Title.

P51 .H29 2002

418'.0071'2–dc21

2001034239

Vice President and Publisher: Jeffery W. Johnston
Acquisitions Editor: Debra A. Stollenwerk
Editorial Assistant: Mary Morrill
Production Editor: Kimberly J. Lundy
Production Coordination: Carlisle Publishers Services
Design Coordinator: Diane C. Lorenzo
Cover Designer: Bryan Huber
Cover Image: SuperStock
Production Manager: Pamela D. Bennett
Director of Marketing: Kevin Flanagan
Marketing Manager: Krista Groshong
Marketing Services Manager: Barbara Koontz

This book was set in Times Roman by Carlisle Communications, Ltd. and was printed and bound by Maple Vail Book Manufacturing Group. The cover was printed by Phoenix Color Corp.

Pearson Education Ltd., London
Pearson Education Australia Pty. Limited, Sydney
Pearson Education Singapore Pte. Ltd.
Pearson Education North Asia Ltd., Hong Kong
Pearson Education Canada, Ltd., Toronto
Pearson Educación de Mexico, S.A. de C.V.
Pearson Education—Japan, Tokyo
Pearson Education Malaysia Pte. Ltd.
Pearson Education, Upper Saddle River, New Jersey

10 9 8 7 6 5 4 3 2 1
ISBN 0-13-087910-X

Preface

Methods for Teaching Foreign Languages: Creating a Community of Learners in the Classroom provides a comprehensive approach to designing curriculum, instruction, and assessment for foreign language programs in middle schools and high schools. Based on a sociocultural understanding of language and development, the book attempts to bridge pedagogical theory and practice, and thus provides a principled basis for making curricular, instructional, and assessment decisions about classroom foreign language learning.

The text first presents a conceptual framework built on theoretical insights and recent empirical findings from a wide range of studies on communication and communicative development in both first and second languages. It then uses this framework to lay out an approach to designing foreign language pedagogy organized around the new *National Foreign Language Standards.*

The text is intended for preservice and in-service teachers of modern foreign languages who aspire to teach or already teach in middle and high school language programs, and who are unfamiliar with a sociocultural approach to teaching and learning. Its purpose is to help these teachers develop the knowledge and skills needed to create and sustain classroom communities of successful foreign language learners.

Readers will be guided through discussions on such essential concepts as communication, communicative development, communicative competence, and multicompetence. They will also be guided through the processes of designing curriculum based on the national foreign language standards, creating instructional activities that are linked to their curricular goals, and devising effective tools for assessing student learning. Finally, throughout most of the text, they will be guided in the design of projects for researching issues that are of particular concern to them in their teaching contexts.

TEXT ORGANIZATION AND COVERAGE

The book consists of nine chapters. Chapter 1 presents an overview of a sociocultural perspective on communication and language. Chapter 2 discusses current understandings of communicative development and the implications for the middle and high school foreign language classroom. Chapter 3 reviews research on practices that have been shown to lead to the establishment of effectual communities of learners. It also includes a discussion on the importance of teacher research. Chapter 4 addresses the role of classroom discourse in learning in general, and, more specifically, in foreign language learning. Chapter 5 presents guidelines for planning instruction and designing effective assessment tools.

Discussions in Chapters 6, 7, and 8 draw together the diverse concepts and ideas presented in Chapters 1 through 5 and apply them to the design of effective instruction and assessment around the three modes of the Communication Standards: Interpersonal, Interpretive, and Presentational. Each chapter reviews the relevant research on one of the three modes and presents a framework for crafting effective pedagogy. Finally, Chapter 9 discusses the nature of professional development and provides ideas for becoming an active member of the foreign language education profession and for sustaining lifelong learning.

FEATURES

Each chapter begins with a set of Preview Questions intended to get the reader thinking about the topical content. The questions are followed by a list of Key Words and Concepts that are presented in the chapter. Key words and concepts appear in boldface type when first mentioned.

The body of each chapter opens with an Overview of the chapter's content and organization. Each chapter concludes with a Summary of the ideas and concepts presented in the chapter, and a list of Discussion Questions and Activities that can be used for in-class discussions or assigned as project work to be completed outside of the regular class. In addition, beginning with Chapter 3, guides for two Teacher Research Projects based on the chapter's content follow the Discussion Questions and Activities. Following the research project guides is a list of Additional Readings and a list of Internet Resources that are pertinent to the topics discussed in the chapter.

TEXT AUDIENCE

The text is intended for use in undergraduate and graduate programs that prepare students of modern languages other than English to teach in middle and high school language programs in the United States. The decision to focus on this particular audience was based on a number of considerations. First, while it is recognized that some middle and high school programs may teach a few less commonly taught languages such as Japanese and Chinese, three Indo-European languages—French, German, and Spanish—are the predominant teaching languages in most programs. Consequently, the majority of students who enter teacher preparation programs across the United States come for their certification to teach one or more of these languages in grades K–12. Thus, this text addresses their needs as teachers of modern foreign languages. While those who teach less commonly taught or classical languages may find some of the information contained in this text useful, they will also require additional texts that address their unique needs.

Second, although second and foreign language learning share considerable theoretical similarities, there is at least one main practical difference: the learners' needs and motivations for learning the additional language. In most literature, the term *second language learner* commonly refers to students who are learning English as an additional language in school programs in the United States, and who need English in order to succeed academically.

Consequently, their reasons for learning English, and the kinds of instructional environments they are likely to be in, are considerably different from those of English-speaking students who study another language. Learners of English are likely to be in classrooms in which most of the instruction occurs in a language with which they are unfamiliar and with many students with whom they cannot converse or have little in common. Moreover, their language needs are likely to be centered on the communicative components needed to master the core academic subjects of math, science, English language arts, and social studies.

On the other hand, *foreign language learners'* interests may range from the minimal need to meet program requirements to the desire to become fluent in the language so that they can travel to places where the language is used as the primary code. However, since they do not need target language skills to succeed in other academic subjects, nor to be successful outside the classroom, their needs are not urgent.

Moreover, exposure to and opportunities for target language interaction are far more restricted for *foreign language learners* than they are for *second language learners*. Many *foreign language learners* have few opportunities to use the target language with target language speakers outside the classroom. This makes the environments created in their classrooms of critical importance to their communicative development in the target language.

In contrast, most *second language learners* must use the language not only for school learning, but also for everyday real-life situations. Most *second language learners,* then, are immersed in the target language and culture both inside and outside school, and thus have greater opportunities for using the target language in different contexts, with different interlocutors, and for a wide range of purposes. These differences create student populations with very different needs.

Consequently, the conditions fostering effective communities of learners in second and foreign language classrooms will differ, in many cases, considerably. For this reason, students who are preparing to be second and foreign language teachers need different kinds of texts. As noted previously, this text is geared specifically to those who aspire to teach or are teaching a modern language other than English to middle and high school learners. Those who want to teach English as a second language require different texts, which are addressed to their specific pedagogical needs. Fortunately, there are many high-quality texts for this group already on the market.

The third reason for focusing on teachers of middle and high school students is because of their especially important role as foreign language teachers. For many learners of foreign languages, at least in the United States, their only exposure to another language is in the foreign language classroom. For many students, their *first* and, sometimes, *only* exposure occurs in a middle or high school program. As we know, the beginning years of language learning are of crucial importance to learners' communicative development in the target language. What the students learn in the beginning years of instruction, both in terms of what counts as language and as the process of learning, sets the foundation upon which their subsequent communicative development is based.

In other words, the learning environments created in middle and high school classrooms—and the teachers who help to create them—are of great consequence to students' development as language learners and users, and more generally to the maintenance of successful foreign language programs. Given the crucial importance of preparing teachers who can create effectual communities of learners in these classrooms, teachers of middle and high school students deserve a text that is addressed specifically to their needs. Those who are preparing to teach children in elementary foreign language programs or, on the other end of the academic spectrum—young adults in university programs—may find some of the information in this text useful and pertinent to their needs. However, it is likely that they will need additional texts that address their unique learning environments and the distinguishing characteristics of their learners.

ACKNOWLEDGMENTS

Methods for Teaching Foreign Languages: Creating a Community of Learners in the Classroom was written after more than 15 years of working with preservice and in-service foreign language teachers in teacher preparation programs and education courses, plus many more years of being a Spanish language learner. My own foreign language learning experiences began in the seventh grade with Sister Margarita, who in her Spanish classroom opened the door to new worlds and exciting adventures. It continued in high school with Mrs. Lee, for whom Spanish language learning was an endless source of joy and delight. The strong communities of Spanish language learners these teachers created in my middle and high school foreign language classrooms formed the foundation of my language-learning experiences and instilled in me a love of Spanish, and the worlds it opens onto, that continues to this day. I am deeply grateful to them and to my lifelong teacher and friend, Sonia Suazo.

Several people have been instrumental in helping me complete what has been a prolonged, but, in the end, exciting and pleasurable experience. In developing the ideas found here, I have benefited immensely from discussions over the years with many friends and colleagues who have served as mentors and models of scholarship. I am indebted, in particular, to Jim Lantolf, Alan Purves, Bob Sanders, Merrill Swain, and Rose-Marie Weber. In addition, I am grateful to Diana Boxer, Pete Brooks, Florencia Cortes-Conde, Rick Donato, David Shea, Steve Thorne, and Lorrie Verplaetse for some of the more intellectually interesting and entertaining conversations on language and learning that I have had the pleasure of participating in.

For the preparation of this book, I am grateful to Teresa Wise and Hyun-Woo Lim for their help with the finer details of editing, and to my department head, Joel Taxel, for affording me the time to write. Two people in particular, Bob Flannigan and Lucinda York, were gracious enough to wade through earlier drafts and provide me with feedback and encouragement. I extend special gratitude to the group of graduate students—all foreign language teachers themselves—who spent an entire semester working with me on fine-tuning the ideas found here. Thanks to Judson Bridges, Lucy Bush, Nacky Fukunaga, Rachel Locey, Sandra Mancusi, Martin Sekanina, Kimberly Sewell, Itsue Tanigawa, and Meghan Walsh. I would also like to thank the text reviewers for their very detailed and helpful comments, including Frank B. Brooks, Florida State University; Julie G. Cruz, California State University–Stanislaus; Christian Faltis, Arizona State University; Maurice Funke, Defense Language Institute; Jay P. Kunz, Mississippi State University; Michael Newman, Queens College; Denise Overfield, State University of West Georgia; Deborah Wilburn Robinson, Ohio State University; and Karen Willmore, University of Alaska–Anchorage. A special thank you to Debbie Stollenwerk, Penny Burleson, and others at Merrill/Prentice Hall for their editorial and other assistance. Finally, with their patience, good humor, and affection, Bill, Katie, and Kelly have, once again, been an endless source of emotional support. No words can express my appreciation.

Brief Contents

CHAPTER 1
Communication   1

CHAPTER 2
Communicative Development   24

CHAPTER 3
Creating Communities of Learners in the Classroom   44

CHAPTER 4
Classroom Discourse   77

CHAPTER 5
Planning Instruction and Assessment   106

CHAPTER 6
The Interpersonal Mode   135

CHAPTER 7
The Interpretive Mode   168

CHAPTER 8
The Presentational Mode   198

CHAPTER 9
Professional Development   228

Contents

CHAPTER 1

Communication 1

Preview Questions 1

Key Words and Concepts 1

Overview 1

Communication 2
  Linguistic Resources 3
  Social Identities 4
  Conventionality and Creativity 7

The Study of Communication 9

Communicative Competence 11

Multicompetence 16

Intercultural Communicative Competence 18

Communication Goal for the Study of Foreign Languages 19

Summary 19

Discussion Questions and Activities 20

Additional Readings 22

Internet Resources 23

CHAPTER 2

Communicative Development 24

Preview Questions 24

Key Words and Concepts 24

Overview 24

A Sociocultural Perspective on Language Learning 25
  Mediational Means 29
  Zone of Proximal Development 30
  Scaffolding 31
  Private Speech 34
  Imitation and Repetition 34
  Play 36

Summary: Principles for Learning Additional Languages　38

Discussion Questions and Activities　41

Additional Readings　42

Internet Resources　43

CHAPTER 3　*Creating Communities of Learners in the Classroom*　44

Preview Questions　44

Key Words and Concepts　44

Overview　45

Communities of Learners　45
　Definition and Goals　45
　Characteristics of Middle and High School Students　46
　Contextual Characteristics of Effective Communities of Learners　48
　Role of the Teacher　48

Organizing Instruction for Effective Foreign Language Learning　50
　Designing Learning Opportunities　51
　Participation Structures for Learning　56
　Content Standards for Foreign Language Learning　57

Designing Curricular Activities Around the Communication Goal　59

Integrating Technology Into the Foreign Language Curriculum　60

Teacher Research　64
　Overview of the Process　64
　Some Final Concerns　69

Summary　69

Discussion Questions and Activities　70

Teacher Research Projects　72

Additional Readings　75

Internet Resources　75

CHAPTER 4　*Classroom Discourse*　77

Preview Questions　77

Key Words and Concepts　77

Overview　78

Classroom Discourse 78
Typical Patterns of Classroom Discourse 80
Instructional Conversations 83

Teacher Questions 88

Input, Negotiated Interaction, and Output 91

Learning Strategies 92

The Role of L1 in the L2 Classroom 94

Linguistic and Interactive Means for Creating and Sustaining Community 96

Summary 98

Discussion Questions and Activities 100

Teacher Research Projects 101

Additional Readings 104

Internet Resources 104

CHAPTER

5

Planning Instruction and Assessment 106

Preview Questions 106

Key Words and Concepts 106

Overview 107

Goals and Objectives 107

Preparing Instructional Plans 109
Course Syllabus 109
Unit Planning 109
Lesson Planning 110
Role of Textbooks and Other Materials in Planning for Instruction 113

Dimensions of Assessment 113
Sources of Data for Assessment 113

Designing Effective Assessment Tools 118
Issues of Validity 118
Norms and Standards for Evaluation 119

Grading 125

Summary 126

Discussion Questions and Activities 127

Teacher Research Projects   129

Additional Readings   132

Internet Resources   133

CHAPTER

6

The Interpersonal Mode   135

Preview Questions   135

Key Words and Concepts   135

Overview   136

The Interpersonal Mode   136

Cognitive and Social Underpinnings of Interaction   138
   Familiarity with, and Experience in, the Activity   138
   Social Identities   139
   Accommodation   141

Guidelines for Designing Instruction Around Interpersonal
Communicative Activities   142
   Choosing Communicative Activities   142
   Identifying the Communicative Components   146
   Creating Instructional Activities   146

Designing Assessment   155

Summary   161

Discussion Questions and Activities   162

Teacher Research Projects   163

Additional Readings   166

Internet Resources   166

CHAPTER

7

The Interpretive Mode   168

Preview Questions   168

Key Words and Concepts   168

Overview   169

The Interpretive Mode   169

Role of Background Knowledge, Genre Familiarity, and Past Reading
Experiences   171

First and Second Language Skills   171

Listenability 172

Visual Literacy 173

Guidelines for Designing Instruction Around Interpretive Communicative
Activities 174
   Choosing Communicative Activities 174
   Identifying the Communicative Components 177
   Creating Instructional Activities 178

Designing Assessment 187

Summary 191

Discussion Questions and Activities 192

Teacher Research Projects 193

Additional Readings 196

Internet Resources 196

CHAPTER

8

The Presentational Mode **198**

Preview Questions 198

Key Words and Concepts 198

Overview 199

The Presentational Mode 199

Cognitive Aspects of Writing 201

Social Aspects of Writing 202

Guidelines for Designing Instruction Around Presentational
Communicative Activities 203
   Choosing Communicative Activities 204
   Identifying the Communicative Components 207
   Creating Instructional Activities 207

Designing Assessment 219

Summary 220

Discussion Questions and Activities 222

Teacher Research Projects 223

Additional Readings 226

Internet Resources 226

CHAPTER *Professional Development* *228*

9
Preview Questions   228

Key Words and Concepts   228

Overview   229

Professional Development   230

Possibilities for Professional Development   231
Professional Development Centers   231
Mentoring   232
Professional Organizations   232
Professional Electronic Networks   236

Summary   238

Discussion Questions and Activities   238

Teacher Research Projects   239

Additional Readings   241

Internet Resources   242

Appendix: National Standards for Foreign Language Learning   *245*

References   *247*

Author Index   *261*

Subject Index   *267*

Note: Every effort has been made to provide accurate and current Internet information in this book. However, the Internet and information posted on it are constantly changing, so it is inevitable that some of the Internet addresses listed in this textbook will change.

Chapter 1

Communication

Preview Questions

Before you begin reading this chapter, take a few moments to consider the following:

- What are your reasons for studying a foreign language?
- What kinds of skills and abilities are you interested in developing?
- What are some of the important aspects of communication that you feel are especially vital to learners of another language?
- Do you feel your additional language learning experiences have enhanced your communicative skills and abilities? If yes, how so?

Key Words and Concepts

National Standards for Foreign Language Learning
Communication
- Linguistic resources
- Social identities
- Conventionality and creativity
Ethnography of speaking
Contextualization cues
Communicative competence
- Discourse competence
- Linguistic competence

Actional/rhetorical competence
Sociocultural competence
Strategic competence
Multicompetence
Intercultural communicative competence
Communication goal
- Interpersonal mode
- Interpretive mode
- Presentational mode

Overview

Ask most middle or high school students beginning the study of another language why they are studying it and they will likely tell you that it is a required subject. However, if you press them further you are likely to find that in addition to needing the credits, most students have some personal interest in the language. Some will tell you that they know native speakers of another language and would like to be able to communicate with them in that language. Others feel that learning to use another language will help them get into a highly regarded college and ultimately help them secure a good job when they graduate. Still others dream of traveling to different parts of the world and feel that being able to use the native language will enhance their experiences. For many middle and high school learners, then, interest in expanding their communicative worlds is a key reason for studying another language.

Recognizing this need, an 11-member task force representing various sectors of the foreign language education field across the United States created the **National Standards for Foreign Language Learning** (National Standards in Foreign Language Education Project, 1996). The standards are organized around five goals: Communication, Cultures, Connections, Comparisons, and Communities (see the Appendix for a complete list of the goals and their standards). While all of these goals are considered important, **communication** is considered the "heart" (p. 27) of additional language study.

Proposing communication as a primary goal of additional language learning is certainly not a novel idea. As a primary organizing principle of the communicative language teaching approach, communication has long been considered an essential goal in the field of second and foreign language learning. What has changed, however, is the conceptual understanding of communication on which the goal is based.

As noted by the task force, foreign language instruction has traditionally defined communication as a simple process of transmission whereby ideas, carried by words, are passed between speakers and receivers (Reddy, 1979). In this view, the four skills of listening, speaking, reading, and writing serve merely as conduits for sending and receiving messages. Such a view, the task force argued, is inadequate to account for recent theoretical and empirical advances on the nature of communication and learning.

The aim of this chapter is to present an overview of the current understandings of communication forming the foundation of the Communication Goal. In addition to a discussion of the concept of communication, the chapter includes discussions on communicative competence, multicompetence, and intercultural communicative competence and their importance to the goals of foreign language education.

COMMUNICATION

Communication is the foundation of all social life (Wittgenstein, 1966). As we go about our everyday lives, we communicate for a multitude of purposes. We engage with others in order to reach individually defined goals, to help others reach theirs, and to negotiate and work toward the accomplishment of a set of mutually constructed goals. It is through our communication with others that we simultaneously develop and manage our individual identities, our interpersonal relationships, and on a broader level, our memberships in various sociocultural groups and communities.

Contrary to some commonly held assumptions, our communicative activity does not entail the spontaneous, unpredictable expression of ideas. Rather, much of the language we use is conventionalized, tied to the contexts, or communicative activities, in which it is used. When we approach these activities, the goals, our social roles, and the uses and interpretations of the language we use are familiar to us. We know what is involved in a greeting, for example, and can easily distinguish a greeting from a complaint. Likewise, we can often predict with some accuracy what will appear in an advertisement about a particular product and how it might differ linguistically and rhetorically from, say, a lecture on the same product. We generally share knowledge about our communicative activities with members of our sociocultural groups and communities, and when we communicate with them, we use the knowledge as "readymade frameworks on which to hang the expression of our own ideas" (Becker, 1975, p. 17).

Linguistic Resources

Part of the knowledge we share with others resides in the **linguistic resources** we use to engage in our communicative activities. These resources consist of a wide range of elements, including lexical, grammatical, and topical choices; speech acts; rhetorical structures; and, specifically for oral activities, turn-taking patterns and prosodic and paralinguistic features such as intonation, stress, tempo, and pausing.

The resources we use to communicate do not come to us as neutral containers, ready to be filled with our personal meanings. Instead they come with meanings already embedded within them, meanings that induce or encourage others to see the communicative moment, and themselves as participants in it, in particular ways (Gumperz, 1982; Hymes, 1972a, 1972b; Kramsch, 1993). These meanings, or sets of expectations, develop over time in the repeated use of the resources in specific communicative contexts. In their habits of use the linguistic resources develop particular visions of the world, "specific complexes of values, definitions of the situation, and meanings of possible actions" (Morson & Emerson, 1989, p. 22). As Bakhtin (1981) notes:

> . . . there are no "neutral" words and forms—words and forms that belong to "no one". . . . All words have the "taste" of a profession, a genre, a tendency, a party, a particular work, a particular person, a generation, an age group, the day and hour. Each word tastes of the context and contexts in which it has lived its socially changed life; all words and forms are populated by intentions. (p. 293)

We use the expected meanings embedded in our resources to make sense of, and negotiate participation in, our communicative encounters. For many native English speakers, the utterance "hi" calls to mind a particular communicative activity—a greeting. It also evokes a particular relationship between the person who utters the word and the person or persons for whom it is intended and a particular kind of response. Thus, along with placing us in a particular kind of communicative encounter, the utterance provides us with a kind of map for figuring out what is going on and knowing how to act. Likewise, the directive "take out your homework" is conventionally linked to certain schooling practices for some sociocultural groups. When those who are familiar with the utterance hear it, a particular goal-directed activity and a typical teacher–student relationship are called to mind. This utterance also evokes a set of expectations about what is likely to follow, about possible sources of misunderstanding, and the likely consequences of responding to the directive in unexpected ways.

From this perspective, then, linguistic resources are one of our central forms of life. We use them not only to refer to, or represent, the world in our communicative activities. They are also forms of action by which we bring our cultural worlds into existence, maintain them, and shape them for our own purposes.

Social Identities

In addition to the conventional meanings attached to linguistic resources, participation in our communicative activities is influenced by the expectations we hold about our own **social identities** and those of others, and the role of relationships we form with them as we engage in our activities (Gee, 1996; Hall, 1996). Some aspects of our identities are ascribed to us at birth and include gender, race, and social class. That is, we are born male or female, Caucasian, African American, or a member of another racial group, and we are born into a particular level of economic status such as poverty or middle class.

A second layer of identities includes both the social roles into which we are appropriated and those we create for ourselves over time through our involvement in the activities of our various social groups and communities. School, church, community, and the workplace are some of the primary social institutions that give shape to these activities and to our identities as participants in them. Informal institutions, such as families and friendship circles, also mold our social identities and the role of relationships we establish with others.

The knowledge of our social group memberships in terms of our multiple identities, together with the values associated with them, comprise our social identities (Tajfel, 1981, 1982). Our expectations of the conventional or communally agreed-upon sets of actions associated with both ascribed and appropriated identities guide both our interpretations and uses of language at any communicative moment. In communicative activities typically associated with families, for example, we take on such roles as parents, children, cousins, and in-laws. In our communities, we come together as neighbors, school board members, or social club associates. In the workplace, we assume roles such as colleagues, administrators, and employees. The linguistic resources we use to communicate are shaped by the role we are playing at any particular moment. We enter into our communicative activities with expectations of how, in our role relationships, we are likely to act. We then use these expectations to work out our own participation in our activities.

The response of a parent to a child when faced with an inappropriate action by the child is likely to be quite different from the response a daughter-in-law would have to an inappropriate action by her mother-in-law. Likewise, in school-oriented activities, such as faculty meetings, club advising, team coaching, classroom teaching, and parent–teacher conferencing, we take on roles as students, teachers, administrators, coaches, and staff members and use our expectations to contribute to and interpret others' contributions in these events. Similarly, when we walk into a classroom as experienced teachers, we have a set of expectations about the kinds of activities that can occur in the classroom. We know what we as teachers can reasonably say and do as we go about setting up and carrying out these activities. Moreover, we anticipate probable student responses and other actions, and even have plans for dealing with the unexpected. Experienced students enter the classroom with similar sets of expectations about the purposes for being there, and the roles that both teacher and student are likely to play, and they use the plans to negotiate their way through their class activities. Students know, for example, the cues the teacher is likely to use to request attention or to reprimand. They know, too, the ways they can display active involvement in or, alternatively, resistance to the activities themselves.

When we participate in communicative activities, then, we use the sets of expectations we hold of our various social identities, of the activities themselves, and of the conventional meanings of the linguistic resources as navigational tools to help us synchronize our actions and interpretations with others. Our expectations give us a sense of what is going on, and we use them to come to a mutual understanding of the event with the other participants (Gee, 1996).

Two final points need to be made concerning the significance of social identities to our communication. First, even though we each have multiple, overlapping social identities that we bring to our communicative interactions with others, it is not the case that all of our identities are relevant at any given moment. Instead, the particular identity or set of identities that becomes significant to the communicative encounter depends minimally on the activity in which we are involved, the goals we are attempting to accomplish, and the identities of the other participants. If, for example, we are on a vacation trip and find ourselves interacting with others from different geographical regions, it is likely that our regional identities will be more relevant than our gender, race, or professional identities. So, we are likely to interact with each other as northerners and southerners or Americans and Italians. In a classroom situation, on the other hand, our professional identities as teacher and students are likely to be more relevant, and thus, the nature of our communication will differ.

Second, as with the meanings of our linguistic resources, the relevance of our identities is dynamic and responsive to the conditions of the moment. If, for example, one were both the parent and teacher of a student, it is likely that during class time, the two would communicate with each other as teacher and student. However, at any time during class, a situation may arise that calls forth their identities as parent and child.

The ways in which we enact any particular identity are also fluid. As an example, Phillipsen (1975) revealed the various ways in which a group of men enacted their identities as males in a town he called Teamsterville. When members of the group considered their relationships with other men symmetrical in terms of age, ethnicity, or occupational status, "speaking" was a dominant focus of their social events. That is, they considered it appropriate to engage in much talk with each other. However, when the relationship was considered asymmetrical, that is, when the men were with others of different ages, ethnic groups, or occupations, a high quantity of talk between them was considered inappropriate. The ways in which this group of men realized their identities depended in large part on those with whom they were interacting.

Expectations of the conventional meanings of our resources, our activities, and our social identities not only help guide our participation in many of our oral communicative activities, but also facilitate participation in our groups' and communities' literate activities (Barton & Ivanic, 1991; Barton & Hamilton, 1998). We approach any particular text as readers and writers with a set of expectations about the structural organization of different text types, the purposes typically associated with our reading and writing activities, and our roles as readers and writers. We use these expectations to guide our behaviors in that particular activity. We know, for example, that a story on gossiping in a popular magazine is likely to differ from a report on gossiping found in a research journal. We are likely to find differences not only in terms of the kind of information that is provided, but also in the lexical and grammatical elements used. Thus, our approach as readers of each text, and the kinds of information we take from them, will likely vary. Likewise, how we read or write a newspaper article on a particular topic differs from how we read or write a text-book excerpt on that same topic. Not only are the purposes for reading or writing the two texts likely to be different, but the kinds of information, and the linguistic forms and rhetorical structures used in the presentation of the information, are likely to differ as well.

It is important to remember that all of our expectations are culturally bound and tied to the groups and communities of which we are members. Expectations for what we as a parent might say to our child at any particular moment depend heavily on what counts as possible parental actions *within our own social groups.* Some groups, for example, do not consider it practical or wise for a parent to tell a child how to do something. Instead, the child is expected to watch and listen. Other groups, however, consider it important for the parent to involve the child in a discussion about the task before the child is allowed to attempt it (Harkness, Super, & Keefer, 1992). Therefore, our language use can perform an action only to the extent to which its expected meaning is shared among the participants. Given the wide range of social groups and communities that comprise the United States, the diversity of group memberships many of us hold, and the range of individual motivations for language use within groups and communities, we can expect these meanings and the values attached to them to be equally varied.

Figure 1–1 illustrates the various dimensions involved in the process of communication. As shown, when individuals engage in a communicative activity, they bring with them

FIGURE 1–1 Dimensions of
the Process of Communication

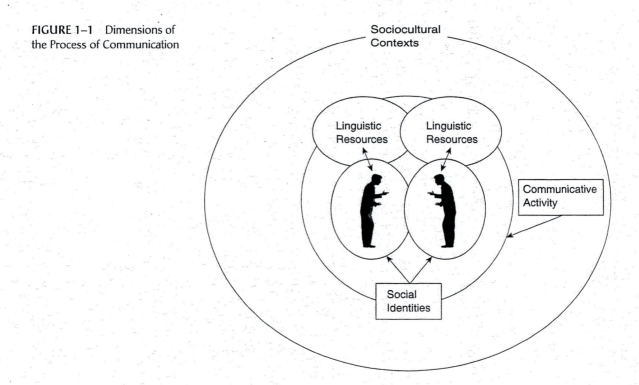

their own sets of linguistic resources. These resources come with meanings developed from their past uses in other sociocultural contexts. In addition, individuals bring with them their various social identities. Together, individuals work with the meanings embedded in the linguistic resources and their social identities to negotiate their goals and work toward the mutual accomplishment of a particular communicative activity.

Conventionality and Creativity

As discussed previously, the **conventional** meanings embodied in our linguistic resources and our social identities help us to navigate our way through communicative encounters. With these sets of expectations, we are disposed to participate in our activities and perceive the involvement of others in certain ways. There are few communicative activities, oral or written, in which we engage on a daily basis for which we do not have some understanding of the conventional meaning attached to their resources. Such understanding helps us to figure out what is going on, and negotiate and work toward the accomplishment of the activity. Indeed, we become quite accustomed to participating in everyday activities in very particular ways, and take for granted others' willingness and competence to do so as well. As noted by Wray (1992, p. 19), in our communicative activities, we rely "not on the potential for the unexpected in a given utterance but upon the statistical likelihood of the expected."

While the conventionalized nature of our communication may at times be perceived as constraining, it is also facilitative, serving both cognitive and social purposes. More specifically, the conventionality of communication provides us with the tools needed to coordinate our actions with others both socially and cognitively, and helps us sustain and transform the goals, values, and customs of our social groups and communities. Moreover, by helping us participate socially and connect with others in mutually intelligible ways, communicative conventions greatly diminish our need to continually renegotiate meaning or understanding of each other. This in turn provides psychological benefits that greatly reduce the amount of uncertainty and unpredictability we must deal with daily. Imagine having to create or figure out the meaning behind every word every time we entered into a communicative encounter with another. Even a simple "hi" could cause us cognitive distress. We would have to ask ourselves at every communicative juncture, "What does that mean?", "Why was it said now?", "How do I respond?", and so on. Our communicative lives would become drudgery.

Although it is true that much of our communication is conventionalized, it is not the case that we are unable to engage in nonroutine activity. Indeed, at any communicative moment there exists the possibility of **creativity.** As individuals, we participate in our communicative activities not as speakers and listeners, but as social actors, each with different motivations for participating in the activities. In choosing particular linguistic resources we are choosing "a particular way of entering the world and a particular way of sustaining relationships with others" (Duranti, 1997, p. 46). In most instances, we choose to use our linguistic resources in expected, conventional ways. If a colleague passes us in our school hallway, for example, and says "Hi, how are you?" we most often respond "Fine, and you?" We recognize the activity as a simple greeting between colleagues at work and play our part in the activity by responding as expected.

We are rarely restricted, however, to using our linguistic resources in expected ways. Rather, our options range from the more conventional to the more creative. For example, we may decide to return the greeting of our colleague with an unexpected request for clarification, "You mean how am I right now, or how am I in general?" Likewise, to the directive "take out your homework," a student may decide to respond with a simple "no" rather than responding in the expected way. Similarly, a teacher may decide to respond to a request by a school administrator to attend a faculty meeting with the utterance "I ain't goin'," choosing a syntactic form and prosodic pattern that may be considered atypical for a teacher to use in a professional encounter.

However, while we may have a range of options to choose from when participating in a communicative activity, the options are not always equivalent in terms of their consequences. Some may be more acceptable than others. In some cases, the linguistic resources we choose to use may produce humor. If we are close friends with the colleague extending the greeting in the hallway, for example, he or she may think we are trying to be humorous by asking for clarification of the question. In this case, our creative response is likely to create goodwill. Likewise, as in the case of poetry, our creative uses of language may engender artistry. While the syntax of the sentence "Light into the window creeps" is considered unconventional in standard American English, if written as part of a narrative or poem, it is likely to be considered lyrical, perhaps even romantic by some readers.

On the other hand, while our creative use of language can generate approval or enthusiasm, it can also create ill will, or anger. The consequences of the choices we make are influenced in part by the degree of sociocultural authority embedded in the activity and its resources, and by the kind of role relationship established between the participants. For example, the more institutionalized the activity, or the more unequal the relationship between participants, the more likely that the consequences for deviating from the conventional use of the resources will be negative. To use the previous example, the consequences for replying "I ain't goin'" to a directive issued by a school administrator are likely to be more negative than if uttered as a response to a directive issued by a close colleague. The school administrator is likely to interpret the individual's utterance as disrespectful, and perhaps even ignorant. Similarly, given that communicative activities associated with religious or civil ceremonies such as weddings, citizenship vows, and organizational pledges are often formal, serious events, overly creative use of their linguistic resources is likely to be viewed with disapproval.

A final noteworthy point concerns the development of creativity. Our understanding of, and ability to creatively play with, our linguistic resources can only come about after we display our ability to use them in conventional ways. To state this another way, the conventionality of our communicative resources provides us with a comfortable sense of predictability about our communication with others and thus lends a sense of order to our lives. It is only through such familiarity with our communicative actions that creative reconstruction can emerge and be acknowledged as such by members who share knowledge of these conventions. If we cannot or do not understand or recognize the conventional meanings associated with particular linguistic resources, it will be difficult, if not impossible, to recognize the creative ways in which they are being used.

This is perhaps most apparent to learners of additional languages. Take the case of humor. Humor often depends on our knowing the conventional meanings of the resources that are being manipulated. Therefore, understanding the humorous intent behind the communicative actions of someone using a language that is unfamiliar to us is one of the more difficult aspects of additional language learning, particularly for less-experienced language learners. Surely, most adults who have learned or are learning another language have had the experience of being in a group of target language speakers and have felt puzzled or bewildered by the laughter engendered by the use of an unexpected word or phrase.

Individual creativity then is the ability to understand and play with conventional meanings of our linguistic resources in unexpected ways. The more experience we attain in using the resources with their conventional meanings, the more expertise or authority we develop, and the more able we are to put them to our own uses, to use them consciously and with volition (Vygotsky, 1978). In the process, we may imbue them with our own voices, expanding, and at times even changing, the meanings conventionally associated with the resources (Bakhtin, 1981, 1986).

THE STUDY OF COMMUNICATION

While connected to several schools of thought, the notion of communication as goal-directed and conventionalized is perhaps most strongly rooted in the research on language use made popular by Dell Hymes and John Gumperz in the field of linguistic anthropology. Their approaches to the study of communication have enabled us to understand more fully the concept of language as culturally situated social behavior.

Defining language as social action, Hymes (1964, 1972a, 1972b) calls for an approach to the study of language that connects linguistic forms with social functions, and on a broader level, with the communal uses to which sociocultural communities put language. Hymes considers the communicative activity, or what he terms the communicative event, to be central to understanding the connections. Thus, the primary focus of his approach to the study of language use, which he calls the **ethnography of speaking,** is on the communicative activities that constitute a community. A major concern of research framed by this approach has been to describe "the ways in which speakers associate particular modes of speaking, topics, or message forms with particular settings and activities" (Hymes, 1972a, p. 92).

To capture the major components of a community's communicative events Hymes proposed the SPEAKING model. Each letter of the model represents one of the components. They are as follows:

- the *situation* including the physical and temporal setting and scene.
- the *participants* including their roles and responsibilities.
- the *ends* or goals of the event.
- the particular speech *acts* constituting the event.
- the *key* or tone underlying the event (e.g., humorous, serious, playful).
- the *instrumentalities* used to realize the event including the code and channel (e.g., written versus oral).
- the *norms* for participation and interpretation.
- the *genre* with which the event is most closely associated.

Examples of communicative events include formal events like sermons, prayers, lectures, and storybook readings, as well as less formal events such as writing letters to friends, griping, chitchatting, and joke telling. Knowledge of these context-specific features constitutes in part the communicative plans with which we approach and make sense of our communicative activities.

Much research in the fields of linguistic anthropology, communication, and education has used the ethnography of speaking approach to investigate the communicative events and activities of particular groups and communities. Specific research has focused on events of less familiar communities, such as criminal trials in Thailand (Moerman, 1988), gossiping among the men of Zinacantan (Haviland, 1977), and ways of speaking among the Kuna (Sherzer, 1983). Other research has focused on more familiar everyday worlds. Katriel (1987), for example, investigated the ritual of treat sharing among children in Israel. Sims-Holt (1972) studied the conventional features of sermons as enacted by African American preachers. Foster (1989) investigated the speech events occurring in the classroom of an African American teacher in an urban community college, and Heath (1983) investigated three communities' ways of communicating in and outside of school. Additional studies have investigated the conventional components of everyday communicative activities such as service encounters (e.g., Lamoureux, 1988/89), radio talk shows (e.g., Panese, 1996), and medical interviews (e.g., Fisher, 1991).

In addition to studies of oral communicative events, there have been several investigations of the conventional features of different groups' literate activities. McCarty and Watahomigie (1998), for example, studied both home and school literacy activities in American Indian and Native Alaskan communities. Similarly, Torres-Guzman (1998) investigated literacy activities in Puerto Rican communities and Dien (1998) looked at literacy activities in Vietnamese American communities.

Basing his work on similar assumptions about language use and culture, Gumperz (1981, 1982) has explored the communicative functions of what he terms **contextualization cues.** According to Gumperz, our communicative plans are constituted in part by knowledge of these cues. These cues, which for the most part are conventionalized but rarely consciously attended to, include features of language and related communicative conventions used by participants to initiate and sustain conversational involvement. Gumperz argues that the use of the cues helps participants make sense of, and at the same time contribute to sense making in, an event by providing them with recognizable markers for the mutual adjustment of perspectives. The cues operate at various levels of speech production and include the choice of lexical and syntactic forms, prosodic cues such as intonation, stress and pitch, paralanguage (e.g., creaky voice, laughter), turn-taking patterns, and even the language code itself.

In contrast to studies using the ethnography of speaking approach, which examine the communal norms and patterns of participation, studies using Gumperz's concept of contextualization cues typically investigate the missteps that occur when participants in a communicative activity use different cues to signal meaning or misinterpret the cues of the other participants. Tyler and Davis (1990), for example, investigated an interaction that resulted in a misunderstanding between a native-speaking American English undergraduate student and an international teaching assistant. They located the sources of miscommunication in the different uses and interpretations of the cues used by each participant in their exchange over a grade the student had received. Along similar lines, Erickson and Shultz (1982) looked at how differences in the timing of turns between a counselor and individual students in advising interviews affected the counselor's evaluation of the students' abilities. They argue that it was the mismatch between the counselor and students' sense of interactional timing that created the miscommunication.

To be sure, all miscommunication between members of different cultural groups cannot be explained as mismatched cultural styles (Sarangi, 1994). Sometimes we knowingly use different cues or misunderstand others' use of cues in order to distance ourselves from them. Nevertheless, studies examining the use of contextualization cues highlight the important role that conventional meanings of linguistic and paralinguistic resources play in framing our communicative encounters. Although varying slightly, the primary concern of both the ethnography of speaking approach and the study of contextualization cues has been to understand the conventional uses of language within and across groups, and more specifically, how group members coordinate their communicative actions in ways that are meaningful to each other.

More recently, research on language use has been concerned with the creative ways in which participants use the resources of particular communicative events. Hall (1993), for example, revealed how one woman was able to positively transform the nature of her involvement in a communicative activity considered important to her group of friends. She did so by creatively manipulating some of the resources conventionally used to enact the activity. Her play with the conventions generated a great deal of humor among the other participants, and thus helped raise her status within the group.

Others have investigated the creative formation and dissolution of conventions and social identities as groups are formed and re-formed in multilingual and multicultural communities. Rampton (1995) investigated the creative, unexpected ways in which adolescents from mixed-race peer groups used the languages associated with each other's ethnic and racial identities to serve both individual and collective purposes.

The findings from these different approaches to the study of communication show the varied and complex ways in which our language use is inherently linked to the cultural, institutional, and historical settings of our social worlds. Because our involvement in the communicative activities of our everyday lives is usually with others who share our expectations, these links are often transparent. Thus, we oftentimes find it difficult to perceive their vitality. Researching investigations like the ones referred to, as well as engaging in our own investigations on the use of language, can help us to stand apart from our communicative worlds and transform their taken-for-granted status. By doing so, we will more fully understand the culturally constructed nature of communication and the roles we play in its construction.

COMMUNICATIVE COMPETENCE

As previously noted, the findings from studies of these different approaches to the study of language use demonstrate the varied and complex ways in which our language use is embedded in our social and cultural worlds. The findings also reveal the range of knowledge we as individuals have that enables us to participate in our communicative activities with members of our groups and communities. In an effort to capture this totality of knowledge Dell Hymes (1972b) proposed the concept of **communicative competence.** Hymes introduced the concept more than 30 years ago as an alternative to the concept of linguistic competence as first proposed by Chomsky (1965, 1966). According to Chomsky's theory of language, we are born with a universal grammar, a mental blueprint, for processing and generating language. Presumed to be a fixed property of the human mind, this innate capacity for language is thought to consist of sets of principles and conditions from which the grammatical rules for language systems are derived. As defined by Chomsky, linguistic competence consists of those sets of principles, conditions, and rules for generating the structural components of a language, which any "speaker of a language knows implicitly" (1966, p. 9).

For Hymes, Chomsky's definition of language was too restrictive in that it did not consider the social knowledge shared by members of a speech community needed to produce appropriate utterances. According to Hymes, an individual's competence to use language effectively is intimately linked to his or her knowledge of such social conditions as the setting, the participants, and the goals constitutive of particular communicative activities. He stated, "It is not enough for the child to be able to produce any grammatical utterance. It would have to remain speechless if it could not connect utterances to their contexts of use" (Hymes, 1964, p. 110).

Drawing on rich ethnographic data on language use from a variety of social groups, Hymes called for a more encompassing theory of communication. Such a theory, Hymes argued, should account for the knowledge that an individual needs to produce and understand utterances that are structurally sound, referentially accurate, and contextually appropriate within the different groups and communities of which the individual is a member. Hymes labeled this knowledge communicative competence.

In the fields of second and foreign language learning, Canale and Swain (1980) were among the first to attempt to develop a framework of communicative competence for the purposes of curriculum design and evaluation. Their initial model of communicative competence contained three components of resources. A description of these components can be found in Table 1–1.

Canale and Swain acknowledged that their model was more concerned with oral skills. Consequently, Canale (1983) added to the model a fourth component, **discourse competence,** that addressed some of the competence needed to participate in literacy activities. In order to determine which components to teach, Canale and Swain argued that each should be addressed in terms of their probability of occurrence as based on authentic texts. That is, choices for what to include in a curriculum for additional language classrooms should be based on an analysis of the linguistic, sociolinguistic, discourse, and strategic components comprising those communicative activities in which learners of additional languages were interested.

TABLE 1–1   *Components of Canale and Swain's Early Model of Communicative Competence.*

- **grammatical**, which includes knowledge of lexical items and rules of morphology, syntax, semantics, and phonology.
- **sociolinguistic**, which includes knowledge of the rules of language use.
- **strategic**, which includes knowledge of strategies to compensate for breakdowns in communication.

Around the same time that Canale and Swain's model of communicative competence appeared, Van Ek (1986) was developing the notion of communicative ability as part of the work he was doing for the Council of Europe. His model contained six components, descriptions of which can be found in Table 1–2.

More recently, in an attempt to link the concept of communicative competence to language testing, Bachman (1990) proposed a model of communicative language ability containing two primary components: language competence and strategic competence. The first component is further divided into two types of knowledge. The first, organizational knowledge, comprises the ability to recognize and produce grammatically accurate sentences in the construction of oral and written texts, and thus integrates grammatical knowledge with textual knowledge. The second type of language competence is pragmatic knowledge. This combines the knowledge of language functions, or illocutionary knowledge, with sociolinguistic knowledge, which is knowledge of how to use functions appropriately in a given context. The second primary component of Bachman's model of communicative language ability, strategic competence, is comprised of three kinds of metacognitive strategies—assessment, planning, and execution—for managing the process of communicating. Table 1–3 summarizes Bachman's model.

TABLE 1–2   *Components of Van Ek's Model of Communicative Ability.*

- **linguistic competence**, defined as the ability to produce and interpret utterances using appropriate forms and conventional meanings.
- **sociolinguistic competence**, defined as the awareness of the relation between linguistic symbols and their contexts of use, including setting, participants, goals, and so on.
- **discourse competence**, defined as the knowledge and ability to use appropriate resources in the construction and interpretation of texts.
- **strategic competence**, defined as strategies such as requesting clarification and rephrasing needed to avoid breakdowns in communication.
- **sociocultural competence**, defined as knowledge of the social components of larger contexts within which communicative activities occur.
- **social competence**, defined as the ability and willingness, including motivation, attitude, confidence, and empathy, to communicate with others.

TABLE 1–3   *Bachman's Model of Communicative Language Ability.*

- **language competence**, which contains two types of knowledge:
  - *organizational knowledge*, which is the ability to recognize and produce grammatically accurate sentences in the construction of oral and written texts
  - *pragmatic knowledge*, which combines
    - *illocutionary knowledge:* the knowledge of functional conventions of language
    - *sociolinguistic knowledge:* the knowledge of appropriate use of functions
- **strategic competence**, which consists of three strategies used in the process of communication:
  - *assessment*
  - *planning*
  - *execution*

FIGURE 1–2 Celce–Murcia
et al.'s Model of Communicative
Competence

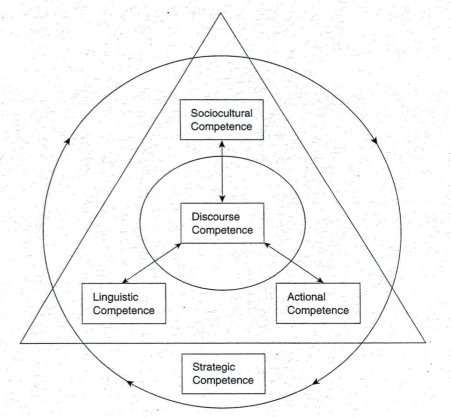

Building upon these previous models, Celce-Murcia, Zoltan, and Thurrell (1995) have proposed what is perhaps the most comprehensive typology of communicative competence to date in the field of second and foreign language learning. Their model, illustrated in Figure 1–2, comprises five interrelated areas of knowledge and skills: discourse competence, linguistic competence, actional/rhetorical competence, sociocultural competence, and strategic competence.

Discourse competence is considered the core of communicative competence. It deals with "the selection, sequencing, and arrangement of words, structures, sentences and utterances to achieve a unified spoken or written text" (Celce-Murcia et al., 1995, p. 13). Included here is knowledge of, and the ability to use, linguistic resources to create cohesion and coherence in both oral and written texts. This involves, for example, knowing how to signal chronological order through the use of such linguistic resources as "first," "then," and "after that." Discourse competence also includes knowledge of conversational conventions such as turn-taking patterns and adjacency pairs. Adjacency pairs are speech actions that involve a sequence of two speech acts, including an opener and both the preferred and dispreferred responses to it. For example, in the case of an apology, for some sociocultural groups, the preferred sequence is apology–acceptance, as in the following:

Bob: I'm sorry.
Mary: That's ok.

A dispreferred sequence is apology–rejection as in:

Bob: I'm sorry.
Mary: Too bad.

In addition, discourse competence includes conversational skills such as knowing how to hold on to the conversational floor, how to interrupt, and how to provide backchannel or "listener feedback" cues such as "umm" and "uh huh" when appropriate. Three additional components give shape to, and are shaped by, discourse competence.

The first of these is **linguistic competence,** which is the aspect of communicative competence that has been given the most extensive coverage in foreign language class-rooms. It consists of the basic elements of the linguistic system that are used to interpret and construct grammatically accurate utterances and texts. Included here is knowledge of syntax including sentence patterns, word order, coordination, subordination, and em-bedding. Also included is knowledge of morphology, phonology, vocabulary, and or-thography, which includes spelling and other mechanics of writing such as punctuation and capitalization.

A second component linked to discourse competence is **actional competence,** which is defined as the knowledge and ability to interpret and produce both direct and indirect speech acts. It is, as noted by the authors, "matching actional intent with linguistic form based on the knowledge of an inventory of verbal schemata that carry illocutionary force" (Celce-Murcia et al., 1995, p. 17). Thus, actional competence entails knowing how to use language to do something, to perform certain functions, such as making a promise, giving orders, complaining, and so on.

Celce-Murcia et al. group speech acts, or language functions, into seven key areas:

- *interpersonal exchanges,* which include greeting, leave-taking, and introducing.
- *information,* which includes asking for information, reporting, and explaining.
- *opinions,* which include expressing opinions, agreeing, and disapproving.
- *feelings,* which include expressing pleasure, happiness, and relief.
- *suasion,* which includes suggesting, advising, and persuading.
- *problems,* which include complaining, blaming, and apologizing.
- *future scenarios,* which include expressing aspirations, promising, and predicting.

Actional competence also involves knowing how to combine individual acts into larger speech act sets to create an appropriate communicative activity such as making a purchase, setting up an appointment, recounting a story, and so on. When discussing written texts, Celce-Murcia et al. prefer the parallel term **rhetorical competence.** This aspect includes knowledge of the speech acts and speech act sets typical of a particular written genre.

The third component linked to discourse competence is **sociocultural competence,** which comprises the nonlinguistic, contextual knowledge that communicators rely on to understand and contribute to a given communicative activity. This aspect of competence is broader than actional or rhetorical competence in that it includes knowledge of the rules, norms, and expectations governing the larger social context of the activity. The relevant elements are divided into four areas:

- *Social contextual factors,* which include participant identity variables such as age, gender, and social status, and situational variables such as time and place.
- *Stylistic appropriateness factors,* which include politeness conventions, degrees of formality, and affiliation. It also includes register, or linguistic characteristics associated with specialized fields of talk like "computerese" or "journalese."
- *Cultural factors,* which include background knowledge of the target language community's ways of living, social conventions, and beliefs, values, and norms.
- *Nonverbal communicative factors,* which include body movements, gestures, facial expressions, eye contact, use of space, and paralinguistic features such as laughter.

Weaving through all four components is the fifth component, **strategic competence.** This competence is comprised of the knowledge and skills needed to resolve communicative difficulties and enhance communicative effectiveness. Included here are the following six strategies:

- *avoidance strategies* such as topic avoidance or message abandonment.
- *achievement strategies* such as circumlocution (e.g., "Give me the thing that goes on the top," for *lid*) or approximation (e.g., using the word *animal* instead of the more specific word *dog*).
- *time-gaining strategies* such as fillers and hesitation devices (e.g., uttering "umm" and "well" while speaking).
- *self-monitoring strategies* such as self-initiated repair (e.g., stating "I mean . . ." before correcting what was just said).
- *interpretation strategies* such as inferring and predicting what will happen next.
- *interactional strategies* such as appealing for help (e.g., "What is the word for this?") and checking for comprehension (e.g., "Does this make sense?").

In summary, the Celce-Murcia et al. (1995) model of communicative competence helps us to appreciate the many types of knowledge, skills, and abilities that foreign language learners need to master to become fully proficient in the target language. Because it is the most comprehensive model to date, it will form the basis for designing foreign language curriculum based on the three modes of the Communication Standard. A more thorough discussion of the standard can be found later in this chapter. See Chapters 6, 7, and 8 for detailed discussions on designing curriculum around the three modes using the Celce-Murcia et al. model.

MULTICOMPETENCE

It is clear that competent participation in our various communicative activities involves a range of knowledge and abilities. As previously discussed, over the last several years various models articulating the components of communicative competence for teaching and testing purposes have been proposed in the field of second and foreign language learning. While not arguing against the notion of communicative competence as an important concept in our understanding of communication and language use, several scholars have begun to question whether it captures fully the competence that learners of additional languages develop (Cenoz & Genesee, 1998; Cook, 1992, 1996, 1999a). Remember, the term was originally proposed by Hymes to reflect the knowledge and abilities that native speakers possess. As Kramsch (1993, 1998) and others (e.g., Cook, 1999a, 1999b; Firth & Wagner, 1997; Valdes, 1998) have pointed out, however, the goal of additional language learning is not to become like native-speaking members of target language groups. Rather, it is for learners to add alternative ways of making sense to their already established repertoires of sense-making knowledge and abilities. This is so that learners can broaden their communicative experiences, their worldviews, and their understandings of the active, creative roles they as individuals play in constructing these worlds. In fact, Cook (1999a) argues that if we accept the definition of native speaker as someone who learned the language as her first language, then additional language learners can *never* be native speakers "without being reborn" (p. 187).

As an alternative way of understanding the competence that additional language users possess, Cook (1992, 1995, 1999a, 1999b) proposes the concept of **multicompetence.** In a review of research on multicompetence, Cook concludes that the communicative competence of those who know more than one language is intrinsically more complex than the competence attained by monolinguals, or those who know only one language. Bilinguals, for example, have been shown to have different cognitive abilities from monolinguals. For example, they are more metalinguistically aware (Cummins, 1979; Diaz, 1985) and score higher on tests of divergent thinking, which value such traits as flexibility, originality, and fluency (Bialystok, 1991). They also make more flexible use of language-learning strategies than monolinguals do (Nation & McLaughlin, 1986; Nayak, Hasen, Krueger, & McLaughlin, 1989). In terms of pragmatic knowledge, bilinguals have been shown to be more sensitive and responsive to their interlocutors than monolingual speakers are (Nicoladis & Genesee, 1996, 1998).

Cook notes that it is not that bilinguals necessarily perform better than monolinguals in all cases. Rather, they perform differently. In recent research comparing grammar knowledge of both monolinguals and bilinguals, Cook (1996, 1999b) revealed that English speakers who know French judge grammatical constructions such as English sentences with null subjects (e.g., Is pretty.) differently from monolinguals. Thought processes also differ for multicompetent language users. Those who know two languages have been shown to perform a bit more slowly on language-related cognitive tasks than monolinguals do. This difference is attributed to the fact that those who know two languages have more than one response available and so need more time to consider their options before responding.

Thus, Cook concludes, learners of two or more languages do not merely add what they learn to do in the target language to what they already know how to do in their primary language. Rather, the new communicative knowledge and skills they develop in the target language interact with and transform the knowledge and skills of their first language. Consequently, users of additional languages are more aptly understood as possessing unique competencies in both their first and second language that "manifest specific characteristics that distinguish it from monolingual competence" (Cenoz & Genesee, 1998, p. 19).

From this perspective, learners of additional languages are more appropriately viewed as acquiring something extra, something that "increases the L2 user's capabilities beyond those of a monolingual" (Cook, 1992, p. 578). If this is the case, then, while the communicative knowledge and skills of a monolingual native speaker of the target language are important to additional language learners, they cannot form the substance of our pedagogical standards. Instead, as Cook (1999a) notes, "The ultimate attainment of L2 learning should be defined in terms of knowledge of the L2" (p. 191), and the model for setting goals should be the bilingual user of both languages. While additional research on the nature of multicompetence is clearly needed, the concept is important because it asks us to recognize the unique status of additional language users as "successful multicompetent speakers, not failed native speakers" (Cook, 1999a, p. 204).

INTERCULTURAL COMMUNICATIVE COMPETENCE

Byram (1989, 1997) and his colleagues (Byram & Morgan, 1994; Byram & Zarate, 1997) have also argued for the need to consider the competence that additional language learners develop as being qualitatively different from the competence that members develop as native speakers of social groups and communities. Learners, they argue, should be treated not as aspiring native speakers but as developing intercultural communicators (Byram, 1997). In an effort to capture some of the knowledge and skills that users of more than one language develop, Byram proposes the concept of **intercultural communicative competence.** He defines this concept as the knowledge and abilities needed to participate in communicative activities where the target language is the primary communicative code and in situations where it is the common code for those with different preferred languages. Specific knowledge and abilities comprising intercultural communicative competence can be grouped into three areas: cognitive, affective, and behavioral. The cognitive dimension includes:

- knowledge of the conventional ways in which one's own communicative activities are accomplished.
- knowledge of the conventional ways communicative activities are carried out among groups who use the target language.
- the ability to sort through, reflect on, and use one's understanding of the differences and similarities in the formation of open, flexible communicative plans and perspectives.

The affective dimension includes the following abilities:

- to tolerate ambiguity and failure with minimal discomfort.
- to take risks.
- to persevere.
- to understand and be sensitive to the perspectives of others.

In addition to the ability to use linguistic resources in the target language in conventional ways, the behavioral dimension includes the following abilities:

- to initiate encounters with strangers in unfamiliar settings.
- to establish interpersonal relationships.
- to deal effectively with different communicative styles.

As we can see, rather than replacing the notions of communicative competence, or multicompetence, intercultural communicative competence builds on and extends them.

COMMUNICATION GOAL FOR THE STUDY OF FOREIGN LANGUAGES

The perspective on communication and the related concepts of communicative competence, multicompetence, and intercultural communicative competence presented in this chapter are the foundation on which the **communication goal** for learning additional languages is based. From this perspective, the goal of foreign language learning is not the assimilation of new language systems into already existing mental structures. Nor is it the acquisition of isolated skills. Rather, it is the development of knowledge and skills needed to understand and participate in a wide range of intellectual and practical communicative activities realized through the target language (Leontiev, 1981).

To capture the context-embedded nature of language use, developers of the standards have organized the communication goal into three general modes: the interpersonal, the interpretive, and the presentational. The **interpersonal mode** is characterized by communicative activities accomplished through direct interaction with others for the purposes of creating and maintaining interpersonal relationships or accomplishing a particular task. The **interpretive mode** is characterized by activities that involve "appropriate cultural interpretation of meanings that occur in written and spoken form where there is no recourse to the active negotiation of meaning with the writer or speaker" (American Council on the Teaching of Foreign Languages [ACTFL], n.d., p. 4). The **presentational mode** is characterized by communicative activities in which the primary purpose is to present or express ideas, information, feelings, and experiences through both the spoken and written word. Each of these modes is more fully defined and their importance to curriculum design addressed in greater detail in Chapters 6 (interpersonal mode), 7 (interpretive mode), and 8 (presentational mode).

SUMMARY

Following is a brief summary of some of the key concepts and ideas discussed in this chapter.

- The National Standards for Foreign Language Learning in the United States Project (1996) has set five goals for language learning: communication, culture, connections, comparisons, and communities. Of these, communication is considered the core.
- The language we use in our communicative activities is embedded in a complex cultural system. Its use is simultaneously constitutive of our social identities, our interpersonal relationships, our memberships in various sociocultural groups and communities and, more generally, our particular beliefs and values. Changing our language use necessarily means changing the way we live our lives.
- Much of our language use is conventionalized, organized around communicative plans of action. The particular meanings of our linguistic resources in any communicative activity come from their past uses, the social identities of the participants, and the local conditions of the moment.

- The conventionality of our communicative resources provides us with a comfortable sense of predictability about our communication with others and thus brings some order to our lives. However, at any communicative moment there exists the possibility of creative language use, where we play with the conventional meanings of language use in unexpected ways. The more experience we gain in using the resources with their conventional meanings, the more able we are to put them to our own uses, to be creative, and to imbue the meanings with our own voices.

- The study of communication has taken several fruitful directions ranging from the ethnography of speaking, to the study of contextualization cues used to create meaning, to the examination of the creative ways in which language is used by individuals for their own purposes. Such studies help us understand more fully the culturally constructed nature of communication and the roles we as individuals play in its construction.

- Communicative competence is an essential concept to foreign language learning. First proposed by Dell Hymes (1964), and most recently expanded by Celce-Murcia et al. (1995), it captures the range of knowledge, skills, and abilities we possess that enables us to participate in our communicative activities. As such it is a key element in designing foreign language curriculum around the national standards.

- Multicompetence, another key concept, captures the unique competencies that learners of more than one language develop in both their first and second languages and thus distinguishes them from native-speaking monolinguals. Given their unique characteristics, Cook (1999a) argues that the more appropriate model for setting goals in foreign language learning is not necessarily the native speaker. Rather, we should focus our attention on the proficient user of both languages.

- Intercultural communicative competence further expands the notions of communicative competence and multicompetence by including knowledge, abilities, and attitudes needed to interact in culturally different communicative contexts.

- The communication goal for foreign language learning is organized around three modes of communication: the interpersonal, the interpretive, and the presentational. From the perspective of communication embedded in this goal, the ultimate aim of learning other languages is best understood as broadening our communicative experiences and worldviews by adding alternative knowledge, skills, and abilities for understanding and participating in a wide range of intellectual and practical activities.

DISCUSSION QUESTIONS AND ACTIVITIES

1. Compile a list of communicative activities in which you participate on a daily basis, using the following short list to help you begin. Group the activities according to how conventionalized or routinized their communicative plans are. Compare your lists to a classmate's. How similar are they? Can you detect any patterns of daily activity? Together choose one activity to describe using Hymes' SPEAKING model. Share your descriptions with your classmates.

Communicative Activities

More routinized

Reading the newspaper
Writing a paper for class
Making a doctor's appointment

Less routinized

Talking with friends at lunch
Chatting with a neighbor

Listening to the radio
Sending e-mails to friends
Making purchases

---

2. As a class choose a communicative activity from the list compiled for question 1. Get together with a partner and describe the components of the activity using Celce-Murcia et al.'s (1995) model of communicative competence. Compare your description with those of other pairs. How similar or different are they? If different, what could account for their differences? Were some of the components easier to articulate than others? Speculate as to why that might have been so. What conclusions can you draw for foreign language learning?

3. Breaches and disagreements in interpretations are key times to observe otherwise tacit cultural knowledge and expectations. Choose one time when you are together with friends, family, or conducting everyday business and do something unexpected. For instance, do not look your interlocutors in the eye. Or, sit too close and stare intently at the other person. Give an unexpected response to a greeting or a question your friend asks. Talk too much or not enough. Spend at least 20 minutes engaging in such unexpected behavior and note the others' reactions. If you can, interview them afterwards, asking them how they felt. Write a three-page report in which you describe what you did, how the others responded to your "breaking of the rules," and how you felt about doing it. What can you conclude about the connection between culture and communication? What implications are there for learning to communicate in another language?

4. According to Cook (1999a), users of more than one language are different from monolingual users. The next page shows a list of skills and abilities composed by a group of foreign language teachers that they felt represented their unique skills and abilities as users of more than one language. In small groups, examine the list and check those that you feel describe your own skills and abilities as multicompetent language users. Add any additional skills and abilities not included here that you feel distinguish you from monolinguals. Compare your lists with those of your classmates. What did you find? What can you conclude?

   To extend this activity, interview bilingual speakers who are not teachers about their views on multicompetence. What are some important skills and knowledge bases they feel distinguish them from monolingual speakers? How do their lists compare to the ones created in your classroom? What conclusions can you draw about the concept of multicompetence?

List of knowledge, skills, and abilities of multiple language users

- enhanced strategic competence including, for example, ability to use circumlocution, guess meaning from context, and detect and respond to communicative breakdowns
- broadened sociocultural understanding
- increased empathy and receptivity to others who are culturally different
- enhanced metalinguistic awareness of first and second language skills
- extended social identities
- more communicative resources on which to draw
- more flexible and creative with language
- enhanced analytic abilities

---

5. Using the list of key concepts and ideas found at the beginning of the chapter, choose one or two on which you would like more information. Do a search of the Internet or library databases for relevant sources of information. Compile an annotated list of five or six resources for each concept or idea. Prepare to share the list with your classmates.

ADDITIONAL READINGS

Agar, M. (1994). *Language shock: Understanding the culture of conversation.* New York: William Morrow.

Cenoz, J., & Genesee, F. (Eds.). (1998). *Beyond bilingualism.* Clevedon: Multilingual Matters.

Hanks, W. F. (1996). *Language and communicative practices.* Boulder, CO: Westview Press.

Kress, G. (1989). *Linguistic processes in sociocultural practice.* Oxford: Oxford University Press.

Le Page, R., & Tahouret-Keller, A. (1985). *Acts of identity.* Chicago: Chicago University Press.

Lvovich, N. (1997). *The multilingual self: An inquiry into language learning.* Mahweh: Lawrence Erlbaum.

Scollon, R., & Scollon, S. (1995). *Intercultural communication: A discourse approach.* Oxford: Oxford University Press.

Zentella, A. C. (1997). *Growing up bilingual.* Oxford: Blackwell.

INTERNET RESOURCES

http://www.sietarinternational.org/   The International Society for Intercultural Education, Training, and Research (SIETAR)

This is the Web site of an international professional association comprised of consultants, trainers, educators, researchers, and other professionals from a wide range of disciplines who share a common interest in international and intercultural relations.

http://www.geocities.com/~wilson_pam/culture/   Resources for Teaching

This site is a repository of resources and pedagogical strategies for developing cultural competence, multicultural awareness, and tolerance of cultural diversity, and for developing skills for intercultural communication. It is addressed to both academic and business communities. It is maintained by Pamela Wilson, Department of Communications, Robert Morris College, Moon Township, PA.

http://www.peacecorps.gov/wws/   World Wise Schools

This is the site of World Wise Schools, an education program sponsored by the Peace Corps whose aim is to broaden learners' perspectives of the world and promote cultural awareness. The site has links to a broad range of educational resources for educators including teacher-tested lesson plans, guides, maps, and stories by former volunteers.

http://www.worldwide.edu/index.html   World Wide Classroom

This site contains a compilation of intercultural and educational programs around the world that welcome international visitors. The programs include University Study, Adult Enrichment, Foreign Language Immersion, Teen Camps, Volunteerism, Internships, and Cultural, Craft, and Heritage Programs.

http://www.sil.org/lingualinks/   Summer Institute of Linguistics International Lingua-Links

This Web site provides an extensive set of resources on communication, communicative competence, and additional language learning. Descriptions of language skills are given along with recommendations of techniques and activities to develop these skills. The site also contains an extensive collection of reference information.

Chapter 2

Communicative Development

Preview Questions

Before you begin reading this chapter, take a few moments to consider the following:

- As a learner of one or more additional languages, what learning experiences have been most meaningful to you? Why?
- What experiences have you found most frustrating? Why?
- Based on your own experiences, what do you consider to be some of the more important components of the language learning process?

Key Words and Concepts

Sociocultural perspective on language learning
    Mediational means
    Zone of proximal development
    Scaffolding
    Private speech
    Imitation
    Repetition
    Play
Principles for learning additional languages

Overview

Our success as educators in preparing our middle and high school students to meet the challenges set out by the communication goal depends on our understanding not only of such concepts as communication and communicative competence but also of the processes by which we become communicatively competent.

Traditionally in foreign language classrooms, language has been treated as a set of autonomous, structured systems comprised of fixed symbols and rules for their combination. Learning additional languages has been viewed as an individually based, internal process involving the assimilation of new knowledge about the structural components of target language systems into preexisting mental structures. Based in large part on Chomsky's theory of language (Chomsky, 1957, 1965), this perspective has assumed the process to be linear, sequentially organized, and influenced primarily by the quality of an individual's innate knowledge structures (Krashen, 1982, 1985). Because language learning is thought to be a natural, universal process, it is assumed that language is not actually teachable. Rather, it is acquired. The role of teaching is to create acquisition-rich conditions in the classroom that would optimize the individual's ability to assimilate and ultimately manipulate the new language structures. Most typically this has involved presenting the systemic components of the language system across four separate skill areas of listening, speaking, reading, and writing in friendly, low-anxiety-producing environments in which students' "affective filters" are low (Krashen, 1982).

Recent theoretical insights and investigations of communicative development and language learning across disciplines have broadened, and in many ways, transformed our understanding of language learning. Current conceptualizations are based on the premise that much of our linguistic, social, and cognitive knowledge is intimately tied to our extended participation and active apprenticeship in sociocultural events and activities. Recognizing the narrowness of the more traditional perspective, the national goals of foreign language learning are based on an understanding of learning that draws from this broader, sociocultural perspective (Hall, 1999; Phillips, 1999).

The purpose of this chapter is to present an overview of communicative development and learning on which the communication goal is based. A discussion of some of the major premises of a sociocultural perspective on language learning is followed by several key concepts. The chapter concludes with a discussion of a set of principles for additional language learning that draws on the theoretical insights and empirical evidence presented in the chapter.

A SOCIOCULTURAL PERSPECTIVE ON LANGUAGE LEARNING

A **sociocultural perspective on language learning** is based on theoretical considerations and empirical investigations of learning drawn from a variety of disciplines. Vygotsky's (1978, 1981, 1986, 1987) theory of learning, first proposed more than 50 years ago, is probably the most well known. One of his major contributions was to link both the nature and development of psychological character to its socioculturally formed environments. More recent theoretical formulations on the substance of knowledge and its development have built on, and in some cases modified and extended, this earlier work (e.g., A. A. Leontiev, 1981; A. N. Leontiev, 1981; Tulviste, 1991; Wertsch, 1991, 1994; Wertsch & Tulviste, 1992).

There are several key premises of this perspective that are particularly relevant to the learning of additional languages. The first concerns the nature of development. According to this perspective, our language development begins in our material and social worlds. Constituting these worlds is a heterogeneous mix of goal-directed, regularly occurring, communicative activities that utilize cognitive and linguistic means for their accomplishment. Through our repeated participation in these activities with more capable members within our sociocultural environments, we acquire the linguistic, sociocultural, and other knowledge and competencies considered essential to full participation. That is, we learn not only the grammatical, lexical, and other structural components of our language, but also how to perform with our words. In the process of acquisition, we transform the specific linguistic symbols and other means for realizing these activities into individual knowledge and abilities. At the same time, we acquire the communicative intentions and specific perspectives on the world that are embedded in them (Tomasello, 1999). It is our eventual internalization or self-regulation of the specific means for realizing our activities, including the particular worldviews embodied in them, that characterizes psychological growth.

From this viewpoint the essence of mind does not exist separately from the varied worlds it inhabits. The communicative contexts in which we spend our time do not simply enhance the development of mental processes that already exist, but instead, they fundamentally shape and transform them. As noted by both A. N. Leontiev (1981) and Vygotsky (1981), our innate abilities to learn, including perceiving, categorizing, taking a perspective, and making patterns and analogies constitute only the necessary preconditions for learning language. In the process of development, these abilities dynamically merge with our sociocultural experiences constituted by the myriad of activities available to us, and, through our actions with others we learn to make sense of and take part in them. In this way, the conditions for and the consequences of, our individual development—what is generally conceived as our psychological nature—are fundamentally tied to social life. The essentially social nature of development is captured succinctly in Vygotsky's (1981) genetic law of development:

> Any function in the child's cultural development appears twice, or on two planes.
> First it appears on the social plane, and then on the psychological plane. First it appears between people as an interpsychological category, and then within the child as an intrapsychological category . . . Social relations or relations among people genetically underlie all higher functions and their relationships. (p. 163)

Substantial research on first language development in a variety of cultural contexts provides compelling evidence on the social nature of development (e.g., Berman & Slobin, 1994; Bruner, 1990; Levy & Nelson, 1994; Ninio & Snow, 1996; Ochs, 1988; Peters & Boggs, 1986; Pine, 1994a, 1994b; Snow, 1989; Snow, Cancino, de Temple, & Schley, 1991; Sokolov & Snow, 1994; Tomasello, 1999; Tomasello, Conti-Ramsden, & Ewert, 1990). It has been shown, for example, that children acquire both the forms and meanings of their linguistic resources from repeated and frequent experience using these resources in regularly occurring, predictable communicative activities with their primary caregivers. In their joint activities the caregivers provide the children with a substantial amount of input in which they highlight the more important cues. Caregivers draw children's attention to these cues through the use of such nonverbal actions as gazing and gesturing, or through verbal actions such as repeating the cues or changing their tone or pitch patterns. They also provide verbal instructions that direct the children to perceive or notice these cues and make connections between them and their contexts.

Initially, as children and adults interact, the adults assume responsibility for doing most of the communicative work. However, this does not mean that the children remain passive in the process. Rather, from the beginning, they are intrepid explorers of the complex structures of their activities. They actively observe and hypothesize, selecting and attending to very specific kinds of information, looking for patterns, testing their hunches and reorganizing their understanding of the activity and their involvement in it. Over time, children learn to recognize the activity taking place, the linguistic resources conventionally associated with the activity, and the communicative intentions residing within them. The children's initial linguistic actions begin to approximate the conventional forms used by the more expert participants to express similar communicative intents.

As the children assume more responsibility in using language to accomplish the activity, they shape their context-specific patterns or habits of language use into prototypes for action and ultimately internalize them for their own use. In this way, the habits of language use become the tools with which the children make sense of, and participate in, their communicative worlds. Through involvement in a diversity of communicative contexts the children learn to anticipate a variety of linguistic actions, and to choose the appropriate elements needed in the formulation of a response. As Vygotsky (1978) notes, through their sustained participation in their linguistically structured activities, "The child begins to perceive the world not only through its eyes but also through its speech. And later it is not just seeing but acting that becomes informed by words" (p. 32).

Based on a substantial set of cross-linguistic data, Berman and Slobin (1994) propose a form-function, interactive process of language acquisition in which the following factors play a significant role: (1) the frequency with which particular features appear in the input, (2) their functional saliency and transparent form-function relationships, (3) the children's regular engagement in the activity, and (4) its connection to their interests. According to these researchers, the frequent, regular, and predictable use of linguistic resources increases the likelihood that what is important to the realization of the activities will be noticed and ultimately learned. Because different communicative activities are comprised of different arrangements of linguistic resources, different conditions for communicative development are created (Wertsch, 1991). In turn these different conditions, the varied means of assistance in recognizing and using the linguistic cues, and the children's individual responses to them give rise to distinct developmental outcomes.

A study by Pine (1994b) illustrates this process. In an analysis of mother–child interaction Pine showed how the different placements of syntactic elements in the speech of mothers provided different learning conditions for their children. More specifically, he showed how the frequent use of nouns and verbs in the mother's speech, their functional saliency, and their connection to the children's interest and focus of attention created different patterns of language use. As a result of sustained interaction with their mothers using these patterns, the children not only appropriated these different patterns of language use, but their understanding and ability to use these elements in communicative situations also differed.

In another study that looked at caregiver–child conversation (Tomasello et al., 1990), it was shown how children developed different ways of communicating from their participation in different communicative contexts. In looking at the differences between mother–child and father–child interaction, the authors found, for example, that when conversational breakdowns occurred, children elaborated upon their utterances if their mothers did not initially acknowledge them while they repeated their utterances or abandoned talk if their fathers did not acknowledge them. The authors concluded that through extended interactions with each parent the children learned to assume different intentions in their parents' lack of acknowledgment. Because mothers usually followed up on their children's utterances when a breakdown in communication occurred, the children learned to interpret their mothers' lack of initial acknowledgment as a need for more information and so learned to elaborate. On the other hand, because fathers usually did not return to the conversation after a breakdown, the children learned to interpret their fathers' lack of acknowledgment as indifference and so learned to give up.

While much research has been concerned with first language development, a few studies, most notably by Snow and her colleagues (Snow et al., 1991; Wu, de Temple, Herman, & Snow, 1994) provide equally compelling data on the relationship between the communicative activities in which one is engaged and the L2 that is subsequently acquired. In the 1991 study, Snow et al. found that the ability of children in grades 2 through 5 to produce formal definitions in both English and French was tied to the children's involvement in activities that included the use of words and syntactic and discourse structures typical of such definitions. They concluded that the development of children's skills in an additional language, if not first acquired in L1, is strongly related to their involvement in activities employing those skills in the second language rather than to access some generalized notion of the language itself.

Similarly, Wu and others (1994) looked at performance differences across tasks in which students used either English or French. They found that those restricted to learning French in the classroom showed a difference in written and oral performances across conditions, doing better in all writing tasks, and doing most poorly on oral contextualized tasks. More specifically, they found that the children's abilities in French were tied to their involvement in particular activities constituted in French, which did not include opportunities to develop oral contextualizing skills. They concluded that the activities constituting the learning environments of additional language learners fundamentally shape their abilities and skills in that language.

More recent studies examining communicative activities found in second and foreign language classrooms have reached similar conclusions. Kinginger (2000), for example, examined computer-mediated communication between university learners of French and a group of French native-speaking peers. Her study revealed how, in the context of developing interpersonal relationships with the French speakers over the course of the semester, the students appropriated the use of the *tu* form for the expression of solidarity with their interlocutors. In a study of the instructional conversations found in an elementary school Japanese language program, Takahashi, Austin, and Morimoto (2000) revealed how the young language learners appropriated and made active use of specific strategies that the teacher used to assist learning. A particular song, for example, was used by the teacher as a mnemonic device for helping students remember how to conjugate a particular verb. At the beginning of the year, the teacher often broke into song when a student needed some assistance in coming up with a correct form of the verb. Eventually, the students appropriated the song's use as a strategic tool for remembering, singing it aloud without prompting by the teacher when they or one of their classmates needed help in remembering the verb forms.

The findings from these and other studies highlight the connection between additional language development and its sociocultural contexts of use. We learn structures of language, the conventions for using and interpreting its components, and the social meanings, values, and attitudes attached to those conventions in the process of interacting with others and being aware of the means by which the communication is accomplished. The ability to recognize what is going on and to contribute independently to a communicative activity constitutes a major accomplishment in our communicative development and thereby facilitates the development of more complex and creative communicative behaviors.

Mediational Means

A key concept to understanding development from a sociocultural perspective has to do with the **mediational means** with which the more competent members assist children and other novices in noticing, ordering, representing, and remembering their involvement in their socioculturally constructed activities. Mediational means can be verbal, visual, or physical and can include, in addition to linguistic resources, computational resources such as calculators, computers, and counting systems, and graphic resources such as maps, diagrams, drawings, and writing systems. We use calendars, for example, to help us remember upcoming activities, maps to help us get from one place to another, and calculators to help us complete tasks involving computations. In the classroom we use particular seating arrangements to facilitate particular kinds of participation in class, and seating charts to help us remember students' names. Similarly, we may require students to use schedules or assignment notebooks as a way to help them remember and organize their time commitments.

These meaning-making resources are "the 'carriers' of sociocultural patterns and knowledge" (Wertsch, 1994, p. 204). According to Vygotsky (1981, 1986, 1987), the means we use in realizing our activities structure both the environment within which development occurs as well as individual developmental outcomes of our participation within these environments. In other words, the means themselves and the ways in which we use them in the pursuit of action with others do not simply enhance our individual development, but rather, they fundamentally shape and transform it. Development is distinguished by our autonomy or self-regulated use of the means. Vygotsky (as cited in Van der Veer & Valsiner, 1994) explains the essential role mediational means play in development:

> The greatest characteristic feature of child development is that this development is achieved under particular conditions of interactions with the environment, where the ideal and final form (ideal in the sense that it acts as a model for that which should be achieved at the end of the developmental period; and final in the sense that it represents what the child is supposed to attain at the end of its development) is not only already present and from the very start in contact with the child, but actually interacts and exerts a real influence on the primary form, on the first steps of the child's development. (p. 344)

The mediational means we use in our activities are of critical importance to our communicative development. They are the structuring agents of both the form and content of what is learned. In other words, they structure not only our activities but also the values and meanings attached to them as well, inducing us "to construe certain perceptual/conceptual situations—to attend to them—in one way rather than in another" (Tomasello, 1999, p. 128). At the same time, we use the means to negotiate our way through the processes of learning to become a competent, full-fledged participant (Wertsch, 1991). The more experience we attain in using the means to realize our activities and to accomplish our goals, the more fully competent we become at using them.

As noted earlier, the means we use to engage in our communicative contexts can vary, sometimes widely, across groups. Likewise, the uses to which we put similar-appearing means can also vary. Because our communicative development is tied to the nature of the means and the uses to which they are put, the paths it takes are equally varied. Thus, understanding development entails investigation of the cultural, historical, and institutional contexts in which it originates.

Since for many middle and high school students their first experiences learning other languages occur in their foreign language classrooms, these contexts, and more specifically, their language-based activities and means with which they are accomplished create specific conditions for the learning of the target language. Thus, they are crucial sites for the investigation of additional language development.

A final point concerns the learning of new mediational means. According to Wertsch (1991), the learning of new means requires two processes. First, it entails engaging in communicative contexts in which these new means are required for their accomplishment. Second, it requires that we become conscious or aware of the means themselves, their typical patterns of use, and the psychological processes associated with the ways they are used. Only through such conscious reflection can we understand fully the connections between language use and development, and imagine the many possibilities for doing different things with our words, bringing to life "new connections and relations between and within them" (Shotter, 1996, p. 303).

Zone of Proximal Development

Another concept that is important to a sociocultural perspective of development is the **zone of proximal development,** or the ZPD as it is more commonly referred to. As noted earlier, learning is a dynamic process by which the mediational means of one's communicative activities are transformed into individual knowledge and skills. According to Vygotsky (1987), this process takes place in the zone of proximal development. This site of development is defined as "the distance between the actual development level as determined by independent problem solving and the level of potential development as determined through problem solving under adult guidance or in collaboration with more capable peers" (p. 86).

The ZPD pertains to any situation that is jointly enacted between experts and learners and in which the goal is for individuals to develop mastery of a skill or understanding of a topic. This does not mean, however, that the teacher or adult is the sole source of assistance in the ZPD. Peers can also act as resources, guiding and extending each other's ideas as they work toward the conclusion or resolution of an issue. Students can help other students; children can help their friends. As noted by Wells (1999, p. 308), "Providing assistance in the ZPD is a function, not of role or status, but of the collaboration itself: Each participant can potentially act in ways that assist the others, and all can learn from the others' contributions."

Recent formulations of the ZPD conceptualize it not as an attribute of an individual but as a dynamic site of learning. It exists not *within* individuals but *between* them, constructed in interaction between the learner and the more capable partner (Lave & Wenger, 1991;

Moll, 1990; Wells, 1999). In this process, learners use knowledge, skills, and other abilities that are beyond their levels of competence with the assistance of more capable others. Effective assistance requires that the more capable individual understands, and is responsive to, the learners' current levels of development.

In the process of assisted learning in the ZPD, the more competent member and learners begin by doing the task together. At first the more capable individual does most of the work, gradually handing over to the learners the responsibility for contributing particular actions until the learners can perform them without help. With such socially mediated assistance, the learners' performances are raised to a level they could not have achieved on their own. The use of the song by the Japanese teacher, noted earlier, is a good example of assisted performance in the ZPD. Remember, the teacher sang the song to help students call to mind particular verb forms needed to accomplish particular activities. Her singing helped raise the young learners' performance in Japanese to a level they could not have attained on their own. Eventually, as the students in the Japanese class did, learners take over the task, appropriating the requisite skills and abilities along with the meanings, values, and attitudes attached to them—no longer needing the assistance of the more capable member.

It is important to note that while biological factors provide the range of an individual's learning potential, it is the mediational tools and the uses to which they are put in the ZPD by which higher mental processes are formed. In other words, "We grow into the intellectual world of those around us" (Vygotsky, 1978, p. 88). For foreign language learning, this means that while the capabilities individuals bring to the classroom are important, the level of competence they ultimately attain in the target language is tied to the mediational means they are given access to and the opportunities provided for using them.

It should also be noted that the extent to which an individual internalizes particular mediational means and their values depends on the degree of consonance or compatibility that exists between the learner and the cultural tools. Learning in the ZPD is more likely to occur when the mediational means are sanctioned or approved by the larger sociocultural environments of school and community. Learning is also more likely to occur when learners find the means personally meaningful and are predisposed to, or invested in, moving toward a particular goal and to using the means in the pursuit of that goal (Wells, 1999).

Scaffolding

As stated earlier, learning occurs in the ZPD through joint activity with more expert participants. However, it is not simply joint activity alone that creates the ZPD. Rather, promoting independent task mastery requires strategically guided assistance by the more capable other. A key aspect of the process by which experts provide help is known as **scaffolding.** First coined by Wood, Bruner, and Ross in 1976, scaffolding is defined as a process of negotiated interaction in which experts first assess the learners' levels of competence and determine the types of assistance they need to accomplish a particular task. They then take control of those portions of a task that are beyond the learners' current level of competence, gradually handing over the responsibility for completing the task to the learners as their competence grows.

Six specific strategies for providing such assistance constitute this process. They can be found on the following page.

1. *Recruiting:* This entails drawing the learners' attention to, and engaging their interest in, the activity.
2. *Reducing the degrees of freedom:* This involves simplifying the demands of the task to meet the needs of the learners.
3. *Maintaining direction:* This requires keeping the learners motivated and focused on the task.
4. *Marking critical features:* This entails emphasizing all relevant features of the activity and highlighting discrepancies between actual and expected behaviors.
5. *Controlling frustration:* This involves helping to reduce the stress that learners develop when trying to participate in something in which they are not yet fully competent.
6. *Modeling expected behavior:* This involves performing the expected behaviors for the learners to notice, observe, and imitate.

Excerpt 1, as follows, contains a simulated example of scaffolding. Here a parent and a child are engaging in an activity considered to be typical of many middle-class American parent–child interactions—labeling. The parent actively works to bring the child into full participation and thus helps the child perform above the level where the child would be able to perform alone.

Excerpt 1

recruits	1. Parent:	(pointing to a picture) What's this?
reduces degrees of freedom		Is this a cat?
	2. Child:	No.
reduces degrees of freedom	3. Parent:	Is it a dog?
	4. Child:	Dog.
maintains interest	5. Parent:	Yes, sweetie (hugs the child). It's a dog. That's right.
maintains direction	6.	What's the doggie say?
reduces degrees of freedom	7.	Does the dog bark? (silence)
models	8.	Does the dog go "ruff ruff"?
	9. Child:	Ruff-ruff.
	10. Parent:	Yes, the dog says "ruff ruff." You're a smartie.

As we can see, in line 1 the parent first *recruits* the child's attention to the task by pointing to a picture and asking "What's this?" Without waiting for a response, the parent *reduces the degrees of freedom* by simplifying the question to one that requires only a yes or no answer. In so doing, the parent attempts to meet the child at the child's level and provide an opportunity to participate fully in the task. After the child provides an appropriate response in line 2, the parent continues with a similarly simplified question in line 3, again helping the child to provide an appropriate response. The parent affirms enthusiastically the child's response verbally and nonverbally (with a hug), and in so doing helps *maintain the child's interest* in continuing. In line 6 the parent *maintains the direction* of the activity by asking a related question, and then proceeds to simplify or *reduce the degrees of freedom* in a subsequent question (line 7). In the third iteration of the question (line 8), the parent *models* the expected answer for the child, which, as we see in line 9, the child repeats. The child's response is both confirmed and aptly rewarded by the parent in line 10.

Eventually, with regular participation in similar activities, the child will be able to manage the activity alone. That is, the child will be able to point to and describe a picture with little or no help from the adult. Once the child has appropriated these skills and abilities the parent can expand the activity to include more complex actions like, for example, narrating a story about the picture or comparing features of two different pictures.

Successful scaffolding, then, entails focusing learners' attention on the task, directing their attention to essential and relevant features, modeling expected behaviors, and keeping the learners motivated throughout. As Wells (1999) has argued, to be considered a scaffolding interaction requires the deliberate intention to move the responsibility for competent performance in an activity from the expert to the novice. However, this does not mean that knowledge is simply handed down to another. That is to say, the task of the expert is not merely to tell the other what to do. Rather, the process is mutually constitutive with all participants, expert and novice alike, active in the process.

In such an interaction, van Lier (1996) notes, "The agenda is shaped by all participants, and educational reality may be transformed" (p. 180). This notion of learning as moving from peripheral to full participation, from assisted guidance to open dialogue, stands in marked contrast to the notion of learning as the transmission of decontextualized bits of knowledge (Lee & Smagorinsky, 2000; van Lier, 1996).

Recent research has examined the processes and outcomes of scaffolding in second and foreign language classrooms. McCormick and Donato (2000), for example, revealed how a teacher of English to university-level nonnative speakers made effective use of particular questions to scaffold students' participation, comprehension, and comprehensibility in their classroom tasks. Along similar lines, in an examination of an advanced, university-level ESL class, Aljaafreh and Lantolf (1994) revealed the various levels of assistance that a tutor provided to a group of learners in helping them notice and correct their syntactic errors.

Other research has examined the role that peers can play in providing assistance to their classmates. Swain and Lapkin (1996), for example, showed how middle school students of French were able to help each other use the target language accurately in the collaborative reconstruction of a story. Similarly, Ohta (1995, 1997) revealed how peers in a university-level Japanese language class were able to help each other complete an instructional task. She concluded that as a result of their collaborative interaction, learners were able to perform at a higher level of competence. As a final example, in a study of a university-level Spanish language class, DiCamilla and Anton (1997) revealed the strategic use of repetition by learners to help each other complete a task. As a whole these studies demonstrate the opportunities that peer collaborations provide for assisted learning. When working together learners are "individually novices and collectively experts, sources of new orientations for each other" (Donato, 1994, p. 46). Together they can achieve what they could not have achieved alone.

Private Speech

Another important aspect of the dynamic process of development, and of special significance to the learning of additional languages, is the concept of **private speech.** Private speech is language that learners address to themselves to aid their participation in an activity. It is labeled *private* not because it contains confidential or secret information, but because it is addressed to the self only and thus not intentionally directed to or in need of a response from others.

According to Vygotsky (1978, 1986), the appearance of private speech indicates that learners are actively engaged in the process of learning. Learners use it as a way to think through and become more self-regulated and less dependent on others for help in accomplishing an activity. For example, in completing a puzzle, a child might say to herself as she searches through the pieces, "Ok, I need to find the corner pieces first. Where are the pieces that have straight edges?" Likewise, in doing a crossword puzzle, an adult might say to himself in a low voice, "Hmm, I need an eight-letter word for *lively* that begins with *v*. Vivacious? No, that has nine letters." Another adult might murmur to herself as she is grocery shopping, "What kind of cheese was I supposed to get?" The content of these utterances reflects the particular locus of each individual's attention in relation to the task at hand. Talking to themselves "in private" helps both the child and the adults focus on the task and call to mind the specific actions needed to complete it.

A great deal of research has examined the use of private speech among children to regulate their involvement in their activities (Berk & Garvin, 1984; Diaz, 1992; Vygotsky, 1978, 1987). However, it is not the case that its use disappears once an individual reaches a certain level of maturity. Rather, anyone—child or adult—who is faced with a difficult or unfamiliar task will engage in private speech.

Several recent studies of second and foreign language learning have highlighted the use of private speech by adults to facilitate the process of learning another language. In a study of a university-level Japanese language class, for example, Ohta (2000) revealed how some learners used private speech to help themselves learn. During large-group teacher-directed interaction, several students whispered to themselves, repeating the teacher's utterances, or changing ill-formed utterances offered by other students in response to questions by the teacher. These private self-whisperings, Ohta argued, helped these students take notice of differences between ill-formed and accurate utterances, and make whatever corrections were needed to their own formulations.

In another study, Lantolf (1997) investigated the extent to which adult learners of Spanish engaged in some form of private speech such as "talking out loud to yourself in Spanish" or "imitating to yourself sounds in Spanish" (p. 9). He found that most of the participants in his study reported engaging in such language and that doing so reduced their reticence to speak Spanish. In a review of the literature on private speech, McCafferty (1994) concluded that it serves important cognitive, social, and affective functions in the learning of additional languages.

Imitation and Repetition

From a sociocultural perspective both **imitation** and **repetition** also serve important functions in learning. Here, imitation is defined not as the simple, mechanical formation of habits but as a complex, significant act of meaning-making in the ZPD (Newman & Holzman, 1993; Tomasello, Kruger, & Ratner, 1993; Vygotsky, 1987). For Vygotsky (1987) imitation "is the source of all the specifically human characteristics of consciousness that develop in the child" (p. 210). By imitating or copying the action of the expert the child or novice is able to do something that he or she cannot yet do on his or her own. As noted earlier, a crucial part of the ZPD entails orienting to learners as competent others, guiding them from dependent, jointly constructed action to independent action. In the ZPD, particularly in the initial stages of learning, imitation is a primary means by which learners perceive and come to master the communicative means and other linguistic and nonlinguistic resources needed for competent engagement in their activities.

Recent research reveals that repetitions and recasts or reformulations of others' words play an equally significant role in the process of learning. In first language contexts, for example, they have been shown to serve multiple cognitive, communicative, and social functions such as helping students take notice of what is to be learned and establishing discursive and topical coherence in interaction (Halliday & Hasan, 1976; Johnstone, 1994; Tannen, 1989).

Research in second and foreign language learning contexts has confirmed and, in some cases, extended findings on the usefulness of repetition and recasts. DiCamilla and Anton (1997), for example, demonstrated how a group of university-level Spanish language learners used repetition to accomplish a task together. By repeating to each other those syntactic forms they found problematic, the learners were able to hold their collective attention on the forms while they worked to construct more accurate versions. The authors argue that repetition did more than increase students' exposure to the target language. It enabled them to hold on to what they had together constructed in order to think about, evaluate, and revise accordingly. In this way it helped to create a collectively constructed "cognitive space in which to work (think, hypothesize, evaluate, and from which to build, i.e., generate more language)" (p. 628).

Duff (2000) also reported cognitive benefits for repetition. In a study of university-level English and Hebrew foreign language classrooms, she found that teacher repetition of terms served multiple functions. It helped to validate the concepts and ideas initially raised by students and to draw their attention to key concepts or linguistic forms. In addition, it helped the learners process the lexical and syntactic components of the utterances and build a base of shared knowledge by making topical and rhetorical connections among the many contributions to the interaction. Other studies in both second and foreign language classrooms (e.g., Boyd & Maloof, 2000; Sullivan, 2000; Verplaetse, 2000) have reported similar findings demonstrating that repetitions of teacher and student utterances help to focus group attention on relevant aspects of individual utterances, and thereby facilitate student appropriation of new words, concepts, and ideas.

Findings from several studies have also revealed communicative and social benefits deriving from repetition and recasts. Duff (2000) and Sullivan (2000), for example, both showed how their use fostered a humorous, lighthearted side to learning in which classroom members were able to use their collectively constructed knowledge to play on each other's words and ideas. This humorous use of repetitions and recasts increased the learners' enjoyment in their interactions with each other. This in turn, the authors note, helped teachers and students build strong interpersonal relationships and, in a more general way, created a sense of community among them.

It should also be noted that while these studies have shown repetition to be beneficial to additional language learning, Duff (2000) points out that not all forms of repetition may be helpful. As she shows in some of her data, persistent, intentional repetition in classroom interaction that focuses exclusively on form can be mind-numbing and thus likely to counteract any possible social, cognitive, or communicative benefits. Excerpt 2, from Duff's study of a university-level German foreign language class, is one example of ineffective repetition. As Duff points out, the repeated utterances—noted in bold—have little to do with affirming student contributions or making topical connections. Instead, they are designed solely to elicit grammatically correct forms. While short, focused sequences of repetition for such purposes are not necessarily bad, the effects of *extended* sequences of repetition, Duff argues, can lead to boredom, frustration, and lack of motivation on the students' part.

Excerpt 2 (from Duff, 2000, p. 127)

1. Teacher: Mhm. Was machst sie?

   What does she do?

2. Student 1:   Uh, sie **zeht?**

   She dresses? (mispronounces third-person form)

3. Teacher: **Zieht.**

   Dresses.

4. Student 1:   **Zieht dich an.**

   Dresses yourself.

5. Teacher: Mhm. **Zieht.**

   Dresses.

6. Student 1:   **Zieht.**

   Dresses.

7. Teacher: **Zieht sich an.**

   Dresses herself.

8. Student 1:   **Zieht sich an.**

   Dresses herself.

Play

The final aspect of communicative development is **play,** particularly fantasy or imaginary play, in which learners take on roles in "make-believe" or imagined situations. In *role* play, for example, learners are provided with opportunities to use their mediational means, or communicative resources, to accomplish myriad goals without being constrained by real-time requirements of interpersonal interactions or task goals. Moreover, they are exposed to roles that they might not experience outside of the classroom, and thus have the opportunity to use language in ways that real-life situations may not provide. For example, they can take on the role of teacher, parent, or counselor. They can become a waiter, a banker, or even the president of a country.

Because the consequences of such play are likely to be nonthreatening or inconsequential, learners are not likely to experience much frustration in their verbal interactions. Rather, taking on different roles can provide them with the freedom to indulge in explorations of language use. They can try out different voices, take on new social identities, rehearse new constructions, and eventually master a broader arena of communicative means to which the learners may only have indirect access outside of the classroom. Such opportunities for divergent language use are especially critical to foreign language development, since, unlike second language learners who live in communities where the target language is spoken, opportunities for foreign language learners to engage in language explorations are pretty much limited to the classroom.

It was Bruner (1986) who emphasized the intimate connection between play and language development most clearly, noting that complicated grammatical and pragmatic aspects of language appear first in play. This happens because, according to Vygotsky (1978), the norms for actions associated with various roles taken up in play help learners organize their behavior in particular ways. When they take on the roles of shopkeeper, teacher, or news broadcaster, for example, they act in accordance with the norms and expectations associated with these characters. Thus, they use words and concepts that under normal conditions—as, say, middle or high school students—they would not have an opportunity to use. In this way, the play conditions allow learners to act at higher linguistic, cognitive, and communicative levels than they could otherwise and thereby help to create a ZPD for their development of higher mental functions. In Vygotsky's (1978) words, "In play the child is always behaving beyond his age, above his usual everyday behavior; in play he is, as it were, a head above himself" (p. 74).

In addition to fantasy or role play, language play is considered important to communicative development. Here learners play with, contemplate, and in other ways enjoy the sounds and images of language. Word or sound play and repartee or verbal dueling are just a few of the activities that, as noted by Cook (1997), learners are engaged in primarily for the pure pleasure of doing so. This deliberate playful use of language reveals not only learners' developing metalinguistic abilities, but also their attitudes toward the value of language for its own sake.

In their examination of successful language-learning lessons for children learning English as a second language, Wong Fillmore, Ammon, McLaughlin, and Ammon (1985) noted the use of such playfulness and its role in bringing learners' attention to forms. They state, "The final characteristic of the language used in successful lessons is that of richness and occasional playfulness as well . . . .The teachers in successful classes tended to use language in ways that called attention to the language itself" (p. 42).

Sullivan (2000) notes that language play can include word coinage—making up new words for humorous purposes—and using words or sounds playfully in inappropriate contexts. Excerpt 3 illustrates one form of word play engaged in by a teacher and a group of learners in an English as a foreign language classroom in Vietnam. In this excerpt the teacher and students are engaging in a game of playful, collaborative repartee. According to Sullivan, the researcher unknowingly triggered the game by commenting that the question asked by the teacher is a "major" one (line 5). This is picked up by the teacher with the words "very big," and followed by students who expand it to "huge," "gigantic," "enormous," and finally, from the teacher, "titanic."

Excerpt 3: Titanic (adapted from Sullivan, 2000, p. 85)

1. Teacher:	Uh huh? Right. Now 14. "What problems do you	
2.	think a developing country may face in its	
3.	social and economic development?"	
4. Students:	*(Several repeat the question in Vietnamese.)*	
5. Researcher:	A **major** question. h-h-h-h.	
6. Teacher:	Yes. A **very big** question uh.	
7. Student 1:	A **huge** question.	
8. Teacher:	**Huge** question. OK.	
9. Students:	[It's **very big.**]	
10. Students:	[A **gigantic** question.]	
11. Teacher:	*(laugh)* A **gigantic** question. OK.	
12. Student:	*(unintelligible)*	
13. Teacher:	OK.	
14. Student 2:	An **enormous** question.	
15. Teacher:	A **titanic** question. OK.	

Sullivan concludes that such banter exemplifies real-life interactions that more often take place outside of the classroom. By encouraging such language play in the classroom, Sullivan argues, the teacher helped to create meaningful and motivating contexts for language use among the class members, and thereby helped to increase their group solidarity. This, in turn, enhanced the learners' interest in continuing to use the target language to interact with each other and the teacher, thus reinforcing and expanding their vocabulary knowledge.

SUMMARY: PRINCIPLES FOR LEARNING ADDITIONAL LANGUAGES

The goal of this chapter was to present an overview of communicative development from a sociocultural perspective. As noted earlier, many of the assumptions about language and learning embodied in this perspective differ significantly from a more traditional perspective. A summary of some of the more significant differences can be found in Table 2–1.

Several **principles for learning additional languages** can be derived from the theoretical insights and empirical evidence presented in this chapter. The first concerns our understanding of the process of additional language learning. We know that the process cannot be explained fully as an innate process of acquiring and controlling a system of isolated, context-free linguistic structures. Rather, it is best understood as an inherently social process of developing a repertoire of cognitive, social, and communicative skills, abilities, and knowledge for engaging in a wide variety of activities in which the target language is the common code. It is, as A. A. Leontiev (1981) notes, learning to participate meaningfully in "distinct types of intellectual and practical pursuits" (p. 99) as they are realized in that language.

TABLE 2–1 *Comparison of Assumptions between Traditional and Sociocultural Perspectives on Language Learning.*

	Traditional	Sociocultural
Language	structural systems, knowledge of which precedes use	tools for social action, systems of which result from use
Mind	universal, innate device from which linguistic knowledge of individual languages is derived	joint creation of biological and cultural processes, originating in material worlds of individual, with the use of mediational means
Learning	internal activation of language acquisition device	process of being acculturated or socialized into intellectual and practical activities of a particular sociocultural group
Goal of Teaching	to optimize assimilation of new knowledge structures into existing structures of mind	to increase access to and skill in using communicative means of variety of sociocultural activities
Focus of research	to uncover universal properties of innate language capacity and role of internal processes in the assimilation of new language systems	to examine consequences of participation in particular communicative activities in terms of individual language development

For middle and high school learners of another language, then, the goal of foreign language learning moves beyond the mere learning of grammar rules to encompass the full appropriation of a wide range of communicative means and resources. Only through such learning can they add new voices to those they already have, create new identities and new roles, and ultimately expand their possibilities for becoming more fully involved in their social worlds both in and outside of the classroom.

A second principle has to do with the source of learning. As discussed earlier, the process itself does not begin in the individual mind. Rather, it is inherently social, originating in participation with others in communicative contexts in which individuals are oriented to as legitimate learners and users of the target language (Lave & Wenger, 1991). In addition to situated participation, learning requires guided assistance by more capable participants in the zone of proximal development through scaffolding. On the part of the learners, it involves an investment in learning, and the ability to monitor and reflect critically on their involvement.

For middle and high school students of other languages, this means that they must be provided with multiple opportunities in which teachers actively work to help them accomplish tasks that bring them to new levels of competence. Furthermore, as pointed out earlier, since they will grow into the intellectual environment that is provided for them, these opportunities must challenge the students cognitively, socially, and communicatively. At the same time, middle and high school learners must be given opportunities to collaborate with one another and in other ways be afforded the chance to serve as "sources of new orientations for each other" (Donato, 1994, p. 46).

A third principle for learning additional language entails understanding the intrinsic link between the cognitive and affective dimensions of learning. As Wells (1999) points out, learning involves not only the development of knowledge and skills needed to be competent participants in important sociocultural activities, but also the development of new identities as legitimate participants in those activities. The success of this involvement is tied to learners' interests, beliefs, and motivations for learning.

For beginning learners of other languages, this involves taking on new identities as users of the target language, which can sometimes be a face-threatening, socially awkward process. For middle and high school students, many of whom are first-time foreign language learners, the process may be even more uncomfortable or difficult since their self-perceptions are already fairly fragile. Thus, in addition to providing cognitively and communicatively challenging learning environments, it is important to provide opportunities for play in which learners feel safe to explore new identities and new opportunities for using language.

A fourth principle concerns the important roles that the routinization and predictability of communicative activities play in the learning process. As noted earlier, many of our communicative activities are organized around a set of communicative plans that include a predictable sequence of exchanges, predictable goals, and predictable norms and expectations for the enactment of our social roles in the activities. In addition to helping participants stabilize and coordinate their thoughts and actions, these plans help them develop a familiarity and a sense of security about their participation in the activities. This familiarity in turn helps them develop a shared base of knowledge and strong interpersonal bonds with each other. Using the mutually constructed knowledge and interpersonal relationships as a base they are subsequently able to construct more complex and creative ways of participating.

In order to help middle and high school learners of other languages develop the same levels of familiarity and sense of security about their use of the target language, it is important to structure their learning around predictable, routinized classroom activities. In addition to helping them coordinate their thoughts and actions in the target language, these activities can help them develop prototypes for action on which more complex and creative uses of the target language can be built.

A fifth principle concerns the role of the teacher in language learning. In most middle and high school language classrooms teachers are the only expert users of the target language to which learners are exposed; therefore, their role in structuring and managing the intellectual and practical contexts in which the students learn the target language is of great consequence to learner development. In the kinds of activities they make available to their students, these teachers provide models of what counts as "the target language" and as "target language learning."

If, for example, the primary activities of the classroom consist of written grammar exercises, students are likely to develop an understanding of the target language as consisting primarily of grammar and of language learning as doing exercises. On the other hand, if students are involved in a variety of activities that involve diverse social, communicative, and cognitive skills and knowledge, their understandings of language and learning are likely to be more encompassing. Moreover, in structuring both the quantity and quality of the opportunities that the students have to participate in and learn from their activities, these teachers make visible their own attitudes toward the activities and toward the students' involvement in them. In doing so, they play a significant role in shaping the degree of individual learning that can occur.

A final principle has to do with the study of additional language learning itself. As we have discussed, our communicative activities are the locus of all learning. The process itself moves from the social action that takes place between persons, which in the case of classroom learning is between the teacher and his or her students, and between students, to the psychological action that occurs within each individual through the varied processes of appropriation and transformation. The study of additional language learning then becomes the study of the processes by which learners' involvement in their classroom activities is shaped, and how, over time, such involvement affects the development of their social and psychological identities both as learners and users of the target language.

Understanding the learning that occurs in foreign language classrooms requires that we identify and characterize the constellations of activities, including the means for their accomplishment, that comprise our classrooms. We must also examine the complex webs of communicative activities and the varied developmental paths created by teacher and learner involvement in and across these activities, within and across classrooms. Findings from this research will lead us to a fuller understanding of the intrinsic link between the kinds of communicative environments we are creating in our foreign language classrooms and the developmental consequences they give rise to. Such an understanding, in turn, will enhance our abilities as teachers to create learning environments that help to shape learners' communicative development in the target language in ways that are considered appropriate to their social, academic, and other needs.

DISCUSSION QUESTIONS AND ACTIVITIES

1. Choose two concepts from Table 2–1 and write down your own views of each. For example, what do you believe language is? How do you view the nature of mind? The nature of learning? In small groups, compare your views with those of your classmates. How do they compare to those presented in the table? In your small group examine the chapter and find three statements that provided you with evidence or information that either confirmed or changed in some way your view of each concept. Then find one or two statements that differ from your understandings, but that you feel do not provide enough evidence or information for you to change your thinking. What further evidence would you need? How might you go about obtaining that evidence?

2. As stated by Wertsch (1991), "Because different communicative activities are comprised of different arrangements of linguistic resources, different conditions for communicative development are created. In turn these different conditions, the varied means of assistance in recognizing and using the linguistic cues, and the children's individual responses to them give rise to distinct developmental outcomes."

   With a partner rewrite these statements using active voice and more familiar vocabulary. Share what you have written with other members of the class, and together provide at least one example of how your experiences as additional language learners relate to the statements. What implications can you draw for teaching another language?

3. To get an idea of how to use language to scaffold or guide the performance of another in a task, join with a partner and choose or create a task in which one of you is more expert. One of you might, for example, instruct the other in how to do a puzzle, build a model with manipulatives, or complete a grammar exercise. Tape-record the interaction as it occurs and then, together, transcribe and identify the purposes of the different utterances. Use the list of scaffolding actions found earlier in the chapter to code the utterances. How successful was the interaction in terms of scaffolding? Provide evidence for your claims.

4. Provide some examples of the ways in which imitation, repetition, and play can contribute to the learning of additional languages. Consider, too, the ways in which they might hinder learning. Draw from your own experiences as both a teacher and student of another language. What implications can you draw for creating effective conditions for foreign language learning in the classroom?

5. With a partner write down as many ideas as you can about the role that private speech plays in language learning. Give examples from your own experiences as language learners of how you have used private speech. Share your ideas with your classmates. What implications can you draw for foreign language learning by middle and high school students?

6. Choose two concepts presented in this chapter on which to gather further information. Search the library for relevant sources of materials and provide annotations of three articles (published in the last 3 years) that address each of the two concepts.

ADDITIONAL READINGS

Bodrova, E., & Leong, D. (1996). *Tools of the mind: The Vygotskian approach to early childhood education.* Upper Saddle River, NJ: Prentice Hall.

Cole, M. (1996). *Cultural psychology.* Cambridge, MA: Harvard University Press.

Dunn, W. E., & Lantolf, J. P. (1998). Vygotsky's zone of proximal development and Krashen's 'I + 1': Incommensurable constructs, incommensurable theories. *Language Learning, 48*(3), 411–442.

Forman, E., Minick, N., & Stone, C. A. (1993). *Contexts for learning: Sociocultural dynamics in children's development.* New York: Oxford University Press.

John-Steiner, V., & Mahn, H. (1996). Sociocultural approaches to learning and development: A Vygotskian framework. *Educational Psychologist, 31*(3/4), 191–206.

Newman, D., Griffin, P., & Cole, M. (1989). *The construction zone: Working for cognitive change in school.* Cambridge: Cambridge University Press.

Reed, E. (1996). *Encountering the world: Toward an ecological psychology.* New York: Oxford University Press.

INTERNET RESOURCES

http://communication.ucsd.edu/MCA/index.html   The Mind, Culture, and Activity Homepage

This is the site of an interactive forum for a community of interdisciplinary scholars who share an interest in the study of the human mind in its cultural and historical contexts. Participants come from a variety of disciplines, including anthropology, cognitive science, education, linguistics, psychology, and sociology. On the homepage you will find links to current and past issues of the journal *Mind, Culture, and Activity,* personal profiles of the participants, and links to other related Web sites.

http://www.iscrat.org/   International Society for Cultural Research and Activity Theory (ISCRAT)

This site is the homepage for the ISCRAT organization, which brings together researchers in both Eastern and Western European countries who work within Activity Theory, including Vygotsky's work, and its connection to teaching and learning.

http://www.cudenver.edu/~mryder/itc_data/soc_cult.html#vygotsky

This Web site, from the University of Colorado School of Education, provides a comprehensive set of links to articles and books on Vygotsky and sociocultural theory including concepts such as the zone of proximal development and scaffolding. The site also includes links to, and comparisons with, other theories.

Chapter 3

Creating Communities of Learners in the Classroom

Preview Questions

Before you begin reading this chapter, think about your own classroom experiences as both a student and teacher.

- What were some of the characteristics of the classrooms where you felt challenged as a learner and at the same time free to take risks?
- What role did the teacher play in creating these classrooms?
- What influenced your decision to become a foreign language teacher? Why do you want to teach middle and high school students?
- What technological knowledge and skills do you have that you feel will enhance your abilities as a foreign language teacher?
- Have you ever participated in a research project on teaching and learning? What role did you play? What were the benefits of participating in the research? What were the difficulties?
- Based on your experiences, what implications can you draw for the role of research in the lives of foreign language teachers and students?

Key Words and Concepts

Communities of learners
  Teacher expertise
    Content knowledge
    Pedagogical content knowledge
    Pedagogical knowledge
Learning opportunities
  Situated practice
  Overt instruction
  Critical framing
  Transformed practice
  The role of grammar teaching
Participation structures
  Individual instruction
  Whole-group instruction

Peer tutoring
Team learning
Learning center
Communication modes
Technology standards
  Basic skills
  Critical literacies
  Construction skills
Teacher Research
  Data sources
    Interviews
    Questionnaires
    Field notes
    Participant observation

Overview

The concepts of communication and communicative development, presented in Chapters 1 and 2, highlight the significant role that our social institutions play in shaping the form, the content, and the value of our communicative activities. Because schools are one of our more significant institutions, the activities formed in their classrooms are especially important to learner development.

A fairly large body of research has examined classroom life from a sociocultural perspective (e.g., Bowers & Flinders, 1990; Gutierrez, 1994, 1995; Lemke, 1988; Moll, 1990; Smagorinsky & Fly, 1993). The findings of these studies make clear the consequential roles that both teachers and students play in creating their classroom communities. More specifically, they reveal how, through regular engagement in their recurring classroom activities, teachers and students develop habits of participation that define particular norms and expectations for their roles and role relationships. For example, together they define the kinds of verbal and nonverbal behaviors they consider appropriate and inappropriate for displaying attention to each other. In addition, through their jointly constructed activities, teachers and students define what counts as subject matter content and how students are to demonstrate their understandings of this knowledge.

For many middle and high school students, their first introduction to the study of another language occurs in their foreign language classrooms. Thus, these classrooms play an especially significant role in their development in that the conditions created in these classrooms are the birthplace of what comes to be known as "foreign language," and "foreign language learning." What the students learn here in terms of language and learning sets the foundation upon which their subsequent development in the target language is based. Given their significance, the creation of effectual learning environments in these classrooms is essential to the development of foreign language teacher expertise.

This chapter focuses on creating communities of foreign language learners in which a high level of learning is supported and academic success is common. After first defining the concept of a community of learners, a discussion on the conditions that promote the establishment of effectual communities and the means for designing them is presented. Included in this discussion is an overview of four dimensions of learning opportunities and ways to structure learners' participation in them. This is followed by a discussion on the foreign language content standards and the integration of technology in classroom learning. The chapter concludes with an analysis of teacher research and the role it plays in helping teachers create effective communities of learners.

COMMUNITIES OF LEARNERS

Definition and Goals

From a sociocultural perspective on learning, a major goal of education is to foster the development of **communities of learners** in classrooms. In such communities, learning is viewed as a socially situated, collaborative, mutually beneficial process of transformation of both the academic and the social. The role of the teacher in the process of transformation is twofold. First, it is to assist learners in appropriating the knowledge, skills, and meanings they need to gain entry into the sociocultural activities considered important to full participation in their larger social worlds (Rogoff, Matusov, & White, 1996). Second, it is to help learners become fully aware of the knowledge and skills they are developing so that they may act responsibly and creatively in achieving their goals (Wells, 1999).

In addition to building meaningful and challenging academic learning environments, teachers are responsible for developing strong social bonds among the members of their classroom communities. Together with their students, teachers build strong interpersonal connections, develop an interdependence, and, more generally, cultivate feelings of solidarity and fellowship among themselves.

Creating communities of foreign language learners entails the collaboration of teachers and students in the creation of an environment in which learners are provided with opportunities to develop the knowledge and abilities needed to participate in a wide variety of communicative activities in the target language. In addition, teachers and learners together engage in developing a classroom community in which interpersonal bonds and feelings of mutual appreciation and respect are fostered.

Characteristics of Middle and High School Students

Part of what teachers need to know to develop effective communities of foreign language learners entails understanding the larger contexts of school outside of the foreign language classroom, and understanding the identities that learners, as members of these contexts, bring with them. As specific environments of learning, middle schools and high schools have particular characteristics that are significant to the kinds of communities of learners that can be developed in them.

Middle schools commonly include grades 6 through 8. Their focus is on serving the intellectual, social, emotional, and physical developmental needs of young adolescents. Core instructional programs include language arts/reading, social studies, science, and math. In addition to the core programs, students have the opportunity to take exploratory courses in a wide range of areas including foreign languages, technological arts, consumer education, and music.

According to recent research on middle schools (National Middle School Association, 1995), exemplary middle schools share three characteristics. First, teachers are generally organized into interdisciplinary teams that are assigned to the same group of students. The purpose of such teams is to create manageable learning communities within a school. In some schools teams are grade specific and consist of one teacher per subject. In others, teams consist of teachers from different grades. In addition, some schools consist of multi-graded houses comprised of two or three sixth-grade teams, two or three seventh-grade teams, and two or three eighth-grade teams. Because team teachers share the same students and, in many cases, have a common planning period, they are able to respond more quickly to the needs of individual students. Moreover, teaming makes it easy to meet jointly with parents, design interdisciplinary units, and establish common grading practices.

A second feature of exemplary middle schools is the student advisory group. These groups consist of a small number of students who are assigned to a teacher, administrator, or other staff member. They meet at a regularly scheduled time to discuss topics of concern to students. The purpose of these groups is to provide opportunities for the students to develop strong interpersonal bonds with teachers and other adult members of the school and, in so doing, to increase their feelings of self-esteem and affiliation. A third feature shared by exemplary middle schools is their use of varied instructional approaches in the classroom. These approaches focus on real-life issues relevant to the student, actively engage students in problem solving, and emphasize collaboration, cooperation, and community.

High schools include grades 9 through 12. They differ from middle schools in that their focus is on preparing students to meet the social, political, and economic challenges they will face as adults (Kellough & Kellough, 1999). Thus, their organizational structure encourages more independence and responsibility on the part of the students. Teachers are typically grouped by subject area departments and are expected to teach five to six periods a day, each lasting from 45 to 60 minutes, although some schools have adopted block scheduling in which classes range from 70 to 120 minutes. Like middle school programs, the four areas generally considered to be part of the core curriculum are English/language arts, mathematics, science, and history/social studies. In addition, there are special fields of study that include foreign languages, the arts, and physical education.

While the organization of middle schools and high schools may vary, the students themselves share many characteristics. The following is a list of some of the more significant features (Kellough & Kellough, 1999).

Intellectual Characteristics

1. They consider their personal concerns more important than academic concerns.
2. They display a wide range of intellectual development.
3. They are interested in learning what they consider useful and relevant to their lives.
4. They prefer active over passive learning experiences.
5. They enjoy peer interaction.

Physical Characteristics

1. They are very aware of their own and each other's appearance.
2. They mature physically, socially, and emotionally at varying rates.

Psychological Characteristics

1. They are easily offended and sensitive to criticism.
2. They can be moody, restless, and self-conscious.
3. They occasionally experience emotional outbursts.

Social Characteristics

1. They sometimes display unusual behavior by acting, for example, aggressively or argumentatively.
2. They fear or distrust unfamiliar settings and people.
3. They can feel deep loyalty to their peers.
4. They need frequent affirmation from adults.
5. They may feel rebellious toward authority figures and will sometimes test the limits of social acceptability.

Contextual Characteristics of Effective Communities of Learners

A growing body of research on effective communities of learners has revealed several essential characteristics of such contexts for learning (e.g., Brown, Ash, Rutherford, Nakagawa, Gordon, & Campione, 1993; Brown & Campione, 1994; Cabello & Terrell, 1994; Carlsen, 1992; Cope & Kalantzis, 2000; Lee & Smagorinsky, 2000; Wells, 1999). First, successful communities of learners are characterized by an atmosphere in which both collaborative group work and individual effort are encouraged.

Thus, students, with guidance from the teacher, are responsible for creating and working toward individual goals, for helping peers work toward theirs, and for negotiating and working toward and sharing in the achievement of mutually beneficial goals. Second, affective concerns are considered as important as intellectual and academic ones. Thus, there is an atmosphere of mutual respect and trust in which students are challenged to develop their interests and abilities. At the same time, everyone is treated seriously and held to the same high level of expectations.

A third characteristic involves the kind of activities found in these communities. For the most part, the classroom is organized around familiar, regularly occurring, and consistently enacted activities that students can easily recognize and, in which they understand the roles expected of them. The routinization of activity has a dual purpose: it helps learners stabilize and coordinate their thoughts and actions and, in doing so, fosters feelings of familiarity and security about the expectations for their classroom participation. This, in turn, helps learners develop strong interpersonal relationships and a shared memory of their learning experiences, which can be used as scaffolds for the development of more complex and creative knowledge and skills. It also promotes a safe environment in which students feel free to take both academic and social risks.

Fourth, effectual communities of learners are distinguished by the use of a wide range of engaging and challenging discourse participation opportunities. Students are encouraged, for example, to discuss, question, interpret, offer opinions, predict, and reason. These opportunities incorporate and build on the background knowledge and experiences students bring to the classroom. Moreover, they allow students to act as peer experts, thus helping them develop confidence in their abilities as learners. Finally, teachers have been shown to play an especially significant role in establishing and maintaining effectual communities of learners. In the next section, we look more closely at the concept of teacher expertise, and the specific ways that teachers foster the development of such communities in their classrooms.

Role of the Teacher

While it is true that both teachers and students play an active role in their learning communities, research findings on classroom learning have shown that the teacher's role is especially consequential (see, for example, Green & Dixon, 1993; Gutierrez, 1994; Gutierrez, Larson, & Kreuter, 1995; Lensmire, 1994; Nystrand, 1997; Smagorinsky & Fly, 1993; Toohey, 1998; Wortham, 1992). In the kinds of learning environments that they design, teachers provide formulations of what they consider appropriate content knowledge and ways to go about acquiring that knowledge. In other words, in the kinds of instructional opportunities they bring to the classroom, teachers create the conditions for certain cognitive and communicative processes to occur. By spending an equal amount of time on teacher-directed instruction and small-group work, for example, they can make student to student interaction as important to learning as the interaction between teacher and student. Likewise, by spending more instructional time on activities requiring, say, reflection, application, and analysis teachers make these cognitive processes more important to student learning than others on which they spend less time, such as recall.

In addition, in the kinds of learning environments they create, teachers lay the groundwork for the development of particular kinds of teacher–student and student–student relationships and particular ways for learners to connect their classroom lives to their larger social worlds. Learners draw on these constructions to make sense of, and participate in, their classroom events. Thus, their learning environments become consequential not only in terms of what and how the students learn in those classrooms, but also, on a broader level, in their future educational activities (Pianta, 1992). Learning to value participation in small-group work in their early learning opportunities, for example, sets up learner expectations for similar kinds of participation in later learning activities.

Because teachers of additional languages assume the role of expert users of the target language in their classrooms, their role in structuring and managing the intellectual and practical contexts in which the students learn the target language is of particular consequence to learners' development. In the kinds of activities they make available to their students, teachers provide models of what they consider appropriate activities and communicative actions. Moreover, in mediating both the quantity and quality of opportunities the students have to participate in and learn from, teachers make visible their own attitudes toward the activities and toward the students' involvement in them. In doing so, they play a significant role in shaping both the form and degree of learning that individual learners can achieve in the target language.

Given the significance of the teacher in constructing effectual communities of foreign language learners, knowing how to be an effective teacher is essential. Research on expertise in teaching (Carter, 1990; Grossman, 1990; Shulman, 1987; Sternberg & Horvath, 1995) has found that the constitution of teachers' knowledge is vital to their effectiveness as teachers, and that this knowledge is both specialized and domain specific. Three domains—content knowledge, pedagogical content knowledge, and pedagogical knowledge—comprise teacher knowledge.

Content knowledge is knowledge of the subject matter to be taught. For foreign language teachers, this includes knowledge of the linguistic resources—both oral and written—needed for successful participation in a wide range of communicative activities in which the target language is the common code. In addition, it includes knowledge of the literature, history, art, politics, and the social issues relevant to communities in which the target language is the primary code. A final aspect of content knowledge includes an understanding of key concepts and principles underlying language use and communication including communicative competence, intercultural communicative competence, and communicative development.

Pedagogical content knowledge is knowledge of how to transform the subject matter—the key ideas and concepts, sets of knowledge, skills, and abilities—so that it is accessible and appropriate to the various abilities and interests of the students. Included here for foreign language teachers is knowledge of relevant pedagogical theories and methods for facilitating their learners' development of the knowledge, skills, and abilities needed to be effective communicators in the target language. It also includes knowledge of how best to help students develop their conceptual understandings and metalinguistic knowledge, skills, and abilities.

The third domain, **pedagogical knowledge**, is knowledge that teachers need to be viable members of their schooling communities. This includes knowledge of the administrative, social, and political operations of middle schools and high schools, theories and practices of classroom management and motivation, and general educational research on such matters as designing and implementing effective lessons and developing effective teacher–student and student–student relationships. It also includes knowing how to engage in the systematic exploration, reflection, and action on issues and concerns pertinent to their specific contexts of teaching and learning.

In their review of the literature on **teacher expertise,** Sternberg and Horvath (1995) note that expert teachers' knowledge, organized specifically for use in teaching, is "extensive and accessible" (p. 11), and that teachers are able to use this knowledge "to adapt to practical constraints in the field of teaching" (p. 12). Expert teachers, for example, are able to articulate clearly the purposes of their instruction. This includes setting clear goals for their instructional activities, making it apparent to students what they are to learn, and arranging space and time conditions so that students can realistically reach those goals. In addition, expert teachers have well-developed management routines for such everyday activities as checking homework, presenting new material, and practicing. In their consistent and regular use of these routines, they make it easy for students to know what is expected of them on a day-to-day basis. Expert teachers are also insightful in that they can easily distinguish information and events that are relevant to facilitating student involvement from those that are irrelevant.

Less effective teachers, on the other hand, are not able to articulate clear goals. Likewise, they do not make consistent use of routines for managing the class, nor are they good at discerning what is pertinent from what is not. In addition, less effective teachers tend to provide fewer opportunities for student involvement in classroom activities. Instead, they hold the floor for long periods of time and try to control students' behavior rather than engage them in learning.

ORGANIZING INSTRUCTION FOR EFFECTIVE FOREIGN LANGUAGE LEARNING

So far we have defined communities of learners, discussed some general characteristics of middle and high school students along with several features of effective communities of learners, and noted the importance of the teacher and teacher expertise in creating such communities. In this section, we address how to organize and develop instruction for effective foreign language learning. The first part of the discussion is concerned with the learning process. Using the theory of pedagogy proposed by the New London Group (1996), a four-component framework for designing learning opportunities is presented. This is followed by discussions on the National Foreign Language Content Standards, which describe what students should know and be able to do in the target language as a result of their learning, and on the integration of technology into the foreign language curriculum.

Designing Learning Opportunities

Using research and insights into the concepts of communities of learners and teacher expertise as a base, the New London Group (1996) has created a theory of pedagogy, one they call a socioculturally responsive pedagogy, that helps us understand how to connect a sociocultural perspective of learning to classroom teaching.

According to this group, a socioculturally responsive pedagogy is comprised of four interrelated spheres of **learning opportunities:** situated practice, overt instruction, critical framing, and transformed practice (see Figure 3–1). Together, these four spheres of learning opportunities lead to the learners' development of a complex web of understandings and perspectives, knowledge and skills, and values and motivations needed for full personal, social, and cultural participation not only in their classroom communities but also in their larger social communities as well.

As pointed out by the New London Group (1996), the four opportunities are not to be viewed as hierarchical stages of learning. Rather, they are complexly interrelated, "elements of each [which] may occur simultaneously, while at different times one or the other will predominate, and all of them are repeatedly revisited at different levels" (p. 85). Each of the four opportunities is explained in more detail as follows.

Situated Practice

As findings from recent research on learning have revealed, developing competence depends in part on the opportunities learners are given to actually participate in authentic versions of those activities in which they are expected to become competent (see, for example, Fischer, Bullock, Rotenberg, & Raya, 1993; Forman et al., 1993; Lave & Wenger, 1991). The New London Group labels such experiential learning **situated practice**. According to

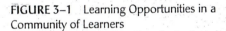

FIGURE 3–1   Learning Opportunities in a Community of Learners

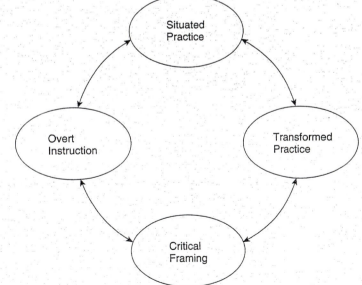

the group, situated practice gives students the chance to learn on their own, to figure out what they need to do and know as they attempt to accomplish something, and to assess their success and make changes or at least recognize where changes are needed. Unlike a more traditional approach to teaching, in which learners are provided opportunities to participate in authentic versions of activities only after they have mastered a range of skills, it is assumed that mastery of skills and knowledge needed for competent performance is, to a large degree, dependent on learner involvement in the very activities in which they wish to become competent.

For foreign language learning, this means involving language learners in legitimate communicative activities using the target language from the beginning of language instruction. If language learners are expected to master certain kinds of academic literacy skills like reading informational texts or writing research reports in the target language, for example, part of their learning experiences must involve being fully immersed in the activities of reading texts and writing papers from the start. Likewise, if learners are expected to be able to exchange letters or e-mail messages on a variety of interpersonal or social topics, then, from the beginning, they must be given opportunities to exchange letters and e-mail messages with others using the target language.

As expert-mentor, the teacher's role in situated practice is to model the linguistic actions the student-apprentices are expected to master, to guide them in recognizing and understanding the meanings of these actions, and to help them produce their own. At the same time, the teacher is responsible for creating an environment where learners feel safe to take on different roles and explore the use of alternate linguistic actions for accomplishing the activity's goals.

Through multiple and varied opportunities, learners build up meaningful communicative plans that will help them make sense of and participate in activities in ways that are likely to have few negative social, academic, or other consequences. Such learning opportunities are invaluable for foreign language learners since the personal and social consequences of inexperience or risktaking in target language activities outside the classroom are likely to be significant. Providing opportunities in the classroom for learners to participate in target language communicative activities that they are likely to encounter outside of their learning environments allows learners to explore fully the various opportunities with few negative consequences. It should be noted that in addition to the teacher, experts from outside the classroom, including peers who are more competent in those target language activities, can serve as guides and mentors in situated practice learning opportunities.

Overt Instruction

Immersion in authentic activities with experts provides learners with ample opportunity to develop familiarity, or a "feel" for these activities, including the means for accomplishing them and learners' roles as participants. However, such engagement alone can make it difficult for learners to focus deliberate attention on these activities, and to practice and gain control of the specific skills and knowledge needed for competent engagement. For this reason, **overt instruction** learning opportunities are needed. The purpose of this second sphere of learning opportunities, then, is to engage learners in intentional, systematic practice of the skills and knowledge needed for competent participation in their communicative activities.

As discussed in Chapter 2, the communicative competence needed to be full participants in any activity involves a range of knowledge and skills. Writing a story, for example, involves not only knowing certain grammatical conventions, but also knowing the conventions of spelling, punctuation, and vocabulary. In addition, it involves knowing the conventional ways to open and close the story and to organize the telling of events and ideas so that the story is coherent. Likewise, seeking information from someone involves more than knowing which grammatical and lexical items to use. One also needs to master the conventional ways to get the interlocutor's attention, to take turns, to use those speech acts considered appropriate to the particular roles of the participants, to understand the norms for participation and interpretation of behavior, and to identify and resolve misdirected talk.

Systematic intervention activities constituting overt instruction are designed to provide learners with opportunities to mindfully abstract, reflect upon, and practice the use of these conventions and other relevant features. In addition to helping learners become conscious of and control the forms used to communicate in their activities, overt instruction leads students in the development of a metalanguage for describing language functions and forms (New London Group, 1996). This means learners gain mastery in using formal terms such as rhetorical structures, speech acts and speech act sets, verb inflections, definite and indefinite articles, and prefixes and suffixes. Being able to extract and consider conventional aspects of communication apart from their particular contexts of use is as important to language learners' communicative development as their learning to use the forms and functions appropriately and accurately.

Traditionally, in the foreign language classroom, overt instruction has taken place in the form of drills and form-focused exercises, often with repeated rehearsal of the form or forms of particular linguistic conventions. In an effort to articulate optimal conditions for such learning, a growing body of research has been concerned with investigating alternative means of overt instruction. For example, studies investigating teacher-directed activities such as "input enhancement," "focus-on-form" instruction, and "consciousness-raising tasks" have yielded useful findings (see, for example, Doughty & Williams, 1998; Ellis, 1992; Fotos, 1994; Long & Robinson, 1998; Van Patten & Cadierno, 1993). They have shown how drawing learners' attention to the structural aspects of the target language and helping them reflect on the uses of the forms to make whatever changes are necessary to their own understandings speeds the rate at which learners gain control of the forms.

Likewise, recent work on classroom tasks has documented the conditions that foster the emergence of "negotiated interaction" through which learners' awareness of particular syntactic and lexical items is promoted (e.g., Crookes & Gass, 1993a, 1993b). In these tasks learners are led to identify gaps in their language knowledge, and through negotiated interaction with their peers, fill the gaps with the appropriate forms. Additional findings from research on collaborative learning tasks reveal that engaging learners in small-group work on tasks requiring conscious attention to communicative forms can also be effective in helping students gain control of their use, and develop metacommunicative skills (e.g., Donato, 1994; Kowal & Swain, 1994).

A primary concern of most of these studies has been with the instruction of one particular aspect of communicative competence, namely, grammar. However, there has been increased interest in examining similar approaches for the teaching of other aspects of communicative competence including speech acts, sociolinguistic markers, and discourse conventions (see, for example, Bouton, 1994; LoCastro, 1996; Lyster, 1994). Moreover, while each of the strands of research noted takes a slightly different tack in looking at how to facilitate the learning of forms, they all agree that some form of overt instruction is an essential component to learning a foreign language.

Critical Framing

The third sphere of learning opportunities essential to a sociocultural approach to teaching is **critical framing.** The purpose of these opportunities is to help learners stand apart from and understand their activities in terms of their historical, social, cultural, political, and ideological contexts. As noted by the New London Group (1996, p. 87), "Through critical framing learners can gain the necessary personal and theoretical distance from what they have learned, constructively critique it, [and] account for its cultural location." In so doing, they come to see their everyday worlds in a new light.

Critical framing learning opportunities are particularly relevant to the achievement of the *National Foreign Language Comparisons and Cultures Standards*, the goals of which are to develop insight into the nature of intercultural knowledge and understanding (National Standards in Foreign Language Education Project, 1996). Here foreign language classrooms become unique sites of cross-cultural fieldwork in which learners act as both informants and ethnographers. As participating members in activities of their own social groups, including those that are indigenous to their classroom communities, learners can use their "insider" knowledge to gain analytic insight into the nature and complexity of these activities. They can then use this information as a basis for comparison with the different intellectual and practical activities constituted in the target language outside of the classroom that are of interest to them.

In their explorations of the various activities in the target language, learners not only develop a broader perspective of their larger contexts, including the social, political, historical, and ideological meanings embedded in the activities, but also gain an understanding of the ways in which these meanings both converge and diverge from the learners' own worldviews. They also develop a critical awareness of language use; they learn to recognize that meanings and rules for the use of communicative resources are arbitrary and tied to their contexts of use in complex ways.

This awareness enables learners to make informed choices about their participation, and, more specifically, about how to use the communicative resources in ways that will enhance their negotiations with others as well as the realization of their own individual goals. Moreover, they develop the discipline and skills needed for intellectual inquiry. They learn how to raise questions about their worlds, how to go about gathering the information needed to answer them, and how to organize, explain, and compare the data. Just as importantly they learn how to judge their own processes of inquiry by evaluating, for example, the effectiveness of their methods for collecting, analyzing, and comparing their data in light of the questions they ask.

Transformed Practice

The knowledge and skills learners develop in critical framing form the basis for the final sphere of learning opportunities—**transformed practice.** All learners need ample experience in situated practice, overt instruction, and critical framing learning opportunities in which the purpose is to lead them to new understandings. In addition, they need learning opportunities in which they can take the lead, using what they know to chart alternative courses of action for realizing their personal goals. This is the purpose of transformed practice.

The focus of this last sphere of learning opportunities is particularly relevant to meeting the *National Foreign Language Communities Standard,* in which students are expected to be able to use the language within and outside of the school setting for personal enjoyment and enrichment (National Standards in Foreign Language Education Project, 1996). As noted by the New London Group (2000), in transformed practice "teachers need to develop ways in which the students can demonstrate how they can design and carry out, in a reflective manner, new practices embedded in their own goals and values" (p. 35).

In these opportunities, then, students apply their new understandings, knowledge, and skills both to create new contexts and to transform familiar ones in creative and insightful ways. The more occasions they have to play with language and through language, to indulge in explorations of language use, to discover and try out different voices and invent new means and goals for self-expression and connecting with others, the richer and more complex their communicative development in the target language will be. As noted by John-Steiner and Meehan (2000, p. 35), "Working with, through and beyond what one has internalized and appropriated is part of the dialectic of creative synthesis."

Together, when aimed at the upper reaches of learners' zones of proximal development, these four learning opportunities—situated practice, overt instruction, critical framing, and transformed practice—make possible the development of a complex range of knowledge, skills, and abilities in the target language. In addition to learning how to communicate in a wide range of practical and intellectual activities, learners gain critically important metacommunicative and metacognitive abilities. Moreover, they develop the ability to see from multiple perspectives, to be flexible in their thinking, to direct their own learning, to solve problems creatively, and, ultimately, to develop new ways of becoming involved in their worlds.

The Role of Grammar Teaching

Because **grammar teaching** has been considered a mainstay of foreign language learning, it warrants a brief discussion on its place in a socioculturally responsive pedagogy. Before the communicative movement of the 1980s, grammar was considered the primary if not sole focus of language teaching. Some of the more common means for teaching it included audio-lingual and grammar-translation methods.

With the arrival of the Natural Approach (Krashen & Terrell, 1983) and other, more communicatively oriented approaches in the 1980s, foreign language teaching moved away from an almost exclusive focus on teaching the formal properties of language to a focus on meaning-based activities. The basis for doing so derived in large part from Krashen's assertions about the learning of other languages. Drawing from Chomsky's theory of language (Chomsky, 1957, 1965), Krashen (1982, 1985) hypothesized that acquiring a second or foreign language was an unconscious process. It occurred when learners were provided with ample comprehensible input, or input containing language structures that are one level beyond those held by the learners, and when they were open and responsive to the input.

With the help of his colleague Tracey Terrell, Krashen incorporated his hypotheses into an approach to language teaching called the Natural Approach. Because acquiring other language was considered unconscious and "natural" or inevitable when provided with the right conditions, Krashen and Terrell (1983) argued for a noninterventionist approach to language teaching in which the direct or overt teaching of grammar was discouraged. This noninterventionist approach became a main feature of many communicatively oriented language teaching approaches in the 1980s and 1990s (Whitley, 1993).

Recent research on the learning of both first and second languages, summarized in Chapter 2 and the following chapters, makes apparent the fact that the learning of grammar, or indeed any concept or skill, does not just emerge "naturally" from one's immersion in a linguistic environment. In addition, it requires intentional focus on what is to be learned. Activities like the ones mentioned previously under overt instruction that help students take notice of particular forms, that provide direct instruction, and that help students restructure their understandings have all been shown to aid in the learning of grammar.

From the perspective of a socially responsive pedagogy, the overt instruction of grammar is as important to learning as immersion in meaning-based learning opportunities of situated and transformed practice. What distinguishes a socially responsive pedagogy from earlier approaches to grammar teaching is that grammar is now conceptualized as "a tool or resource to be used in the comprehension and creation of oral and written discourse rather than something to be learned as an end in itself" (Celce-Murcia, 1991, p. 466). Thus, rather than returning to the teaching of grammar as isolated elements, it is integrated into a pedagogy that also provides learners with opportunities to critically reflect on the varied forms, functions, and other resources used in communication, and to use them in legitimate, real-world activities.

Participation Structures for Learning

In addition to providing a wide range of learning opportunities in our classrooms, a socially responsive pedagogy requires organizing opportunities for student participation in ways that enhance interaction and learning. Five particular **participation structures** to encourage learner involvement are discussed here.

Perhaps the two most common structures of the mainstream American classroom are individual and whole-group instruction. **Individual instruction** entails having students work on their own, and usually at their own pace. In **whole-group instruction**, the teacher directs the teaching to the entire group of learners. Teaching to the whole class can create a positive learning environment in that it allows the teacher to interact with and monitor the progress of all students. At the same time, it allows students to observe and learn from each other as each interacts with the teacher and with each other.

While both individual and large-group participation structures facilitate student learning, by themselves they cannot support fully the goals on which a community of learners is based. For this, additional participation structures are needed. Three in particular have been shown to be effective in promoting learning. One such structure is **peer tutoring.** Here, one student is paired up with and assists another in learning. The one-on-one instruction provided by tutoring has been shown to be highly effective in enhancing student achievement (e.g., Bloom, 1984; Graesser, Person, & Magliano, 1995).

Another useful participation structure is **team learning**. In this structure, learners are arranged in small cooperative groups in which they work together on specified tasks. Based on the premise that each individual brings different abilities to a task, and that these abilities constitute a valuable resource for learning, small-group work has been shown to be particularly effective for classrooms with a diverse mix of learners (Cohen, 1994; Lotan, 1997).

Features of effective small-group work include using open-ended tasks that tap into a full range of abilities, minimize teacher involvement, maximize opportunities for student participation, and foster accountability at both the group and individual levels. Team learning promotes learning by increasing opportunities for learners to build strong interpersonal relationships with each other, to draw on each other's strengths in accomplishing tasks, to take responsibility for their own learning, and to engage in exploratory talk in which they can work out their ideas in a relatively stress-free environment.

A final participation structure is the **learning center**. Learning centers, which are usually organized around themes, are specially designated areas in the classroom where, depending on the goal of the center, individuals or small groups of students can learn more about a specific topic, improve specific skills, and explore new paths of knowledge. In a reading and writing center, for example, students can enhance their linguistic knowledge and abilities by working on crossword puzzles, creating rhymes and word games, reading magazines and newspapers, or writing plays and stories. A center that provides opportunities for students to create autobiographies, develop portfolios that display their achievements, or maintain diaries in which they reflect on their classroom experiences can enhance development of learners' metacognitive and metalinguistic skills. Table 3–1 summarizes key information on the five participation structures.

Content Standards for Foreign Language Learning

In addition to knowing how to design effectual learning experiences in the foreign language classroom, we must know what it is we want the students to learn. As pointed out in Chapter 1, in the 1990s a task force comprised of members from many sectors of the foreign language education field undertook the task of defining "what students should know and be

TABLE 3–1 *Student Participation Structures for Learning.*

Participation Structure	Key Feature
Individual	The learner proceeds at his or her own pace. Interaction is between *individual student* and *teacher.*
Whole-group	Learners move together through an activity. Interaction is between the *teacher* and an *entire class or group.*
Peer tutoring	Learners work in pairs on an activity. Interaction is *student to student.*
Team learning	Learners work together in small groups. Interaction is within *small cooperative groups of students.*
Learning center	A *specific physical space* for learning; often theme oriented. Learners can work alone, in pairs, or in small groups on projects and other activities.

able to do" (Phillips, 1999, pp. 1–2) as a result of their foreign language learning experiences. The work of this group resulted in the formation of 11 content standards organized around five main goals: communication, cultures, connections, comparisons, and communities (National Standards in Foreign Language Education Project, 1996). The purpose of these standards is to "tell everyone in the educational system what is expected of them" (Ravitch, 1995, p. 27). The foreign language standards were generated from the premise that "to study another language and culture gives one the powerful key to successful communication: knowing how, when, and why to say what to whom" (National Standards in Foreign Language Education Project, 1996, p. 11).

Although there are five goals, communication is considered the organizing principle for the study of additional languages. Thus, meeting the standards of the communication goal is essential to the accomplishment of the other four goals. Through *communication* learners develop an understanding of the *cultures* for which the target language is the common code. They make *connections* to other bodies of knowledge that would otherwise be unavailable to them as monolingual speakers of English. They engage in analytic *comparisons* and develop insight and perspective into their own and others' languages and cultures. Ultimately, they develop new ways of understanding and participating in their worlds that allow them access to, and even membership in, multilingual *communities*.

Although there can be a variety of ways to characterize the concept of communication, the Standards document has organized it around three **communication modes** that frame the purposes for learning to communicate in another language: the interpersonal, the interpretive, and the presentational. As noted by the creators of the Standards, organizing them as modes is "a richer and more natural way of envisioning communication than the traditional four skills of listening, speaking, reading and writing" (ACTFL, 1998., p. 4).

The *interpersonal mode* involves those communicative activities accomplished through direct interaction with others for the purposes of creating and maintaining interpersonal relationships or accomplishing particular tasks. Thus, interpersonal communicative activities are characterized by active negotiation in interaction. While the activities are most often accomplished through face-to-face interaction, they can also involve the exchange of personal letters or e-mail messages.

The *interpretive mode* involves communicative activities in which the primary focus is on understanding spoken, written, and visual texts for the purposes of developing new meanings, new ideas, new feelings, and new experiences and using them to transform those we have. Through their participation in interpretive communicative activities, learners develop the biliteracy skills needed to appropriately interpret a diversity of texts from a variety of contexts.

The third mode, the *presentational mode,* frames those communicative activities in which the primary purpose is to present or express ideas, information, feelings, and experiences through language. Presentational communicative activities are characterized by the lack of opportunity to actively negotiate meaning during the presentations themselves. Here, then, learners develop the skills needed to create oral, written, and visual documents using not only standard pen and paper or audio- and video-recording formats, but also a variety of high-tech electronic media.

It should be noted that although the interpersonal, the interpretive, and the presentational modes are oriented to different communicative purposes, they are not categorical. In other words, they do not involve communicative behaviors that are mutually exclusive. It is more realistic to think of them as interconnected, each influencing and being influenced by the development of the other. Each communication mode is discussed in greater detail in Chapters 6, 7, and 8.

DESIGNING CURRICULAR ACTIVITIES AROUND THE COMMUNICATION GOAL

The foreign language content standards describe the communicative goals students are expected to achieve in the target language. Thus, they serve as a useful guide for classroom instruction. Because the activities we make available to our students in our foreign language classrooms fundamentally shape their development as learners and users of the target language, the choices we make about the kinds of communicative activities to include in the curriculum are of great consequence. In designing curricular activities around the communication goal, then, there are two important issues to consider.

First, as noted earlier, foreign language classroom communities are unique learning environments. A primary goal of learning another language is to be able to participate in communicative activities outside the classroom where the target language is the primary or common code of communication. At the same time, to be successful learners of the target language, learners need knowledge and skills in the target language that will help them be full participants of their foreign language classroom communities.

Thus, for each of the communication modes, the interpersonal, the interpretive, and the presentational, we need to design two types of instructional activities. The first type is comprised of activities that foster the building of skills for full participation in activities involving the target language outside of the classroom. The second type of instructional activity includes activities that foster the development of communicative knowledge and skills needed to be active members in classroom-based communities of foreign language learners. In other words, learners need tasks that prepare them to be active explorers of and participants in the social worlds outside the classroom. They also need activities through which they can develop interpersonal relationships and shared memories as members of communities of learners.

Second, as pointed out in Chapter 1, the activities in which we engage are tied to and shaped by such important institutions as family, school, community, and the workplace. If our aim is to develop well-rounded language learners and users, then we need to design the curriculum around a wide variety of family, academic, social, and work-related communicative activities. As part of our design, we must be mindful of our learners' needs and aspirations for using the target language.

For example, a set of curricular activities typically found in many traditional foreign language textbooks involves the student as tourist to a country where the target language is the common code. Students learn the communicative skills needed to shop, eat in restaurants, and plan trips. Although these are activities that learners may encounter in their travels outside the classroom, they are not the only ones nor are they necessarily the most important ones. Nor are they the ones in which all students are likely to have the most interest. Some learners may

FIGURE 3–2   Framework for
Designing Curricular Activities

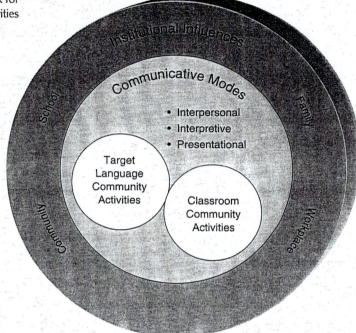

Institutional Influences

School

Family

Community

Workplace

Communicative Modes

- Interpersonal
- Interpretive
- Presentational

Target
Language
Community
Activities

Classroom
Community
Activities

be more interested in learning the knowledge and skills needed to engage in community service activities with a target language community. Others, perhaps those who have friends who speak the target language, may be more interested in learning the communicative knowledge and skills needed to sustain social relationships among friends.

It is important to remember that the communication modes and their constitutive activities do not exist in any kind of hierarchical relationship. That is to say, no one mode is more important than another. Activities in the interpersonal mode can be as meaningful to learning as those connected to the interpretive and presentational modes. Likewise, within each mode, social activities can be as important as those activities whose purposes are more business or academically oriented. All have the potential for the development of complex communicative behaviors. Figure 3–2 lays out the framework for designing activities around the communication goal in the foreign language classroom.

INTEGRATING TECHNOLOGY INTO THE FOREIGN LANGUAGE CURRICULUM

Over the last several decades, various forms of electronic media such as the computer and electronic network capabilities have changed the ways in which we make sense of and communicate in, our everyday worlds. We now use a wide range of symbolic systems and media to communicate in addition to the more traditional printed text and face-to-face interaction. For example; we use electronic mail to correspond with friends and family, we shop via the Internet, we write, produce, and circulate personal Web pages, and we meet and make connections with others who live around the world in electronically connected, virtual communities.

To respond to these changes a national group, the Panel on Educational Technology, was organized in 1995 to make recommendations for the integration of technology into the K–12 curriculum (Panel on Educational Technology, 1997). Based on these recommendations, the Technology and Literate Thinking Research Strand of the National Research Center on English Learning and Achievement (Swan, 1999, p. 6) created "a possible set of performance-based, non-print media and technology literacy competencies." The list of competencies is meant to be used as standards for guiding and assessing the integration of technology across the K–12 curriculum. It was derived from three sets of national standards, the *National Educational Technology Standards for Students, Information Literacy Standards for Student Learning,* and *Standards for the English Language Arts.* The competencies are grouped into three categories: basic skills, critical literacies, and construction skills.

Basic skills are competencies involving the use of nonprint media and the recognition of their common conventions. **Critical literacies** involve the ability to interpret, analyze, and evaluate nonprint texts and other kinds of media, and to apply them in solving problems and increasing personal understandings. **Construction skills** are used to transform familiar means and create new pathways of ideas and opinions, to communicate with others, to enhance problem solving and, in other ways, to reach personal fulfillment. According to Swan (1999), the skills are cumulative; by the completion of high school, students should have acquired all of them.

How well we prepare learners of additional languages to meet the social, political, and economic challenges of the next several decades will depend in part on our success in integrating technology into the foreign language curriculum. At the very least, it should entail expanding the communication goal so that it includes knowledge of and ability to use multiple media resources in interpersonal, interpretive, and presentational activities realized through the target language. In integrating technology into the foreign language classroom, we should remember that the issue is not how we can use technology to enhance language learning, but rather how we can use computers and other electronic media to enable our learners to become full participants in multiple literate activities (Murison-Bowie, 1993; Warschauer, 2000).

Table 3–2 contains an abridged list of the **technology standards** developed by the Technology and Literate Thinking Research Strand of the National Research Center on English Learning and Achievement (Swan, 1999). They are included here to serve as a basis for discussion about technological knowledge and skills that foreign language learners *and* teachers should have, and as a guide for documenting the integration of technology into the foreign language curriculum. No one can disagree with the fact that the technological revolution is here to stay. Thus, it behooves foreign language educators to become well informed about the pedagogical issues at stake and to develop a high level of expertise in multimedia communicative skills in both English and the target language.

TABLE 3–2 *Standards for Integrating Technology.*

Basic Skills

Elementary School
Use a mouse to successfully operate a computer
Use a keyboard to successfully operate a computer
Use a computer monitor
Use a computer printer
Use a scanner
Use developmentally appropriate multimedia encyclopedias
Use content-specific educational software to support learning
Use a word processor
Use computers to compose texts
Use computers to compose graphical representations
Use computers to search a variety of databases
Use e-mail
Participate in online discussions
Use a browser to navigate the World Wide Web
Use search engines to locate and access remote information

Middle School
Use content-specific computer simulations to support learning
Use computers to search the Internet
Use communications and computing technologies to locate information efficiently

High School
Use online information resources for research
Use technology tools and resources for managing personal/professional information
Use technology tools and resources for communicating personal/professional information
Discuss real world applications of expert systems
Explore a range of sources to find information of personal/professional interest

Critical Literacies

Elementary School
Make sense of simple computer programs
Make sense of WWW pages
Use computer-based puzzles and logical thinking software to support problem-solving activities
Use a variety of computer-based resources to acquire information
Discuss and critique computer programs
Discuss and critique WWW sites
Use a variety of nonprofit media to understand cultures
Discuss basic issues related to the responsible use of technologies
Select and use appropriate technology tools to complete a variety of tasks

Middle School
Distinguish the uses of WWW sites
Select and use appropriate technology tools and resources to complete a variety of tasks
Demonstrate knowledge of current information technologies
Demonstrate an understanding of the effects technological changes have on society and the workplace

TABLE 3–2 *(continued)*

Critical Literacies

Middle School—*continued*

Discuss the consequences of the misuse of information and/or technologies

Demonstrate an understanding of the concepts underlying hardware, software, and connectivity tools

Apply strategies for identifying and solving routine hardware and software problems

High School

Recognize and compare different media genres

Evaluate the electronic information seeking process as it evolves and make appropriate adjustments

Discuss and evaluate technology-based options for lifelong learning

Identify capabilities and limitations of current and emerging technologies

Assess the potential of current and emerging technologies to address personal and workplace needs

Make informed choices among technology systems, resources, and services

Analyze the advantages and disadvantages of the widespread use of technology in society

Advocate for ethical and legal behaviors when using information technology

Use online resources to enhance personal/professional productivity

Explore a range of sources to find information of personal/professional interest

Construction Skills

Elementary School

Use computer-based writing tools to communicate thoughts, ideas, and stories

Use computer-based drawing tools to illustrate thoughts, ideas, and stories

Use multimedia authoring tools in the creation of knowledge products

Use presentation software in the creation of knowledge products

Use WWW authoring tools in the creation of knowledge products

Use technology resources for self-directed and/or extended learning

Use technology resources for problem solving

Use telecommunications technologies to participate in collaborative projects

Middle School

Choose appropriate media formats for presenting a variety of information

Use nonprofit media to create information products related to topics of personal interest

Express information and ideas creatively in nonprint formats

Use telecommunications and collaborative tools to collaborate with peers, experts, and others on curriculum related problems

Works collaboratively over distance to create and evaluate complex information

High School

Use technology to collaborate with others to contribute to a content-related database

Select and apply technology tools to support research in content learning

Select and apply technology tools for decision making in content learning

Select and apply technology tools for problem solving

Select and apply technology tools for information analysis

Collaboratively create complex information over distance

Collaboratively evaluate complex information over distance

Swan, K. (1999). *Nonprint media and technology literacy standards for K-12 teaching and learning.* Report series 12013. Albany, NY: National Research Center on English Learning and Achievement.

TEACHER RESEARCH

A final component of the expertise that foreign language teachers need to create effective communities of learners involves the ability to engage in systematic exploration, reflection, and action on issues and concerns related to teaching and learning. This process is commonly referred to as **teacher research**. Viewed as "an extension of professional work, not an addition to it" (Winter, 1996, p. 14), teacher research helps teachers bring awareness to the significant issues and concerns they deal with on a daily basis in their particular schooling contexts for conscious reflection and subsequent action toward improvement. Indeed, teachers who use knowledge produced from systematic investigations into their own worlds of teaching as a basis for reflective inquiry, renewal, and innovation are as Larsen-Freeman (2000) notes, "scientists in the best sense of the role" (p. 20).

There are at least two immediate benefits to engaging in teacher research. Perhaps most importantly, organized and reflective inquiry helps teachers make sense of their own practices. Standing apart from, and analyzing their teaching contexts from, multiple perspectives helps teachers develop insight into the myriad of conditions that affect their day-to-day lives as teachers, and, ultimately, how they might effect change. Understanding the process by which foreign language textbooks are adopted in a school system, for example, can help teachers understand how such decisions are made, and how they might become an integral part of the process. Findings from teacher research can also serve as a source of empirical data to substantiate and justify requests for action made to school administrators and other authorities. These can range from requests for changes in curriculum materials to requests for increased funding for student programs, to requests for structural improvements to classrooms.

On a more general level, engaging in teacher research gives individual teachers access to a larger professional community of foreign language educators who have an interest in foreign language education including teachers and scholars of all levels from kindergarten to university, and students, parents, and administrators. It does so by providing a forum where members of these groups can work together to generate and explore concerns with all aspects of foreign language teaching and learning.

Overview of the Process

Teachers can engage in research projects either individually or as part of a collaboration among a small group of teachers, of teachers and students, or even of teachers, students, and parents. As illustrated in Figure 3–3, the research process is a five-step cycle that involves raising questions, gathering data needed to answer them, reflecting on the findings, determining what to do next, and sharing what was learned with others. It is cyclic in that the findings and reflections arising from one project can help raise new questions and concerns for further exploration. General instructions for engaging in each of the five steps are presented here.

1. *Pose a Problem.* Identifying problems, concerns, or issues arising from and important to one's everyday life as a teacher is the first step. Once a problem or concern has been identified, the next step involves generating a list of questions about it. For example, if a teacher is interested in the general problem of student motivation in lower-level high school

FIGURE 3–3 Five-Step Cycle
for Engaging in Teacher
Research

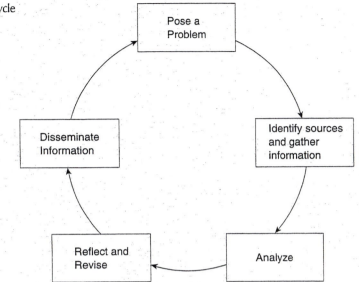

foreign language classrooms, he or she might ask, "What motivations for learning another language do the students bring with them to the class? How is student motivation for learning related to the structures of participation in their learning opportunities? Do they, for example, enjoy working and thus produce a better written project when they are in small groups, when they are in pairs, or when they work individually?"

As questions are generated, it helps to map and rank them, connecting related questions and deciding which questions are particularly interesting or relevant to the situation. Once a question or set of questions has been chosen, the teacher needs to consider whether the questions are researchable given whatever constraints the teacher may have in terms of time and other resources, and solvable, and thus worth the effort to investigate. It may be, for example, that the question is both significant and directly relevant, but the time and resources needed to answer it adequately are more than one can provide.

2. *Identify Sources and Gather Information.* Once a decision on the question or set of questions to research has been made, the next step is to formulate a plan for gathering information to help answer them. The first step in making such a plan involves deciding on the group of participants. Depending on the questions, participants may include all of one's language classes or be limited to just one small group. Likewise, the teacher-researcher may include all foreign language teachers in his or her school or may limit the focus to one teacher.

Another decision to be made concerns how information needed to answer the research questions will be gathered. There are several sources from which data can be collected, each of which will provide a particular perspective of the problem. A discussion of these possible sources of data follows:

Interviews. The **interviews** are typically grouped into three kinds: structured, semi-structured, and open. *Structured interviews* are considered more formal in that the questions are written beforehand and ask for specific kinds of information on a specific topic. There is little room for discussion beyond the set of questions. Both the interviewee and interviewer are expected to stay on the task of addressing the preformulated questions. This kind of interview is helpful when the interest is in others' perspectives on a particular question such as the benefits of after-school peer tutoring on test performance.

While the focus in *semistructured interviews* is also on a set of preformulated questions, here, the interviewee is often asked to expand upon his or her answers. The interviewer is free to follow the direction of this discussion before coming back to the next round of questions.

Open interviews are similar to, but even less structured or formal than, the semistructured interview. Here the interviewer can direct the discussion as he or she wishes, expanding on some issues, raising others for discussion, and so on. Semistructured and open interviews are useful if the interviewer is interested in discovering others' ideas on a broad topic such as the kinds of peer help participants feel are beneficial to student performance on tests.

An advantage to both semistructured and open interviews is that the teacher researcher may end up with unexpected insights into or perspectives on the research questions. A disadvantage is that the interview data can be difficult to code and analyze, especially if each of the interviewees decides to address a different aspect of the topic. Interviews are typically audio- or videotaped and then transcribed by the teacher-researcher for analysis.

Questionnaires. These are similar to interviews except that they ask for written responses from the participants. Like interviews, **questionnaires** can be structured, semistructured, or open. *Structured* and *semistructured questionnaires* ask respondents to give specific kinds of information in short answers or to choose one response from several options. *Open questionnaires* ask the participants to provide opinions or information on a particular topic in their own words.

(Participant) Observation and Field Notes. **Observation** involves the presence of the teacher-researcher at the particular site of interest. If, for example, the interest is in certain classroom management techniques used by one's peers, the teacher-researcher may decide to sit in on one or more of their classes for a period of time. If, during the observations, the teacher-researcher also acts as a bona fide member of the classroom, helping students complete a task, for example, he or she is considered a **participant observer.**

Written records, or **field notes,** are usually kept on these observations. The notes can take different forms. For instance, the teacher-researcher may make a list of behaviors he or she is interested in documenting prior to the period of observation. During the observation the teacher notes on the list whether the behaviors occur and the contexts of their occurrence.

Alternatively, the teacher-researcher may be interested in discovering the kinds of behaviors used by other teachers, irrespective of whether they conform to a particular list. In this case, the teacher-researcher writes rich, detailed accounts of the events that occur during the observation period. Also included as part of the field notes are one's reflections on the observed events.

In writing field notes it is important to remember the distinction between descriptive and evaluative statements. Descriptive statements strive to report exactly what was observed without judging its occurrence or attributing an intention to it. Thus, a statement such as "The teacher looked at the student who was talking for about 4 seconds before asking another student to answer" describes in neutral words what took place.

In contrast, *evaluative statements* use words that place a value on, judge the worth of, or attribute an intention to an observed behavior. Changing the word looked to glared in the preceding statement places an intention in the teacher's action that may or may not be a fair assessment of the teacher's behavior. Good note-takers strive to be descriptive, not evaluative.

Personal Reflection Journals. These are written records of incidents, readings, observations, or other events considered significant and the teacher-researcher's personal reactions and reflections on them. They are typically written on a regular basis, and, depending on the research questions, can be written at the end of the teaching week, after department or school faculty meetings, or after student–teacher conferences. Journals typically consist of two parts. In the first, detailed descriptions of the events are given; in the second, personal feelings, reactions, and opinions are recorded.

Logs. These are accounts of recurring events in which the data are typically recorded numerically. If, for example, there is interest in tracking student attendance at foreign language club meetings, the number of students at each meeting is counted and recorded. Depending on the questions being asked, an accounting of other relevant aspects such as the gender, race, and language level of each attendee may also be kept.

Comments on the data can also be included in the log. For example, assume that a snowstorm occurred on a day that fewer students than normal attended an after-school club meeting. This information should be noted in the log as it could have influenced the number of attendees. If the number is significantly different from attendance on other days, the information provided can help explain the discrepancy.

Official Documents. These include reports, records, curriculum guides, newsletters, and other related materials that are considered pertinent. Such data can provide different perspectives on a topic, and can be used to justify a particular approach or to compare perspectives across contexts. Say, for example, the teacher-researcher wants to compare his or her local foreign language curriculum to those of other schools or states. The sources of data could then include written materials produced by the teacher-researcher's department or school as well as those from other institutions.

Literature Review. This source of data includes published reports of empirical research related to the research questions. It usually entails a library search for journals and other written documents that contain these reports, and a review of them in order to synthesize and evaluate the findings. If interest is in documenting the cognitive benefits of foreign language study, for example, a primary source of data can be found in a review of research on that same topic.

Tests and Records of Performance. Measures of student or teacher achievement can include both traditional and alternative assessments. They are useful in diagnosing individual or program needs and in determining whether changes have occurred, and the effectiveness of the means for facilitating change.

Once the sources of data have been identified, the time period, including length of time for data collection, must be decided. Like the others, these decisions depend on the questions asked. If, for example, the questions concern students' initial perspectives of foreign language study, then the data should be collected during the initial stages of language learning, such as the first week or weeks of the academic year. Likewise, if the teacher-researcher is concerned with his or her own development as a teacher, then data is best collected over an extended period of time so that enough evidence can be gathered to document any changes that occur. Once the sources of data have been identified, the time period decided upon, and any tools needed to collect data constructed, the actual process of data collection can begin.

3. *Analyze.* This step involves coding and examining the data. Coding involves converting the data collected into another format for analysis. How one codes depends on the kinds of data collected. If, for example, a count is kept of how often female students raise their hands to answer teacher questions, the average number can be computed and compared to the average for all students. Alternatively, the teacher-researcher can decide to translate the numbers into percentages and display a frequency distribution of a set of occurrences. If the source of data is text-based, the data can be coded according to the themes or topics contained in the text. However one decides to code, it is important to note the coding scheme and to use it consistently across similar sources of data.

Once the data are coded, the next step involves searching across data sets, looking for patterns and asking what the data reveal about one's particular set of questions. If, for example, the questions concern student motivation, and the data was gathered through semi-structured interviews, the teacher-researcher can ask, "What are the particular themes brought up in student interviews on motivation? Which are most frequently mentioned?"

Likewise, if the interest was in documenting student involvement according to structures of participation and the data was gathered through observations of classes, the teacher-researcher may ask, "What is the average number of times that female students raise their hands to participate in whole-group discussion for any one class meeting? Does this number change over time? Does this number change according to the kind of participation structure?"

4. *Reflect and Revise.* Once the data have been adequately analyzed, the next step is to reflect on the findings and, where appropriate, begin to identify steps for using the findings. If the research project was undertaken by a group of teachers, this step can take the form of a group discussion. Some questions to guide the process of reflection include:

What were the anticipated findings?
Were there some unanticipated findings?
Were the questions answered adequately?
Were there obstacles that prevented completing the project?
Could the project have been done differently?
What have we learned from this?
What might we have to re-learn or unlearn in our work?
How can the findings be used to make a difference to the teaching context?
What are the next steps?

5. *Disseminate Information.* The final step involves sharing the findings with others. No matter how the project turns out, there will be something worthwhile to report from which others can learn. How and with whom information is shared depends in part on the

consequences the teacher-researcher would like the project to engender, whether they be changes at the personal or program level, and the degree of support he or she feels is needed to help ensure their realization. The more people that can be involved in the project, the more impact the findings are likely to have.

Means for sharing can range from the more formal to the informal. More formal approaches include making an oral presentation to department heads or school faculty, to the student body, or to parents of the students. In addition, the findings can be presented at a meeting of the local school board or to members of a professional organization at a local, statewide, regional, or even national gathering. They can also be published in such documents as a school newsletter, the local newspaper, or a professional journal. More informal approaches can include sharing project ideas and findings with others in an electronic chat room of professional educators, as postings to members of an electronic listserv or bulletin board related to foreign language education, or in conversations with colleagues, administrators, students, parents, and other important stakeholders.

Some Final Concerns

It is important to remember that any action taken as a teacher-researcher must be done within the existing organizational guidelines of one's school. Before beginning any project, teachers should become familiar with the procedures required by their schools for undertaking such an activity. At the very least, they will likely require the following guidelines:

- Official permission from school authorities, such as the department head or school principal.
- Permission from all participants from whom or about whom data will be collected. This entails informing the participants of all procedures and possible risks involved in the research. Of course, participation in any research project should be voluntary; no one should ever be coerced into taking part.
- Guarantee of confidentiality of participation for all participants. When sharing findings with a wider audience, if there is a need to mention names, pseudonyms for participants should be used unless permission to use their real names is given.

SUMMARY

Several ideas and concepts important to creating communities of learners in foreign language middle and high school classrooms are summarized here.

- Creating effectual communities of learners in middle schools and high schools is essential to meeting the National Foreign Language Standards for foreign language learning. The notion of communities of learners is based on the assumption that learning is a socially situated, jointly constructed, and transformative undertaking in which learners gain entry into the valued sociocultural activities of their communities. This understanding of learning is a significant change from the more traditional view of learning as transmission.

■ To be effectual, communities of learners must include a range of participation structures that move beyond the individual and whole group to include peer tutoring and collective tasks, either in small groups or as participants in learning centers.

■ In creating effectual learning contexts, the foreign language teacher plays a critical role. Expert teachers know that in any kind of activity, they must make the purpose of the lesson clear. They must model all communicative behaviors and attitudes students are expected to learn and clearly distinguish between essential and nonessential information. In addition, they must help students make connections to what they already know and encourage students to participate, interact with each other, and collaborate.

■ Designing effective curriculum based on the National Foreign Language Standards involves organizing activities around the three communication modes—the interpersonal, the interpretive, and the presentational—and the four learning opportunities—situated practice, overt instruction, critical framing, and transformed practice. Moreover, to be effective instruction must move from what students know and are familiar with to that which involves them in the exploration of new worlds. Finally, instruction must provide a foundation for developing the communicative competence necessary for full participation in a range of practical and intellectual activities in communities who use the target language as a common code. At the same time it must provide opportunities for learners to use the target language to create a sense of belonging in their classrooms and, ultimately, invest in the classroom as valued members of a community of learners.

■ The varied use of multiple electronic technologies is changing the ways we communicate in our worlds. In order to keep pace with these changes, we must integrate technological knowledge, skills, and abilities into the foreign language curriculum from the beginning levels of instruction.

Figure 3–4 summarizes the many features that are essential to creating successful communities of foreign language learners.

DISCUSSION QUESTIONS AND ACTIVITIES

1. Investigate the scheduling options at a few middle schools and high schools that are located in your area. Find out how long the periods are, how many teachers teach, and what other duties they have when they are not teaching. Interview some foreign language teachers and students at the schools to find out what they consider to be the advantages and disadvantages to their particular schedules. What implications can you draw for your own teaching?

2. In a small group of your peers, review the list of characteristics of middle and high school students discussed earlier in this chapter. Do they seem reasonable and reflective of what you know about middle and high school students? Can you add others? What implications can you draw for teaching foreign languages to these groups of students? Share the main points of your discussion with your classmates.

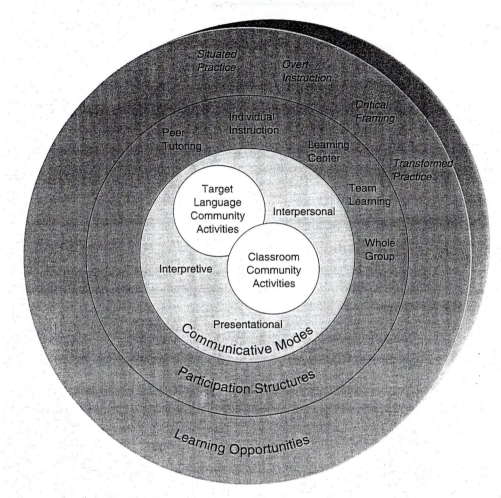

FIGURE 3–4 Summary of Features for Designing Curriculum for a Community of Foreign Language Learners

3. Describe the kinds of participation structures in which you have the most experience as a university student. Compare your participation experiences as a university student to those in which you were most frequently involved as a high school student. What do you feel is the value of each different structure for foreign language learning? Which structures do you feel most comfortable in? Most uncomfortable in? What implications can you draw for your own teaching?

4. Use the list of technology skills and abilities discussed earlier to reflect on your own level of skills and abilities in using various electronic technologies. Mark those areas in which you feel fully proficient, and those in which you feel you need improvement. How does your level of expertise compare to your classmates? What steps can you take

to improve your own technology skills? How important do you think it is for all teachers to be technological experts? Provide reasons for your opinions.

5. How might middle and high school students with whom you are familiar feel about being part of a teacher research project? How might other teachers feel about being part of a project? What are some ethical and practical concerns they might have? Discuss ways that you can effectively involve different groups in a project while maintaining high standards and minimizing potential obstacles or negative feelings.

6. Choose one of the Web sites described in the "Internet Resources" section and explore it. Write a two-page report summarizing the findings of your explorations to share with your classmates.

TEACHER RESEARCH PROJECTS

A. Metaphors of Teaching.

The purpose of this project is to help foreign language teachers bring to awareness, reflect on, and articulate their beliefs and attitudes about teaching, about their role as teachers, and about the role of their students.

Pose a Problem

Metaphors are a useful way for conceptualizing your beliefs and attitudes. To uncover some of your assumptions about teaching and the roles that you perceive you and your students to play you might ask yourself the following: To what particular roles and positions does a foreign language teacher compare? To what particular roles and positions do students compare? What assumptions about teaching underlie my perceptions? How are they reflected in my daily practices?

Identify Sources and Gather Information

You can do this project on your own or you may decide to invite a group of peer teachers to collaborate with you. Ask each to complete the worksheet contained in Figure 3–5.

Analyze

If you are working alone, once you have completed the worksheet ask yourself the following questions: Which of the metaphors you have chosen describe conflicting images? Which are compatible? What assumptions about teaching underlie the metaphors? If you are working with a group, compile the responses and search for patterns. How similar or dissimilar are they? How do the choices made individually compare with those made by the other group members?

Reflect and revise

Once you have analyzed the choices, consider the following questions: How might any conflict across individually chosen metaphors be eliminated and compatibility enhanced? What changes can you make to your teaching practices that will best reflect your assumptions about teaching, your role as teacher, and the roles of your students?

A. Circle up to 5 metaphors that describe the way you see yourself as a teacher.

actor	doctor	minister
advocate	encyclopedia	orchestra conductor
animal trainer	entrepreneur	parent
artist	farmer	police officer
boss	friend	politician
coach	guide	prison warden
comedian	judge	referee
counselor	master	student

B. Circle up to 5 metaphors that describe the way you see your students.

actor	enemy	pawn
advisee	farm crop	prisoner
athlete	friend	questioner
audience	jury	sheep
ball of clay	monster	sponge
client	musician	teacher
cup	obstacle	tourist
customer	patient	wild animal

C. Circle up to 5 metaphors that describe the way you see your classroom.

animal den	courtroom	jungle
battlefield	factory	party
cage	family	playground
carnival	farm	prison
church	fishbowl	resort
circus	gym	small business
community	home	stage
concert	hospital	zoo

D. List the metaphors you selected:

Teacher Metaphors	Student Metaphors	Classroom Metaphors
1._____	1._____	1._____
2._____	2._____	2._____
3._____	3._____	3._____
4._____	4._____	4._____
5._____	5._____	5._____

FIGURE 3–5   Metaphors of Teaching

Disseminate Information

Share what you have learned about your own beliefs and assumptions with other teachers in your school. Perhaps those in other departments would be interested in completing the worksheet and comparing their responses to yours and those of your group. You might also ask a group of students to complete the worksheet and then use a comparison of their responses to yours as a basis for discussion and reflection on the different perspectives.

B. Significant Learning Experiences.

The purpose of this project is to help preservice and in-service teachers examine the assumptions affecting their expectations and preferences in teaching, and to articulate their teaching philosophies.

Pose a Problem

Teachers' perspectives on teaching are drawn in part from their own experiences as students. Reflect on your past learning experiences and consider the degree to which they have influenced your teaching experiences. In doing so you might ask yourself the following question: How have my own experiences as a learner influenced my understanding of my roles and responsibilities as a teacher?

Identify Sources and Gather Information

Your reflections on prior learning experiences can serve as the primary source of data. Think back on all of your learning experiences and write about two or three of the most positive learning experiences you have had and two or three of the most negative learning experiences. For each experience note the context, the other participants, the focus of the learning experience, your stance or position in the experience at the time it occurred, and reasons why you considered the experience to be either positive or negative. The following box lists some possible contexts where learning can take place.

church	home
community organization	school
counseling session	social club meeting
friendship circle	team or individual sport
group game	workplace

Analyze

Look across the experiences and identify the significant conditions of the positive learning experiences. Do the same for the negative experiences. Make note of all patterns.

Reflect and Revise

Use the following questions as a guide for reflection on your experiences: How do your learning experiences, both positive and negative, compare to your experiences as a teacher? What assumptions about teaching and learning are embedded in them? How do they compare to what research tells us about effective teaching? What conclusions can you draw?

Disseminate Information

You might consider writing a personal narrative about what your experiences as a learner have taught you about teaching and submitting it for publication in the newsletter of your local or state professional organization. You might also try posting it on an electronic bulletin board serving foreign language educators and asking others to respond with feedback or with narratives of their own.

ADDITIONAL READINGS

Alexander, W., Carr, D., & McAvoy, K. (1995). *Student oriented curriculum: Asking the right questions.* Columbus, OH: National Middle School Association.

American Association of School Librarians. (1998). *Information literacy standards for student learning.* Chicago: American Library Association. http://www.ala.org/aasl/ip_nine.html.

McNiff, J., Lomax, P., & Whitehead, J. (1996). *You and your action-research project.* London: Routledge.

Queen, J. A. (1999). *Curriculum practice in the elementary and middle school.* Upper Saddle River, NJ: Prentice Hall.

Tyner, K. (1998). *Literacy in the digital world: Teaching and learning in the age of information.* Mahweh, NJ: Lawrence Erlbaum.

U.S. Department of Education. (1991). *America 2000: An educational strategy.* Washington, DC: United States Department of Education.

Warschauer, M. (Ed.). (1996). *Telecollaboration in foreign language learning.* Honolulu, HI: University of Hawaii Second Language Teaching and Curriculum Center.

INTERNET RESOURCES

AELACTION@ael.org   Appalachia Educational Laboratory

This is a discussion list for teachers and other educators who are interested in classroom-based action research. To subscribe, send this message to Majordomo@aelliot.ael.org: subscribe aelaction <your email address>. For help contact owner-aelaction@aelliot.ael.org.

www.clcrc.com/   Cooperative Learning Center

This is the Web site for the Cooperative Learning Center at the University of Minnesota. This research and training center focuses on how to make classrooms more cooperative places and on the teaching of cooperative skills such as leadership, decision making, trust building, and conflict resolution. The site includes links to essays on cooperative learning and lists of resources.

http://www.cal.org/   Center for Applied Linguistics (CAL)

CAL is a private, not-for-profit organization whose purpose is to promote and improve the teaching and learning of languages, identify and solve problems related to language and culture, and serve as a resource for information about language and culture. There are links on a variety of topics and to numerous sites including the ERIC Clearinghouse on Languages and Linguistics, the Foreign Language Assessment for the National Assessment of Educational Progress (NAEP) project, and the Heritage Language Initiative.

http://www.oise.utoronto.ca/~ctd/networks/   Networks: An Online Journal for Teacher Research

This is an online journal dedicated to teacher research. The journal provides a forum for classroom teachers to share their experiences and learn from each other.

http://www.ed.gov/Technology/

This is the site of the U.S. Department of Education Office of Technology. The goals of this agency are to expand and improve access to technology and to bring effective uses of technology to the classroom.

http://www.whatis.com

Whatis® is a knowledge exploration tool about information technology, especially about the Internet and computers. The site contains a glossary of over 2,000 terms related to electronic technology and a number of quick-reference pages.

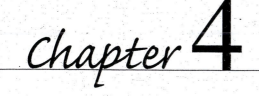

Chapter 4

Classroom Discourse

Preview Questions

Before you begin reading this chapter, think about your current experiences as a language student.

- What kinds of discourse patterns are typically found in your classroom?
- What are the expectations for students in terms of, for example, turn-taking, and ways of contributing to the classroom activities?
- How effective is the teacher in getting all of the students to participate? What are some ways the teacher does this? Alternatively, how could the teacher improve on the means used to involve students in the classroom interaction?
- How do your current experiences compare to your language classroom experiences as a middle or high school student?
- How might your past experiences shape the kinds of classroom environments you plan to construct as a teacher?

Key Words and Concepts

Classroom discourse
Initiation–Response–Evaluation (IRE)
Instructional conversations (ICs)
  Modeling
  Feeding back
    Corrective feedback
  Contingency managing
  Directing
  Questioning

Role of teacher questions
  Probing questions
Input
Negotiated interaction
Output
Learning strategies
Role of L1
Means for enhancing affective
        dimensions of learning

Overview

This chapter focuses on the important role of teacher–student and student–student discourse in the creation of effectual communities of learners and ultimately in the shaping of individual learners' development in the target language. Understanding classroom discourse helps us understand how the practices of a classroom contribute to the construction of knowledge. Since oral communication is both a primary medium of learning and an object of pedagogical attention in foreign language classrooms, the discourse of these classrooms plays an especially significant role in shaping learners' understanding of, and ability to, communicate in the target language. Middle and high school foreign language teachers are usually learners' first, and sometimes only, exposure to expert users of the target language, especially at the beginning levels of language study. Consequently, these teachers' knowledge of, and ability to, manage the classroom discourse is particularly crucial to the development of their students' communicative competence. The kinds of linguistic and communicative environments the teachers create in their interactions with their students help shape the students' knowledge, skills, and abilities as learners and users of the target language.

At the beginning of the chapter, the concept of classroom discourse is defined and findings from recent research on classroom interaction and learning are summarized. This is followed by a discussion on the nature and importance of instructional conversations in creating active learning communities. Also included are a discussion of the role of teacher questions and a summary of research on three types of classroom talk: input, negotiated interaction, and output. After a discussion of the connections between classroom discourse and learning strategies, the chapter concludes with a brief analysis of some discursive means for building effectual communities of language learners.

CLASSROOM DISCOURSE

Classroom discourse is the oral interaction that occurs between teachers and students and among students in classrooms. Through their interactions with each other, teachers and students construct a common body of knowledge, understandings of their roles and relationships, and the norms and expectations for their involvement as members in their classrooms. To be successful at learning students must develop the communicative competence that is specific to their roles as participants in their classroom discourse. They need to know, for example, how to listen or appear to listen at appropriate times, how to take turns, and when and with whom it is appropriate to speak. They also need to identify the cues in the teacher's talk that make apparent what it is they are to learn, and how to display their developing knowledge and skills in ways that are deemed appropriate by the teacher (Edwards & Westgate, 1994).

Findings from recent research on classroom discourse link students' involvement in their classroom interaction to their communicative development (see, for example, Baker, 1992; Cazden, 1988; Chang-Wells & Wells, 1993; Gutierrez, 1994; Gutierrez, Larson, & Kreuter, 1995; Nystrand, 1997; Smagorinsky & Fly, 1993; Wells, 1996). More specifically, they demonstrate how the patterns of interaction that are established in the classroom socialize students into particular understandings of what counts as the official curriculum and of themselves as learners of that subject matter. The patterns of interaction also help define the communicative activities through which learning occurs and the norms by which individual student achievement is assessed. Students draw upon these patterns and norms to participate in subsequent classroom activities. Thus, they are consequential in terms of not only what students ultimately learn, but also, more broadly, their participation in future educational events and the roles and group memberships that they hold within these events.

For example, students who engage most often in instructional contexts for literacy instruction in which they are expected to provide one word or brief responses to the teacher develop an understanding of literacy learning as an activity of recalling literal detail of stories they read (Gutierrez, 1994). Moreover, they come to understand what the teacher expects of them in terms of appropriate displays of behavior toward the teacher and each other and what they can expect from the teacher in terms of individual attention and responsiveness to their needs and concerns (Edelsky, 1996).

Additional research has shown how differences in discourse patterns across classrooms and across activities within the same classroom in terms of the kinds of learning opportunities available to the students lead to distinct individual developmental outcomes (see, for example, Cazden, 1988; Eder, 1982; Hall, 1998; Poole, 1992; Sperling & Woodlief, 1997). Smagorinsky and Fly's (1993) investigation of large- and small-group discussions on literature in two high school English language arts classrooms provides compelling evidence of this link between classroom discourse and student development. They found that students' beliefs about the nature of the activity of "literature discussion" and their own discussions on literature in their small groups reflected the values and processes that were evident in their teachers' discourse in the large-group discussions.

In one classroom both teacher-directed large-group discussions and student-directed small-group discussions were characterized by brief, unelaborated interactions that did not draw on external knowledge sources. In contrast, in the other classroom both large- and small-group discussions were characterized by lengthy, detailed interactions that drew on a variety of external sources. Smagorinsky and Fly concluded that the different ways in which literature discussions were accomplished in the two classrooms led to the creation of two distinct communities of learners with different interpretive frameworks and communicative means for engaging in discussions on literature.

Regarding differential discourse patterns within the same classroom, in a study conducted by the author of a high school Spanish classroom, it was demonstrated how the use of different turn-taking patterns in a particular instructional activity led to the development of two groups of Spanish language learners (Hall, 1998). Looking in particular at how a group of students participated in a "speaking practice" activity during one semester, the author was able to show that the different opportunities the teacher provided to individuals within this group resulted in the formation of two different status groups—a primary and a secondary group. In their interactions with the teacher, each group developed different participatory roles and rights to the floor. The students in the primary group received more interactional attention from the teacher. For example, she actively encouraged these students to participate, allowing them opportunities to initiate talk and even to take over others' turns.

The students in the secondary group were provided with different opportunities. While they were able to respond to the teacher's inquiries almost as often as the primary group, their responses were sometimes ignored. Moreover, they were not given many chances to initiate interactional exchanges. When they were, their initiations were not acknowledged by the teacher as frequently as those of the other group.

Interestingly, the teacher used these differences as a partial basis for her evaluation of the learners' midyear performances in this activity. Those in the primary group were thought to be more active, creative learners of Spanish than those in the secondary group. These findings led to the conclusion that the communicative inequalities resulting from differential teacher attention to student turns led to differences in the development of these students' communicative abilities and attitudes toward speaking Spanish.

Typical Patterns of Classroom Discourse

Much of the research on classroom discourse has shown that although discourse activities may differ from classroom to classroom and school to school, one particular pattern, the teacher-led three-part sequence of **Initiation–Response–Evaluation (IRE),** typifies the discourse of Western schooling from kindergarten to the university (Barnes, 1992; Cazden, 1988; Mehan, 1979; Nystrand, 1997). Commonly referred to as recitation script, the pattern involves the teacher asking a question to which the teacher usually already knows the answer. The purpose of such questioning is to elicit information from the students so that the teacher can ascertain whether they know the material. Students are expected to provide a brief but "correct" response to the question, which is then evaluated by the teacher with such typical phrases as "Good," "That's right," or "No, that's not right." After completing one round of interaction with a student, the teacher typically moves right into another round by asking either a follow-up question of the same student or the same or a related question of another student. This pattern is exemplified in Excerpt 1.

> **Excerpt 1**
>
> 1. Teacher: Who can tell me the answer to the first question? Angela?
> 2. Angela: Turkey.
> 3. Teacher: Yes, that's right, turkey. Who can answer number two? Mary, what do you have?
> 4. Mary: I put apples.
> 5. Teacher: Apples? Tom, what did you put?

As we can see, the teacher begins by directing a closed, known-answer question to Angela, to which Angela provides a short response. With the phrase, "Yes, that's right, . . ." in line 3 the teacher positively evaluates Angela's response, and then follows with a related question to another student. Like Angela, Mary gives a short response. As we see in line 5, rather than responding with an evaluative phrase, the teacher repeats the student's response using a rising intonation, indicated by the question mark. Repeating a student's response in this way is commonly used by teachers in the I-R-E sequence to indicate that the student response is incorrect and thus needs to be repaired (McHoul, 1990). The teacher then poses the same question to a different student.

Excerpt 2 is an example of an I-R-E sequence typically found in a foreign language classroom. This excerpt is taken from Hall (1998). The English translation appears in italics immediately following each line.

Excerpt 2

1. T: oye amigo qué te trajo Santa Claus

   listen friend what did Santa Claus bring you

2. J: aw Santa Claus mi trajo uhm ropa

   aw Santa Claus brought me uhm clothes

3. T: me trajo ropa sí ropa bueno muy bien excelente

   he brought me clothes yes clothes good very well excellent

In this excerpt the teacher begins by asking a question designed to elicit a list of items. After the student to whom the question is directed provides a response, the teacher first recasts the student's response into a more syntactically appropriate one, and then provides positive evaluation of the student's effort. In this way the teacher provides feedback to the students on what she considers an appropriate response to the question.

A great deal of research has examined the consequences of prolonged participation in the I-R-E sequence of interaction. Using data from her own and others' classrooms, Cazden (1988) shows how the use of this pattern in reading lessons more often facilitated teacher control of the interaction rather than student learning of the content of the lesson. Similarly, based on examinations of classroom discourse from several classrooms, Barnes (1992) found that the frequent use of the I-R-E sequence reflected a constricted transmission model of learning. The extended use of this pattern, Barnes argues, did not allow for complex ways of communicating between the teacher and students.

More recently, Gutierrez (1994) examined "journal sharing" in nine different classrooms. She found that in classrooms in which the activity was based on a strict use of the I-R-E sequence of interaction, the teacher did most of the talking and provided few opportunities for the students to participate in the activity. Thus, the students' opportunities to expand their learning about the topics on which the journal sharings were based were limited to responding briefly to the teacher's questions. It was the teacher, rather than other students, who commented or elaborated on the specific student's journal entries. This "recitation script" is exemplified in Excerpt 3.

Excerpt 3 (from Gutierrez, 1994, p. 348)

1. (T calls on Louisa: Louisa reads her journal)

2. T: Very nice Louisa . . . great . . . okay . . . she told us how he got burned and the [title

3. L: [Oh yeah . . . and it took place at the house

4. T: At the house . . . great . . . Yolanda

5. (T calls on Yolanda: Yolanda reads her journal)

Gutierrez concluded that prolonged participation in this script gave students few opportunities to develop the skills needed to construct extended oral and written texts.

In one of the most comprehensive studies of classroom discourse, Nystrand (1997) examined 112 eighth- and ninth-grade language arts and English classrooms. He found that the overwhelming majority of teachers used the recitation script almost exclusively in their classrooms and that its use was negatively correlated with learning. Students whose learning was accomplished almost exclusively through the recitation script were less able to recall and understand the topical content than were the students who were involved in more topically related open discussions. Moreover, he found that the use of the I-R-E sequence of interaction was more prevalent in lower-track classes, leading to significant inequalities in student opportunities to develop intellectually complex knowledge and skills.

The author's own investigations of a high school Spanish language classroom (Hall, 1995, 1998) revealed similar findings on the links between language learning and the use of this pattern of classroom discourse. In an instructional activity in which the goal was to provide opportunities for students to practice speaking Spanish, the author found that the teacher used the I-R-E pattern of interaction almost exclusively. The teacher was most often the initiator of the sequence, and the responses to students—the third part of the three-part sequence—were almost always an evaluation of the grammatical correctness of the students' responses to the initial question. The sample of classroom interaction found previously in Excerpt 2 typifies the kind of interaction that took place in this classroom over the course of an academic semester. The author found that the pervasive use of this pattern of discourse led to mechanical, topically disjointed talk and limited student involvement to recalling, listing, and labeling. It was concluded that extended student participation in exchanges of this type limited their communicative development to cognitively, linguistically, and socially simple skills in the target language.

In a comparison of the I-R-E sequence of interaction with other, more open, complex patterns of interaction, Wells (1993, 1996) found that what differed most often was how the third part of the sequence was realized. When it was limited to an evaluative comment like "That's right" or "Very good," it stifled rather than maximized student participation. However, when the third part followed up on a student's response by adding an example or elaboration of the student response, or invited the student to do so, it stimulated student involvement in the interaction. Examples of such utterances are "That's an interesting idea. Can you tell how you arrived at your understanding?" or "How does that compare to the lists that Jim and Mary compiled?"

In the Gutierrez study (1994) mentioned earlier, two additional orientations to journal sharing—responsive and responsive/collaborative—were found in the other classrooms. In classrooms with these orientations, students were encouraged to ask questions and to respond to and elaborate upon each other's contributions. In addition, the teachers more often expanded upon rather than evaluated the students' responses. Excerpt 4 contains an example of the interaction found in a classroom with a responsive/collaborative orientation. Here, the students attempt to decide together how one student, Maria, should revise her text.

Excerpt 4 (from Gutierrez, 1994, p. 359)

1. (Maria reads her paragraph aloud again)
2. S: How come you have to . . . like . . . like when you said the part about Olivia . . . and . . . and she likes Cesario, oh . . . she doesn't like Cesario . . . then . . . um . . . is that Malvolio that?

3. M: No no. Malvolio . . . Malvolio is like thinking that . . . what she says.

4. L: But isn't . . . but isn't Cesario Viola, you mean? You should put Cesario Viola (demonstrates what she's trying to say).

5. S: Maria . . . Maria . . . I got kinda . . . kinda messed up right there (points to Maria's text).

Gutierrez concluded that in such orientations to journal sharing, students are more actively involved in the activity, more topically related discourse is produced, greater opportunities for joint problem solving are created, and learning is enhanced. Similar conclusions have been reached in examinations of discourse in such content areas as English (Lee, 1995), math (Forman, 1996), and science (Warren & Rosebery, 1996).

Wells argues that the choices teachers make about the kinds of interactional patterns they use in their classrooms are linked to their pedagogical beliefs. Teachers who view themselves as leaders of communities of learners, and who view students as active agents in the learning process and thus take student involvement seriously, are more likely to engage their students in intellectually challenging interactions. Conversely, teachers who perceive themselves as authorities of knowledge and students as passive recipients of their knowledge are more likely to use the transmission-oriented I-R-E pattern of interaction.

Given what we know about classroom discourse we can conclude, as Wells (1993), Nystrand (1997), and van Lier (1996) do, that creating conditions for student learning through classroom discourse does not depend so much on whether the teacher controls the discourse but on their expectations for student involvement. Where teacher-produced questions and comments are limited to evaluating student displays of knowledge, and student contributions are limited to short responses to teacher queries, the classroom discourse is not likely to lead to active student involvement and complex communicative development. Rather, student participation will be limited to simple kinds of activity like recall, recitation, listing, and labeling. However, where teacher questions and comments are probing and open-ended, and students are allowed to ask questions and expand on the talk in addition to responding to the teacher, participation in classroom discourse will facilitate learning. As noted by Nystrand (1997, p. 72), "What ultimately counts is the extent to which instruction requires students to think, not just report someone else's thinking."

Instructional Conversations

Using the findings from the research on classroom discourse, Tharp and Gallimore (1991) and their colleagues (Goldenberg, 1991; Patthey-Chavez, Clare, & Gallimore, 1995; Rueda, Goldenberg, & Gallimore, 1992) have developed guidelines for creating developmentally rich patterns of teacher–student interaction in the classroom. Labeled **instructional conversations (ICs),** the purpose of this type of interaction is to assist students' understandings of, and ability to communicate about, concepts and ideas that are central to their learning. ICs stand in marked contrast to the more traditional recitation pattern discussed previously. Drawing on Vygotsky's (1978) notions of the ZPD and scaffolding, ICs are based on the idea that classroom discourse that engages students in challenging, intellectually complex interaction helps them to develop complex knowledge and communicative behaviors at the same time that it helps them assume responsibility for their own learning. Extended negotiation of concepts and ideas with others helps students to internalize the meanings of these concepts and ideas. It also helps them to connect their own experiences to the concepts; thereby developing deeper conceptual understandings as well as the communicative behaviors needed to display and use this knowledge in meaningful ways.

In regard to foreign language learning, Takahashi, Austin, and Morimoto (2000) noted that ICs constructed in the foreign language are important not only because they convey target language content, but also because they promote learners' understanding of how to use language to build knowledge and achieve shared notions of interpretation. They argue, "Through their participation over time, learners not only develop expectations of the content focus of the lesson; just as important, they learn about the process of communication itself" (p. 143).

In combining both instructional and conversational elements, instructional conversations are distinguished by several features:

- The focus is always on an intellectually challenging topic or theme that is of interest to the students.
- The discussion is managed in such a way that all class members are highly involved. This does not mean that the teacher does most of the talking or maintains tight control of the students' turns at speaking. Nor does it mean that the teacher relinquishes control to the more talkative and assertive class members. Rather, the teacher acts as discussion leader and facilitator, allowing students to initiate turns while making sure that all student voices are included in the discussion.
- Students are encouraged to produce intellectually challenging contributions and are helped by the teacher to articulate clearly their thoughts and the reasoning behind their stated opinions and assertions.
- The teacher helps the students link their background experiences and prior knowledge to the current discussion by making sure that the contributions are highly responsive and interconnected and that they build upon each other's contributions by challenging or extending them.

There are several communicative actions by which teachers can facilitate students' conceptual and communicative development in the ICs. They are discussed in the following sections.

Modeling

In **modeling,** the particular communicative and cognitive behaviors that are needed to do a particular activity are modeled or demonstrated to the students. Teachers may talk aloud about their own thinking on a particular issue or task, letting students listen to how they connect given information to new information, how they construct an argument to defend a position, or how they think through the solving of a problem or exercise. Students are expected to observe, note, and imitate the actions performed by the teacher. In addition to live performances, students can be provided with audio and video recordings of an activity they will be expected to perform. Along with the cognitive strategies students need to engage in the activity, modeling exposes students to the words, phrases, and other linguistic cues they are likely to need to accomplish the task on their own.

Research on modeling (Bandura, 1977) has shown it to be an effective means of establishing abstract or rule-governed behavior. By watching what others do or having a model to work from, we learn, among other things, linguistic styles, conceptual schemes, information-processing strategies, cognitive operations, and standards of conduct. Reciprocal Teaching (Palincsar & Brown, 1984) is an example of an approach in which modeling plays a central role. Here the teacher models strategies that have been shown to be necessary to successful reading comprehension. The teacher uses the language skills students will need to ask questions about a text, to clarify a point, to summarize the reading, and to predict what is to happen next. The teacher then guides the students in these same tasks, gradually decreasing assistance as the students' abilities develop.

Another example of effective modeling is the use of the strategy "wondering aloud." In her study of a middle school science teacher, Verplaetse (2000) showed how in his large-group discussions with both native and nonnative English-speaking students, "Mr. Wonderful," the name Verplaetse gave to this teacher, modeled the kinds of questions he expected students to ask. The teacher did this by stating the questions in such a way that they "spoke aloud a curiosity as if it were a question inside the students' minds" (p. 237). Excerpt 5 is an example of the kinds of questions the teacher wondered aloud. The modeled questions are in italics. The larger discussion from which this excerpt is taken was centered on the concepts of chromosomes, cell division, and reproduction.

Excerpt 5 (from Verplaetse, 2000, p. 233)

1. T: Now, you guys seem to be talking about X and Y. And people seem to be talking about X and Y like they're these old friends, like you understand exactly what they are. *Can somebody let me in on this?* (Hands raise) *Are we just choosing X and Y randomly?*

2. Ss: Yes, Yeah,

3. T: Could, *why don't we choose G and B?*

According to Verplaetse, the question in line 33 was posed by the teacher "as if he did not understand" (p. 234). Moreover, through his use of *we* in line 35, he spoke collectively "as if he had become one of the students" (p. 234).

Feeding Back

Feeding back is a communicative behavior that lets students know the particular standards with which their performances are being evaluated and how well their actions at a given point in time compare to these standards. According to Wiggins (1998), effective feedback is descriptive. It provides a clear model of an expected performance, and helps the student compare his or her performance to the model in order to figure out what can be done to improve that performance. Moreover, effective feedback is timely, frequent, and ongoing. Ineffective feedback, on the other hand, only indicates vaguely, if at all, the expected actions and how the student's performance compares to them. It includes nonspecific comments such as "keep trying" or "you didn't study enough." In addition, feedback is ineffective when it is given infrequently or comes long after the student can make effective use of it.

There has been a great deal of research examining the connection between **corrective feedback,** a primary purpose of which is to focus learners' attention on grammatical forms in the second language, and the learning of additional languages (e.g., Lightbown & Spada, 1990; Lyster & Ranta, 1997; Lyster, 1998; Ohta, 2000). In a study of four primary immersion classrooms in Canada, for example, Lyster and Ranta (1997) found the following types of corrective feedback were used by teachers in their interactions with students: *recasts, explicit correction, repetition, metalinguistic feedback,* and *clarification requests.* Of these, recasts, in which the teacher reformulated students' ill-formed utterances, did not lead to any student-generated forms of repair, at least as indicated in their responses immediately following the recasts. Lyster and Ranta speculated that recasting student utterances may not have helped because they "already provide correct forms to learners" (p. 53) rather than asking students to provide them. They concluded that feedback strategies that highlight student errors and at the same time require learners to reformulate or recast their own utterances with the correct forms are more effective in facilitating the learning of these forms than is feedback that provides the correct answers to the student.

A more recent study on teacher recasts, however, demonstrates that in some circumstances they can also be an effective feedback strategy. In an examination of university-level learners of Japanese, Ohta (2000) found that teacher recasts were a source of data that students used to compare and ultimately reshape their own ill-formed utterances. Most of the students did this work on their own, in private speech, rather than making their corrections public through oral responses to the teacher.

More specifically, Ohta found that as the teacher interacted with an individual student, other students attended to those instances when the teacher reformulated ill-formed utterances produced by the student. As the teacher directed her talk to the individual, other students whispered the reformulated utterance to themselves, practicing, as it were, the correct formulation. For these students, Ohta argues, teacher recasts were an effective form of feedback. She concludes that both teachers and researchers need to be careful not to judge the effectiveness of recasts on whether students immediately and publicly produce a corrected oral response. Rather, they should be aware that providing feedback in the form of corrected models can be equally effective in helping students learn language forms.

Ohta's findings add to those of MacKey and Philp (1998) who found in their study on recasts that although students did not immediately produce accurate utterances in response to teacher recasts, they eventually corrected their forms in subsequent interactions. Like Ohta, these authors concluded that although the effect may be delayed, teacher recasts can be beneficial.

Contingency Managing

Through **contingency managing,** the teacher makes clear the connections among the various turns, incorporates student voices into the ongoing discussion, and helps learners elaborate and build upon each other's contributions. Managing the interaction includes the use of such communicative actions as confirmations, back channel cues (e.g., "oh," "really"), affirming responses such as "that's great" and "that's very well stated," repetitions, elaborations, and recasts or reformulations of what students say. Through the regular use of such actions, teachers help keep the conversation going and at the same time help students construct a coherent and intellectually meaningful discussion.

A study by Boyd and Maloof (2000) of a university-level ESL classroom exemplifies the nature of contingency managing. In their investigation of the discourse they show how the teacher actively orchestrated opportunities for student talk by incorporating the individual student contributions into the large-group discussion. For example, specific words that were used by the students were adopted by the teacher and used in the teacher's subsequent contributions to the discussion. In this way, the authors argue, the teacher affirmed student contributions and ultimately increased their participation in the literature-based discussions.

Directing

This particular communicative action focuses learner attention on what is to be learned in a task or activity by directly teaching a skill or concept. Rather than having students try to figure out how to do something on their own, it is sometimes helpful to provide the students with the information and the particular linguistic tools they need to complete a task successfully. This can be done through lectures, demonstrations, and coaching. Evidence from research on **direct teaching** in first-language content classes (e.g., Light & Butterworth, 1993; Stone & Forman, 1988) and in second-language learning (Schmidt, 1994) shows that direct or overt teaching helps learners notice and subsequently learn the salient features of a task or activity. A more extended discussion on the utility of direct instruction in the learning of additional languages can be found in Chapter 3.

Questioning

Assisting learning through **questioning** is perhaps the most common means of assistance in classrooms. Teacher questions have two general functions. The first is to *assist* students in accomplishing a task or activity. This is done by eliciting extended student discussion on a particular topic or helping students activate and make connections to relevant background knowledge. The second function of teacher questions is to *assess* learners in terms of their understandings and abilities to perform without assistance. The importance of teacher questions in facilitating learning is discussed in more detail later in the chapter.

Explaining

This particular means of assisted performance involves specifying or making comprehensible the underlying conceptual framework or structures of what is being learned. The act of **explaining** can include defining or illustrating the meaning of a concept or term, offering reasons for some actions or beliefs, or making clear the causes of an event. Explaining also involves justifying statements and opinions with evidence and relevant details that can help learners organize and make sense of new information, knowledge, or skills. As research on learning (Detterman & Sternberg, 1993) has shown, helping students make sense of what they are learning by providing them with explanatory frameworks for organizing the new knowledge or skill greatly facilitates their learning.

Task Structuring

Task structuring involves arranging tasks so that the essential aspects are clearly distinguished from the nonessential, and that they are cognitively and communicatively accessible and challenging to the learners. Tasks that are too easy can lead to frustration, lack of motivation, and disinterest in much the same way as tasks that are too broad or too difficult.

Through their effective use of ICs in the classroom, teachers can help students reach the upper levels of their ZPD. Weaving instruction into their conversations with students, teachers make their own thinking explicit, modeling for the students the strategies they use to work through an issue, solve a problem, or accomplish a task. They also help students make connections and build upon what they already know. Students then are able to develop a shared base of knowledge and set of skills upon which more complex knowledge and skills can be built.

Goldenberg (1991) notes that although teachers may seem less directive in ICs, they are as deliberate in their instruction, organizing their actions around "facilitating and guiding students' understanding in the course of extended verbal interactions" (p. 6). It should also be noted that instructional conversations are not meant to replace other kinds of instructional activities but rather to complement them. In addition to the more traditional forms of instruction, ICs help students develop their target language knowledge and skills by involving them in problem solving and inquiry-based learning in the context of shared conversations. Because their primary goal is to help students "comprehend text [content], learn complex concepts, and consider various perspectives on issues" (Goldenberg, 1991, p. 17), ICs are particularly appropriate for use in two kinds of learning opportunities: overt instruction and critical framing.

TEACHER QUESTIONS

Teacher questions are particularly important for creating effective instructional conversations. The different kinds of questions teachers ask function as resources for creating supportive conditions for comprehension and participation, thereby helping students move forward in the learning process. Questions can assist students during difficulties with complex classroom tasks, help them maintain focus on the task, and guide them in producing their own contributions to the interaction. They can also help teachers assess where students are in terms of their learning.

The kinds of questions used by teachers can require different levels of student involvement, ranging from questions that ask students to recall already stated facts or ideas, to questions that ask students to draw relationships between ideas, or imagine new solutions for familiar problems. The taxonomy of cognitive objectives proposed by Benjamin Bloom (1984) provides a useful framework for talking about the cognitive work teacher questions can help stimulate in students. Bloom initially created the taxonomy as a way to differentiate what he considered to be the level of abstraction needed to perform particular cognitive activities. For our purposes here the taxonomy serves as a useful framework for developing teacher questions that elicit from students a range of linguistic, communicative, and cognitive skills. The actions are arranged into the following six domains:

- *Knowledge:* This domain refers to action words that ask students to remember, recognize, and recall concepts, ideas, terms, facts, rules, procedures, and all other knowledge and skills previously learned.
- *Comprehension:* This domain refers to action words that ask students to display their grasp of the meaning of the material by, for example, explaining, translating, or summarizing the material.

- *Application:* This domain includes action words that ask students to use the knowledge and skills learned in meaningful, concrete ways. This includes having students apply rules, concepts, ideas, theories, or methods in specific situations.
- *Analysis:* This domain refers to words that ask students to separate the learned material into its component parts, to identify the relationships between these parts, and to recognize the organizational principles underlying the structure of the material.
- *Synthesis:* This domain refers to action words that ask learners to bring together various aspects of the material to create a new, meaningful whole. This can involve, for example, having them create a new plan, proposal, or activity in which the focus is on the formulation of new patterns.
- *Evaluation:* This domain refers to action words that ask learners to judge the value of the material for a particular purpose, to justify the valuations, and to evaluate the worthiness and appropriateness of value statements made by others.

Table 4–1 provides a range of action words typically associated with each domain.

While lists like the one found in Table 4–1 can be helpful in constructing questions, it should be remembered that the cognitive complexity of questions is very much tied to their contexts of use. In other words, how complex a question is depends on the larger activity of which it is a part and its institutional setting. In a summary of research on the use of questions, Rymes and Pash (2001) note that a simple yes or no question, when embedded in a larger interaction, may be part of a complex line of reasoning. They go on to show how one

TABLE 4–1 *Taxonomy of Action Words for Developing Teacher Questions.*

Knowledge	Comprehension	Application	Analysis	Synthesis	Evaluation
Complete	Classify	Apply	Analyze	Combine	Argue
Define	Defend	Arrange	Associate	Compose	Assess
Describe	Depict	Classify	Break apart	Create	Conclude
Draw	Distinguish	Compute	Compare	Design	Consider
Identify	Estimate	Demonstrate	Contrast	Develop	Convince
Label	Expand	Dramatize	Debate	Explain	Critique
List	Explain	Draw	Diagram	Formulate	Decide
Locate	Generalize	Develop	Differentiate	Hypothesize	Deduce
Memorize	Give examples	Model	Discover	Integrate	Evaluate
Name	Illustrate	Modify	Examine	Invent	Judge
Outline	Interpret	Plan	Infer	Originate	Justify
Pronounce	Match	Produce	Investigate	Rearrange	Rank
Recite	Paraphrase	Relate	Order	Reconstruct	Recommend
Recognize	Predict	Show	Research	Summarize	Support
Reproduce	Restate	Solve	Separate	Synthesize	Validate
State	Summarize	Use	Survey	Theorize	Weigh

seemingly simple question, "Do you see a lot of men in hats outside of Wal-Mart?" asked to a group of second graders required greater cognitive work that was only made visible when the question was placed in its larger activity structure. The authors conclude that to understand fully the complexity of a question we must consider both its institutional context and the larger argument or purpose of the interaction.

Along similar lines, Cooper and Simonds (1998) point out that while the taxonomy of action words can help us vary the kinds of cognitive activity we ask students to engage in, there are additional types of questions that need to be considered. They call these "probing questions" (p. 157). **Probing questions** push students to elaborate and expand their thoughts, to reflect on their own thinking, and to link their ideas to those of their peers. Questions such as "Can you elaborate?", "How does that relate to what Sarah said?", and "How does that relate to your earlier comments?" are examples of probing questions.

Kellough and Kellough (1999) provide some useful guidelines for effective preparation and implementation of teacher questions. First, teachers must be mindful of their instructional goals and prepare questions with those in mind. Adequate preparation ahead of time ensures that the purposes for asking questions are likely to be well matched to the instructional task. Preparing ahead will also reduce the amount of in-class "trial and error" time. That is to say, the less time teachers take *in* class, trying to figure out what they are doing as they are doing it, the more time there will be for teachers and students to be engaged in actual learning.

Second, teachers need to vary their turn-taking patterns for student participation in response to teacher questions, and be consistent in their application. In many classrooms, teachers often require students to bid for the opportunity to participate by raising their hands. Although this pattern of taking turns may help involve a number of students in the discussion in an orderly way, it is not the only viable pattern. Students should also be given the opportunity to self-select. That is, there should be times when students are allowed to join the discussion at will, much like they would in a conversation outside of the classroom. How and when the different turn-taking patterns are used matter less than their consistent application across students when they are being used. In other words, if the teacher requests that students raise their hands to bid for the floor, then the teacher should use this pattern for all students, rather than allowing some students to self-select and others to raise their hands.

Third, in those situations where students bid for the floor, teachers should ask the question first before calling on a student for response. This allows all the students to hear the question and begin to formulate a response. Calling on one particular student before asking the question often signals to the others that the question is meant only for that student and thus releases them from having to attend to it themselves.

Fourth, teachers should restrict their questions at any one time to a number that can reasonably be responded to. Sometimes when we are trying to hurry through a task, or have not spent adequate preparation time formulating questions, we may overwhelm students with a series of questions as we try to work through our own thinking. For example, asking the questions "What did you think of that character? Why do you think she did what she did? Did you feel her actions were justified? Would you have done the same thing?" one right after the other will make it difficult if not impossible for students to know which question or set of questions they are to focus on. This, in turn, may limit their interest and their ability to follow and participate in the development of the discussion. Finally, provide ample wait-time for students to respond and be sure that the amount of time given is consistent across students and across tasks. The more cognitive work the question elicits from the students, the more time they need to formulate their thoughts.

Teacher questions are dynamic discursive tools for assisting students' active involvement in the process of learning (McCormick & Donato, 2000). The kinds of questions we ask depend on our instructional goals; the more cognitively complex the questions are, the more we will move learners to higher levels of thinking. Through our goal-directed use of questions, then, we can construct academically meaningful paths of learning and guide our students into full, competent performance.

As a final note, as Kellough and Kellough (1999) point out, questions that punish students, embarrass them, or in any way show disrespect serve no meaningful academic or social purpose. We need to be especially careful in middle and high school foreign language classrooms where issues of language use and identity are in the foreground. The target language needs to be used in positive, identity-enhancing ways, since students of this age are easily offended and embarrassed, and particularly sensitive to criticism.

INPUT, NEGOTIATED INTERACTION, AND OUTPUT

As noted in Chapter 3, particularly in the discussion on overt instruction, a great deal of research has been concerned with examining features of classroom interaction that aid the process of learning forms in the target language. While many of the theoretical tenets underlying this research differ—in some cases quite significantly—from those of a sociocultural perspective on learning, nevertheless, many of the findings add valuable knowledge to our understanding of the connection between classroom interaction and language learning (for discussions on these differences, see Donato & Lantolf, 1990; Dunn & Lantolf, 1998; Firth & Wagner, 1997; Hall, 1997). Thus, a more detailed accounting of the research is provided here.

The research on classroom interaction and the learning of target language forms has taken three orientations: input-oriented research, negotiation-oriented research, and output-oriented research. The first orientation has its roots in Krashen's (1982, 1985) theoretical work on comprehensible **input.** As pointed out in Chapter 3, Krashen considered meaningful input central—and sufficient—to the process of language learning. Although in his own work Krashen provided little empirical evidence for this claim, it motivated much interest among others. Much of the work by scholars such as Gass (1997), Gass and Varonis (1985), Long (1981, 1983), Long and Robinson (1998), Pica (1988) and her colleagues (Pica, Kanagy, & Falodun, 1993), for example, has been concerned with defining the features of input that help to make it comprehensible. These investigations have included the examination of such features as the degree of syntactic complexity, the rate of speech, and utterance length. Discourse features of input such as feedback, error correction, and use of questions have also been examined for the roles they play in making input comprehensible.

Building on the findings from this research, additional studies have focused on "input enhancement" and "form-focused instructional talk" (Doughty & Williams, 1998; Fotos, 1994). Of specific concern here are the roles these special genres of teacher talk play in the raising of students' consciousness about the syntactic aspects of the target language, and their subsequent learning of these forms. In a summary of research on consciousness-raising and language learning, Schmidt (1994) concludes that by explicitly focusing the learners' attention on the forms to be learned, such teacher talk facilitates students' learning of these forms.

The second orientation, much of it also stemming from Krashen's (1982, 1985) theory on comprehensible input, has focused on the role of **negotiated interaction** between students. Negotiated interaction is defined as the use of speech modifications such as clarification requests, repetitions, recasts, and comprehension checks. Generally, the concern has been with documenting the conditions fostering the emergence of such speech—more versus fewer modifications—in student–student interaction and less so in assessing the impact such negotiation has had on additional language learning (see Pica, 1994, for a review of this research).

Recent work examining features of classroom task conditions suggests that how tasks vary in terms of, for example, goals and information flow influences the number of modifications used by the students to accomplish the task. Findings show that tasks in which the information flow goes both ways, that is, when neither participant has all the information, and in which the goals are collaborative rather than competitive enhance the use of negotiated interaction by the learners (see Crookes & Gass, 1993a, 1993b).

A third research orientation has examined the outcomes of students' learning as a result of their collaboration on tasks (see, e.g., Donato, 1994; Kowal & Swain, 1994). Swain (1995) calls this talk **output,** and proposes that student output facilitates language learning in at least three ways. First, it can get students to notice or become aware of a gap between what they can communicate and what they want to communicate. Second, it can reveal the students' testing of hypotheses as they try new forms. Third, it can play a metalinguistic role by providing learners with opportunities to actively reflect on their language use.

While much of the research on input, negotiated interaction, and output has been limited to examinations of their role in the learning of syntactic and lexical forms, the findings are useful in that they provide additional evidence for the importance of raising students' awareness of what is to be learned. As Wertsch (1991, 1994) and others (New London Group, 1996) have noted, while the ways in which we are made aware of relevant linguistic resources can vary, the fact remains that for learning to occur we must take notice of them. Moreover, in demonstrating that collaborative group work is as useful to learning as teacher-directed whole-group instruction, the findings on input, negotiated interaction, and output provide additional evidence on the important role that different participation structures play in learning.

LEARNING STRATEGIES

Learning strategies are goal-directed actions that are used by learners to mediate their own learning. Effective strategy use involves not only knowing about a particular strategy, but also when to use it and how to monitor its use. Strategies are typically grouped into three categories:

- *Metacognitive Strategies.* These include previewing main ideas and concepts and planning, sequencing, monitoring, assessing, and revising one's performance.

- *Cognitive Strategies.* These include grouping and classifying, using dictionaries and other external resources, notetaking, visually representing the material through charts, diagrams, and so on, rehearsing, and forming hypotheses and testing them out.
- *Socioaffective Strategies.* These include asking for clarification, repeating, imitating, circumlocuting, cooperating, and engaging in private speech.

One common approach to strategy instruction has been to directly teach these different strategies to learners. Chamot and O'Malley (1994) and Oxford (1990), for example, have developed instructional models for the assessment of students' strategy use and the explicit instruction of effective strategy use. The goal of such overt instruction is to make learners aware of the variety of ways they can help themselves to learn so that they can become increasingly self-directed and ultimately assume full responsibility for their involvement in the process.

Without denying that the overt instruction of strategies can be beneficial, the evidence on learning and classroom discourse makes clear that strategy learning also occurs as an outcome of teacher–student interaction in classroom activities. In their interactions with students, teachers play an especially important role in helping them develop and manage particular strategies for learning. By modeling effective strategy use and scaffolding student participation in their use across the four kinds of learning opportunities, for example, teachers assist learners in the development of a wide range of important strategies for directing their own learning.

Studies of learning in four different foreign language classrooms illustrate this connection between classroom interaction and strategy development. Through the use of a performance-based portfolio assessment tool Donato and McCormick (1994) show how university students learning French were "purposefully socialized into constructing their own strategy learning through dialogue with self and teacher and connections to actual evidence of their growing abilities" (p. 463). During the semester, students were asked to create portfolios in which they regularly reflected on and provided evidence for the strategies they used in learning. The authors argue that "the systematic act of documenting and thinking about performance is the catalyst and mediator for developing and sharpening one's strategies" (p. 462). Rather than being taught learning strategies apart from their experiences, these students were learning how best to learn within the context of their learning activities. Documenting and reflecting on the specific steps they undertook as they went about learning not only promoted critical awareness of the process, but also the appropriation of the strategies they needed to be successful learners.

Another study provides evidence of strategy learning through context-based classroom interaction. In their study of elementary-grade students learning Japanese, Takahashi, Austin, and Morimoto (2000) show how students appropriated one particularly useful strategy initially used by the teacher to help themselves and each other remember previously learned material. In this case, it was the singing aloud of the mnemonic song, "Tai (I want)" that helped students remember certain syntactic features. At the beginning of the year, it was the teacher who sang the song to the students to help cue their recall of specific learned items. The authors show how, as the year progressed, the students used the song themselves to help cue their own memories and those of their peers by singing the song aloud whenever assistance was needed. The authors argue that the singing of the song, learned through their interactions with the teacher, is a compelling indication of the students' appropriation of an important learning strategy.

In addition to appropriating strategies made available to them in classroom discourse, students have been shown to be quite resourceful in creating their own effective learning strategies. In a study of a high school Spanish as a foreign language classroom (Brooks & Donato, 1994), it was shown how students used their first language, English, to help themselves and each other carry out an unfamiliar and difficult task in Spanish. Members of one small group, for example, used English to figure out how to do the task (e.g., "Am I supposed to tell you and you write stuff on your paper?"), and to come up with an appropriate word in Spanish (e.g., "Solamente.", "Ah! Solamente. That's a good word!"). The researchers concluded that the students' use of English served as a useful learning strategy, helping them organize, plan, and coordinate theirs and each other's behaviors in the accomplishment of the task.

As a final example, in the study mentioned earlier by Ohta (2000), it was shown how individual students used private speech as a strategy for mediating their learning in a whole-group activity. Examining utterances learners addressed to themselves, Ohta found that these individuals used both teacher and student utterances they heard addressed to others in large-group interaction as a basis for comparing and reformulating their own responses. By repeating or recasting utterances heard in the interaction between the teacher and other students, Ohta argues, individual learners created their own learning strategies, and thus actively pursued learning, even though they were not the direct focus of the teacher's interactional attention.

In summary, these studies have shown that in addition to the direct teaching of language-learning strategies, students can develop a range of effective strategy use through active, conscious involvement in their classroom activities with the teacher and other students. Even the strategies the youngest learners are able to engage in, indeed, can help to construct intellectually rich interactions in which they are able to mediate their own learning and that of their peers without the explicit help or directed attention of the teacher. Thus, it is essential to provide opportunities in our classroom interactions that enhance the strategic development of learners' ingenuity and skill in the process of learning.

THE ROLE OF L1 IN THE L2 CLASSROOM

Traditionally, foreign language teaching methods have urged the exclusive use of the target language in the classroom from the beginning levels of instruction (Krashen, 1982, 1985; Krashen & Terrell, 1983). In fact, according to Howatt (1984), avoiding the use of L1 has been a feature of foreign language teaching methods for much of the 20th century. Discouraging the use of English by both teachers and students was thought to be beneficial in helping learners keep the two languages separate while developing a reliance on the target language.

The notion of multicompetence (Cook, 1992, 1995, 1996, 1999b) and current research on language development (e.g., Anton & DiCamilla, 1998; Genesee, Nicoladis, & Paradis, 1995; Nicoladis & Genesee, 1996), however, make this position problematic. As Cook (1992) notes, "This [position] is reminiscent of the way of teaching deaf children language by making them sit on their hands so that they cannot use sign language" (p. 584). As we know, learners' first language is always present in their minds as they are learning the second language. Indeed, the two systems are so closely linked that what one does or learns to do in one has a significant impact on what one can do and learns to do in the other (Cook, 1992).

The study of language use by students in a secondary Spanish class by Brooks and Donato (1994), noted previously, highlights the cognitive links existing between learners' first language and the target language. As pointed out earlier, the Spanish learners' use of English helped them orient to, and become involved in, a Spanish language task. As they gained experience and grew comfortable with what needed to be done in the task, their use of English decreased. Thus, as the researchers point out, the learners' use of English did not hinder their learning of Spanish. Rather, it facilitated it by helping them mediate their involvement in their instructional activities.

Along similar lines, Anton and DiCamilla (1998) examined the use of English and Spanish among beginning-level adult learners of Spanish working in small groups to complete a written composition. They found that the learners used their first language, English, in their conversations as a way to hold their collective attention and together figure out how to say something in Spanish. Excerpt 6 shows how two students used English to help themselves and each other access forms and construct a sentence in Spanish.

Excerpt 6 (from Anton & DiCamilla, 1998, p. 322)

G: Or do you want to just say in the afternoon?

D: Let's say . . .

G: Por la tarde?

D: Let's just do 'por . . . la tarde . . . '

G: Por la tarde . . . comen . . . what do they eat?

D: Um . . . frutas.

Anton and DiCamilla (1998) conclude that in addition to helping students access particular forms in Spanish, their use of **L1** helped them to maintain intersubjectivity, or a shared understanding of the task. Both functions were instrumental in helping the students successfully complete the task.

Findings from these studies confirm the important roles that learners' first languages play in bilingual development. It should be noted that the resourcefulness of L1 is not limited to its use by students. Teachers can also use it as a tool in teaching. In fact, Cook (2000) suggests several ways for teachers to incorporate the systematic use of L1 into L2 classrooms. For example, it can be used to convey meaning about a particular concept or term, to explain a grammar point, and to organize the class for learning when the cost of using the target language is too great (e.g., giving instructions, checking homework, and so on). English can also be used to brainstorm vocabulary and other kinds of sociocultural and pragmatic information that students may need to know to complete a task.

According to Cook (2000), several factors need to be considered when deciding on the language to use in a particular activity. Two of the more important include the following:

- Efficiency: Can the activity be carried out more effectively through the use of L1?
- Facilitation of learning: Will using the L1 help students in the learning of the target language?

In deciding whether to use English in the target language classroom, Cook advises that benefits from the use of L1 must always be compared to potential loss of L2 experience. He concludes that although the use of L1 is clearly beneficial to learning the second language, everything else being equal, it is always good to use the L2 as much as possible.

More research on the uses to which teachers and students put English and the target language as they engage in their classroom activities will certainly help make their connections even clearer. For now, it seems safe to assume that using English in the foreign language classroom will not retard or unduly restrict the learning of the target language. Rather, when used to help learners mediate their involvement in their classroom activities, it can promote their learning of the other language.

LINGUISTIC AND INTERACTIVE MEANS FOR CREATING AND SUSTAINING COMMUNITY

Much of this chapter has focused on the cognitive dimensions of classroom discourse and their role in learning. However, as we know, **affective dimensions** of learning are equally important in creating effectual communities of learners. These include feelings of group affiliation and solidarity as well as personal autonomy and confidence. This chapter concludes with a discussion on some ways in which a positive classroom community can be constructed through discourse.

First, affirm student responses. Affirmation involves listening to the students with understanding and empathy, striving to understand their points of view, and incorporating their contributions into the larger discussion. Affirmations can occur through the use of back channel cues such as "oh," "uh huh," and "mmm," which let students know that they are being listened to. They can also occur through repetitions, recasts, or reformulations of student utterances. What makes these utterances affirmations is the way that the teacher conveys respect for the student's contribution through the use of tone and other paralinguistic cues and at the same time makes it clear that the authorship of the utterance is left with the student.

In Nystrand's (1997) study of classroom discourse, mentioned earlier, a close examination of the discourse of one exemplary ninth-grade English teacher whose students not only participated actively in the interaction but also appeared to enjoy their involvement revealed that this teacher frequently and consistently affirmed students' contributions. Likewise, in the Verplaetse (2000) study, also mentioned earlier, affirmation of student contributions was found to be a frequently used strategy by the middle school teacher Verplaetse had called "Mr. Wonderful." In addition to making students feel valued, such discursive actions help to foster students' feelings of autonomy, which, in turn, lead to heightened student interest and motivation in learning (Cooper & Simonds, 1998; van Lier, 1996).

Second, use language to create group bonds and rapport. When referring to classroom activities use inclusive pronouns such as "we" and "us." Use "let's" as an alternative to an imperative, and vary intonational patterns, voice pitch, loudness, and tempo to express immediacy or positive affect (Cooper & Simonds, 1998).

Third, use humor and allow students to use humor to reduce tension, to relieve embarrassment, to save face, or to entertain. It should be remembered, however, that while the use of humor can strengthen the interpersonal bonds between classroom members, when used incorrectly, it can also serve to create divisiveness. Because middle and high school students are especially sensitive to anything that might, even loosely, be perceived as criticism, it is important to use humor with care.

An example from a high school Spanish classroom, taken from Hall (1995), illustrates how the use of humor at the expense of one student can lead to embarrassment and even humiliation. The interaction between a teacher and student found in Excerpt 7 occurred after the teacher had spent several minutes asking the questions *te gusta tocar* (do you like to play [an instrument]) and *te gusta comer* (do you like to eat) to several students.

Excerpt 7

1. T: pero te gusta, Monica, te gusta comer gatos te gusta comer gatos
(*but do you like, Monica, do you like to eat cats*)

2. Monica: sí
(*yes*)

3. T: sí o no, sí, ok, me gusta, me gusta
(*yes or no, yes, ok, I like, I like*)

4. Monica: me gusta
(*I like*)

5. T: comer gatos
(*to eat cats*)

6. Monica: comer gatos
(*to eat cats*)

7. T: comprendes comer comer yum yum gatos Sylvester, Garfield
(*do you understand to eat to eat yum yum cats.*)

8. Student: cats!

9. T: sí, a Monica le gusta comer gatos
(*yes, Monica likes to eat cats*)

10. Student: she likes to eat cats?

11. T: sí, por supuesto
(*yes, of course*)

12. Students: (laughter, simultaneous talk)

13. Student: (to Monica) you been eatin cats

14. Monica: no

15. T: no ahh no ok no me
(*no ahh no ok I don't*)

16. Monica: (*very softly*) no me
(*I don't*)

17. T: comer gatos, sí, no me gusta comer gatos bueno Monica, sí. A mi me gusta comer gatos en pizza, en pizza, solo en pizza, solo en pizza
(*eat cats, yes, I don't eat cats, good, Monica, yes. I like to eat cats on pizza, on pizza, only on pizza, only on pizza*)

As we see in line 1, the teacher asks Monica whether she likes to eat cats. Apparently thinking that, like the students before her, she was being asked if she could eat something that was edible, Monica replies with a "yes." The teacher then repeats the entire utterance, evidently to get Monica to repeat it as well, which she does in lines 4 and 6. Perhaps because he thinks it is funny and wants the other students to share in the humor, the teacher, with the help of a student who translates the teacher's utterance into English, brings Monica's response to the attention of the entire class in lines 9 and 11. As we see in lines 12 and 13, this calls forth laughter and some teasing from other students. Unfortunately, the humor is at the expense of Monica, who realizing what the teacher led her to say, attempts to change her answer. However, she does not engage in the laughter. Rather, she repeats the teacher's utterances softly and, once this interaction is over, does not attempt to participate again.

While it is very likely that the teacher did not intend to embarrass Monica in front of the class, encouraging students to laugh at her attempt to participate did just that. As this excerpt and findings from other studies on the role of humor in language learning demonstrate, to engender feelings of affiliation and group support, the premises on which the humor is based must be shared among all the members rather than just a few (Consolo, 2000; Duff, 2000; Sullivan, 2000). It must also be used to enhance goodwill rather than to rebuke, punish, tease, or make a point.

A final way to foster a positive learning environment has to do with the creation and management of classroom norms and expectations for learning. Given the diversity of life experiences that students bring to the classroom, it is likely that they may have different understandings of appropriate classroom behavior. Differences across national culture groups have been well documented. However, differences can exist even across seemingly similar groups of people.

For example, in many locations in the southeastern United States, it is expected that students address their teachers and other persons of authority using "Sir" or "Ma'am." This is not the expectation, however, in other sections of the United States. Likewise, in some areas, overlapped talk, where one person begins talking before the speaker is finished, is common and thus treated as appropriate conversational behavior. In other places, where it is expected that one person finishes talking fully before another begins talking, such overlapped talk could be interpreted as "interruptions" and thus considered rude or inappropriate.

The important point is not that there is one right way of behaving. Rather, it is to work collectively with the students to decide upon norms for classroom behavior, to articulate them clearly, and to follow them consistently and fairly across all individuals and situations. Explicit, consistent expectations provide a stable, safe learning environment. Safe learning environments, in turn, enhance learners' self-confidence, their interest in learning, and their interest in building strong interpersonal relationships with each other and the teacher.

SUMMARY

Classroom discourse is an essential component of all learning environments. In foreign language classrooms, because the language to be learned is both the object of pedagogical attention and the primary medium of communication, the interaction that occurs between teachers and students, and among students, is especially significant to creating effective communities of language learners. Consequently, understanding key concepts and terms associated with classroom discourse as well as how to construct different patterns of discourse to effect different learning outcomes is a crucial aspect of pedagogical content knowledge for foreign language teachers. A brief summary of some of the key issues relating to classroom discourse presented in this chapter is provided here.

- The initiation–response–evaluation (IRE) is the most common pattern of classroom interaction found in Western schooling contexts. Its use typically exemplifies a transmission model of teaching in which the focus is on delivering a body of knowledge to learners. It more often facilitates teacher control rather than student involvement, and when used exclusively, severely limits student learning.

- Based on Vygotsky's notion of scaffolding, instructional conversations are a cognitively rich pattern of discourse that actively assists learners' understanding and ability to communicate about significant concepts and ideas. While they are primarily teacher-directed, instructional conversations (ICs) are also jointly constructed with learners. That is, learners have ample opportunities not only to actively participate but also to lead the teacher and fellow students in their intellectually challenging conversations. ICs typically involve seven communicative actions: modeling, feeding back, contingency managing, directing, questioning, explaining, and task structuring.

- Teacher questions play a particularly critical role in scaffolding learner involvement in classroom interactions. In their questions, teachers need to challenge learners to think, to draw on what they know, and connect it to what they are learning. In addition, when constructing questions it is important to make clear connections between the questions asked and the instructional goals, and to provide a variety of ways for students to participate in the ongoing interaction.

- Much research on second language acquisition has investigated the roles of teacher input, teacher–student and student–student negotiated interaction, and student output in facilitating student learning of lexical and syntactic forms. In general, findings from the various strands of research have provided useful information on how to construct interaction in overt instructional activities in ways that help students to notice or become aware of, actively reflect on, and ultimately gain control of the various aspects of the target language.

- Recent research on learning strategies shows that in addition to being directly taught strategies for learning, students also acquire them through their active involvement in classroom interaction. Not only do they appropriate strategies that teachers use in the context of their instructional interactions, but they also devise their own strategies in response to their individual needs. Providing time for students to document and reflect on their use of strategies helps them become more aware of their own learning process, and ultimately, more capable language learners.

- Recent research on the use of English in foreign language classrooms has raised questions about traditional assumptions restricting the use of anything but the target language. Findings show, for example, that the use of English helps learners access new forms and functions in the second language and integrate the new knowledge into what they already know. While more research is needed, we can acknowledge the beneficial cognitive role that English can play in helping students mediate their learning of the target language.

■ Finally, affective dimensions of learning are as important as cognitive dimensions. Thus, creating effective communities of language learners requires the use of particular patterns of discourse that foster the development of positive affect, group solidarity, and interpersonal bonds. Some communicative resources for doing so include the use of respectful, affirming responses to student contributions, and of personal pronouns such as "we" and "us." It also involves using humor to foster friendliness and goodwill among all class members, and collectively establishing and adhering to a common set of guidelines for classroom behavior.

DISCUSSION QUESTIONS AND ACTIVITIES

1. In pairs or small groups, analyze the patterns of language found in the following excerpt of teacher–student interaction. What kind of instructional interaction—the IRE or the IC—is it more reflective of? What consequences in terms of learning are likely to result from long-term participation in this pattern? How might you improve upon it? What implications can you draw for foreign language learning?

Excerpt (taken from a middle school English class)

T: What are some characteristics of crows?
S1:   Fly.
T: They fly. What else?
S2:   They're black.
T: They're black. What else?
S3:   They like homework.
T: I didn't call on you George.
S4:   They screech.
T: They screech. They caw. Daniel.
S5:   They squawk really loud.
T: They squawk, they're loud. What else?

---

2. Tape-record 20 minutes of a classroom discussion. It can be from one of your own university courses or from a middle or high school classroom. Be sure to secure permission from the class members before taping. Together with a partner, first transcribe the discussion and then identify and analyze each teacher question using the taxonomy of action words listed in Table 4–1. Based on your analysis, how would you evaluate the effectiveness of the teacher's questions in creating a cognitively rich interaction?

3. State in your own words what instructional conversations are, and their usefulness to learning. How applicable is the concept of instructional conversations to the

discourse found in university classrooms? How well do they reflect the discourse patterns found in your language classes at the university? List the promises and difficulties of using ICs in language classrooms with which you are familiar as a teacher and as a student. Share the list with your classmates. What implications can you draw for using ICs in middle and high school classrooms?

4. It was suggested in this chapter that English can play a role in the foreign language classroom. How closely do the findings on the use of English reflect your own use of English when learning your teaching language? Have you, for example, ever used English when working with a partner on a task to help you both figure out how to do the task? Interview several of your classmates in your university-level language classes about their use of English. Are there patterns to their use? What conclusions can you draw from your small sample of data? What kinds of research on the use of English in foreign language classrooms would be helpful to you, in your role as a teacher of another language? In your role as a language student?

5. Several ways for creating positive affect and building rapport in the classroom were presented in this chapter. Using your own experiences as both teacher and student, discuss how effective you feel these means are. In your opinion, how important is creating group bonds among class members to learning a foreign language? Can you suggest additional ways for enhancing interpersonal relationships and group bonds in the foreign language classroom?

TEACHER RESEARCH PROJECTS

A. Instructional Conversations.

The purpose of this project is to help foreign language teachers develop an understanding of instructional conversations and how they might be used to foster target language learning.

Pose a Problem

As discussed in this chapter, instructional conversations are responsive patterns of classroom interaction in which teachers actively assist students in developing their understanding of, and ability to, communicate about concepts and ideas that are central to their learning. To uncover some of your own patterns of classroom interaction, or if you are not teaching, those of someone who is, you might ask the following questions: What are the patterns of teacher–student interaction typically found in my or my peer's classroom? How well do they reflect patterns typical of instructional conversations?

Identify Sources and Gather Information

Videotapes of your own or a colleague's teaching can serve as the primary source of data. Choose a day or a series of days in which whole-group instruction will be used. Be sure to set the camera in such a way that it captures clearly the movements and sounds of the entire class. If you are using your own classroom, you might enlist the assistance of a colleague to do the videotaping for you.

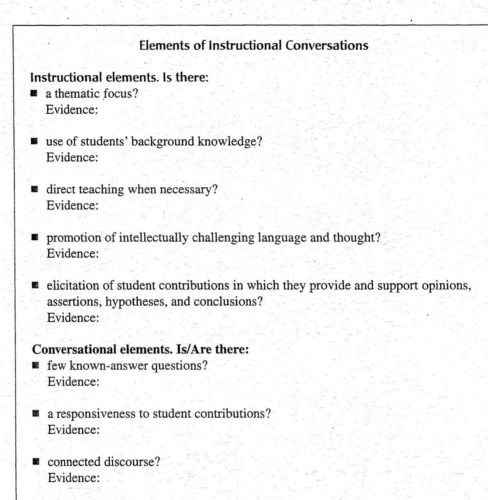

FIGURE 4–1   Framework for the Analysis of Classroom Interaction

Analyze

Observe the videotapes and choose several sections to transcribe. Once the transcriptions of the classroom interactions are completed, analyze them using the framework found in Figure 4–1. The framework is based on a scale for rating instructional conversations designed by Rueda, Goldenberg, and Gallimore (1992).

Reflect and Revise

After completing the analysis, ask yourself the following questions: Which features of instructional conversations were found in the interactions? Which were used most often? Which were used least often? Were all of the students involved in the conversations? How might the interactions be changed so that they more effectively assist the learning of all students?

Disseminate Information

Share what you have learned in a presentation to your classmates or other foreign language teachers from your school or district. Alternatively, conduct a workshop on how to analyze classroom interactions and engage in instructional conversations at a gathering of members from your local or state professional organization for foreign language educators.

B. The Role of L1 in Learning L2.

The purpose of this project is to help teachers examine their own uses of both English and the target language *as language learners* so that they may become aware of the functions that both languages can play in the learning of another language.

Pose a Problem

One helpful source of information on the roles that the use of English can play in the learning of the target language is your own use of English as a language learner. What role does English play in your own learning? When have you found its use helpful to learning the target language? When have you found it to be limiting?

Identify Sources and Gather Information

An effective means for collecting data on your use of English in learning the target language is a combination of a log and personal reflection journal. In the log, record each time you use English in your language class and the context in which it was used. After class, write down your reflections on the events in which English was used. Be sure to note whether you thought its use facilitated or hindered your learning of the target language, and provide reasons for your opinions. In order to capture patterns of use, plan to keep a record over a period of time. If you have daily classes, 2 to 3 weeks of record keeping should provide you with enough data.

Analyze

If the log data are primarily quantitative, compute the average number of times English was used and in what contexts and compare this information across time. Note any patterns. Read through the journal entries and note common themes and topics. Summarize your findings from both sources of data.

Reflect and Revise

What did you find about your use of English? Which findings do you think are most significant? Why? Were you surprised by any of your findings? What questions have these findings raised? What implications can you draw from your experiences as a language learner for language teaching?

Disseminate Information

If you are already a language teacher, use your findings as a point of discussion with your students on the ways in which they can use English as a strategy for learning the target language. If you do not have your own classroom, share your findings with others by posting them to an electronic bulletin board for foreign language teachers, or writing an article about strategy use and language learning for the newsletter of your state foreign language education association.

ADDITIONAL READINGS

Bowers, C. A., & Flinders, D. (1990). *Responsive teaching: An ecological approach to classroom patterns of language, culture, and thought.* New York: Teachers College Press.

Johnson, K. (1995). *Understanding communication in second language classrooms.* Cambridge: Cambridge University Press.

Macaro, E. (1997). *Target language, collaborative learning and autonomy.* Clevedon, U.K.: Multilingual Matters.

Manke, M. P. (1997). *Classroom power relations.* Hillsdale, NJ: Lawrence Erlbaum.

McGilly, K. (Ed.). (1994). *Classroom lessons: Integrating cognitive theory and classroom practice.* Cambridge: MIT Press.

Mercer, N. (1995). *The guided construction of knowledge: Talk amongst teachers and learners.* Clevedon, U.K.: Multilingual Matters.

Oxford, R. L. (1990). *Language learning strategies: What every teacher should know.* New York: Newbury House.

Young, R. (1992). *Critical theory and classroom talk.* Clevedon, U.K.: Multilingual Matters.

INTERNET RESOURCES

Several National Language Resource Centers have undertaken research and training projects that readers may find helpful in advancing their understanding of classroom discourse and language learning. Three specific sites are:

http://carla.acad.umn.edu/CARLA.html   The Center for Advanced Research on Language Acquisition (CARLA)

This is the Web site of CARLA, a National Language Resource Center, located at the University of Minnesota. The center supports a number of coordinated programs of research, training, and development related to foreign language teaching. The Second Language Learning Strategies Project was one of many research projects sponsored by the center. Links to detailed information on this and other projects can be found at the Web site.

http://www.cal.org/k12nflrc/ National K–12 Foreign Language Resource Center

This is the Web site of a National Language Resource Center jointly sponsored by Iowa State University and the Center for Applied Linguistics. Its focus is on the professional development of K–12 foreign language teachers. Its three primary initiatives are performance assessment, effective teaching strategies, and new technologies in the foreign language classroom. Links to these and other projects can be found at the Web site.

http://www.cal.org.nclrc The National Capital Language Resource Center

This center is a collaborative effort by Georgetown University, The George Washington University, and the Center for Applied Linguistics. Part of its purpose is to engage in projects emphasizing the teaching and learning of less commonly taught languages and to provide practical teaching strategies for elementary-, secondary-, and university-level foreign language teachers. Links to related sites can be found here.

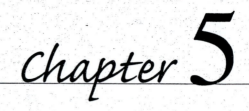

Planning Instruction and Assessment

Preview Questions

Before you begin reading this chapter, think back on any experiences you have had as a teacher.

- How much time did you spend planning your lessons?
- What part of lesson planning did you find most valuable? Least valuable? Why?
- What do you feel are some of the more positive consequences of a well-planned lesson in terms of student learning?
- As a student, with what kinds of assessment tools are you most familiar?
- How important are tests and grades to you? Why?

Key Words and Concepts

Instructional goals and objectives
Syllabus
Unit and lesson planning
Role of textbook
Dimensions of assessment
    Diagnostic
    Formative
    Summative
Traditional assessment
    Standardized tests
    Teacher-made tests
    Norm-referenced tests
    Criterion-referenced tests

Alternative assessment
    Portfolios
    Formative
    Summative
    Webfolios
Designing effective assessment tools
    Validity
        Content
        Systemic
        Face
    Norms and standards
    Scoring rubrics
    Rating scales
    Grading

Overview

As noted in earlier chapters, from a sociocultural perspective foreign language teacher expertise is not just defined in terms of target language competence. It also includes well-organized *pedagogical knowledge,* or knowledge of how to teach. Such knowledge is comprised of several important dimensions.

First, pedagogical knowledge involves knowing how to articulate clear instructional goals and objectives. Research on teacher expertise (Sternberg & Horvath, 1995) has shown that expert teachers are critically aware of the significant role that instructional goals and objectives play in and across all aspects of instruction. They understand how goals drive instruction and, furthermore, they understand that effective teaching depends on their ability to articulate their instructional goals and objectives to learners, and to connect them to their instructional activities.

A second dimension of pedagogical knowledge entails knowing how to plan lessons that meet well-articulated goals and objectives. Here, the research on teacher expertise (Sternberg & Horvath, 1995) reveals that expert teachers know how to create plans that effectively and efficiently integrate knowledge of the content with knowledge of teaching methods. Moreover, expert teachers know how to use their well-developed planning structures to create plans that are responsive to both expected and unexpected events that occur as the lesson unfolds.

A third component of pedagogical knowledge entails knowing how to design and administer tests and other assessment measures, and how to use them to evaluate the effectiveness of instruction both in terms of student learning and in meeting program goals. Expert teachers have extensive, accessible knowledge about assessment that they use in performing and evaluating their day-to-day instructional activities. Moreover, they are able to apply their knowledge to specific situations, identifying relevant information, making insightful connections, and solving problems in ways that are both appropriate and creative.

The purpose of this chapter is to present an overview of the various dimensions of pedagogical knowledge that one needs to develop foreign language teaching expertise. The chapter opens with a discussion of several dimensions of instructional planning. This is followed by discussions of the concept of assessment and the means for designing assessment tools that match instructional purposes. Included here is a set of steps for creating effective evaluative rubrics and rating scales. A short discussion on the important role that grades play in the school lives of middle and high school learners concludes the chapter.

GOALS AND OBJECTIVES

Planning for instruction is a major component of teaching. It involves three general levels. The most abstract level is *long-range planning,* the goal of which is to establish the general scope or direction of a course. For some, a course includes a full academic year; for others, such as those on block scheduling, it includes one academic semester. The second level is *unit planning,* which establishes the skills and knowledge related to specific expectations and learner needs for a particular thematic or topical unit of study within a course. Unit planning includes delineating student tasks, instructional strategies and methods, resources, assessment criteria, and evaluation tools for an extended period of time. The third level is *daily planning,* which establishes teacher and student tasks for the day.

Goals and objectives are essential to effective planning at all three levels. **Goals** are general statements of educational direction or intent and thus serve as organizing principles for the design of classroom instruction. **Instructional objectives** are more specific than goals. They describe what the students are expected to be able to do as a result of their involvement in their learning opportunities.

Well-written instructional objectives contain three components. The first is a description of the behaviors demonstrating the knowledge or skills to be learned. Well-written objectives include clearly articulated behaviors; words that are ambiguous or not easily observed, such as appreciate, believe, or understand, are avoided. A typical source for choosing descriptive behaviors is the list of action words associated with Bloom's (1984) taxonomy of cognitive abilities. A list of words based on this classification scheme, which are often used to write instructional objectives, is presented in Chapter 4, Figure 4–1.

A second component of instructional objectives involves the particular context and conditions of performance. Because all learning is contextual, clearly articulating the setting in which the behaviors are to be demonstrated is essential. Examples of context include "in a letter written to a friend" or "in an oral presentation on the topic to the class."

The third component constituting instructional objectives is the degree of expected performance. This involves stating how well the students should be able to perform the expected behaviors in order for the teacher to determine whether learning has indeed occurred. In some cases, the teacher may expect the student to perform flawlessly, with no errors, in order for the teacher to conclude that learning has occurred. In other cases, occasional errors may be permitted.

Brown (1995) notes several benefits deriving from the use of instructional objectives in language classrooms. Some of the more important benefits include helping teachers clarify and organize their teaching and articulate more clearly the kinds of skills, knowledge, and abilities they expect students to learn. Using instructional objectives also helps teachers develop appropriate assessment measures, and evaluate learners' progress in meeting their expectations.

Instructional objectives can be difficult to write, especially for the novice teacher. Curriculum documents and the materials of more experienced peer teachers are good resources for ideas in developing one's own set of instructional objectives. The important issue to consider when writing objectives is the clarity with which we make our expectations known to students. The more clearly we state the expectations for learning, the easier it is to plan for instructional activities and the more likely the students are to understand and meet the expectations.

It is important to remember, however, that all learning cannot be translated into observable behaviors. Some learning occurs in our mental images, attitudes, and understandings, and thus may not be observable, at least initially. It is also important to keep in mind that we cannot anticipate, observe, and measure all learning that occurs in our classrooms. Thus, we need to be open to, and indeed encourage, unplanned learning.

PREPARING INSTRUCTIONAL PLANS

Course Syllabus

A **syllabus** is a written document that provides a general overview of the entire course, and thus is a good indicator of long-term planning. It includes a description of the course, its major goals and objectives, the topics or units to be covered, and a general overview of the knowledge and skills that students can expect to develop. It also includes a detailed explanation of the grading policy along with descriptions of the activities that will be graded and the procedures for assessment. Other information such as teacher contact information, a list of both required and recommended materials, and general guidelines for classroom behavior should also be included.

By providing the students with a clear plan for the course, the syllabus helps establish familiarity, reduce insecurity, and create rapport between teachers and students and among students, all of which are essential to the establishment of effective communities of learners. It also makes course plans visible to those outside of the classroom and thus helps build connections with other teachers, administrators, and with parents.

Unit Planning

The next level of planning occurs at the **unit** level. One course usually comprises several units of study. Units can be theme- or subject-based and should involve a wide range of activities from the interpersonal, interpretive, and presentational communication modes. Topics and themes of relevance to learners of foreign languages in middle school and high school are usually interdisciplinary and can include politics, youth culture, role of schooling and education, social and community life, tourism and travel, festivities and customs, ethnic relations, working life and employment, and gender roles and relationships. Although less usual in middle and high school foreign language classrooms, units can also be organized around traditional subjects or content areas such as geography, history, mathematics, music, art, and literature.

Developing a unit involves the following steps. First, for each unit, the content standards around which instruction will be organized must be identified. These standards should be written in terms of the three communication modes—the interpersonal, the interpretive, and the presentational—that form the National Foreign Language Standards, and should make clear what students should know and be able to communicate in the target language by the end of the unit.

Next, decisions about unifying themes, concepts, or subject areas for each unit as well as the length of time that will be spent on each unit must be made. Some units can take up to a couple of months to cover. Others may involve only a few weeks. For each unit, specific instructional objectives clearly identifying the knowledge and skills students will be expected to learn must then be developed for each of the standards. For each objective, the instructional activities in which the students will be involved over the course of the unit that will lead them toward achieving the standards must be clearly described. The following should be included in the descriptions:

- The type of *learning opportunity* in which the students will be involved. Is it, for example, situated practice, overt instruction, critical framing, or transformed practice?
- The *structures for learner participation*. Will, for example, the activity involve the whole group, a small group, or pairs of students? Alternatively, will it be an individual activity or made part of a learning center?
- The *materials and other resources* that will be needed to participate in the activity. For example, will students need certain books, pens, paper, or some kind of realia to participate in the activity?

Finally, plans and procedures for assessing whether and how well the students meet the goals and objectives of the unit must be clearly articulated. Depending on the length of the unit, there may be multiple assessments leading to an integrative, culminating activity. Because assessment is a critical component of instruction, it is discussed in more detail later in this chapter. Figure 5–1 contains a sample format for planning a unit of instruction.

Lesson Planning

Planning **daily lessons** is the most detailed level of instructional planning. Effective teaching cannot occur without planning; thus, daily plans are an essential instructional tool. They help teachers mediate their thinking about teaching and learning, and make explicit the connections between their thoughts and ideas and their expectations for student learning. In addition, they serve as useful documents for teacher reflection and self-assessment, for assessment of student learning, and more generally, for the evaluation of course goals and objectives.

While the format of lesson plans can vary, several elements are basic to a well-written plan. First, all plans should state the goal or goals of the unit to which the plan is connected and the instructional objectives for the day's lesson. It is important to remember that the objectives need to be stated in terms of what the students are expected to learn from their participation in the day's activities.

A second essential component is the set of procedures for accomplishing the objectives. In addition to clear descriptions of the teacher actions, the procedures should include an estimation of the amount of time needed for each step or set of steps, descriptions of expected student actions, and a list of materials and equipment to be used. Since the plan serves as a script for teacher action, the steps themselves are most easily written as directives such as "Have students get into small groups" or "Ask them to follow along as I read the directions aloud to them." It is helpful to include as part of the written script whatever reminders are needed to help the teacher make the connections between each step within a particular activity and across each activity clear. Whatever the daily activities are, procedures for all lessons should begin with a clear opening aimed at engaging learners' interest in the day's lesson. They should end with a brief, but clear conclusion that reinforces what the students have learned from participation in the day's activities and prepares them for the next day.

A third element of an effective lesson plan is a description of any homework assignments that are based on the day's lesson. While the actual assignments should be noted in

Unit_____   Estimated Length of Time_____

Goals
    Interpersonal
        1.
        2.
        3.
    Interpretive
        1.
        2.
        3.
    Presentational
        1.
        2.
        3.

Instructional Objectives (match to goal)

    Interpersonal Objective 1
        Activity 1
            Learning opportunity
            Participation structure
            Materials and resources

        Activity 2
            Learning opportunity
            Participation structure
            Materials and resources

Assessment Plans and Procedures

    Sources of data for evaluation

    Rating criteria

FIGURE 5–1   Sample Format for Planning a Unit

a separate section, it is expected that the steps that are taken in making the assignment known to the students will be included as part of the procedures. Finally, a lesson plan should include a section where notes and reflections on the success of the day's lesson can be recorded. These notes and reflections are essential to future planning and, more generally, to building teacher expertise (Sternberg & Horvath, 1995). Figure 5–2 provides a sample format for creating daily lesson plans.

Lesson Plan   Date_____

Class _____   Unit _____

Goals
    1.

    2.

Objectives
    1.

    2.

    3.

Procedures (written as directives). Be sure to include an estimation of the amount of time needed for each step, descriptions of expected student actions, and a list of materials and equipment to be used.
    1.

    2.

    3.

    4.

Homework Assignments

Self-Assessment and Reflections. Ideas for Revisions.

_____

_____

_____

FIGURE 5–2   Sample Format for Planning Lessons

Effective teachers, no matter how experienced they may be, plan for instruction. Because their pedagogical knowledge and skills have become less effortful and more automatic and efficient through their extensive experience, expert teachers may tend to use less complex plans. Novice teachers, however, need plans that are extensive and detailed. Finally, while all daily lessons should be well planned, they should also be flexible enough to allow for contingencies and unexpected developments.

Role of Textbooks and Other Materials in Planning for Instruction

Textbooks are generally considered a significant source of content in foreign language classrooms (Apple, 1992; Grosse, 1993; Luke, 1988). They are useful in that they provide an organizing framework for curricular content and ideas for activities and exercises. However, they should never be used as the sole source of material. Additional resources from which teachers can draw include computer software programs, Internet sources, audiotapes and videotapes, and visual and graphic representations. The World Wide Web, for example, provides access to a myriad of electronic documents, such as newspapers, magazines, and video and audio recordings created by persons around the globe. Because these documents are authentic, natural sources of language, they can be useful pedagogical resources (Walz, 1998).

DIMENSIONS OF ASSESSMENT

According to a sociocultural perspective, **assessment** is the crucial link between teaching and learning. It is perhaps best defined as an ongoing process of collecting data to use in making instructional decisions (Fradd & McGee, 1994). Effective assessment helps teachers and students determine students' progress in meeting their educational goals and, more specifically, their instructional objectives. It also helps teachers to evaluate the effectiveness of their instructional activities, and more generally, their courses and programs.

Assessment is commonly used for three broad purposes. First, it is used to determine students' strengths and weaknesses in a particular area in order to place them at appropriate levels of instruction. This is usually referred to as **diagnostic assessment,** and occurs prior to instruction. A second purpose involves monitoring the students' progress toward meeting the instructional objectives and goals. Such assessment, usually referred to as **formative,** occurs during the learning process, and is used by teachers to help them identify any difficulties learners are experiencing so that they may adjust instruction and assessment methods accordingly.

A third purpose is summative. **Summative assessment** occurs after an instructional segment, which can be a particular lesson, a unit, or a block of time. It involves determining the extent to which students have met their instructional goals or objectives and communicating the results to the students, parents, and other members of the school community. The results can also be used to evaluate and improve the effectiveness of the instructional activities and assessment measures, and, more generally, the curriculum.

Sources of Data for Assessment

Although we may tend to use in our classrooms and programs one assessment tool more than we use others, the consensus is that no single measure can address all aspects of learning or of a program's success. Thus, effective teaching involves the use of multiple assessment tools. In this section, both traditional and alternative means for assessing learning are discussed.

Traditional Means

Traditional assessment measures include standardized and teacher-made tests. **Standardized tests** are those for which there are established uniform conditions for taking and scoring the test. Included are conditions such as the amount of time allowed to complete the test, seating arrangements, and the use of aids or references. Any kind of test, from multiple-choice to written essays to oral interviews, can be standardized as long as uniform testing and scoring conditions are used. Using standardized tests allows for the comparison of individual scores across groups. **Teacher-made tests** are those constructed by the teacher to assess student learning of classroom content.

There are two additional ways to group tests. Tests can be either norm-referenced tests or criterion-referenced tests. **Norm-referenced tests** are standardized tests whose purpose is to compare test-takers to each other. More specifically, it is to rank individual students according to their achievement in broad areas of knowledge with respect to the achievement of others. In order to determine the average test behavior for students at different ages and grades against which individual student performance is assessed, the tests are given to a representative group of students from a variety of racial, ethnic, economic, and regional groups prior to the tests' availability to the public. The scores of this group constitute the *standard* or *norm*. The scores of the students who take the tests after their publication are then compared to those of the norm group.

Thus, a student's score is interpreted in light of the average group score rather than to some agreed-upon, criterion-based score. Comparing the performance of individual test-takers to the performance of the norm and assigning the individual a score ranks him or her within that large group. The score is usually expressed as a *percentile,* a *grade equivalent score,* or a *stanine*. The major reason for using norm-referenced tests is to highlight achievement differences across students and groups of students. Individual rankings are usually meant to discriminate between high and low achievers. School systems find such classifications useful for grouping students according to ability levels.

Established norms are typically used by test publishers for 7 years. All students who take the test during that period have their scores compared to the original norm group. Tests such as the California Achievement Test (CTB/McGraw-Hill) and the Iowa Test of Basic Skills (Riverside) are examples of norm-referenced tests used in elementary and middle school grades. The Scholastic Aptitude Test (SAT) is a common norm-referenced test taken by college-bound high school students. In general, norm-referenced tests have been used to measure what are assumed to be general language or cognitive abilities. They have been criticized, however, for being biased toward mainstream groups, since those who differ in ethnicity, race, and social economic status often perform less well than students from mainstream groups.

Criterion-referenced tests measure student performance with respect to curricular goals or standards. These goals or standards have been identified by teachers and curriculum experts as important to the learning of the content area. Thus, they function as benchmarks of student performance. The purpose of criterion-referenced tests, which can be either standardized or teacher-made, is to measure how well an individual has learned a specific body of knowledge and skills. In other words, the interest is not in determining a student's ranking, but instead to ascertain what a student knows and does not know with respect to a particular set of curricular goals.

In terms of scoring, an individual student's performance is judged with respect to curricular goals rather than to the scores of other students or group of students. He or she must reach a certain agreed-upon level of performance to be considered successful. It may be, for example, that in order to be considered a "pass" a student has to answer 80% of the test questions correctly. The performance of other examinees is irrelevant in determining individual scores.

As noted earlier, these tests are used to measure students' performance against particular program objectives. Consequently, the more directly the test matches the course or program objectives, the better the students are expected to do. On standardized criterion-referenced tests, passing scores are usually set by a committee of experts. For teacher-made criterion-referenced tests, it is usually the classroom teacher who determines what is considered an acceptable score. Scores on criterion-referenced tests are useful for ascertaining how well students have learned the knowledge and skills they are expected to master. They can also be used to help determine how successful a program is in helping students meet curricular goals.

In some school districts throughout the United States, standardized criterion-referenced tests have been created for different content areas and are being used to determine whether students can graduate or be promoted to higher grades. They are also being used to assess overall school performance.

A recent variation of criterion-referenced testing is *standards-based assessment*. Many states and districts have adopted content standards, such as the National Foreign Language Standards (National Standards in Foreign Language Education Project, 1996) that describe what students should know and be able to do in different subjects at various grade levels. To assess how well students meet these content standards, *performance-based standards* have been developed that define how much of the content students should know at each level.

Traditional Means for Assessment in the Foreign Language Classroom.

Traditionally, foreign language classrooms have relied on discrete-point criterion-referenced grammar and vocabulary tests for evaluating student knowledge of the language (Hadley, 1993). Such tests, however, have been criticized for not capturing the full range of communicative knowledge and skills students are learning, and for only tapping into lower cognitive skills such as recall and recognition.

The 1980s saw the beginning of the move toward communicative proficiency-oriented instruction in foreign language classrooms (Hadley, 1993). This move prompted a concern for developing a test that assessed more than students' linguistic knowledge. Specifically, the concern was to develop a performance-based test measuring students' abilities to perform particular language tasks. Born from this concern was the Oral Proficiency Interview (OPI), a standardized measurement tool designed to evaluate oral abilities in the foreign language. This instrument was developed from an assessment tool used by the federal government to evaluate the language abilities of foreign service officers (Clark & Clifford, 1988; Rennie, 1998).

The OPI entails a structured 10- to 25-minute face-to-face interview with a trained examiner who rates students' proficiency on one of four levels ranging from novice to superior. To rate students' proficiency, the examiner uses a set of proficiency guidelines created by the American Council on the Teaching of Foreign Languages (1986). A typical OPI consists of four phases: warm-up, level checks, probes, and wind-down. The interview begins with simple background questions aimed at making the test-taker comfortable. This is followed by a series of tasks designed to assess the interviewee's ability to perform different functions. The interview ends as it began, with a series of simple questions designed to bring the interview to a close.

A variation of the OPI, the **Simulated Oral Proficiency Interview** (SOPI), elicits speech via tape-recorded and text-based prompts and the responses of test-takers are recorded on audiotapes (Stansfield & Kenyon, 1996). All directions in the test booklet and on the tape are in English. They provide the context of each speaking task and any other relevant information. The tasks themselves are in the target language. The test-taker listens to a prompt given by a native speaker and responds accordingly.

In most cases those who take the OPI or SOPI are college-aged students or adults, although in some places, modified versions have been given to high school students. While both the OPI and SOPI have had a positive impact on foreign language assessment, they have been of limited value in assessing students' full development of a range of complex intellectual and communicative knowledge and skills in the target language (Barnhardt, Kevorkian & Delett, 1998; Rennie, 1998). Thus, additional alternative approaches to foreign language assessment have been developed.

Alternative Means.

Alternative assessment measures include procedures and techniques that measure actual performance and can be used within the context of instruction; thus they are easily incorporated into the daily activities of the school or classroom (Hamayan, 1995; O'Malley & Pierce, 1996). These tools typically emphasize both the processes and products of learning. They focus on knowledge and skills needed for real performance in real contexts that learners have encountered in the classroom or are likely to encounter in their daily activities outside of the classroom. Tools for alternative assessment, which has also been termed *authentic assessment,* are organized around particular activities with specific purposes and audiences, and reflect the actual knowledge and skills that learners use to participate in their communicative activities, howsoever they are constructed in their classrooms (Wiggins, 1993).

Several benefits result from the use of alternative assessments. They emphasize higher-order thinking skills, and actively involve students in assessing their own learning processes, and in so doing, encourage students to take charge of their own learning. Moreover, alternative performance assessments can document change over a period of time, allowing teachers to gain valuable insight not only into students' development but also into their own development as teachers. Finally, alternative assessment measures link instruction directly to assessment so that what is assessed is that which has been taught. As Rennie (1998, p. 1) notes, alternative assessment measures "integrate instruction and assessment in such a way that "teaching for the test" promotes good instruction, and good instructional practice is effectively evaluated by assessment outcomes."

There are several kinds of alternative assessment tools that can be used in foreign language classrooms. Some of the more common are:

- *Student journals.* Journals are a useful tool in helping students develop and reflect on their own ideas, interests, and experiences in relation to what and how they are learning. Teachers can use journals to understand student perceptions about learning and to document changes in their thinking and abilities. Journals can either be student-directed or teacher-directed. In journals that are directed by the students, students determine the topic and direction of their writing, while in teacher-directed journals, the teacher decides on the topic and goals for journal writing.

■ *Teacher observations.* Observations are helpful for documenting students' involvement in their instructional activities and any changes that occur over time. Even though we regularly observe our students' classroom behavior, if observations are to be used as assessment measures, they need to be systematically recorded. Records can be in the form of field notes, checklists, or rating scales that focus on particular sets of skills and behaviors.

■ *Demonstrations.* Through demonstrations students display their understanding of particular concepts or skills by illustrating or explaining—orally or in writing—how something works, or is used. With such a tool teachers can assess students' understanding of the concepts and skills as well as their ability to express themselves.

■ *Projects and exhibitions.* Projects showcase a range of knowledge, skills, and abilities and thus can be used to assess the students' ability to bring together or synthesize their understandings, knowledge, and communicative skills and to apply them in new contexts or in new ways in familiar contexts. They can be centered on a particular topic or theme and can include displays or models, inventions or artistic creations, role plays, simulations, or any of a number of similar tasks.

While each of these assessment tools provides a useful window into particular aspects of our students' development, one tool, *portfolio assessment,* is comprised of various components, and thus can help build a more comprehensive understanding of student learning. This tool is described in the next section.

Portfolio Assessment.　A **portfolio** is a systematic collection of work from multiple sources that represents an individual's development and achievements (Barnhardt, Kevorkian, & Delett, 1998; Kieffer & Faust, 1994). There are two kinds of portfolios. The first type, the **formative portfolio,** is a collection of student work that illustrates the process of individual development. Key components of a formative portfolio include (1) samples of student work collected over a specified period of time, (2) students' self-assessments and reflections on their development, (3) teacher assessment, and (4) clearly stated criteria for the assessments.

Student assessments are especially useful as they provide students with the opportunity to become more aware of themselves as learners and their process of development. More specifically, they help students identify their strengths and weaknesses and develop personal goals thus helping them to assume responsibility for their own learning (O'Malley & Pierce, 1996). Peer assessments, while optional, can be useful as they provide opportunities for students to collaborate and learn from each other.

The second type of portfolio, the **summative portfolio,** is meant to showcase what learners know and can do at the end of a specified learning period. The summative portfolio typically contains a set of exemplars of student achievement from multiple sources along with a teacher assessment. Key components include writing samples, audio- or video-taped recordings, projects and other creative work, interview notes, teacher records, quizzes, tests, and student and teacher checklists or collections of reflections.

An alternative to the traditional portfolio is the **webfolio** (Nellen, 2000). A web-based, electronic version of the portfolio, the webfolio provides students with a wider audience for their work. Nellen notes that because of its interactive possibilities, the webfolio provides greater links for learners to communities outside of their schools and thus more fully engages them in the process of learning.

Two key features distinguish portfolios, and their electronic versions, from more traditional measures of development and achievement. The first is the active learner participation in selecting the content of the portfolio, the criteria for selection, and the assessment criteria. Including learners in the assessment process not only makes them more aware of the learning process, but also helps them assume more responsibility for their own development (Barnhardt, Kevorkian, & Delett, 1998). Second, portfolios document what learners can do as opposed to what they cannot. Thus, they provide a clearer understanding of where learners are at every stage of their development.

As a final note, portfolios typically assess individual learning. We know, however, that collaborative work is equally important to learners' development in that it provides learners with opportunities to do something together that they may be unable to do on their own (Bodrova & Leong, 1996; Vygotsky, 1978). Thus, it is useful to include group projects and other collaborative measures that showcase both the processes and products of group learning.

DESIGNING EFFECTIVE ASSESSMENT TOOLS

In the design of adequate and appropriate measures for assessing student learning, three issues need to be considered. The first has to do with the notion of validity. The second concerns the construction of norms and standards for measuring performance, and the third involves the specific steps for designing effective measures including rubrics and rating scales.

Issues of Validity

Assessment validity refers to the appropriateness of an assessment tool. There are three general kinds of validity: content, systemic, and face (Barnhardt, Kevorkian, & Delett, 1998). For an assessment tool to have **content validity,** it must be clearly connected to an instructional purpose and set of objectives and it must be appropriate for its intended group of learners. Questions such as "Is the purpose of the assessment clearly linked to the instructional objectives?", "Does the tool adequately measure what the students should have learned?", and "Is this measure appropriate for this age group and grade level?" help us determine how valid the content of assessment measures is.

An assessment tool that is **systemically valid** helps us determine the effectiveness of our instruction and, subsequently, to make changes to our instruction so that what is taught is that which is assessed. Questions such as "What kinds of changes must I make to my instructional practices so that they are more closely aligned with their assessments?", and conversely, "What kinds of changes must I make to my assessment tools so that they are more closely aligned with my instructional objectives?" can help us determine how systemically valid our assessment tools are.

The third type of validity, **face validity,** refers to "the perception of the instrument by those it impacts" (Barnhardt, Kevorkian, & Delett, 1998, p. 27). In other words, it is concerned with how well the test "on its face," or on the surface, appears to measure what it is supposed to measure. Those who will be administering the test and those who will be taking it usually determine whether an assessment tool has face validity. Questions such as "On the surface does this test appear to measure what it is supposed to measure to those in the field who will be using it?", "How familiar are the students with this particular instrument?", and "Can students determine what is expected of them from looking at the test?" can help determine the face validity of assessment tools.

Norms and Standards for Evaluation

As noted earlier, in the 1980s the American Council on the Teaching of Foreign Languages (ACTFL, 1986) produced a set of proficiency guidelines for evaluating learners' target language proficiency. In addition to speaking, the guidelines assess the traditional skill areas of reading, writing, and listening across four main levels of language proficiency: novice, intermediate, advanced, and superior. They are available for several languages including languages that are typically offered in middle schools and high schools such as Spanish, French, and German, as well as less commonly taught languages such as Russian, Japanese, Chinese, and Arabic.

Used in the field for well over two decades, these guidelines are not without their critics (Bachman, 1988; Barnwell, 1989; Lantolf & Frawley, 1985). It has been argued, for example, that the guidelines lack both a theoretical base and support from research on additional language learning. Nonetheless, they have had a significant impact on foreign language assessment. It should be noted that they are currently being reevaluated and refined (Breiner-Sanders, Lowe, Miles, & Swender, 2000).

The recent move toward standards-based instruction, as indicated by the creation of the foreign language content standards for K–12 learners (National Standards in Foreign Language Education Project, 1996), prompted the need for performance-based standards to assess how well learners are mastering the foreign language content. Using the proficiency guidelines as a base, the American Council on the Teaching of Foreign Languages recently developed a set of standards-based performance guidelines (ACTFL, 1998). These guidelines provide performance benchmarks or expected norms of language use by students at three foreign language program levels: elementary, middle, and high school. Organized around the three communication modes—the interpersonal, the interpretive, and the presentational—the guidelines specify performance standards for three different levels: novice, intermediate, and pre-advanced.

Like the content standards for foreign language learning, these performance standards are designed to "reflect second language learning that begins in kindergarten and continues in an uninterrupted sequence through Grade 12" (ACTFL, 1998, p. 1). Unfortunately, few programs exist in schools around the United States that offer such an extended program of foreign language study. However, according to the creators of the guidelines, the standards can still be useful since they "account for various entry points that reflect most major language sequences found in the United States" (ACTFL, 1998, p. 1).

The definitions of the three levels are meant to reflect the various sequences. *Novice learners* are defined as those in the beginning years of language study, regardless of grade. Thus, they can be used to assess learners in grades K–4, grades 5–8, or grades 9–10. The *intermediate level* refers to learners in grades K–8 or 7–12 while the *pre-advanced level* can be used to assess students in any grade K–12.

For each of the three communication standards, descriptions of expected learner behaviors at each of the three levels are grouped according to six domains. The domains are as follows:

- *comprehensibility:* how well the language learner is understood.
- *comprehension:* how well the language learner can understand.
- *language control:* how accurate the language learner's language is.
- *vocabulary:* how extensive and relevant the language learner's vocabulary is.
- *cultural awareness:* how well the language learner's cultural knowledge is reflected in his or her communicative actions in the target language.
- *communication strategies:* how well the language learner maintains communication.

While these standards can be of some value in helping teachers articulate the range of communicative knowledge and skills and abilities they expect from their students, like the ACTFL Proficiency Guidelines, they have some faults. Primary among these is the lack of theoretical framework or empirical findings underlying the standards and the three levels of performance. We do not know, for example, the basis for creating the distinctions between novice, intermediate, and pre-advanced. Nor do we know the basis for the six domains. It is unclear, for example, how they connect—conceptually and practically—to the domains of knowledge, skills, and abilities distinguished in recent models of communicative competence, such as that proposed by Celce-Murcia et al. (1995). Given the long-term importance of the concept of communicative competence to the field of foreign language learning, the lack of a clear conceptual base makes the usefulness of these six domains somewhat problematic.

Moreover, it is unclear how the norms evaluating learners' communicative performances were created. Is, for example, the assumed norm the native speaker of the target language? If so, given the variety of groups that speak the languages we typically teach in foreign language classrooms, how are exemplars of native speakers of those languages determined? Is a prototypical native speaker of Spanish, for example, considered a citizen of Spain, of Mexico, or of the Dominican Republic? Is the French native speaker a citizen of France or Canada? Do we consider the native speaker to be a man or a woman, an adolescent or an adult, a social elite or someone from the middle class? Finally, is the ideal speaker considered to be monolingual, bilingual, or multilingual?

Given what we know about cultural, linguistic, and other differences that exist across groups that speak the same language, and across social identities within language groups, as well as the cognitive and linguistic differences that exist between monolingual and bilingual speakers of languages, such distinctions are crucial to the clear articulation of norms for judging target language learning. These concerns notwithstanding, we should not be too quick to dismiss the guidelines. Rather, they are more usefully viewed as a fruitful place to begin examining some of these important concerns.

Steps for Designing Assessment Tools

As we have seen, the ACTFL Performance Standards are broad-based descriptions of communicative performance at three different levels of study. While they provide a practical framework for considering broad assessment issues, they cannot account for much of the learning that occurs on a day-to-day basis in classroom contexts. For this, assessment tools are needed that are particular to learning contexts and that assess what the students actually learn. This section presents an overview of the steps for designing such traditional and alternative teacher-made assessment measures for use in middle and high school foreign language classrooms.

The first step in creating assessment tools is to identify the purpose for assessment. Are you seeking to diagnose students' abilities for placement purposes (diagnostic), to monitor learners' progress toward meeting your instructional objectives and goals (formative), or to determine the extent to which learners' have met them (summative)? Next, identify the dimensions of communicative competence to be assessed with the presentation, performance, or product and articulate what you are seeking to assess in terms of performance-level standards. The five-component model of communicative competence proposed by Celce-Murcia et al. (1995) is a particularly useful framework to use to determine the particular aspects of student learning that you are assessing. Note here, for example, whether you are assessing components of students' linguistic competence, actional or rhetorical competence, sociocultural competence, strategic competence, or discourse competence. Also note how students will demonstrate their learning of these components to you. Be sure the standards are closely tied to your instructional objectives.

Next, decide who will choose the source or sources of data for collecting the evidence that documents student learning. Will it be, for example, the teacher, the student or groups of students, the teacher and students together, administrators, parents, or other teachers? Once this is decided, the next step is to select specific sources of data. These can include such measures as interviews, journals, tests, quizzes, presentations, and documented observations. Be sure that the sources of data that are chosen will provide the clearest evidence of what students are learning or expected to have learned. Next, decide when the evidence will be collected. For example, will data be collected on a weekly basis or at the end of a lesson, a unit, or a marking period? The purpose for doing the assessment will help determine when the data is collected.

Once the kinds of data to be collected have been determined, the next step is to determine how the data will be evaluated. To evaluate students' progress and achievement, an accurate rating system is needed. The more traditional measures, such as discrete-item tests and quizzes, are fairly easy to rate and evaluate. This is due in part to the fact that their format usually requires students to select or produce short answers in response to a series of closed-ended display questions, such as "Choose the correct verb ending" or "Fill in the blank with the correct form of the adjective" and so on. If the test or quiz is teacher-made, decisions on the numerical value of each section must be made ahead of time and communicated to the students before they take the test or quiz. If the test or quiz is commercially produced, these decisions are usually made by the producers of the test and included with the test instructions.

Figure 5–3 contains an example of some scoring criteria for traditional criterion-referenced assessment measures. Of course, how scores are determined depends on the teacher or group of experts who construct the tests. They will decide, for example, whether scores should be figured in terms of percentages or points, and what specific guidelines or criteria will be used to determine individual scores.

For alternative assessment measures, **scoring rubrics,** which are a set of guidelines for evaluating students' work, are more appropriate. They set out the criteria or standards for judging a performance along with a rating scale for evaluating how well students meet the criteria or standards. There are two general types of rubrics: holistic and analytic.

Holistic rubrics use multiple criteria to produce an overall score for a product, demonstration, or performance. *Analytical rubrics* isolate the specific elements or components of a product, demonstration, or performance, articulate criteria for evaluating each feature, and assess and score each separately. Thus, each performance or product receives a series of scores. For example, an oral presentation may receive individual scores for content, organization, and delivery. Although analytical rubrics are more time-consuming to create, the feedback they provide is more detailed than that provided by holistic rubrics, and thus, more likely to be of greater value to both students and teachers.

The form of the rubric will depend on the purpose of the assessment. For example, student self-assessment rubrics typically use informal language while rubrics used to determine grades or placements are more formal and more detailed. Thus, it is important to consider the purpose of the assessment when designing a rubric.

After determining whether the rubric to be used will be holistic or analytic, the next step is to specify the evaluative criteria. It is important to be as specific and clear as pos-

Percentage	Criteria
85–100	Outstanding performance; reveals extensive base of knowledge, skills, and abilities.
70–84	Very good performance; reveals fairly balanced base of knowledge, skills, and abilities.
60–69	Fair performance; reveals limited, minimally adequate base of knowledge, skills, and abilities.
Below 59	Weak performance; reveals negligible or inaccurate base of knowledge, skills, and abilities.

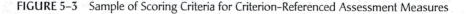

FIGURE 5–3   Sample of Scoring Criteria for Criterion-Referenced Assessment Measures

sible. If the rubric is analytic, determine each of the elements that will be addressed and choose a **rating scale** to measure the extent to which a learner has met each of the criteria. Scales can use descriptive words such as *never, rarely, sometimes, often, always* or *poor, acceptable, excellent,* or even simply *yes* and *no.* They can also use a numerical sequence such as 1 to 5 to distinguish degrees of performance. Numbers and descriptive words can be used together so that the words define the meaning of the number. For example, on a scale of 1 to 5, the number 1 might be labeled "weak" and the number 5 "strong."

It is important to note that no particular scale will fit all assessment criteria and measures. The kind of scale that is used depends on the number of levels of performance that are considered appropriate for the performance. A simple yes–no scale would be a useful scale to use, for example, if one of the criteria for an oral performance called for the use of visuals. Assessing the quality of the visuals used would require another criterion on the rating scale. In this case, a three-level scale such as *poor, acceptable, excellent,* or a five-level scale such as *never, rarely, sometimes, often, always* would be appropriate. An example of an analytic rubric for assessing an oral performance can be found in Figure 5–4.

Good rubrics not only provide criteria but they also provide descriptors or examples of behaviors that meet the stated criteria for each level of performance. Thus, for each point on the rating scale it would be useful to specify expectations for performance, noting, for example, what constitutes terms like *excellent, acceptable,* and *poor* or, if using a numerical scale, what students need to do to earn a 1, 2, 3, 4, or 5. It may help to provide samples of student work that exemplify each of the criteria. Where appropriate, make sure the examples illustrate high-quality work that takes a variety of approaches so that the criteria are not reduced to one particular formula for performing or achieving. Examples of scoring rubrics for assessing learners' knowledge and skills in the target language in each of the three communication modes are included in Chapter 6 (Interpersonal), Chapter 7 (Interpretive), and Chapter 8 (Presentational).

As part of their active involvement in the assessment process, students should be involved throughout the process of developing and using rubrics. By helping to create the rubrics, they gain a fuller understanding of expectations for their learning, and thus, they are likely to be more invested in the task. Students should also be involved in using the rubrics to rate their own and each other's performances. Not only will this help students develop the ability to articulate the direction of their own learning, but it also will help them become actively involved in charting their progress.

Like instructional objectives, when first created, rubrics are likely to undergo significant revision. The more they are used, the more both teachers and students will be able to articulate clearly the knowledge, skills, and abilities the students are expected to learn in the foreign language. When used appropriately, rubrics can be effective classroom tools for helping both teachers and students articulate and reflect on their expectations for learning. This in turn enhances both the students' growth as language learners and the teachers' development as language teachers. Rubrics can also be helpful to teachers and administrators in evaluating and modifying instructional programs. A summary of the steps involved in designing assessment can be found in Figure 5–5.

Evaluation Rubric for Oral Academic Presentation

Content

Clearly introduced topic

Poor	Fair	Average	Strong	Excellent
1	2	3	4	5

Main points were clear

Poor	Fair	Average	Strong	Excellent
1	2	3	4	5

Main points were fully supported

Poor	Fair	Average	Strong	Excellent
1	2	3	4	5

Clearly summarized the main points

Poor	Fair	Average	Strong	Excellent
1	2	3	4	5

Clearly brought presentation to a close

Poor	Fair	Average	Strong	Excellent
1	2	3	4	5

Format

Transitions between ideas were clear

Poor	Fair	Average	Strong	Excellent
1	2	3	4	5

Made appropriate and accurate use of grammar, vocabulary, and discourse structures

Poor	Fair	Average	Strong	Excellent
1	2	3	4	5

Delivery

Used voice (volume, pitch, rate) effectively

Poor	Fair	Average	Strong	Excellent
1	2	3	4	5

Maintained eye contact with audience

Poor	Fair	Average	Strong	Excellent
1	2	3	4	5

Gestures and facial expressions were appropriate

Poor	Fair	Average	Strong	Excellent
1	2	3	4	5

Visuals that illustrated or enhanced the presentation were used effectively

Poor	Fair	Average	Strong	Excellent
1	2	3	4	5

FIGURE 5–4   Sample of an Evaluation Rubric for an Oral Academic Presentation

1. Identify purpose (diagnostic, formative, or summative).
2. Identify the dimensions of communicative competence to be assessed (discourse, linguistic, actional/rhetorical, sociocultural, strategic).
3. Set performance-level standards against which students' presentation, performance, or product will be evaluated.
4. Decide who will choose sources of evidence to document learning (teacher, students, administrators, parents, or an assemblage comprised of representatives of these groups).
5. Select sources of data (interviews, journals, tests, quizzes, presentations, or documented observations).
6. Determine when data will be collected (e.g., daily, weekly, end of a lesson, end of a marking period).
7. Determine the means for evaluating the data (scores and scoring criteria).
8. Devise rating system for traditional test or quiz, if needed, and share with students.
9. For alternative assessment measures, determine whether rubric will be holistic or analytic.
10. Devise criteria and rating system for rubric and share with students.

FIGURE 5–5   Steps for Designing Effective Assessment Tools

GRADING

Grades are an efficient means of summarizing a student's performance. They are not equivalent to assessment, however. Assessment is a multidimensional process involving the collection of data from a variety of sources by which teachers decide whether and how well students are meeting the instructional objectives. These sources of information provide a basis for determining a grade. As you know from your own experiences, grades can significantly impact a student's life. Thus, developing a clear and fair grading policy is essential to effective teaching.

In constructing a grading policy, you will need to determine the particular components to be graded and the weight that each component will carry. For example, say you determined that class participation in large-group work is a significant aspect of learning, and you constructed and used an appropriate assessment tool for measuring and assessing student participation in large-group work. The next issue you need to consider is how much the particular grade received for class participation will figure into the overall course grade. Will it count, for example, as 20% of the course grade? 10%? 5%?

Likewise, if homework assignments are to count as part of the course grade, you need to determine the extent to which the assessment of student performance on these assignments will be considered in determining the overall grade. That is, you must decide what percentage of the overall grade will be determined by the grades received on homework assignments. You may find that the foreign language department in your school or district has guidelines for determining the components of a course grade, and the weight given to each component.

Grading in middle school and high school can either be numerical or letter-based. You may also find that your school or local district has established guidelines for determining the letter equivalent of a numerical grade. These guidelines may stipulate, for example, whether a grade of A is equivalent to 94–100 points or 90–100 points.

As pointed out earlier, along with the instructional objectives and goals, grading policies must be clearly articulated and communicated to the students at the beginning of the course. Issues to consider when developing a grading policy include deciding how to deal with graded activities that need to be made up due to student absence. Remember that the role of the foreign language teacher is to facilitate learning for all students, and to help them become successful learners and users of the target language. Thus, like all other aspects of instruction, effective teaching involves the willingness to negotiate one's grading policy with students.

SUMMARY

To be an effective foreign language teacher involves knowing how to articulate, plan for, and implement instructional goals and objectives. It also entails knowing how to design traditional and alternative means of assessment, and how to use the results to assess not only student learning but also the overall effectiveness of a foreign language program. This section summarizes some of the key ideas and concepts on instructional planning and assessment presented in this chapter.

- Instructional goals and objectives are key components of effective teaching. Goals are general statements of educational direction or intent and thus serve as organizing principles for the design of classroom instruction. Examples of goals that articulate the direction for a content area are the National Foreign Language Content Standards.
- More specific than goals, but equally essential to effective instruction, are instructional objectives. They describe what the students are expected to be able to do as a result of their involvement in their learning opportunities on a daily basis.
- Planning for instruction occurs on three levels: the course level, the unit level, and the daily level. Clear, detailed written plans at all levels help teachers make connections between their ideas on what and how to teach, and their expectations for student learning. In addition, they are useful documents for teacher reflection and self-assessment, for assessment of student learning, and more generally, for the evaluation of program goals and objectives.
- Effective assessment is tied directly to the curriculum. For assessment to be effective it must reflect as closely as possible what is thought to be appropriate instructional practice. From this perspective, good teaching necessarily involves teaching to the test, and conversely, effective assessment involves assessing that which is taught.
- Assessment is commonly used for three purposes: to diagnose or determine students' strengths and weaknesses in order to place them at appropriate levels of instruction; to observe students' progress toward meeting instructional objectives and goals; and to evaluate how well learners have mastered the curriculum.

■ There are multiple means for assessing learning that include both traditional standardized tests and other, newer forms of assessment tools such as teacher observations, student self-assessment logs, and portfolios. The newer forms of assessment are designed so teachers can better align their instructional goals with their assessment of student performance.

■ In the design of adequate and appropriate measures for assessing student learning three issues need to be considered: the content, systemic, and face validity of the measures; the appropriateness of the norms and standards against which student performances are evaluated; and the design and construction of adequate evaluative rubrics and rating scales.

■ The recent move toward the creation of national standards for foreign language learning has sparked interest in creating standards-based assessment measures. These are considered a variation of criterion-referenced tests. Using the ACTFL Proficiency Guidelines as a starting point, a national group of foreign educators has created a set of general performance guidelines for foreign language learners from kindergarten through high school. It is not yet known how well these guidelines will help teachers adequately assess student learning and program goals.

■ Grades provide an overall rating of the performance of an individual student. They are usually calculated on the basis of examining a wide range of student work. Because of the importance of grades to students, it is essential that fair and reasonable grading policies be established, clearly articulated to students and other stakeholders, and that students have a hand in creating them.

DISCUSSION QUESTIONS AND ACTIVITIES

1. Interview a group of novice foreign language teachers (with fewer than 2 years in the classroom) and more expert foreign language teachers (with more than 5 years in the classroom, and who have been identified by colleagues as experts) from either a middle school or high school about how they plan for teaching. Include questions that ask them to discuss long-term unit planning in addition to daily lesson planning. Compile your findings. Are there detectable patterns within each group of teachers? Across the two groups of teachers? What conclusions can you draw for the role that planning plays in the lives of these teachers? What implications are there for your own teaching?

2. Local schools may have their own formats for writing lesson plans. Gather examples of different formats by contacting schools or teachers in your area. In small groups compare the formats to each other and to the ones contained in this chapter. What are the advantages and disadvantages to each of them? Together, try constructing one that you feel captures the best qualities of each of the different formats. Share with your classmates.

3. Find out how foreign language textbooks are adopted in your local middle school or high school. Interview teachers about their opinions of the process. Write a two-page report to share with your classmates.

4. What does "teaching to the test" mean to you? As a teacher, in what cases would you object to having to "teach to the test"? In what cases would you welcome the

Contributions to class discussions (large and small group)
I contribute a reasonable amount to all discussions.

1	2	3	4	5
weak				strong

My comments and questions are clearly articulated, relevant, and substantive.

1	2	3	4	5
weak				strong

I expand upon others' comments in productive ways.

1	2	3	4	5
weak				strong

Content knowledge, skills, and abilities
I can cite and summarize accurately and appropriately published academic articles on course topics.

1	2	3	4	5
weak				strong

I can accurately and appropriately define, explain, and give examples of the essential concepts contained in each of the course chapters.

1	2	3	4	5
weak				strong

I can competently search and locate relevant Internet sites related to course topics.

1	2	3	4	5
weak				strong

Attitude
I show interest, listen attentively, and display support for my peers.

1	2	3	4	5
weak				strong

Punctuality
I attend class regularly, arrive on time, and don't leave early.

1	2	3	4	5
weak				strong

I complete assignments on time.

1	2	3	4	5
weak				strong

FIGURE 5–6 Student Self-Assessment Measure of Class Involvement

opportunity to "teach to the test"? As a student, in what cases do you object to having teachers "teach to the test"? And when do you welcome having teachers "teach to the test"? What implications can you draw from your discussion about the nature of assessment for foreign language learning (or for all learning)?

5. Find out whether your state has adopted content standards for foreign language learning in K–12 public schools. Most state boards of education have Web sites that contain links to state content standards. How do your state standards for foreign language learning compare to the national foreign language standards? Are they, for example, organized around the traditional four skills of reading, writing, listening, and speaking or are they organized around the three communicative modes? Find out how the content standards for your state were developed. Based on your findings, what conclusions can you draw about foreign language instruction and assessment in your state?

6. In small groups, create a self-assessment rubric that you feel adequately addresses your involvement in your methods course. You can use the example in Figure 5–6, which was developed by a group of students in a foreign language methods course, or you can start from scratch and develop your own. How difficult was it to develop a rubric? What implications can you draw for designing rubrics for your foreign language classes?

TEACHER RESEARCH PROJECTS

A. Textbook Analysis.

The purpose of this project is to help teachers develop skills to evaluate curricular materials.

Pose a Problem

Textbooks are a primary source of curricular content in foreign language classrooms. One way to assess whether the communicative information and cultural perspectives provided in the available texts are appropriate and sufficient for your students' needs, interests, and abilities is through a textbook analysis.

Identify Sources and Gather Information

Choose a selection of texts that are available for use in your classes. Choose sections from the text to examine. You may choose to look at every other chapter or a certain percentage of chapters from each text. To record your findings, use the framework of topics provided in Figure 5–7 or one that you have constructed that addresses your particular curricular concerns.

Analyze

Note and classify the content found within each chapter on the analytic framework. Once you have examined each selection, compile the results for each text in order to get a better sense of the text as a whole.

	Text 1	Text 2	Text 3
Topics for Communication Personal House and Home Community Services Family Life Around the Community and Neighborhood Sports Health and Welfare Travel Education The Workplace Current Events **Comments:**			
Cultural Perspectives Personal Life Leisure Religion, Art, the Humanities Social and Political Systems and Institutions Environment **Comments:**			
Aspects of Communicative Competence **Covered in the Exercises** Linguistic Sociocultural Actional/Rhetorical Discourse Strategic **Comments:**			

FIGURE 5–7   Framework for the Analysis of Language Textbooks

Reflect and Revise

Assess the suitability of each text using the following questions as a guide: Are the communication topics relevant to the personal needs and interests of the students? Are the cultural perspectives comprehensive, adequately stated, and pertinent to the program's curricular goals? Are the different aspects of communicative competence given adequate coverage in the text's exercises? Can the text be easily modified to correct perceived deficiencies?

Disseminate the Information

It is likely that your findings will be of interest to those who teach similar courses. Thus, it would be worthwhile to share a summary of your findings with your colleagues, either as part of a faculty meeting or as a posting to an electronic bulletin board for foreign language educators. In addition, many journals publish reviews of materials. You might consider sending your review to a journal for publication consideration.

B. Analysis of Grading Policies.

The purpose of this project is to familiarize novice teachers with different grading policies used in middle and high school foreign language classrooms that they can ultimately use as a base for developing one of their own.

Pose a Problem

Begin this project by first deciding whether you will focus your attention on middle school or high school policies. You can then raise the following questions: What kinds of grading policies are currently in place? How do they compare across classrooms, across grade levels, and across schools?

Identify Sources and Gather Information

Once you have identified the program you are interested in—choosing either middle school or high school programs—you need to decide the number of schools, the grade levels, and the number of classes within each grade from which you will gather information. If there are a number of middle school programs in your area, you may wish to limit your search to these programs. If there are not, however, you may want to extend your search to programs outside your area.

Once you have identified the sources of data, you can then gather your information. If you know some teachers who work in programs in which you are interested, you can enlist their help in gathering policies from their colleagues. You can also consider posting a message to an electronic bulletin board for foreign language teachers to locate teachers who are interested in sharing their grading policies with you.

Analyze

Once you have collected the policies, begin examining them for patterns. The following questions can be used to guide your analyses. Constructing a table or chart in which you summarize the components of each policy you have collected can help you compare the policies.

What activities are graded?
For what percentage of the grade does each activity count?
How are grades computed?
Are there guidelines for making up missed work? If so, what are they?
Are there any additional components to the policy?
How is the policy communicated to the students? To the parents?

Reflect and Revise

Use the following questions to help you reflect on your findings: What components are common to all or most of the policies? How do they differ? In general, what are some of the strengths of the policies? What are some of the weaknesses? How could you improve on these policies? Use your reflections to construct a grading policy that you feel would be most effective for your classes, or, if you are not currently teaching, a group of learners with whom you anticipate working in the future.

Disseminate Information

Consider sharing your findings on the different policies with other foreign language teachers. You can post the chart to an electronic bulletin board for foreign language teachers and ask others to respond or even add to it. You might also consider writing a summary of the project for the newsletter of your statewide professional organization of foreign language teachers.

ADDITIONAL READINGS

Airasian, P. (1994). *Classroom assessment* (2nd ed.). New York: McGraw-Hill.

Chaloub-Deville, M. (1997). The Minnesota Articulation Project and its proficiency-based assessments. *Foreign Language Annals, 30*(4), 492–502.

Corbett, H. D., & Wilson, B. L. (1991). *Testing, reform and rebellion.* Norwood, NJ: Ablex Publishing.

Dixon-Krauss, L. (1996). *Vygotsky in the classroom: Mediated literacy instruction and assessment.* New York: Longman.

Hart, D. (1994). *Authentic assessment: A handbook for educators.* Menlo Park, CA: Addison-Wesley.

Stiggins, R. J. (1994). *Student-centered classroom assessment.* New York: Merrill.

Strickland, K., & Strickland, J. (1998). *Reflections on assessment: Its purposes, methods and effects on learning.* Portsmouth, NH: Heinemann.

Thompson, L. (1997). *Foreign language assessment in grades K–8: An annotated bibliography of assessment instruments.* McHenry, IL and Washington, DC: Delta Systems and the Center for Applied Linguistics.

INTERNET RESOURCES

http://carla.acad.umn.edu/MNAP.html   Minnesota Articulation Project (MNAP)

This is the site of MNAP, a statewide initiative to develop a model for articulating French, German, and Spanish curricular strategies and outcomes with a focus on the transition from high school to postsecondary institutions. Included are links to resources for proficiency-oriented language instruction and a battery of assessments for reading, writing, and speaking in French, German, and Spanish using the ACTFL proficiency guidelines.

http://www.TeachNet.org/   The Teachers Network (TeachNet)

TeachNet is sponsored by IMPACT II, a not-for-profit educational and independent organization that supports classroom teachers in the United States. Some of the major initiatives of IMPACT II include the TeachNet Project and the National Teacher Policy Institute. Links to these and other projects can be found at this site.

http://www.pampetty.com/assessment.htm   Authentic Assessment Techniques in K–6 Classrooms

This site contains large amounts of good information on assessment measures including definitions of different assessment tools and a wide range of links to a variety of professional resources and other Web sites.

http://www.nwrel.org/eval   The North West Regional Educational Laboratory (NWREL)

This is the Web site of NWREL's project on assessment and evaluation. Links are provided to topics such as oral communication assessment and instruction and program planning and evaluation, and to their Assessment Resource Library.

http://cresst96.cse.ucla.edu/   The National Center for Research on Evaluation, Standards, and Student Testing (CRESST)

Funded by the U.S. Department of Education and the Office of Educational Research and Improvement, this center conducts research on important topics related to K–12 educational testing. The site contains links to their projects and other resources.

http://ericae.net/   The ERIC Clearinghouse on Assessment and Evaluation

The center, located at the University of Maryland, Department of Measurement, Statistics and Evaluation, is one of 16 subject-oriented clearinghouses operated by the U.S. Department of Education, Office of Educational Research and Improvement. ERIC/AE is viewed as the central source for assessment and evaluation information. There is a wide assortment of links to assessment and evaluation resources on the Internet for such topics as action research, computer-assisted testing, demographics, elementary and secondary education, and home schooling, to list but a few. There are also links to related journals, newsletters, and reports on assessment and evaluation.

CHAPTER 5

http://www.cal.org/nclrc/fltestdb/   The Foreign Language Test Database

This is a searchable database of secondary- and college-level tests in languages other than English. It currently contains more than 140 tests in 63 languages. It is maintained by the National Capital Language Resource Center, a joint project of Georgetown University, the George Washington University, and the Center for Applied Linguistics. The site can be searched by language, target population, intended test level, intended test use, and areas being assessed.

Chapter 6

The Interpersonal Mode

Preview Questions

Before you begin reading this chapter, take a few moments to consider the following:

- What kinds of interpersonal activities do you engage in on a daily basis?
- How competent do you feel about your participation? What do you think accounts for your feelings of competence?
- What kinds of interpersonal activities do you feel most competent engaging in when using the target language?
- What do you think accounts for your feelings of competence in these activities?
- How might instruction and assessment be organized to develop language learners' communicative competence in a variety of interpersonal communicative activities?

Key Words and Concepts

Interpersonal mode
  Transactional purpose
  Interactional purpose
  Cognitive underpinnings of interaction
    Past experience
    Social identities
    Communicative accommodation
Designing instruction
  Target language community activities
  Classroom community activities

Technological resources
  Synchronous interaction
  Asynchronous interaction
Analysis of communicative
    components
Communicative activities
Instructional activities
Learning opportunities
Participation structures
Designing assessment

Overview

Traditionally, interaction was taught in the foreign language classroom as the separate skills of listening and speaking (Hadley, 1993). It was assumed that learners would first have to control language components before they could actually understand and use them for real purposes in interactions with others. In addition, there was an assumption that a single standard of correctness existed across situations, speakers, and contexts.

With its emphasis on the context–embedded nature of language use, a sociocultural perspective on communication makes visible the narrowness of this more traditional view. It reveals, instead, that communicating with others is qualitatively different from, and thus more than the sum of, the skills of speaking and listening. Moreover, in highlighting the intricate connections between language and the contexts of its use, it reveals the sometimes subtle, but always significant, ways that language use varies across situations, speakers, and contexts, and how it changes with time. Characterized by communicative activities accomplished through interaction with others, the *interpersonal mode* of communication captures this understanding of language use.

This chapter provides an overview of the interpersonal mode. Its purpose is to draw together the diverse concepts and ideas presented in Chapters 1 through 5 and apply them in the design of effective instructional activities and assessment tools. After presenting a discussion on the nature of the interpersonal mode and a review of current research, guidelines for designing instruction and assessment around interpersonal communicative activities are proposed.

THE INTERPERSONAL MODE

The **interpersonal mode** includes communicative activities accomplished through direct interaction with others. Their primary purpose is either transactional or interactional (Ramirez, 1995). In activities with a **transactional** purpose one interlocutor seeks to obtain something from another, such as directions to an unfamiliar location, information on a new program, instructions for doing something, or help with one's homework. Also included are activities whose goal is to identify and resolve a problem or concern, such as the doctor–patient consultation during a health examination, or the negotiation of rules when playing a game. Also, certain service encounters such as those enacted in restaurants, banks, or department stores are considered transactional. In classrooms, transactional activities include debating an issue, participating in an academic discussion on a topic, and even taking roll, and other similar administrative tasks.

Generally, the goals of transactional activities are transparent or obvious, and clearly expressed. Consequently, participation in them is likely to be more conventional or routine than it would be in activities where the goals are less obvious or not as well articulated. As we saw in Chapter 4, much of the interaction geared toward instruction that takes place in effective classrooms is more rather than less planned. Effective teachers make their goals clear and assist the students in meeting them through engagement in fairly well-planned instructional conversations.

Activities whose primary purpose is **interactional** are directed toward the establishment and maintenance of interpersonal relationships. Included here are activities whose purpose is to establish mutual acquaintanceship, such as encounters with new neighbors, classmates, or colleagues. Also included are activities that serve to nurture family bonds, friendships, and other social relationships, such as mealtime talk, gossiping, chatting, "hanging out," and "dropping a line." All of these activities, as mundane as they might seem, are crucial to the nourishment of stable community life. Generally, our participation in interactional activities is more open to moment-to-moment vagaries and contingencies; thus, our language use is likely to be less conventionalized.

It is important to note that the two goal orientations of interpersonal activities are not categorical. Rather, they constitute a two-dimensional continuum along which all activities can be placed. Some activities, such as making an appointment, seeking directions, or engaging in a debate are likely to be more task-oriented, and thus will fall more closely along the transactional continuum. Others, such as chatting with a friend or recounting a personal experience are more likely to be oriented toward maintaining interpersonal relations and, thus, fall along the interactional continuum. Still others, such as roll taking and playing a game, can serve both goals. This two-dimensional goal-oriented continuum is displayed in Figure 6–1.

It should also be noted that while many of the activities framed by the interpersonal mode are accomplished through face-to-face interactions, there are additional ways of accomplishing them. For example, personal letter writing, phone calling, electronic mail, audio, video, and satellite exchanges, and other technology-related modalities can be used to conduct transactions and make connections with others.

FIGURE 6–1   Two-Dimensional Goal Orientation of Interpersonal Activities

Obtaining directions

Discussing health with a professional

Transactional

Engaging the help of a service provider

Discussing current events with a friend

Phoning a friend

Chatting in an electronic chat room

Interactional

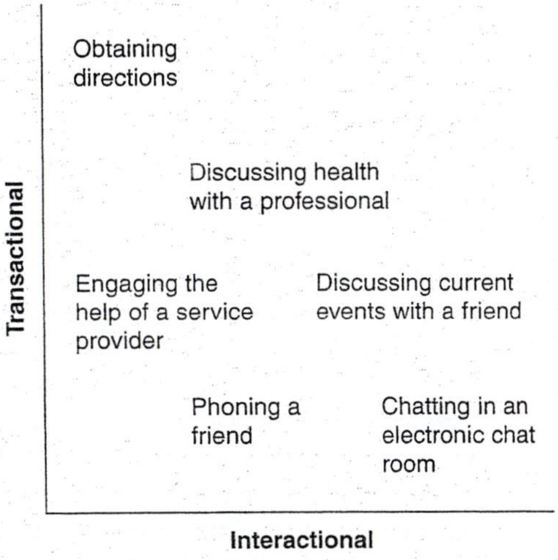

COGNITIVE AND SOCIAL UNDERPINNINGS OF INTERACTION

Research on **interaction** reveals how intricate and complicated interpersonal interaction can be (e.g., Clark, 1996; Goodwin & Goodwin, 1992; Lerner, 1994; Psathas, 1990; Sanders, 1987, 1992; Schegloff, 1982). We enter into direct interaction with others with a set of communicative expectations or plans for the general goal of the activity, the sequence of linguistic actions, and the norms for the enactment of our social roles in the activity. These plans provide us some cognitive security as they provide a structure, however limited, to guide our participation. As Sanders (1987) explains, forming and interpreting communicative acts in an interaction are a kind of problem solving. Regardless of the goal orientation of our interpersonal activities, when we interact we are involved in two general cognitive processes. First, we strive to be understood by others and to have some control over how others understand us. Second, we strive to understand others so that we can act appropriately toward them.

Working through these two processes as the interaction unfolds involves multiple cognitive actions (Clark, 1996; Sanders, 1987). When another is speaking, we monitor the emerging structure (prosodic, grammatical, lexical, etc.) of that person's utterances. At the same time we make general projections about the goal of the activity, and where we think the interaction is heading. We also make more specific projections as to how well what is emerging fits with the activity that we think is unfolding. As we make predictions about what is going on, we monitor situational factors such as the setting and participant roles, and individual factors including features of the participants' personalities and their social identities. Based on our moment-to-moment analysis, we decide how to attend to what is currently being said. Moreover, in addition to signaling attention and understanding to our interlocutors, we formulate and assess our own contributions in terms of how well they fit in with the ongoing interaction. If miscommunication occurs, we attempt to reanalyze prior talk to find out where the misstep might have taken place and then take measures to correct it.

The degree of cognitive complexity needed to participate competently in these two processes depends on at least three conditions. First is our familiarity with, and past experience in, the activity. Second is the number and kinds of social identities we have in relation to the other participants. Third is the degree to which we accommodate to the communicative style of these participants. Each is explained in more detail in the following sections.

Familiarity with, and Experience in, the Activity

A first condition influencing the degree of cognitive complexity involved in interacting has to do with our familiarity with, and **past experiences** in, activities. Generally speaking, the more extensive our prior experiences as a participant in similar kinds of interpersonal activities are, the more developed our communicative plans are. The more developed our plans are, the better able we are to locate quickly the appropriate resources needed to understand what is taking place, to anticipate forthcoming utterances, and to create our own appropriate linguistic actions. Indeed, as experienced participants we can quite often anticipate and begin to respond to a linguistic action before the utterance is actually completed (Goodwin & Goodwin, 1992). Likewise, while producing an utterance, we may decide to change it in midstream if we sense that others may respond to it in inappropriate or unintended ways.

It is important to note that in many of the interpersonal interactions in which we have extensive experience we become quite accustomed to interacting in just one or two particular ways. We take for granted the other participants' experience and prior knowledge as well as their willingness and ability to interact in similar ways. Thus, we enter into these activities assuming the meaning and goals of the interactions to be clear, and our linguistic actions and enactment of role relationships to be routine and unproblematic. In these cases, the need to have to continually renegotiate meaning or make sense of each other as we work through the interaction is greatly diminished. As a consequence, we can accomplish these activities without having to think about, or make our involvement an object of, attention.

If many of our daily interpersonal activities were not like this, we would find ourselves emotionally and cognitively drained by our constant efforts to negotiate meaning. Having to negotiate, for example, the intended meaning of the greeting "How are you doing?" every time someone were to utter it would make even the briefest of interactions a cognitive chore. That we are mindless or inattentive to what we do, however, does not mean that the cognitive actions we undertake are unimportant (Mandelbaum & Pomerantz, 1991). On the contrary, the cognitive work we do as we interact with others is essential to the successful achievement of our interpersonal communicative activities.

Social Identities

A second condition that influences the degree of cognitive complexity of our participation in interpersonal activities concerns the number and kinds of participants involved. The amount of cognitive complexity increases with the number of participants involved, and the number and kinds of **social identities** a participant has in relation to the other participants. Dyadic interactions, which involve just two interlocutors, are those that generally demand less cognitive energy as we only need to attend to the contributions of one other participant. In multiparty interactions, however, possible contributions and interpretations multiply along with the number of participants, thereby increasing the cognitive effort needed to both monitor and produce talk. Monitoring the topical coherence of our and others' contributions to the ongoing interaction and determining when it is appropriate to take a turn, for example, become increasingly more difficult to sustain systematically as the number of participants rises.

The number and kinds of social identities a participant brings to the interaction in relation to the other participants also influences the amount of cognitive energy needed to engage in the interaction. As explained in Chapter 1, we each have a multitude of identities that we bring with us to each interaction. The more varied the relationships are between our identities and those of the other interactants, the more possibilities there are for relevant interactional moves, and the more we must consciously attend to the talk in order to ensure that the interaction proceeds in an orderly fashion.

For example, an interaction that occurs in a workplace setting between an employer and a person who is both an employee and relative of the employer has more complexity built into it than it would if the person had just one relevant identity. Interactional involvement in this case requires from both participants more thought to both interpret and construct utterances that make only one of the identities relevant but that, at the same time, appropriately and tacitly, acknowledge the other relationship.

Furthermore, if all participants agree to what the relevant identities are and how they are to interact in regard to these identities, then the interpersonal activity is more likely to unfold uneventfully; in other words, with fewer missteps. However, say we object to the identity to which the other participants orient, and we assume that the identity that we would like to be more perceptible is known to them. In this case, the cognitive work we need to make this identity relevant and at the same time move systematically through the interaction is greater.

For example, in a transactional interaction between two colleagues, one male and one female, the male colleague may decide to orient toward his colleague's identity as a woman, making the gender identity more relevant than that of colleague and peer. He may refer to her as "honey," for example, instead of using her professional title. Suppose this identity is different from the identity to which the woman wants the man to orient. In that case, the cognitive energy she needs to recognize what is happening and to move the interaction in ways that make her professional identity more relevant than her gender identity without causing the interaction to derail is greater than if her male colleague had initially and solely oriented to her professional identity. The case becomes further complicated if there is an unequal degree of authority attached to the voices. The more institutional authority there is attached to the male colleague's voice, for example, the more complicated it may become for the woman participant to redirect subsequent contributions in ways that move the interaction away from unwanted outcomes but at the same time do not undermine her colleague's authority or the interaction's orderliness.

There is at least one kind of participant identity affecting the amount of cognitive work involved for all parties that is of particular significance to learners of additional languages. It involves novices or newcomers to the activities, such as language learners. In interpersonal interactions between native speakers of the target language and learners of that language, for example, more cognitive energy is usually needed by all participants since they must make public, or put into words, more of what they usually communicate using prosodic and nonverbal contextualization cues. They must do this in order to avoid having the interaction unfold in unintended ways and result in misunderstandings (Sanders, 1987). In other words, as the degrees of linguistic and cultural difference between native and nonnative participants' communicative plans for participating in a particular activity increase, the more self-conscious and deliberate the participants must be in their involvement. They may spend more time, for example, checking for comprehension, assessing preceding contributions for appropriateness, projecting the direction of the interaction, formulating utterances, and detecting and responding to misunderstandings. As a consequence, economy and efficiency of expression are likely to be difficult to achieve (Goodwin & Goodwin, 1992; Sanders, 1987).

This suggests that the kinds of interpersonal communicative activities requiring higher levels of cognitive effort for additional language learners would be those that are used by a target language group to create personal, social, and community bonds. In these activities the subtle yet complex differences in background knowledge, communicative plans, and the social and personal characteristics and attitudes of the participants are usually not made explicit in the propositional content of participants' utterances. Yet, they are powerful influences on the meanings and interpretations of the utterances.

Accommodation

A third aspect of interaction influencing the degree of cognitive complexity involved in our participation is the degree to which we **accommodate** to the interactional style of our interlocutors. In addition to monitoring and assessing our utterances and the utterances of our interlocutors in light of their unfolding meanings when we interact with others, we make decisions regarding whether to synchronize our communicative actions with those with whom we are interacting (Giles, Coupland, & Coupland, 1991; Giles, Mulac, Bradac, & Johnson, 1987).

We can decide to *converge,* whereby we adapt to each other's communicative behaviors. We do so in order to reduce interpersonal and social differences and become more similar to the other, to increase our attractiveness to the other, to gain social approval, to accomplish certain personal goals, or to resist or align ourselves with larger social goals. *Bilateral convergence* occurs when all parties seek to converge. This most often happens in interactions where participants perceive themselves to be on equal footing. Included here are interactional conversations among friends, or transactional conversations between two colleagues. *Unilateral convergence* occurs when only one of the participants seeks to adapt to the communicative style of the other. This usually occurs in interactions where the participants perceive the social roles of the others to be of higher or lower status. In the case of a conversation between a teacher and a school administrator, for example, the teacher may perceive the administrator to have more institutional authority, and thus, may seek to adapt to his or her communicative behaviors in order to gain approval or receive positive feedback from the administrator. Conversely, if the school administrator is seeking to gain the support of the teacher, the administrator can decide to converge to the communicative style of the teacher and thereby reduce the amount of social or personal distance between them.

Alternatively, in our interpersonal activities, we can decide to *diverge* from the communicative style of our interlocutors. When we diverge, we use communicative strategies to accentuate differences and distance between our interlocutors and us. Divergence can help to create or heighten the unequal or separate relationships perceived to exist among the interlocutors. It can also help to create feelings of personal or social distinctiveness.

Convergence and divergence occur in a variety of discourse features ranging from choice of dialect code to particular words or phrases to intonational or phonological patterns. Decisions on whether or how we will accommodate to others in our interpersonal interactions depend on such contextual conditions as the situation, goals, the social roles of the participants, and our social and personal identity characteristics and those of our interlocutors. The more different the styles are, the less familiar the interlocutors are with each other's styles, and the more consequential the goals of the interaction are, the more complex the decisions to accommodate become. Moreover, as with all the decisions we make as we engage in the moment-to-moment unfolding of interaction, these decisions are contextually contingent, fluid, and open to change. Thus, regardless of whether we can articulate the basis for making these decisions as we interact, decisions about whether or how to accommodate to our interlocutors in our interpersonal communicative activities demand a constant level of cognitive effort from us.

In summary, interpersonal interaction is characterized by a wide range of communicative activities accomplished through exchanges with others for the purposes of accomplishing particular tasks or creating and maintaining interpersonal relationships. Our competent participation as communicators in these activities involves a range of social and cognitive complexities. The knowledge of these complexities and the ability to deal with them are essential to learners' participation in interpersonal activities in the target language.

GUIDELINES FOR DESIGNING INSTRUCTION AROUND INTERPERSONAL COMMUNICATIVE ACTIVITIES

The overall goal of instruction designed for the interpersonal communication mode is to help students develop the communicative competence needed to participate in a wide range of transactional and interactional communicative activities. This section presents a set of guidelines for designing classroom instruction around interpersonal communicative activities.

Choosing Communicative Activities

The first step in **designing instruction** for interpersonal communicative activities is to do a *needs analysis*. A needs analysis entails identifying the particular communicative activities in which learners are expected to, or want to, participate in as users of the target language. To help in the selection of activities you may want to ask yourself questions such as the following: In what kinds of activities are you expecting your students to develop competence? Are they interested in participating in activities with speakers of the target language in contexts outside of the classroom? If so, will they be primarily peer-related interactional activities, or will they involve both transactional and interactional activities with participants of different ages, genders, and with varying social roles? Alternatively, is their goal to use the target language primarily for academic-related interactional and transactional activities that occur primarily in schools and with their classmates?

Crucial to this process of identifying particular activities is the selection of topics and themes used to frame both interactional and transactional interpersonal communicative activities. Figure 6–2 contains a list of some common topics and themes.

Activities can be further classified according to two dimensions. In the first dimension, activities can be grouped according to whether they are part of the **target language communities** to which learners are likely to be a part of, or interact with, in the future, or whether they are integral to the creation and maintenance of **classroom communities** of foreign language learners. The second dimension has to do with goal orientation and classifies activities according to whether their main purpose is transactional or interactional.

Figure 6–3 maps some common interpersonal communicative activities onto the two-dimensional matrix. Quadrant I contains transactional activities typically associated with community life in the target language outside of the classroom. Quadrant II includes transactional activities that are typical of the classroom community. Classroom transactional activities are typically those having to do with classroom management, such as taking roll or planning for schoolwide events.

Quadrants III and IV include activities whose primary purpose is interactional. Activities in Quadrant III are those learners are likely to engage in with members of target language communities outside of the classroom, while the activities in Quadrant IV are those

FIGURE 6-2 Topics and Themes Framing Interpersonal Activities

Art
Community and Neighborhood
    Community Service
Current Events
Education
Environment
Entertainment
Geography
Family Life
    House and Home
Health and Welfare
History
Humanities
Personal Life
    Leisure
Politics
    Government
    Political Institutions
Religion
Social Life
    Community Services
    Social Institutions
Sports
Travel and Transportation
Workplace

which learners will engage in with their own classroom communities of learners. It should be noted that these quadrants are not categorical. As illustrated in Figure 6–3, several activities can be considered indispensable to the communicative life of both target language and classroom communities, and so overlap two quadrants. Competent participation in a variety of activities from all four quadrants is necessary for full bilingual development.

Technological Media and Resources for Engaging in Interpersonal Communicative Activities

A last aspect of the process of identifying interpersonal communicative activities concerns the means by which they are accomplished. The advent of new technology has expanded the options for engaging in interpersonal communicative activities. These **technological resources** include such media as electronic mail, electronic bulletin board postings, and audio, video, and computer conferencing. These options are usually grouped into two types of interactions: **synchronous interaction,** in which the interaction takes place in "real time," and **asynchronous interaction,** where there may be a delay of hours, days, or weeks between messages.

Target Language Community Activities	Classroom Community Activities
I Engaging in a service encounter Making a bank transaction Engaging in a job interview Engaging the help of a service provider Giving directions Obtaining directions Ordering in a restaurant Shopping Making a purchase Making an appointment Discussing health with a professional Seeking help	**II** Managing daily classroom life (e.g., roll taking) Debating a political, social, or academic issue Videoconferencing with another class
Participating in an academic discussion Discussing a current event Completing forms	
Transactional	Transactional
III Talking on the telephone with friends and family Getting to know new neighbors	**IV** Getting to know new club members, students, and teachers
Writing letters to friends and family Recounting a personal experience Chatting (in an electronic chat room) Playing a game Engaging in a sport Exchanging jokes, riddles, and repartee Singing songs	
Interactional	Interactional

FIGURE 6–3   Interpersonal Communicative Activities

Synchronous interaction can occur in several ways. In satellite videoconferencing, for example, participants can see each other as they interact through electronic means. In computer-mediated conferencing, although participants may not have visual contact with each other, they can interact with each other through electronic means, and thus share a virtual space.

Some software programs designed for synchronous interaction do not require an Internet connection. Rather, computers can be connected to each other as part of a networked system. These computers are usually housed in the same room or language laboratory, and thus can allow groups of students to interact with each other via computer. Such conferencing can be used for both transactional and interactional purposes. For example, it can serve as an alternative to small face-to-face group discussions on particular topics. It can immerse students in other situated practice learning opportunities, encouraging role play or simulations, for example, as well as facilitate student engagement in overt instruction, critical framing, and transformed practice learning opportunities.

Internet Relay Chat (IRC) is one kind of synchronous communication that requires a connection to the World Wide Web. To interact with others from outside their own classroom or school, students can enter a *chat room* and engage in discussions with others from around the world on a variety of topics and for a variety of purposes. Multi-User Dimension (MUD) is a general term used to describe one kind of text-based synchronous environment in which participants interact in real time. These environments are often quite elaborate, comprising thousands of interlinked settings or rooms. Participants usually take on the identities of fantasy characters in these settings and move about from room to room interacting with other characters.

A MOO, which stands for MUD Object-Oriented, is a variation of a MUD. It was developed as more of a social space for people to come together to interact by connecting users through the Internet to a textual world of rooms and objects in real time with real people for real-world purposes. Depending on the larger social goal of the MOO, participants can take on character roles or remain as themselves. In addition, unlike MUDs, which are already-formed virtual spaces, MOOs are more flexible and allow users to create their own rooms and objects in their virtual environments.

More recent technological developments have produced IRC programs that allow for synchronous audio and video communication in addition to the text-based communication provided by these particular programs. Moreover, additional technologies are emerging that will allow students to use voice input rather than the keyboard to interact not only with other human users of the computer, but also with the computer itself (Godwin-Jones, 2000).

Asynchronous communication includes interactions that do not take place simultaneously. In other words, the interactions take place over an extended time period rather than at the same time. Options here include electronic mail, or e-mail, and postings to electronic bulletin boards or listservs. E-mail is a unique means of communication in that it combines the immediacy of interaction using short, actively negotiated turns, with the more permanent features of written text (Luke, 2000). Posting to bulletin boards and listservs is similar in that participants type messages and send them to a central server where they are displayed either chronologically or topically on a board.

Many of the kinds of interactions one can have via asynchronous media are similar to those via synchronous media. They differ primarily in the amount of time participants have to read and respond to each other's postings. Asynchronous interaction is much slower because message exchanges may be separated by several days. Listservs are similar to bulletin boards because messages sent are posted to an entire group. They differ somewhat from bulletin boards because listservs are usually oriented around a particular topic and the conversations can take the form of multiparty discussions with several members contributing to a discussion on a particular topic. Moreover, the lists are usually restricted to a group of participants that must subscribe to the list to be able to engage in the discussion.

Identifying the Communicative Components

Once it has been determined which topics and themes, and which activities within those topics and themes, are to form the curricular base for the interpersonal communication mode, the next step is to identify the basic **communicative components** and features of each activity that students need to learn in order to successfully engage in that activity. As noted earlier, a useful frame for analyzing the skills, abilities, and knowledge needed is the Celce-Murcia et al. (1995) model of communicative competence presented in Chapter 1. As explained, their model of communicative competence is comprised of five interrelated areas of knowledge, skills, and abilities: discourse competence, linguistic competence, sociocultural competence, actional competence, and strategic competence. Some of the skills and knowledge needed, for example, to initiate and sustain an e-mail partnership might include the following:

Discourse: The linguistic devices for creating a coherent and cohesive message and for linking messages across time, and if the exchange is between more than two people, among participants.

Linguistic: The grammatical structures and vocabulary needed to exchange e-mail messages on particular topics or themes.

Actional: Typical speech act sequences for opening and closing e-mail exchanges.

Sociocultural: The *netiquette,* or guidelines for exchanging messages on the Net in appropriate and polite ways, including knowledge of emoticons, signs made from typographical characters to represent facial gestures such as smiles :-) or frowns :-(, which are used to display affect. Also included here is the knowledge of, and ability to use, linguistic devices to index and create social roles and identities in expected ways.

Strategic: Linguistic devices for expressing confusion, requesting clarification, redirecting the exchange, and resolving communicative misunderstandings.

Creating maps of the components of communicative activities in this way helps to make explicit the substance of the communicative plans that more experienced participants use to guide their own participation in the activities. These maps can then be used as blueprints for the design of instructional activities. It should be noted that the significance of each of the components or subcomponents of communicative competence is likely to differ across activities. In some interpersonal activities, such as greetings or introductions, for example, the speech acts comprising the activity are few. Thus, most of the instructional activities are likely to be focused on elements of linguistic and sociocultural competence. Likewise, the focus of instruction is likely to differ across groups of learners. Instruction for beginning learners is likely to focus on the less complex elements of the five components of communicative competence, moving to the more complex aspects as the learners advance in their learning.

Creating Instructional Activities

Once the analysis of the activities is completed, the next step is to create a set of instructional plans for helping students appropriate the needed knowledge, skills, and abilities for competent engagement. As noted in Chapter 5, a unit plan functions like an organizational map. It lays out the long-term instructional goals and objectives as they pertain to a variety of activities that include all three communication modes, the interpersonal, the interpretive, and the presentational. Daily plans identify the learning objectives and the kinds of instructional activities students will engage in for one class period.

In designing instructional plans, it is essential to keep in mind the distinction between *communicative activity* and *instructional activity*. It is through involvement in our significant **communicative activities** that we live our everyday lives as, for example, teachers, students, parents, children, friends, and colleagues. Becoming competent users of the target language in myriad communicative activities is a primary goal of foreign language learning. Thus, communicative activities form the base of the foreign language curriculum.

In contrast, **instructional activities** are intended to help learners develop the various knowledge, skills, and abilities they need to be successful participants in the chosen communicative activities. Instructional activities are specific to particular learning environments. They are usually constructed by the teacher, although as pointed out in earlier chapters, students should be involved in creating them as well. The kinds of instructional activities found in a high school classroom, for example, will differ from those in an elementary classroom.

Moreover, effective instructional activities involve all four skills in the learning process. So for students to develop the ability to participate fully in academic discussions on a particular topic in the target language, they need to learn, among other things, about the topic, how to take turns appropriately, and how to construct speech acts that include summarizing, explaining, and justifying. Such learning can only happen through engagement in instructional activities that employ all four skills. Likewise, learning to engage competently in a service encounter in the target language requires using the skills of listening, speaking, reading, and writing in instructional activities to develop the requisite linguistic structures, vocabulary, and sociocultural knowledge.

Connecting Instructional Activities to Learning Opportunities

To construct an effective instructional activity, several decisions must be made. The first decision involves the kind of learning opportunity it will be. As we discussed in Chapter 3, full engagement in learning involves participation in four kinds of **learning opportunities:** situated practice, overt instruction, critical framing, and transformed practice.

Situated Practice. In situated practice, the purpose is to experience fully or be immersed in the activity itself without worry of whether one is "doing it right." Immersion in the communicative activity involves full active participation for real, meaningful purposes. For those communicative activities that are part of the classroom community or involve electronic connections, such as exchanging letters with another in or outside of the classroom, developing an e-mail partnership with a classmate or a target-language-speaking peer from another part of the world, or engaging in classroom or electronic discussions on a chosen topic, it may be easy to bring the real experience to the classroom. Other activities that are more typically part of the communities of target language speakers outside of the classroom, such as seeking the help of a service provider, or ordering in a restaurant, may be more easily created as simulations, improvisations, and role plays. The following sections provide extended examples of two situated practice instructional activities. Examples of others can be found in Table 6–1.

TABLE 6-1   *Instructional and Assessment Activities for Interpersonal Communicative Activities.*

Learning Opportunities	Activities
Situated Practice	Conversation cards
	Debate
	Dialogue journals
	Games
	Role plays
	Simulations
	Talking journals
Overt Instruction	Arranging/sequencing of activity components
	Dictionary and thesaurus work
	Information gap tasks
	Language logs
	Matching (vocabulary, speech acts, etc.)
	Minimal pair practice (pronunciation)
	Pattern analysis (grammar, discourse markers, etc.)
	Semantic webs
	Strategy checklist
	Word lists
Critical Framing	Activity analysis and comparison across contexts and groups
	Collection of anecdotal records
	Diary of daily activities
	Ethnographic research
	Interviews with target language speakers
	Self-assessment of skills, strategy use, attitudes
	Survey of attitudes
Transformed Practice	Creative responses
	Improvisations
	Role play
	Simulations
	Student-choreographed productions
	Teaching others

Role Playing.   As noted in Chapter 2, *role playing* provides opportunities for students to immerse themselves in authentic versions of communicative activities in safe or inconsequential environments where they can make mistakes as they learn. Role playing can be as simple as two people playing out an unprepared scenario such as, for example, friends meeting on the street. On a more sophisticated level it can involve well-defined scenes reflecting real-life situations outside of the classroom environment. Eating out, taking a guided tour of a museum or gallery, or participating in a job interview are just a few examples of situations that can be role played.

One concern with creating role plays of everyday communicative activities from target language communities outside the classroom is how to provide students with models of these activities for them to observe and imitate in the classroom. In some cases, it may be possible to provide students with videotapes of the activities. Another possibility is using books. A recent study (Kim & Hall, 2000) provides an example of how everyday interpersonal activities from the target language culture can be brought into the classroom through books and used as a foundation for students' role playing.

In this study, the researchers involved young children learning English in Korea in shared book readings about schooling activities that occur in American English-speaking schools. The shared book readings involved reading the stories aloud to the children while actively involving them in the process. For example, as the teacher read the stories, the students were asked to elaborate on the action and were prompted for their opinions.

The researchers found that the story lines and dialogues provided in the storybooks served as models of role-based language that the young learners were able to appropriate and use in their role plays about that context. In their role plays, they took on the roles of teacher and students, friends on the playground, and parents and children, and acted out scenes they had read about. Kim and Hall found that in the young learners' role plays they not only appropriated the story lines and dialogues from the books but they did so with no overt instruction from the teacher.

Examination of the children's language use during play over a 4-month period revealed positive changes in their language abilities. It was concluded that involving learners of other languages in shared readings about particular communicative contexts found in communities who use the target language *outside* the classroom can help them simulate these experiences *in* the classroom and that such simulations positively affect communicative development in the target language.

Talking Journals.   In this situated practice activity the students carry on extended conversations with the teacher, or other more expert users of the target language, through the use of a tape recorder. *Talking journals* are similar to dialogue journals in which students correspond with the teacher and, in some cases, other students by writing in journals and exchanging them with each other, except that rather than writing, students and teachers corresponded by exchanging recorded messages on audiotapes (Foley, 1993). Beginning with a prompt from the teacher, such as "Tell me about yourself," students talk into their audio journals much as they would if they were carrying on a face-to-face conversation with the teacher. The intent is not to have students prepare scripts ahead of time, but rather to gain experience in engaging in social conversation in the target language. In response to the students' entries, teachers can ask the students to elaborate on something they said. They can also add their own personal experiences and stories.

Through such exchanges, teachers provide authentic experiences in carrying on social conversations to the students. Such conversations can also help the teacher and students form strong interpersonal bonds that can foster the development of group rapport and further strengthen their classroom community of learners.

It should be noted that because of the situated practice nature of this activity, the exchanges are not the place to point out errors of grammar, word choice, or pronunciation to the students, unless concerns with accuracy and other communicative matters arise naturally from the exchanges themselves. Instead, it is more appropriate to take note of recurring errors and to make them the focus of overt instructional activities.

Whether they are real or simulated experiences, the teacher's role in situated practice instructional activities is to apprentice students into these activities. They do so by modeling the appropriate linguistic actions and providing guided support where necessary yet without constraining the students' involvement. While it is expected that initially learners may have to rely on their first language when engaging in the activity, they should strive to use the target language in situated practice activities to the fullest extent possible.

Overt Instruction.   The purpose of the second learning opportunity, overt instruction, is to examine the underlying systems and structures of meaning in order to develop appropriate and accurate use of them. This means giving systematic, analytic, and conscious attention to the various grammatical, lexical, discourse, sociocultural, actional, and strategic components needed to engage in those communicative activities forming the curriculum. The communicative components needed to engage in e-mail exchanges, given in the previous section, are examples of what would become the focus of overt instruction activities designed to develop such competence in learners.

As noted in earlier chapters, much instruction in foreign language education has traditionally focused on this particular kind of learning opportunity, with a primary focus on the drill and practice of grammar knowledge and skills. Recent formulations of overt instruction activities, however, have moved away from heavy reliance on mechanical drills and toward the use of more engaging techniques such as information gap activities and focus-on-form tasks. They have also included activities for the teaching of skills and knowledge in addition to grammar and vocabulary. See Table 6–1 for an abridged list of some overt instruction activities that can be used in middle and high school classrooms. Extended descriptions of two activities appear in the following sections.

Language Logs.   One innovative overt instruction activity involves having students keep *logs of language* they hear, or in the case of e-mail exchanges or written letters, language they come in contact with that they do not understand, and to reflect on its use. If, for example, they come across a word or words they do not know in an e-mail note from their pen pals, they note the words in their log, along with the sentence or phrase from which the words were taken. Next to the entry, in a separate column, they note their guesses as to the meanings of the words. In a third column they note the meanings attributed to the words, ascertained either by asking the original user of the words or another person who is a more competent user of the target language, or by looking them up in a dictionary. A fourth column could be added in which they note their own use of the words, perhaps in a subsequent e-mail message or in a conversation with another person.

This activity provides learners with ample opportunities to actively attend to language and reflect on its use. At the same time it helps them notice the gap between what they know and do not know about forming particular linguistic structures for particular purposes. This, as noted in Chapter 3, helps to raise their consciousness and subsequently leads to their learning to form these structures on their own.

Dictionary Use.   Dictionaries are useful tools in language development. However, students, particularly middle and high school students, may not necessarily know how to use them effectively. Students need to understand the conventions used in dictionary definitions and know how to make sense of the information provided in them. Dictionary definitions usually contain the following information: part of speech, pronunciation key, origin, past tense ending (verb) first meaning, second meaning, and example sentence. This activity helps students learn how to use the various kinds of information contained in dictionaries to further their target language learning for use in a particular communicative activity.

One way to start is to make a list of the words students need to know in order to engage in a particular interpersonal activity. For each word contained in the list, ask the students, either as individuals, in pairs, or as a group, to look up the words and locate the particular elements of the definition as it appears in their dictionaries. Then they can be asked to create their own sentences using the words. They can also be asked to locate synonyms and to replace the words in the passage with the synonyms.

The teacher's role in any overt instruction activity is to provide multiple opportunities for students to examine, reflect upon, and practice the formation of these various components, providing assistance and direct instruction when necessary.

Critical Framing. Critical framing, a third learning opportunity, is intended to allow students to stand back from the activities and reflect on the connections between the communicative resources of an activity and their social and cultural contexts. As noted in Chapter 3, the purpose of these opportunities is to facilitate learners' development of intercultural knowledge and understanding, and intercultural communicative competence. The development of such understanding comes about through learners' participation in critical framing instructional activities such as conducting and analyzing interviews or surveys on others' perceptions of their uses of language in particular contexts. They can also involve students in analyzing their own language use and comparing it to their classmates' or researching the use of language in activities that appear to be similar across contexts and across groups using, where possible, video and written archives.

While serving as both informants and ethnographers in their explorations of language use, learners may find, for example, that the linguistic means for creating solidarity in the target language in e-mail exchanges may differ depending on whether learners are interacting with peers, with strangers, with interlocutors having more authority, or with other types of interlocutors. They may also find differences across language groups; how solidarity is created among peers in English, for example, may differ from how it is created among peers in the target language. Following are examples of two critical framing activities that can be used to help students understand the social and cultural contextual conditions framing particular interpersonal communicative activities. A list of additional activities is contained in Table 6–1.

Speech Act Pattern Analysis. This activity engages learners as ethnographers in the examination of patterns of language use. Here students are provided with a series of openers in the target language for a variety of interpersonal activities, such as interactional routines like greetings and leave-takings, or transactional activities such as service encounters. Examples of openers in English include utterances such as "Can I help you?", "How are you today?", and even a simple "Hey."

Using these openers, students are expected to survey a variety of speakers of the target language on how they might respond to the openers. Depending on the availability of target language speakers in the area, they may also conduct the survey via e-mail or electronic chat rooms. Students log the responses and code each of them in terms of the social identities of the speakers (e.g., age, gender, place of residence, etc.). Once they have gathered their data, they then analyze the responses for patterns of use, ascertaining whether, for example, they vary according to the social identity of the respondent. Given their findings, they can be asked to speculate about the reasons for variation in language use.

Activity Analysis.   The goal of this instructional activity is to help students develop a researcher's stance toward involvement in particular communicative activities. It involves standing apart from and learning to observe and analyze the linguistic and other actions that comprise the communicative activities of interest. Here students watch a short clip or set of clips of a scene taken from a target-language-speaking community. This can include, for example, a scene from a restaurant or a service encounter in which two or more people are interacting.

As they watch they are asked to note features of the context. In the case of the restaurant scene this would include noting features such as overall appearance and atmosphere, the manner in which the host or waiter interacts with the customers, how ordering takes place, and so on. The students can use both English and the target language to do this. They can also note specific vocabulary words and phrases that are used by the participants.

After multiple viewings, students can compile their findings, compare their lists with each other, and together create what they would consider to be a typical enactment of this particular encounter. This can be used in subsequent critical framing activities as a base for examining other service encounters (or other interpersonal communicative activities) and analyzing them for differences in language use.

The teacher's role in any critical framing instructional activity is to challenge learners to expand their understandings of the activity. This includes helping students examine alternative linguistic means for meeting the same goals, visualizing other options that students may not find on their own, redirecting their learning where necessary, and in other ways, assisting the learners to reach full intercultural communicative understanding.

In both overt instruction and critical framing instructional activities, the use of the target language will vary. As noted in Chapter 4, quite often students will use their first language, English, to help them organize, plan, and coordinate their thoughts and actions, particularly when they are introduced to a new concept or asked to complete an unfamiliar or difficult task. Thus, it is expected that the students will use more of the target language in some activities and less in others, particularly at the beginning levels. As they gain experience in their activities, their ability to use the target language to participate in the activity and to help themselves learn will develop as well.

Transformed Practice.   The purpose of the final learning opportunity, transformed practice, is to provide opportunities for students to use the newly developed skills and knowledge in new contexts or in new ways. Transformed practice instructional activities, then, allow students to try out their new knowledge and skills in new, unfamiliar contexts, making connections between seemingly different activities in innovative and creative ways. This could mean, for example, providing opportunities for students to create new e-mail partnerships and developing them in ways that are of particular significance to individual students. Alternatively, it could mean having the students use their new perspectives on e-mail exchanges to expand or in some way transform the kinds of partnerships they have already established.

Students can also be asked to teach what they know to less expert learners. For example, a group of students may decide to create their own set of guidelines for participating in e-mail exchanges and to share them with other groups in their schools or on the Internet. A list of possible transformed practice activities can be found in Table 6–1. Examples of two such activities can be found in the following sections.

Improvisations.　When using *improvisations* as transformed practice, students are not expected to enact particular social roles and communicative activities in conventional ways. Rather, the purpose is for them to be creative, to try out alternative portrayals, or invent new ones. They can be asked to improvise a scene at a restaurant, for example, in which they choreograph and direct the unfolding activity. They decide who the characters will be, what motivations lie behind each character's interactions, and the particular conventions the characters will use to enact their roles.

Such creative enactments come about only after learners have developed the knowledge, skills, and abilities needed for conventional displays of communicative competence. Thus, only after students have been given ample opportunities to role play and learn the conventions typical for engagement in a particular communicative activity can they be asked to innovate through the creation of improvisations of the activity.

Talking Journals.　This activity is similar to that for situated practice except that here it is the student who takes the lead, asking the questions, providing the prompts, and moving the conversation along. Students can also be asked to expand upon the activity itself. They can be asked to create alternative ways of using tape recorders for their own enjoyment. For example, a student could create a running story in which the student begins the telling of a tale, passing the recorder to other students who are expected to add to the story. After each student is provided the opportunity to contribute, as a group, they can listen to (and appreciate their creativity in) the collectively created stories.

In transformed practice instructional activities the teacher's role is to act as coach and facilitator, providing new experiences to the students where possible, assisting them in their endeavors, and in all other ways encouraging learners' explorations into using language for their own purposes. As in situated practice activities, language use in transformed practice is expected to be primarily in the target language.

Choosing a Particular Participation Structure

Once it has been decided what kind of learning opportunity the instructional activity will be, the next decision to be made concerns **participation structure.** As noted in Chapter 3, student participation in the instructional activity can be geared to the individual, to pairs or small groups of learners, or to the whole group. It can also be organized around learning centers.

Because of the interactive nature of activities in the interpersonal communication mode, situated and transformed practice instructional activities necessarily involve at least one other person. To take the example of e-mail exchanges, to be immersed in the real activity of exchanging e-mails, individual learners need at least one other interlocutor with whom they can interact. The interlocutor can be another student or group of students, in which case, the activity would involve pairs or small groups of learners. Alternatively, the interlocutors can be target-language-speaking contacts established through the Internet with whom learners interact on an individual basis.

Participation in overt instruction and critical framing instructional activities, on the other hand, do not necessarily involve others. Thus, they can be organized around any of the five possible participation structures. Individuals, for example, may be assigned to analyze different communicative components of the e-mail exchanges taken from the entire class. Once they have completed the tasks on their own, they can be placed in small groups and asked to share their findings with their peers. Another possibility would be to make the analysis itself the focus of a learning center where the students could work together in pairs or small groups.

As pointed out in Chapter 3, no one structure is more valuable than another. Rather, the important point is to make available to the students a range of options for participating in their learning opportunities. How they participate in any one particular activity depends on

---

Steps for Designing Instruction for the Interpersonal Mode
A. Conduct a needs analysis
>   What themes and topics are important?
>   What kinds of activities are important?
>   target language community
>   classroom community
>   transactional
>   interactional
>   What means will be used to engage in activity?
>   Face to face
>   Electronic
>   Other
B. Create a blueprint of communicative activity by identifying components to be learned
>   Discourse
>   Linguistic
>   Actional
>   Sociocultural
>   Strategic
C. Create instructional activity
>   Choose type of learning opportunity
>   Situated practice
>   Overt instruction
>   Critical framing
>   Transformed practice
>   Choose type of participation structure
>   Individual
>   Pair
>   Small group
>   Whole group
>   Learning center

FIGURE 6–4   Designing Instruction for the Interpersonal Mode

the goal of that activity as well as on other considerations that are determined by the teacher to be significant, such as space options. Figure 6–4 summarizes the steps involved in designing instruction for the interpersonal communication mode.

DESIGNING ASSESSMENT

As pointed out in Chapter 5, **assessment** is the crucial link between teaching and learning. Effective teaching involves the use of multiple assessment tools that are linked directly to the objectives of learners' instructional activities. Traditionally, foreign language learning of interpersonal knowledge and skills in middle schools and high schools has been evaluated primarily with criterion-based, teacher-made, discrete-point grammar and vocabulary tests. This is not surprising since for the most part, the learning opportunities in foreign language classrooms have centered on the overt instruction of grammar and vocabulary.

As we noted earlier, the focus of overt instruction is on separating, examining, and practicing the accurate and appropriate formation of the many communicative components of communicative activities. Because the measures traditionally used in foreign language classrooms can be compatible with these instructional objectives, they should not be abandoned in favor of alternative measures. Rather, they should be improved upon to ensure that what is evaluated is closely tied to the focus of the instructional activities. In addition, the tests should be expanded so that they measure student learning of other components of communicative competence such as discourse, sociocultural, actional, and strategic competence in addition to grammar and vocabulary.

Chapter tests that accompany commercially published foreign language textbooks often include criterion-referenced, discrete-point test items such as multiple-choice, fill-in-the-blank, sentence and paragraph completion, matching, and short answer to evaluate student learning of grammar and vocabulary. These can certainly be expanded to suit the purposes of overt instruction assessment of the other communicative components as well. Moreover, any of the instructional activities used to directly teach the various components of communicative competence can also be used as assessment tools. Indeed, any of the activities categorized by learning opportunities found in Table 6–1 can also be used for assessment purposes.

Because situated and transformed practice instructional activities involve the learners' use of all the communicative components of a communicative activity, they are more difficult to assess using traditional, discrete-point measures. As noted in Chapter 5, current measures for assessing students' face-to-face speaking abilities include the OPI and the SOPI. These tests evaluate learners' ability to orally perform functions such as giving directions, describing items, and narrating a sequence of events. However, as pointed out in that discussion, these tests are of limited value in assessing students' full development of the knowledge and skills needed for engaging in a wide range of communicative activities accomplished through the target language and that are specific to particular learning communities. For this, additional performance-based measures are needed.

Figure 6–5 includes an example of a rubric that can be used as both a formative developmental evaluation, and as a summative measure of performance in interpersonal

	NOVICE	INTERMEDIATE	COMPETENT	DISTINGUISHED	EXPERT
Discourse Competence	Displays a limited understanding of the gist of the interaction. Has difficulty making a coherent contribution.	Has difficulty understanding, selecting and arranging utterances to achieve a coherent interaction. Can sustain the interaction only with help.	Is able to sustain interaction through the appropriate interpretation, selection, and sequencing of utterances, although may occasionally need some help, especially if the interaction moves away from the expected or conventional means associated with the activity.	Has a clear understanding of the activity and is able to initiate and sustain the interaction through the appropriate interpretation, selection, and sequencing of utterances until the task or activity is completed.	Can understand and use a variety of linguistic resources to create and sustain a cohesive, coherent interaction. Can lead other, less expert interlocutors in sustaining a coherent interaction, providing assistance where needed.
Linguistic Competence	Displays limited understanding of, and ability to use accurately, vocabulary, grammar, pronunciation, and prosodic knowledge and skills associated with the interaction.	Displays understanding of, and can use some, basic vocabulary and grammar, but it is generally not enough to sustain the interaction beyond a fairly basic level. Relies heavily on nonverbal gestures to communicate. Has difficulty pronouncing words and using appropriate intonational patterns.	Displays understanding of, and can use the, conventional vocabulary and grammatical structures associated with the activity. Pronunciation and intonational patterns are adequate, and thus do not impede communication.	Can understand, use, and elaborate on conventional vocabulary and grammatical structures. Pronunciation and intonational patterns are appropriate and accurate.	Understanding and use of grammar, vocabulary, pronunciation, and intonation patterns are precise. Displays understanding of, and can use a variety of, grammatical structures and vocabulary words to construct similar meaning utterances.
Actional Competence	Displays limited understanding of the communicative activity. Has great difficulty understanding or constructing the speech acts needed to perform functions required by the communicative activity; can contribute only on a very limited basis.	Displays a basic understanding of the typical speech acts associated with the activity, but has difficulty understanding, responding to, and initiating conventional speech acts in interaction. Relies heavily on nonverbal gestures.	Displays a solid understanding of the typical speech acts associated with the activity and can understand, respond to, and crate speech acts for performing expected functions in interaction.	Displays a solid understanding of the typical speech acts associated with the activity and can understand, respond to, and create speech acts for performing expected and unexpected functions in interaction.	Can interpret, respond to, and create a variety of speech acts to perform similar functions in the interaction. Can also move the interaction in unexpected, creative directions through the use of a variety of speech acts.

Sociocultural Competence	Displays limited understanding of the norms and expectations for behavior associated with particular social roles and identities of the participants, and of any extralinguistic factors needed to contribute to the interaction.	Displays a basic understanding of the norms and expectations for behavior in the interaction associated with particular social roles and identities of the participants, but has difficulty putting that understanding into action.	In addition to understanding the norms and expectations for behavior associated with particular social roles and identities of the participants, displays a solid understanding of the extralinguistic factors as the context, stylistic appropriateness, and the nonverbal and other background cultural knowledge needed to contribute to the interaction.	Displays an understanding of, and ability to use, norms, expectations, and other extralinguistic factors to contribute to the interaction in expected ways. Displays and interprets such stylistic features as politeness, formality, and affiliation in appropriate ways.	Displays an understanding of, and ability to use, norms, expectations, and other extralinguistic factors to contribute to the interaction in both expected and novel ways. Displays and interprets such stylistic features as politeness, formality, and affiliation appropriately, accurately, and, where possible, creatively.
Strategic Competence	Involved in the interaction on a very limited basis. Has difficulty identifying or resolving communication glitches or missteps. Has limited use of resources for enhancing his or her involvement.	Shows some difficulty in understanding but frequently asks for repetition or clarification. Needs some help to notice and correct errors, to notice and resolve communication missteps, and to enhance the effectiveness of his or her involvement.	Displays a basic understanding of, and ability to use, strategies such as circumlocution, avoidance, approximation, and comprehension requests needed to resolve communicative difficulties and to enhance the effectiveness of the interaction. Notices and self-corrects errors fairly consistently.	Makes appropriate and effective use of strategies for resolving communicative difficulties and enhancing the effectiveness of the interaction. Notices and self-corrects errors consistently and accurately.	Makes appropriate and effective use of strategies for resolving communicative difficulties and enhancing effectiveness of the interaction. Can anticipate possible misunderstandings and takes steps to resolve them before they actually occur. Notices and self-corrects errors consistently and accurately, and helps others to repair their utterances.

FIGURE 6–5 Rubric for Evaluating Student Performance in Situated and Transformed Practice Activities

Criteria for Evaluation of a Research Report

Content
The purpose of the report is clearly articulated.
1   2   3   4   5
weak   strong

Date source(s) are clearly articulated and appropriate.
1   2   3   4   5
weak   strong

Methods of data collection are clearly articulated and appropriate.
1   2   3   4   5
weak   strong

Findings are clearly articulated and supported with ample evidence from the data.
1   2   3   4   5
weak   strong

Conclusions are appropriate, given the findings and clearly articulated.
1   2   3   4   5
weak   strong

Format
Report is written in academic prose.
1   2   3   4   5
weak   strong

Report is well organized (clear transitions between paragraphs and between sections and appropriate use of headings and subheadings).
1   2   3   4   5
weak   strong

Report makes appropriate and accurate use of grammar, vocabulary, and discourse structures.
1   2   3   4   5
weak   strong

Format is appropriate.
1   2   3   4   5
weak   strong

If used, citations and reference list are accurate, appropriate, and consistent in style.
1   2   3   4   5
weak   strong

FIGURE 6–6   Rubric for Evaluating a Written Research Report

situated practice and transformed practice activities. It uses the Celce-Murcia et al. (1995) model of communicative competence as a framework, and thus is compatible with the curricular framework set out in this chapter.

Because a primary concern of critical framing instructional activities is to develop students' intercultural knowledge and communicative competence, assessment of these activities can take a variety of shapes including both traditional and alternative means of assessment. If the goal of a critical framing activity is for students to identify and compare a variety of options for creating solidarity in e-mail exchanges, for example, they might be asked to conduct an action research project that includes interviews, surveys, analysis of collected e-mail exchanges, and so on.

Learners can also be asked to keep journals documenting their explorations of language use in other contexts. They might keep records on the ways they collect and analyze new information, noting, for example, the sources of their information and their observations about it, as well as any comparisons they can make. They might also note the particular strategies they use in gathering and analyzing their information, rating each on its usefulness for helping them accomplish their tasks. They can be asked to create graphs, diagrams, narratives, and other kinds of records to display the information they collect and their own analyses of the information. Moreover, they can be asked to create dictionaries of words, phrases, and grammatical or other communicative features that they uncover in their explorations. Possible student-produced products resulting from their research can include a portfolio of the various artifacts that were developed as part of the activities previously listed or a more conventional written report.

Performance-based rubrics and student self-assessment tools would be appropriate summative measures for evaluating their learning in the project. Figure 6–6 contains an example of a rubric that can be used to evaluate a conventional written report. In addition, students can be given traditional criterion-referenced exams in which they are asked to display their understanding of the social and cultural contexts of particular interpersonal communicative activities by matching, selecting, filling-in-the-blanks, or completing short or long essay responses to questions.

Finally, in addition to assessing learning in particular instructional activities, it is suggested that students' general development as learners be assessed. This would include, for example, assessing students' daily class attendance, participation, and organizational skills. Figure 6–7 provides one example of an analytic rubric that can be used to assess learners' general participation in their classroom community.

There are two final points to make about designing assessment for evaluating student learning. First, all assessment tools should be reviewed and revised on a regular basis. This will enable both teachers and students to revisit their instructional goals and objectives and evaluate their success in accomplishing them. Second, no one tool can adequately assess all dimensions of communicative development in foreign language classrooms. Consequently, effective teaching involves the use of a varied assortment of both traditional and alternative means of assessment. As noted earlier, when used appropriately, assessment can not only help enhance students' development as language learners, but it can also strengthen teachers' development as language teachers.

	NOVICE	INTERMEDIATE	COMPETENT	DISTINGUISHED	EXPERT
Attendance	Attendance is limited.	Attendance is somewhat sporadic.	Attends the majority of classes, only missing occasionally.	Rarely misses a class.	Has a perfect or near perfect attendance record.
Participation	Is usually underprepared for class, and contributes to class discussions or activities only on a limited basis.	Preparation for, and participation in, class discussions or activities is somewhat sporadic.	Is regularly prepared for class and is a regular participant in class discussions and activities.	Is almost always well prepared for class and consistently participates in class discussions and activities.	Is always well prepared for class and is an active participant in class discussions and activities, frequently taking the lead, encouraging and helping other students to participate.
Completion of Assignments	May forget from time to time to hand in required assignments or make up missed assignments.	Hands in required assignments, although is late from time to time. Is sporadic in making up missed assignments.	Regularly hands in required assignments, although occasionally misses the deadline; makes up most missed assignments.	Almost always hands in required assignments on time, only infrequently missing deadlines; makes up almost all missed assignments.	Always hands in all required assignments on time and always makes up missed assignments.

FIGURE 6–7 Rubric for Evaluating General Student Participation in Learning

160

SUMMARY

The interpersonal mode is one of three modes around which the communication goal is organized. Several key concepts and ideas related to this mode were presented in this chapter and are summarized below. Also summarized are guidelines for designing effective instructional activities and means of assessing student learning.

- Two general purposes for engaging in interpersonal communicative activities are transactional, in which one interlocutor seeks to obtain something from another or to resolve a problem or concern, and interactional, in which the primary concern is with the establishment and maintenance of interpersonal relationships.
- Regardless of the purposes behind our interpersonal activities, when we interact with another we are involved in two general cognitive processes. We seek to be understood by others and to have some control over how others understand us and, we seek to understand others so that we can act appropriately toward them.
- The degree of cognitive complexity involved in interaction depends on at least three conditions. First, it depends on our familiarity and past experiences in the activity. Second, it depends on the number and kinds of social identities we have in relation to the other participants. Third, it depends on the degree to which we accommodate to the communicative style of these participants.
- In designing effective instruction for interpersonal communicative activities, the first step involves conducting a needs analysis. Knowing which activities our students want or need to become communicatively competent in will help determine which communicative activities will form the foundation of the curriculum.
- In choosing interpersonal communicative activities it is important to note the distinction between two types of communities. The first is the target language community or communities that use the target language as a common code and which learners are likely to be a part of or interact with in the future. The second is the classroom community or communities in which the target language is used for interactional and transactional activities that primarily occur in learners' language classrooms.
- The growing arena of electronic technology has expanded the options for engaging in interpersonal communicative activities to include electronic mail, electronic bulletin board postings, and audio, video, and computer conferencing. These options are usually grouped into two types of interactions. In synchronous interaction the interaction takes place in "real time." In asynchronous interaction there may be a delay of hours, days, or weeks between messages.
- Once it has been determined which activities will form the curricular base for the interpersonal mode, the next step is to identify the basic communicative components and features of each activity that students need to learn in order to successfully engage in that activity. A useful frame for analyzing the skills, abilities, and knowledge needed is the Celce-Murcia et al. (1995) model of communicative competence.

- The next step involves creating instructional activities organized around the four types of learning opportunities. These opportunities are situated practice, overt instruction, critical framing, and transformed practice.
- Also important to the design of effective instructional activities is selecting a particular structure for student participation. Will the activity be geared, for example, toward whole-group instruction or individual students? Alternatively, will students be asked to work in small groups or in pairs, or will the activity involve a learning center where students can work at their own pace in groupings of their choosing?
- Equally important to effective pedagogy is the construction of multiple assessment tools. These should include both traditional and alternative means of assessment that are linked directly to the objectives of learners' instructional activities.

DISCUSSION QUESTIONS AND ACTIVITIES

1. In performing a needs analysis in order to determine which interpersonal communicative activities will form part of the curriculum, whose needs do you think should be taken into account? The teachers? The students? The larger foreign language learning community? Provide reasons for your opinions.
2. Explain in your own words the distinctions that are made in this chapter between a communicative activity and an instructional activity and between classroom communities and target language communities. Can you provide examples of each of these? How useful do you think these distinctions are? Provide reasons for your responses.
3. In small groups, examine Figures 6–2 and 6–3. Can you add other topics and themes that can frame interpersonal communicative activities? Can you add additional communicative activities to each of the four quadrants? Share your revisions to the figures with your classmates. How similar or different are they?
4. Examine Table 6–1. Can you add other instructional activities to each of the four learning opportunities? Choose one instructional activity from one of the learning opportunities on which to gather additional information. For example, locate a sample of an information gap task or a semantic web. Prepare to present what you have learned about the activity to your classmates. Give examples of how they might use the instructional activity in their own language classrooms.
5. Divide into small groups according to the language you are teaching. Together, choose one interpersonal communicative activity from one of the four quadrants and do the following:
   - Identify some of the elements of each of the five components of communicative competence to be learned in the target language.
   - Create two instructional activities based on two different kinds of learning opportunities (be sure to identify the learning opportunity and participation structure for each).
   - Create an assessment measure for evaluating student learning in one of the two instructional activities.

TEACHER RESEARCH PROJECTS

A. Needs Analysis.

The purpose of this project is to help teachers uncover some of the ways in which learners want to use the target language so that their needs and interests can be incorporated into the curriculum.

Pose a Problem

Part of planning a curriculum entails assessing your learners' needs and interests in learning the target language. What do learners want to do with the target language? In what activities do they want to be able to use the target language? How do their interests in using the target language compare with the activities they regularly engage in as English language users?

Identify Sources and Gather Information

Using a survey is one effective way to gather information on learners' needs and interests in learning the target language. On the survey, students can be asked to identify particular activities in which they wish to be competent target language users. Asking them about their activities in English in addition to their interests in target language activities will provide you with some information on how familiar or experienced they are in particular activities, and how much background knowledge they bring to the classroom.

Figure 6–8 contains a sample of a survey that you can use. It can be used as is, modified to better suit your group of learners, or you can create your own. Depending on how your foreign language program is configured, you can survey all learners of a particular level (e.g., beginners, intermediate, advanced), a particular grade (e.g., grade 6, grade 9, and so on), or even just one class. Because the findings can help in curricular planning, it is a good idea to collect the data early on in the academic year, perhaps even the first week or two of school. If you do not have your own classes yet, you might undertake this project with a teacher or group of teachers.

Analyze

Once you have gathered the completed surveys, you can compute the average number of times each activity under each language code is checked. You can also compile a list of activities provided by students in the "other" category, and compute the average number of times these activities are mentioned by students. You might also create a graph comparing the activities according to their reported frequency across the two languages.

Reflect and Revise

Use the following questions as a basis for reflection on your findings: What activities do your learners most often engage in when speaking English? In what activities are they interested in becoming competent users of the target language? How do their activities compare across

Survey of Communicative Activities		
Check all that apply.		
	Activities I do in English	**Activities I'd like to do in (language)**
Chat in electronic chat rooms		
Discuss current events		
E-mail friends		
Explore the Internet		
Fill out forms		
Keep a daily diary		
Listen to the radio		
Music		
News		
Talk programs		
Read magazines		
Read newspapers		
Read novels		
Read textbooks		
Talk to neighbors		
Talk to friends on the phone		
Watch TV		
Cartoons		
News programs		
Soap operas		
Sports		
Talk shows		
Weekly series		
Write letters to friends		
Write papers for classes		
Other: _____		
_____		
_____		

FIGURE 6–8   Sample of Needs Analysis Survey

the two languages? In what additional activities do you, as a foreign language teacher, feel the students need to become competent target language users? How can you use these findings to improve your program curriculum? Is there anything else you feel would be helpful to know from students based on their responses to this survey?

Disseminate Information

Share the findings with your department and districtwide colleagues, or, if you do not have your own classes yet, with the colleagues of the teacher or teachers with whom you worked on this project. Together, develop a plan for integrating student target language interests and needs into the curriculum. You might also share the survey you used and the findings with others at a local, state, or regional meeting of a foreign language professional organization.

B. Video Exchange Project.

The purpose of this project is to discover how video exchanges can be used to establish interpersonal and intercultural relationships between learners of another language and peers who are users of the language being learned.

Pose a Problem

Videos can be an effective resource for connecting adolescents and young adults from around the world. Having your students create their own video in which they document their views, opinions, daily activities, and other aspects of their lives that they consider culturally meaningful, and exchanging it with a group of peers from another community, can help lay the groundwork for cross-cultural understanding.

Identify Source and Gather Information

This project is best done by a group, comprised of the teacher and a group of language students. First, identify the group or class of students with whom you wish to work. Explain the goal of the project to them, and together develop a description of what you would like to include in your video to send to the target-language-speaking group and what you would like that group to send you. Many middle and high school students are likely to be interested in sharing information on their lifestyles and learning about those of their peers.

If you have contacts in a community that uses the target language, see if you can arrange to exchange videos with a group of students from that community. Explain to them what your intention is, and the kinds of information you would like to get from the group. If you do not have any contacts, you can try to locate a group on the Internet. The site of GOAL (Global Online Adventure Learning, http://www.goals.com/gle/ope/default.asp) has a link to a video exchange project for teenagers from different countries. The aim of the project is to promote intercultural tolerance, world citizenship, and caring. You might be able to secure a contact from this site. Together with the students, make a video and exchange it for that made by your contact group.

Analyze

As a large group, view the video sent by your contact group. After the viewing, separate into small groups and have each student describe what he or she found significant, interesting, and thought-provoking. Compile the lists made and as a large group point out places of convergence and divergence. Using the information provided in the videos, compare the lifestyles of the target language group with those of the target language learner group.

Reflect and Revise

Once the analysis of the videos is completed, together as a group, reflect on what was learned from the project. Based on the similarities and differences found in the videos what can the students conclude about their own lives as adolescents or teenagers? About the lives of their counterparts? What more would they like to know? If they were able to redo their own video, what would they do? What kinds of activities in the target language are they interested in pursuing based on their involvement in this project?

Disseminate Information

Together with the students, prepare a program for other classes, for parents of the students, or for some interested community groups. As part of the program organize a presentation of both videotapes, after which a student panel can discuss the advantages and disadvantages of working on the project. The students can also address the benefits they felt they derived from their participation; in particular, the project's effectiveness in enhancing their intercultural understanding. You and the students might also develop a workshop demonstrating how others might create a similar project.

ADDITIONAL READINGS

Andrews, L. (1998). *Language exploration and awareness: A resource book for teachers.* Mahwah, NJ: Lawrence Erlbaum.

Blyth, C. S. (1999). *Untangling the Web: Nonce's guide to language and culture on the Internet.* New York: Nonce Publishing.

Coulthard, M. (Ed.). (1992). *Advances in spoken discourse analysis.* London: Routledge.

González-Bueno, M. (1998). The effects of electronic mail on Spanish L2 discourse. *Language Learning & Technology, 9*(2), 55–70.

Holmevik, J. R., & Haynes, C. (2000). *MOOniversity: A student's guide to online learning environments.* Boston, MA: Allyn & Bacon.

Lindstromberg, S. (1997). *The standby book: Activities for the language classroom.* Cambridge: Cambridge University Press.

Schiffrin, D. (1987). *Discourse markers.* New York: Cambridge University Press.

Tanaka, K. (1997). Developing pragmatic competence: A learners-as-researchers approach. *TESOL Quarterly, 6*(3), 14–18.

Wilkinson, A., Davies, A., & Berrill, D. (1990). *Spoken English illuminated.* Milton Keynes, U.K.: Open University Press.

Woods, J. C. (1998). Edu MOOs: Virtual learning centers. *Technology Connection, 5,* 24–25.

INTERNET RESOURCES

http://polyglot.lss.wisc.edu/lss/lang/teach.html   Teaching with the Web

This Web site provides a compilation of ideas for using Web resources as language teaching tools. It also offers links to sites with pedagogical information.

http://www.daedalus.com/net/moolist.html   Educational MOOs and MUDs

This site has links to a variety of MOOs, MUDs, and other text-based virtual realities. The links are grouped into three categories, one of which is ESL/EFL and foreign languages. It is a good place to start looking for and experimenting with some MOOs for use in the language classroom.

http://www.iecc.org   Intercultural E-mail Classroom Connections (IECC)

This is a free service to help teachers link with partners in other countries and cultures for e-mail classroom pen pal and project exchanges. IECC is intended for teachers seeking partner classrooms for international and cross-cultural e-mail exchanges.

http://www.europa-pages.co.uk/index.html   Resource for Pen pals

This is a commercial site that provides information on language schools in Europe and foreign language materials. It includes a pen pal service.

http://www.call.gov/   Center for Advancement of Language Learning (CALL)

The Center for Advancement of Language Learning Web site provides foreign language resources for a diversity of languages. For each language there are links to newspapers, magazines, radio broadcasts either from the target country or Voice of America radio broadcasts in the target language, and transcripts of these broadcasts. The General Language Learning Resources section contains references to instructional materials, instructional programs, general language information sites, and conference schedules.

http://www.awesomelibrary.org/   The Awesome Library

This site provides links to 15,000 carefully reviewed resources for K–12 programs. In addition to general education and other content-based connections, it contains links to an incredible array of resources for the teaching of French, Spanish, and German, in addition to about 25 other languages.

Chapter 7

The Interpretive Mode

Preview Questions

Before you begin reading this chapter, take a few moments to reflect on the kinds of interpretive communicative activities you engage in on a daily basis.

- For what purposes do you read books and other texts?
- How much of what you read involves electronic texts?
- For what purposes do you listen to performances or programs on the radio or watch them on television?
- How do your interpretive activities in English compare with those in the target language?
- What kinds of instructional activities do you, as a language learner, find useful for developing the communicative competence you need to successfully engage in interpretive communicative activities in the target language?

Key Words and Concepts

Interpretive mode
    Aesthetic purpose
    Efferent purpose
    Background knowledge
    Genre familiarity
    Past reading experiences
    First and second language skills
    Listenability
    Visual literacy

Designing instruction
    Target language community activities
    Classroom community activities
    Technological resources
    Analysis of communicative
        components
    Communicative activities
    Instructional activities
    Learning opportunities
    Participation structures
Designing assessment

Overview

A traditional perspective of reading and listening in another language defined them primarily as a process of decoding a set of linguistic symbols. It was believed that the skills needed to read or to comprehend aural text were best learned by breaking the process of decoding into its smallest constituent parts, and then teaching them as discrete skills to the students (Haneda & Wells, 2000). Moreover, because it was thought that skill development proceeded linearly—moving from listening, to speaking, to reading, and finally, to writing—students were seldom taught how to read in another language until they first developed their aural and oral skills.

In contrast to this narrow view, current research has revealed that reading and listening in another language are complicated, multidimensional processes involving a complex interplay of a number of factors (e.g., Bernhardt, 1991; Carrell, Devine, & Eskey, 1988; Carrell & Eisterhold, 1983; Grabe, 1991; Hall, 1997; Hammadou, 1991; Haneda & Wells, 2000; Rubin, 1993; Rubin, Hafer, & Arata, 2000; Weber, 1991). To derive meaning from any kind of text, either oral or written, we use both bottom-up and top-down processes. This means that we draw upon our previous emotional and intellectual experiences and our knowledge of the subject matter and the target language, as well as skills and strategies we have learned in our first language, to give shape to and derive meaning from aural and written texts in the target language.

Also shaping our interpretive experiences are the attitudes and motivation with which we approach the task. The understandings and knowledge we derive from our experiences, in turn, transform our past experiences, knowledge, and skills, and help create new frames for textual interpretations (Rosenblatt, 1938/1995; Scholes, 1989). It is this understanding of reading and listening that underlies the interpretive mode of communication.

This chapter presents an overview of the interpretive mode, which includes communicative activities whose purpose is to effect an understanding of the intent of a variety of texts. After a discussion on the nature of reading and listening, including a review of current research, frameworks for designing curriculum, instruction, and assessment geared to the interpretive mode are presented. Included in the discussion on instructional design are examples of different kinds of instructional activities and assessment tools.

THE INTERPRETIVE MODE

The **interpretive mode** is comprised of communicative activities accomplished through the reading, listening, or viewing of written, audio, and visual texts and whose primary purpose is either *aesthetic* or *efferent* (Rosenblatt, 1938/1995). Activities with an **aesthetic** purpose involve reading, listening, or viewing for pleasure, where the focus is on exploring a range of possible meanings as well as on the feelings, ideas, and attitudes that emerge as we read, view, or listen. The reward for participating in such an activity is the enjoyment derived from participating in the activity itself. Viewing movies with friends, listening to music, and watching favorite television programs are examples of such activities. In foreign language classrooms, activities with an aesthetic purpose can include reading books for pleasure or listening to music performed by a musical artist or group from a target-language-speaking community.

The purpose of **efferent** interpretive activities is to seek new information or understanding. The focus here is on particular meanings we carry away from our involvement with texts. Efferent activities involve a variety of expository text types including descriptions, narratives, comparisons and contrasts, chronological order, cause and effect, and persuasive essays. Reading textbooks, newspapers, or instruction guides, watching the evening news, surfing the Internet in search of information, or listening to or viewing a lecture are examples of interpretive activities that typically have an efferent purpose.

It should be remembered that these two general purposes are not categorical. Rather, they constitute a two-dimensional continuum as illustrated in Figure 7–1. Our purpose for reading the newspaper, listening to the news on the radio, or attending a lecture may be primarily to gain understanding. Thus, these activities are closer to the efferent continuum. On the other hand, we may engage in other activities such as reading a mystery novel or watching a movie for the sheer pleasure of doing so. These fall closer to the aesthetic continuum. It can also be the case that we participate in some activities for both purposes. We can listen to a speaker, for example, and become drawn into the presentation through the speaker's play with words and the cadence of speech. At the same time that we are learning something about the topic, we can also appreciate the aesthetic qualities of the presentation. Such activities occupy the space where both dimensions come together.

In any activity at any given moment, the purpose that takes precedence depends on our stance as reader/interpreter, and the larger social context in which the activity is embedded. Our purpose for engaging in the activity, in turn, determines our approach to the activity including the amount of attention we pay, the time we spend, and the features or parts of the

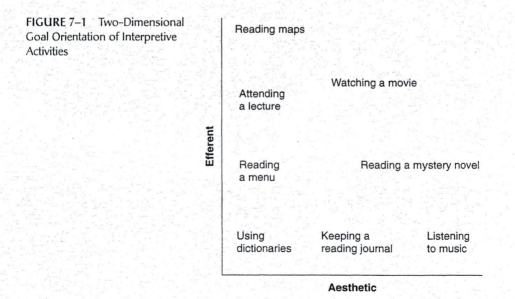

FIGURE 7–1 Two-Dimensional Goal Orientation of Interpretive Activities

text we focus on (Knutson, 1997). As noted earlier, interpretive communicative activities in the target language involve not only written but also audio and visual texts. The following section reviews current research on the knowledge and skills needed to engage in different interpretive activities.

ROLE OF BACKGROUND KNOWLEDGE, GENRE FAMILIARITY, AND PAST READING EXPERIENCES

Findings from research on reading in another language reveal that **prior topic knowledge** and **genre familiarity** significantly impact comprehension (e.g., Bernhardt, 1991; Carrell & Eisterhold, 1983; Hammadou, 1991). This knowledge and familiarity comprise in part readers' schemata, or frames for interpretation, which they bring to bear on any particular text when reading a written passage. The more substantive readers' schemata are in terms of topic knowledge, rhetorical structures, and other organizational forms, the more readers can make sense of and recall the meaning embedded in the written symbols of the text. In addition, the more able they are to connect the meaning to and transform what they already know (Carrell, Devine, & Eskey, 1988).

It has also been shown that knowledge of the topic and familiarity with text organization can help readers make sense of written texts even if their general language proficiency in the target language is low (Chen & Donin, 1997). This means, for example, that knowledge of rhetorical structure and plot development developed through extended readings of mystery novels can help readers make sense of a mystery novel they are reading for the first time. Using their schemata, they are able to anticipate what is likely to happen next and to guess the meanings of unfamiliar words, phrases, and syntactic structures. Likewise, the more knowledge they have about a topic, the greater their ability to understand and glean information from a lecture or a book on this topic.

Also significant to learning to read in the target language are learners' **past experiences** with reading in their first language. For example, if they are experienced first language readers and typically find their experiences pleasurable, they are likely to bring their investment in and enthusiasm for reading to their experiences in the target language. Equally important is the role that reading occupies in learners' personal lives (Heath, 1983; Tharp & Gallimore, 1988).

FIRST AND SECOND LANGUAGE SKILLS

In addition to topical and rhetorical knowledge and prior experiences with reading, the skills and strategies used to decode and comprehend text developed in the first language have been shown to influence the development of reading skills in the target language (Aebersold & Field, 1997). Thus, if learners are highly skilled English readers, they are likely to develop into skilled foreign language readers. Conversely, if they are poor readers in English, they will likely be poor target language readers (Alderson, 1984; Jiménez, García, & Pearson, 1995). If, however, learners are skilled readers in English but struggle in the foreign language, the difference may be due to a variety of factors. These include the degree to which the two languages are similar, to readers' level of general language proficiency in the target language, or to a combination of both conditions (Alderson, 1984; Fitzgerald, 1995; Jiménez, García, & Pearson, 1995; Miramontes, Nadeau, & Commins, 1997).

In terms of language similarities, it has been shown that the more similar the writing systems of the two languages are, the greater the degree of transfer of reading skills. Thus, the time and effort involved in learning to read in the target language is reduced. Durgunoglu, Nagy, and Hancin-Bhatt (1993), for example, found that children's phonological awareness and word recognition skills in Spanish, their first language, predicted their word recognition abilities in English, their second language. In another study, Calero-Breckheimer and Goetz (1993) found that Spanish-English bilingual readers used the same strategies to read regardless of language, suggesting that these learners had transferred the strategies from one language to the other.

Conversely, the greater the degree of difference between the two systems, the more difficult it is to transfer reading skills developed in the first language to developing skills in the target language. It has been shown, for example, that because of the significantly different orthographies between their first language and English, Japanese learners of English have difficulty transferring the skills they use to read Japanese to reading in English (Koda, 1988, 1989; Sasaki & Hirose, 1996).

In terms of general language proficiency, it has been shown that proficiency in particular oral language activities in the target language is connected to the development of target language literacy skills. More to the point, it has been shown that successful performance in target language activities typically associated with academic language use, such as providing formal definitions and providing explanations, is related to the development of both reading and writing skills in the target language (Snow, 1994; Snow et al., 1991). This suggests, then, that the more proficient students are in performing certain literacy-based oral activities in the target language, the less difficulty they may experience in learning to read in the target language, regardless of the differences in written systems. In turn, the more fluent one becomes in reading in the target language, the more the reader is able to use both bottom-up and top-down skills to construct meaning (Grabe, 1991; Stanovich, 1980).

LISTENABILITY

Much of the research on the interpretive communication mode has focused on the skills needed to interpret written texts. However, there is some recent research that deals with skills needed to comprehend aural texts (Rubin, 1993). According to Rubin (1993; Rubin et al., 2000), reading and listening are similar in that several factors are involved in effective interpretation of both kinds of texts. These factors include memory capacity, cognitive complexity of the text, and learners' prior conceptual and organizational knowledge. In terms of memory capacity, both reading and listening involve similar sensory, attentional, decoding, comprehending, and inferential activity. Involvement in these various activities eventually leads to long-term information storage.

Where reading and listening differ is in terms of specific textual features that place constraints on short-term memory. When reading written texts, readers can more easily control the pace of information flow, rereading when necessary to help process language and content. Thus, the potential for remembering what was read is great. When listening to certain "live" texts such as lectures or televised programs, however, the potential for controlling the processing of language and content is limited, at best. Thus, the potential for remembering information is limited as well.

To capture the degree to which features of "live" aural texts affect listeners' ability to interpret and remember effectively, Rubin (1993) proposed the notion of **listenability.** According to Rubin, several features characterize a highly listenable text. First, it contains less rather than more complex syntactic constructions. Second, lexical density and diversity are relatively low. That is, there are not a lot of different words used, and those that are are not overly complex. Third, the text is arranged so that the information is clearly introduced and logically arranged. These features make it easy to infer the organizational and conceptual structure of the text and thereby help activate the listener's presumed background knowledge.

Moreover, discourse markers are used in such a way that meaning relations between phrases or thought groups are clear. For example, conjunctions are used regularly to signal relationships such as cause and effect (e.g., *because, due to, consequently*), extension (e.g., *and, in addition to*), and time sequence (e.g., *before, after, then*). Finally, prosody is used to point to or highlight crucial junctures in the aural text. For example, more vocal stress is put on words and phrases that are important. The higher the degree of a text's listenability, the more listeners are apt to comprehend and remember.

VISUAL LITERACY

In addition to reading and listening, **visual literacy** is important to full development of the knowledge and skills needed to engage in interpretive communicative activities. Visual literacy is defined as the ability to discriminate and interpret visual objects, images, and symbols in addition to the written word. Studies examining learners' ability to interpret texts that include visual as well as auditory cues, such as video programs, have shown the process to be similar to learners' comprehension of written texts. That is, learners' knowledge of the topic, familiarity with the particular genre of film or show, and their general proficiency in the target language influence their ability to interpret visual texts (Herron, Cole, Corrie, & Dubreil, 1999). Also shown to play a role is learners' knowledge of nonverbal and other extralinguistic features (Swaffar & Vlatten, 1997).

In summary, engagement in interpretive communicative activities accomplished in the target language is a complex process. We draw on factors such as our past experiences with interpretive activities, and our knowledge of the subject matter and the target language, to give shape to and derive meaning from aural and written texts in the target language. Our attitudes toward the activities and our motivation for participating in them also help shape our involvement. The understandings and knowledge we derive from our experiences, in turn, transform our past experiences, knowledge, and skills and help create new frames for textual interpretations.

GUIDELINES FOR DESIGNING INSTRUCTION AROUND INTERPRETIVE COMMUNICATIVE ACTIVITIES

The overall goal of instruction designed for the interpretive communication mode is to help students engage with aural, written, and visual texts in order to contemplate not only the ideas contained in the texts but also the language that is used to convey that meaning. At the same time, it helps learners understand themselves and each other as active explorers or interpreters of their own cultures and those of the target language groups (Purves, Rogers, & Soter, 1995). This section presents a set of guidelines for designing classroom instruction around interpretive communicative activities.

Choosing Communicative Activities

In designing instruction around the interpretive communication mode, the first step is to decide on those **communicative activities** for which students will be expected to develop competence. Together with the chosen interpersonal communicative activities, these activities will form the core of the foreign language curriculum. Figure 7–2 lists some typical interpretive communicative activities in which middle and high school students might be expected to engage. The activities are grouped according to two dimensions: the primary purpose for engaging in the activity, and the community to which the activities most appropriately belong.

Quadrant I contains efferent activities that are typically associated with the real world, which exists in the target language community outside of the classroom. Quadrant II is comprised of efferent activities that are more typical of the classroom community. Included across the two quadrants are activities that are typical of both communities. As noted earlier, the focus in efferent activities is on the new meanings and information that can be taken from the text and used by the learners to enhance their knowledge and understanding of key concepts and ideas, as well as their participation in other tasks and activities.

Quadrants III and IV include aesthetic activities. In such activities students enjoy texts for the personal meanings, understandings, and satisfaction they can derive from them. Quadrant III contains aesthetic activities that learners are likely to engage in with members of target language communities outside of the classroom. Quadrant IV contains aesthetic activities that learners are likely to engage in with their own classroom communities.

As seen in Figure 7–2, many aesthetic activities are typical to both communities and thus they overlap the two quadrants. Moreover, many of them are fairly generic. For example, the competence needed to engage in the activity of reading a piece of literature can vary, sometimes widely, depending on the topic and genre or text type. Likewise, the competence needed to understand a television program can differ depending on whether the program is a game show, a variety show, a documentary, or weekly drama series. Figure 7–3 contains an abridged list of written text genres and Figure 7–4 contains an abridged list of visual and auditory text genres that would be appropriate for framing interpretive communicative activities geared to middle and high school students.

One criterion to consider using when selecting texts for interpretive communicative activities is their relevance to the students' lives. Choosing written, visual, and aural texts that

Target Language Community Activities | Classroom Community Activities

I	II
Reading maps, graphs, road signs, billboards Reading timetables Reading menus Reading bus/train/subway/plane routes and 　schedules Understanding public announcements Cooking/baking/preparing a food dish from 　a recipe Using phone books Listening to recorded phone messages for 　movie times, guided tour times, etc.	Listening to a lecture and taking notes Reading an article and summarizing it Locating resources on a topic Keeping a reading journal Reviewing a movie, book, article, art work, or 　craft Designing a flowchart of significant historical 　events Using dictionaries and thesauruses

Reading a newspaper
Navigating Web sites
Following instructions to complete a task
Watching a news report

EFFERENT | *EFFERENT*

III	IV
Listening to recorded personal phone messages Watching a television show Listening to a radio program	

Reading a piece of literature
Reading a popular magazine
Reading comic books
Perusing catalogues
Watching a movie, film, or a live performance
Listening to music

AESTHETIC | *AESTHETIC*

FIGURE 7–2　Interpretive Communicative Activities

connect to students' interests is likely to stimulate their motivation to learn the knowledge and skills needed to interpret them appropriately. Thus, asking students about their preferences and interests prior to choosing texts would be of great help to the selection process (Aebersold & Field, 1997). The topics and themes contained in Figure 6–2, and the lists of text types found in Figures 7–3 and 7–4, can be useful starting places in helping students identify areas of interest. As with interpersonal communicative activities, competent participation in a variety of interpretive communicative activities from all four quadrants is necessary for full bilingual development.

FIGURE 7–3 Abridged List of
Text Genres

Autobiographies
Biographies
Children's Books
Comics
Ethnographies
Expository Texts
Fables
Fairy Tales
Folklore
Folktales
Legends
Literature
Magazines
     Computer
     Entertainment
     Home
     Sports
     Travel
Narratives
Newspapers
Plays
Poems
Science Fiction
Scripts
Short Stories
Teenage Novels

FIGURE 7–4 Abridged List of
Auditory and Visual Text Genres

Academic Lectures
Comedy Series
Documentaries
Game Shows
News Reports
Operas
Television Drama
Variety Shows

Technological Media and Resources for Engaging in Interpretive Communicative Activities

Electronic media like television, videotapes and audiotapes, and films have long been used to bring a variety of visual and audio texts into the foreign language classroom. While these forms have certainly facilitated foreign language learning, they have allowed for little interaction between learners and the media themselves. Fortunately, this is changing. The current trend in electronic media is moving toward the use of more interactive media.

The World Wide Web (WWW), an electronic network included in the larger Internet network, is one such medium. The WWW is constructed as a *hypertext*. A hypertext is a document containing links to several other texts. In addition to written text, the links can connect graphics, video clips, photographs, and other images. Unlike the more traditional forms of media, which are inherently linear, hypertext allows students to explore visual, written, and audio texts freely in nonlinear directions, and based on their own interests, to move between written, video, and audio materials as they do. Moreover, it allows for the flexible ordering or associations of semantically and logically related concepts and ideas. In so doing, hypertext challenges students to find or create new relationships among different texts and text elements. The process of creating or weaving together different kinds of texts and text elements helps learners make personalized connections among concepts, ideas and their prior knowledge and experiences.

Using the WWW students can read about current events from a foreign news service or from newspapers that are local to target language communities. They can take a virtual tour of famous art museums such as the Prado in Madrid or gather information about a place from encyclopedias, travelers' guides, and other electronic texts.

Warschauer (2000) has suggested a list of skills that students need for using the Web to do research. First, he states, students need to know how to choose tools such as search engines, online dictionaries and encyclopedias, listservs, and bulletin boards to help them locate information. Next, they need to know how to find information by using browsers and appropriate search keywords, and navigating and searching particular sites. Third, they need to know how to archive information including how to save Web pages, how to cut and paste, and how to save HTML files. A fourth skill involves knowing how to interpret the information. This includes knowing who created the site, when it was created and when it was last updated, and evaluating the credibility of the information. Finally, they need to know how to use and cite online sources appropriately.

As Bangert-Drowns and Swan (1997) have noted, these days most teachers and students get the majority of their news, information, and entertainment through electronic sources. Thus, if one of our goals in foreign language learning is for our learners to develop a full range of interpretive communicative knowledge, abilities, and skills in the target language, they must become active and creative users of electronic technology in the foreign language classroom.

Identifying the Communicative Components

Once it has been decided which activities will form the curricular base for the interpretive communicative mode, the next step is to identify the basic components and features of each communicative activity that students need to learn in order to successfully engage in that activity. As noted in the discussion on the interpersonal communication mode in Chapter 6, a useful frame for analyzing communicative components of interpretive activities is the Celce-Murcia et al. (1995) model of communicative competence. The purpose of identifying the components of interpretive communicative activities is to make explicit the content of the communicative plans that more experienced participants use to guide their own participation in the activities. The components of these plans will form the core of the learning objectives to which instructional activities are oriented.

Some of the skills and knowledge needed, for example, to read a narrative essay might include the following:

> **Discourse:** The linguistic resources needed to create cohesion and coherence including the use of conjunctions to signal temporal relations between clauses, or thought groups, and the use of lexical relations such as hyponyms and synonyms to create semantic ties across the narrative.
> **Linguistic:** Vocabulary relevant to the narrative; knowledge of present and past verb tenses; knowledge of how direct and indirect quotations are structured.
> **Rhetorical:** Knowledge of how speech acts including informing, explaining, and describing, and acts typically used to open and close narratives, are conventionally formed.
> **Sociocultural:** Knowledge of the audience and the larger social context in which the narrative is embedded so that the reader can interpret the significance of the event being narrated.
> **Strategic:** Inferencing skills needed to judge, conclude, or reason from information given in the narrative. Monitoring skills for determining whether the narrative makes sense. Comprehension skills for knowing when to reread, read ahead, look up words in the dictionary, generate questions, or ask someone for assistance.

Creating Instructional Activities

Once the knowledge, skills, and abilities for competent engagement in the selected communicative activities have been identified, the next step is to create a set of instructional plans. An integral part of planning involves constructing appropriate **instructional activities** that will lead students to appropriate the various knowledge, skills, and abilities they need to be successful participants in the chosen communicative activities.

As pointed out in Chapter 6, instructional activities differ from communicative activities in that the former are the activities that are used in class to develop the communicative knowledge, skills, and abilities learners need to be able to engage competently in the latter. Effective pedagogy, then, involves designing instructional activities whose outcomes will lead students to develop the competence they need for engaging in those interpretive communicative activities chosen to form the curricular content of their language classrooms.

Connecting Instructional Activities to Learning Opportunities

Central to designing any kind of instructional activity for the interpretive communication mode is creating a motivating atmosphere in the classroom that values texts, not only written texts but visual and aural texts as well (Tunnell & Jacobs, 2000). This can be done in a number of ways. First, according to Tunnell and Jacobs the emotional climate should be "safe but exciting" (p. 234). This means that students' reactions to texts must be appreciated and not belittled. It is quite likely that their interests and tastes will differ from the teacher's. The point is not to make them like what the teacher likes but rather to help them make "personal connections and new discoveries" (ibid). Allowing them to make choices about what to read, listen to, or watch and to voice their opinions helps create such a climate. Making a variety of written, visual, and aural texts available in the classroom, either in a special center or displayed around the room, also helps to create a motivating atmosphere. Finally, communicating the teacher's own excitement about engaging with texts by reading, listening to music, or watching programs in the target language and *by sharing experiences, opinions, and feelings with the students* is a powerful influence on the students' developing enthusiasm and motivation.

For learners' development of the communicative competence needed to be full participants in their interpretive communicative activities, instruction must include all four types of learning opportunities: situated practice, overt instruction, critical framing, and transformed practice.

Situated Practice. The purpose of situated practice instructional activities is to provide opportunities for students to be immersed fully in the communicative activity. Through their involvement, learners are encouraged to act as readers or interpreters of the target language and are treated as such. Spending time fully immersed with texts, both written and visual, has been shown to significantly benefit learners' communicative development (Fielding & Pearson, 1994; Weyers, 1999).

Provided here are descriptions of two examples of situated practice instructional activities. Examples of others can be found in Table 7–1.

Shared Readings. One situated practice instructional activity for the interpretive communication mode shown to be beneficial to learners' development in the target language is what is commonly referred to as *shared reading* or *book flooding* programs. Findings from various studies reveal that such programs lead to real gains in learners' interpretive skills including vocabulary comprehension and attitudes toward book reading (e.g., Anderson & Roit, 1996; Cho & Krashen, 1994; Elley, 1991; Elley & Mangubhai, 1983; Krashen, 1995; Romney, Romney, & Braun, 1988).

In shared reading or book flooding programs, the teacher immerses students in book reading by reading stories aloud to them. The role of the teacher as he or she is reading is to actively engage the students in the story by asking them questions and making connections for them that extend beyond the text. In addition, the teacher encourages students to react to the reading by commenting on the story, sharing their own meanings, listening to those of others, and asking for clarification when needed.

In response to the students, the teacher expands upon their ideas and comments, clarifying their contributions, explaining the meaning of a word or structure, and drawing attention to the highlights of the story and its illustrations. By these actions, the teacher helps focus students' attention on relevant cues available in the text. At the same time, the teacher models the use of effective reading strategies. Through such actions the students are made active participants in, rather than passive listeners to, the reading of the stories.

TABLE 7–1 *Instructional and Assessment Activities for Interpretive Communicative Activities.*

Learning Opportunities	Activities
Situated Practice	Dictation
	Games
	Listening to music and oral performances
	Literature circles
	Notetaking
	Reading aloud
	Retellings (with words, pictures, maps, diagrams, etc.)
	Shared readings
	Watching televised programs, films, and videos
Overt Instruction	Arranging/sequencing of text elements
	Character maps
	Cloze tests
	Comprehension questions
	Dictionary and thesaurus work
	Flowcharts
	Essay diagramming
	Information gap activity
	Information maps
	Language logs
	Outlining
	Pattern analysis and practice (e.g., grammar, discourse markers, rhetorical structures and functions)
	Semantic webs
	Story puzzles
	Strategy checklists
	Venn diagrams
	Word lists
Critical Framing	Film/text analysis
	Genre comparison
	Interviews with native speakers
	Reader response journal
	Self-assessment of skills, strategy use, and attitudes
	Survey of attitudes
Transformed Practice	Buddy reading
	Listening to music
	Literature circles
	Log keeping on voluntary activities
	Notetaking
	Outlining
	Reader's theatre
	Reading aloud
	Response journals
	Teaching others

In addition to active teacher and student interaction around the text, another essential component of a shared book reading program is the use of texts that are well illustrated, engaging, and provide good background information. The texts themselves can be either fiction or nonfiction. A final component is that "the topic be something the student is genuinely interested in, that he would read in his first language" (Krashen, 1982, p. 164).

Because learners themselves do not have to know how to read in the target language to benefit from a shared reading program, such an activity can be implemented at the earliest stages of language learning in both middle and high school. Moreover, the activity does not need a teacher to lead the students through the readings to be successful. Learning centers can be designed where, with the use of audiorecordings of the books, groups of students can engage in peer-shared readings with little assistance from the teacher.

Ideally, shared reading should be a regular instructional activity. Moreover, as mentioned earlier, students should have a hand in deciding on the books to be used. Teachers may want to display a suggestion box or folder containing a list of reading possibilities from which students can choose.

Literature Circles.   In this situated practice activity the focus is on having students come together for the purpose of sharing their views on books. Called *literature circles* (Peralta-Nash & Dutch, 2000; Tunnell & Jacobs, 2000), they are similar to adult community book clubs in that groups of students read the same book and meet on a regular basis to discuss what they read. In these groups, students are in charge of their own reading and of leading their own discussions.

To facilitate student-generated discussion, students can be assigned different roles. One important role is the *discussion leader.* This person develops lists of discussion questions for the group and helps to keep the discussion going. Another important role is the *word finder,* who looks up new or unfamiliar words to share with the group. A third role is the *connector.* The task of this person is to help the other group members make connections to their lives or other books they have read. Ideally, these roles should rotate among the group members so that every student has the opportunity to play them.

As in other situated practice activities, the teacher's role in literature circles is to model for the students the kinds of language they need to express their opinions, to ask for others' views, and to keep the discussion on topic. Initially, especially at the early levels of language learning, the discussions are likely to be limited. Through scaffolded interactions with the teacher and each other, the students' skills in the target language will develop and as they do, their ability to sustain topically related discussions will develop as well. As noted in Chapter 6, in situated practice instructional activities, learners are likely to rely on English when first engaging in them. However, with the encouragement and directed help of their teacher, they should strive to use the target language in these activities to the fullest extent possible.

Overt Instruction.   The purpose of overt instruction is to engage learners in the systematic analysis of both the formal and functional components of texts so that they can develop expertise in using them to construct meaning from texts. This includes, for example, helping learners establish a clear purpose for engaging in a particular interpretive communicative activity, and activating and building the topical and rhetorical background knowledge they need to comprehend the text. It also includes identifying key words and phrases that contain main ideas and help build cohesion and coherence within the text. Likewise, it entails using a variety of strategies to construct meaning including previewing the text to build expectations. Finally, it involves building student knowledge of key lexical, grammatical, and discourse words and structures used to construct meaning.

As noted in earlier chapters, a great deal of instruction in foreign language classrooms has traditionally been organized around overt instruction activities in which learners are asked to identify and practice the accurate formation of particular grammatical and lexical items. The exercises found in most foreign language textbooks are examples of such activities.

Generally, the central concern of these activities has been with aspects of linguistic competence. Far less attention has been paid to other components of communicative competence. Thus, while typical textbook activities are useful for developing grammar skills and vocabulary knowledge needed for engaging in interpretive communicative activities, it is important to remember to include overt instruction activities in which students are led to consider components in addition to these.

In the domain of rhetorical competence, for example, students can be asked to identify the functions of particular sentences found in an expository text. They can be asked to determine if the sentence's purpose is to describe a situation, compare two events, explain a set of procedures, and so on. They can then be asked to locate the structure or structures that mark the sentence as one type or another.

In terms of discourse competence, they can be asked to identify discourse features of a narrative text that help build emotional reactions to the story, contribute to its persuasiveness, or mark it for a particular audience. In addition, they can be asked to identify particular words and phrases, such as prepositions of location or conjunctions, that signal logical connections between text segments and help establish topic and theme. Story puzzles in which students are asked to arrange parts of a text in logical order and explain the cues they used to help them put the pieces together is one particularly useful overt instruction activity for teaching discourse and rhetorical competence.

Table 7–1 includes a list of overt instruction activities that can be used to help students become proficient users of the different communicative components of interpretive communicative activities. Descriptions of two overt instruction activities appear in the following sections.

Semantic Webbing Activity.   One particularly useful overt instruction activity for building vocabulary and content knowledge is the *semantic webbing activity* (Anderson & Roit, 1996). In semantic webbing, students graphically organize vocabulary from their texts into related groups of words. This is done by first having students select words from the text that are central to the topic or the story. This can be done with or without the help of the teacher.

Using these words as a base, the teacher then leads the class in a discussion on the words in which meanings and uses of the words are identified and ideas are clarified. Of course, the discussion can be supplemented with dictionaries, thesauruses, and other tools considered helpful to the building of word meaning. Next, the students are asked to construct a map or web that groups the selected words and phrases according to a classification scheme. If they are reading a story, for example, they can be asked to group the words and phrases by character, choosing those that best describe each of the characters appearing in the story. Alternatively, they can focus on one character, and arrange the words and phrases according to the character's strengths and weaknesses.

Students can be invited to generate as many words as possible in addition to those found in the text. They can also revisit their webs as they read or reread the text, adding to or modifying them as needed. These webs are useful resources for students because they help students identify key topical elements, summarize information, develop conclusions, and expand on the ideas contained in the text. They also help students better understand the text by activating their background knowledge, helping them organize new concepts, and connecting them to what they already know.

Information Maps. A useful activity for helping students become aware of the different parts of a text is creating *information maps*. Creating information maps requires students to first read a text or listen to or watch a program for specific information and then sketch, diagram, or in some way illustrate the main events of the story. If the text is about history, students can be asked to create a time line of main events. If the text is a narrative, students can be asked to draw pictures that illustrate the story. If it is a description of a place, students can be asked to draw a map or blueprint according to the specifications given in the text. They can also be given maps and asked to locate specific points based on directions contained in an aural or written text.

At the beginning stages, students can be provided with partially completed maps. For example, for a text describing how something works, students can be given a drawing that illustrates only part of the process. They can then be asked to read or listen to the text to complete the rest of the drawing. As their interpretive skills improve they can be asked to provide more of the information themselves.

As in any overt instruction activity, the teacher's role is to provide guided assistance and direct instruction to students as they examine, reflect upon, and practice the formation of the various components needed for successful engagement with the texts.

Critical Framing. The purpose of critical framing instructional activities is to help students develop a critical, informed understanding of how different readers' transactions with texts can lead to multiple perspectives and interpretations of the same texts. Such learning requires having learners stand back from the object of inquiry and reflect on their own particular historical, social, and cultural positionings. In doing so, they are led to see how their personal readings and interpretations are shaped by the larger contexts to which their interpretive activities are tied. The role of the teacher is to help the students compare and contrast the different cultural contexts and purposes behind the activities, to raise questions they may not have thought to ask, and to help them construct alternative interpretations. Table 7–1 contains a list of some critical framing instructional activities that can be used with middle and high school students. Two examples are presented as follows.

Predicting. The activity of *predicting* asks students to predict or anticipate events of a text by drawing on textual and other available cues and their own background knowledge and experiences. Because it requires a sense of expanded context it can help students make connections between specific events and their cultural meanings (Anderson & Roit, 1996).

The activity involves presenting the students with a set of clues about a particular text they are to read, listen to, or watch, such as the text title and illustrations, and then asking them to speculate or guess what the text is about. Asking students to provide reasons for their predictions can help them make their own cultural leanings explicit and available for analysis and critique. If their predictions are written down, they can be revisited several times while reading, viewing, or listening to the text. In addition to asking students for their predictions, they can be asked to analyze and critique the illustrations. What, for example, do they feel the illustrations represent? How well do they feel the illustrations capture the essential parts of the text? What are some of the social and cultural assumptions embedded in the illustrations?

Some texts, like fairy tales, if found in both languages, can be used for a comparative analysis of illustrations. Students can be asked to find similarities and differences across the illustrations and to compare their findings with those of their classmates and other groups of students.

Text Analysis.   The purpose of *text analysis* is to have students examine the cultural perspectives found in a particular genre of texts. The texts can be written, visual, or auditory. The lists contained in Figures 7–3 and 7–4 can help in selecting a particular genre for examination. Once a particular genre and set of representative texts have been chosen, the students need to construct an analytic framework that addresses their particular concerns, and which they will use to record their findings.

If they have chosen children's literature, for example, they may decide to examine the pictures or illustrations of individual books, looking for patterns of representation. They may note, for example, who is represented in terms of social groups and gender. They may also examine the topics of the stories noting what kinds of stories are told, and whether the roles the different characters play vary by gender, age, or social group.

If they have chosen advertisements, they may decide to examine the ads in terms of intended audience, main message, and language patterns used to persuade the reader. As a final example, if they have chosen television news broadcasts in the target language, they may wish to examine patterns of language use. They may look at, for example, the use of titles such as Mr., Mrs., Doctor, or the use of first and last names when newscasters are both talking to and talking about people. They can note whether the use of titles varies by gender, status, or age of the person being referred to.

The findings from these analyses can serve as a springboard for discussions on the varied ways that language use is tied to its contexts of use. They can also serve as a comparative base for other analyses, either across genres, or, staying with the same genre, across English and the target language.

As noted in earlier chapters, students' use of both English and the target language will vary in overt instruction and critical framing instructional activities. When they are first engaged in unfamiliar activities, or asked to do something for which they do not have the language, they are likely to rely more heavily on English to organize and coordinate their thoughts and actions. As they become more experienced in both kinds of activities, and with the teacher's directed assistance, their use of the target language for talking about learning (for overt instruction) and engaging in critical analyses (for critical framing) will increase.

Transformed Practice.   Transformed practice is the final learning opportunity. The goal of this type of instructional activity is to provide students with the chance to use their developing skills and knowledge for their own purposes. By the time students arrive at this point, they should have a fairly well-developed understanding of themselves and the target language. In addition, they are aware of their myriad of identities as language users in relation to the target language and its varied contexts of use, developed from their participation in situated practice, overt instruction, and critical framing learning opportunities.

In transformed practice instructional activities, students bring their new knowledge, experiences, and insights to inform their participation in unfamiliar or new contexts. They can also create new voices or in other ways transform those communicative environments with which they are already deeply familiar.

Transformed practice instructional activities for the interpretive mode, then, involve students in designing their own spaces for interpreting texts and generating their own responses and interpretations. They can also involve learners in rewriting parts of stories, songs, or other kinds of texts and retelling them from the viewpoints of different characters, which perhaps the learners create themselves. Learners may also create their own text-based clubs, meeting to discuss their opinions of music, performances, or other texts from target-language-speaking communities that the learners have discovered from their own explorations. A list of additional transformed practice activities can be found in Table 7–1. More detailed descriptions of two activities are provided in the following sections.

Sustained Silent Reading. *Sustained Silent Reading (SSR),* or free reading, is time provided for both students and teachers to read, listen to, or watch texts that they have chosen based on their own interests (Cho & Krashen, 1994; Krashen, 1995). SSR provides opportunities for learners to apply their interpretive skills and knowledge in the exploration of new or unfamiliar texts in ways that are personally meaningful to them.

The role of the teacher is to provide students access to a wide variety of materials that represent a range of genres and student interests and can meet a range of independent reading abilities (Rothlein & Meinbach, 1991). It is also to engage in the activity as an equal participant, by reading a book, listening to some music, or otherwise engaging with a text at the same time that students do. This demonstrates to the students that such activity is as valuable and meaningful as other more traditional instructional activities.

Based on a review of successful SSR programs, Tunnell and Jacobs (2000) make two additional suggestions for creating a successful SSR activity. First, they note that students must always be allowed to choose their own texts. If someone begins a book and decides he or she is not interested in it, the student should not be required to finish it. Second, while students may choose books for which they have an assigned activity, the teacher must not make any assignments based on the texts or the time spent engaged with the text, such as requiring students to log their activity or write a report. As Tunnell and Jacobs note, providing the opportunity for students to reengage with a favorite text or to engage with new texts in ways that are personally meaningful to them is one of the best ways to give them practice in applying their developing interpretive knowledge, skills, and abilities.

Reader's Theatre. *Reader's Theatre* is an oral reading activity in which students take on the roles of characters in their favorite books and stories. Readers stand or sit in a semicircle, and, using scripts they have developed, read aloud their parts. Because the focus is on reading rather than acting, physical movement is minimal. Instead, action is conveyed through each reader's speech.

Reader's Theatre gives learners the chance to use their comprehension and interpretation skills to express their understanding of the author's purpose, the characters' personalities, and the events of the story. *Reader's Theatre* can also be used with expository texts. In this case, it gives learners the opportunity to bring the information to life, so to speak, highlighting what they consider the significant aspects of the text through the use of intonation and other prosodic uses such as word stress, pausing, and pitch.

Creating scripts for the theatre involves converting passages from the text into dialogue, indicating speakers, and adding, where needed, a narrator to explain the situation or action. Students can create their own scripts or work in pairs or small groups to create scripts for particular scenes or excerpts from texts.

A successful theatre performance requires attention to at least three conditions. First, students must be given many opportunities to practice. They can take the scripts home or arranged in pairs or small groups, they can practice together in class. Second, readers need to be coached on oral reading. They need to know how they can use their voices to portray different feelings and emotions experienced by the characters or to highlight significant information in expository texts.

Finally, having a small audience for the *Reader's Theatre* can enhance student performance. In addition to the other class members, the audience can include students from other language classes, parents, or other members of the school. The role of the audience is to listen and encourage readers with positive responses to their performances, perhaps asking questions about the information, event, or character being portrayed. Alternatively, audience members can be asked to write down a one- or two-sentence observation to be shared with the readers about something they will take away from the performance.

As with many transformed practice activities, *Reader's Theatre* closely resembles a situated practice activity, in this case, shared reading. The difference is that instead of the teacher leading the book readings, the students lead the activity, performing the stories aloud for the teacher and their peers. As student readers, they are expected to bring their own voices to the activity, presenting the information, taking on characters, and in other ways portraying the events of the text from their personal perspectives. In so doing, the students have the opportunity to take the reading in new directions, making new connections to the stories, and in other ways transforming the nature of the activity itself.

As in other transformed practice activities, the teacher's role is to act as coach and facilitator, providing new experiences where possible and helping students apply and revise what they have learned. On a more general level, the teacher works with the learners in effecting the positive transformation not only of the activity but also, most importantly, of themselves as members of their larger community of learners (Wells, 1999). As noted in Chapter 6, given the nature of situated and transformed practice activities, language use is expected to be primarily in the target language.

Choosing a Particular Participation Structure

The second important component in the design of effective instructional activities for the interpretive mode involves deciding how students will participate in the activity. As noted in earlier chapters, activities can be organized around the individual learner, pairs or small groups of learners, or around the whole group. They can also be organized around learning centers.

Some of the instructional activities may lend themselves to one particular structure. Sustained Silent Reading, for example, is best realized as an individual activity. Other activities can be realized in a variety of structures. *Reader's Theatre,* for example, can involve small groups of learners or, depending on the size of the class, the entire group of learners. How activities are structured for student participation depends in part on their goals, the number of students in the class, and other considerations that the teacher determines to be significant.

DESIGNING ASSESSMENT

Up until now, we have discussed how to develop a foreign language curriculum based on the interpretive mode of the communication goal. More specifically, we have discussed how to articulate curricular objectives, or intended learning outcomes, in terms of selecting particular interpretive activities, and articulating their communicative components. In addition, we have discussed how to design instructional activities to facilitate student learning of the desired outcomes.

In this section, we discuss the last process essential to effective pedagogy for the interpretive mode, **designing assessment.** As noted in earlier chapters, to be considered effective, assessment measures must correspond closely to classroom instruction. Up until recently, most measures of students' reading and other interpretive abilities in middle and high school foreign language classrooms have been limited to traditional tests of comprehension and discrete-point measures of linguistic competence. As noted in Chapter 6, given the traditional focus on the overt instruction of grammar and vocabulary in foreign language classrooms, such measures have had legitimate, although seriously limited, uses.

The recent move in education toward the use of alternative methods of assessment in the classroom, and the more recent creation of content and performance standards for foreign language learning, has made apparent two needs in the area of foreign language assessment. First is the need to improve traditional measures of evaluation to ensure that they measure the learners' full range of communicative competence and that what they measure closely matches the intended learning outcomes of instruction. Second, the recently developed foreign language content and performance standards have made apparent the need to link these major innovations to alternative assessment measures of foreign language learning in addition to the more traditional end-of-unit pen-and-paper tests and quizzes.

Alternative assessment measures for the interpretive mode include procedures and techniques for assessing students' actual knowledge and skills that they develop from their participation in their instructional activities. Such assessment tools can encompass a diversity of performance-based means. Because situated and transformed practice instructional activities are actual or, if the activity is of a target-language-speaking community, simulated performances of different kinds of interpretive communicative activities, assessing student learning entails using means that closely correspond to those very activities.

Such performance-based measures might include reading (or viewing) logs or response journals in which students record or respond to the books they read or the films, programs, or performances they listen to or watch. Figure 7–5 contains an example of a reading log

MY READING LOG

Title of text: _____

Author: _____

Kind of text: _____
            (e.g., book, article, Web page, other _____)

Genre of text: (circle one)

Autobiography	Literature
Biography	Narrative
Comic Book	News
Computers	Play or Drama
Entertainment	Poem
Fable	Science Fiction
Fairy Tale	Short Story
Folktale	Sports
Legend	Travel
Other _____	

I began reading on _____.

I finished reading on _____.

My reactions:

_____

_____

_____

_____

_____

FIGURE 7–5   Example of Student Reading Log

that students can use to record their reading behavior. As part of the assessment of their reading behaviors, students can be asked to log a certain number of readings from a certain number of genres over a specified period of time.

Alternatively, students can work with different kinds of texts in the classroom or library to create a portfolio of books, films, and programs on a topic of interest. In the portfolio, students can be asked to briefly summarize the essence of each text. This can be done through pictures, drawings, or other modes in addition to writing. They can also be asked to write a paragraph explaining their interest in the topic and their reactions to several of the chosen texts.

Circle the word that you feel best describes your involvement in your Literature Circle.

1. I listened to the other group members and commented on their ideas in positive ways.

not at all   rarely   sometimes   often   always

2. I offered my opinions about the book.

not at all   rarely   sometimes   often   always

3. I fulfilled my role as assigned by the teacher.

not at all   rarely   sometimes   often   always

4. I asked questions for clarification or information.

not at all   rarely   sometimes   often   always

5. When I did not understand what was going on, I asked for help.

not at all   rarely   sometimes   often   always

6. Other (write any behaviors and actions not included here that you used that you feel best reflect your involvement in the Literature Circle).

_____

_____

_____

FIGURE 7–6   Student Self-Assessment of Involvement in a Literature Circle

Because beginning learners may not have the language proficiency needed to write full reactions in the target language, they should be allowed to use English when necessary. Remember, the point of this type of assessment is not to evaluate students' writing skills, but to assess their ability to draw meaning from various target language texts.

Assessment measures can also include teacher assessment and self-assessment of students' behaviors in literature circles or shared reading activities, or of students' comprehension of stories, films, programs, or live performances. To assess students' interpretive abilities, they can be asked to retell what happened, either orally or by drawing pictures, creating charts or montages, or reenacting the story, film, program, or performance. Figure 7–6 contains an example of a rubric that can be used by students to assess their involvement in literature circles. Figure 7–7 provides an example of a rubric that can be used to assess students' comprehension of a narrative through their retellings. It can be used to assess oral retellings as well as retellings accomplished with drawings, pictures, or performances.

	NOVICE	INTERMEDIATE	COMPETENT	DISTINGUISHED	EXPERT
Setting	Provides a limited description of the setting.	Provides a basic description of the setting.	Provides an accurate description of the setting, including all essential elements.	Provides an accurate description of the setting, including the essential components and some of the more minor details.	Provides an accurate and fully detailed description—including all major and minor elements—of the setting.
Characters	Provides limited descriptions of some of the major characters.	Provides basic descriptions of most of the major characters.	Provides accurate descriptions of all major characters, including all essential elements.	Provides accurate descriptions of the major characters, and some of the minor characters.	Provides accurate and fully detailed descriptions of both major and minor characters.
Events	Provides limited descriptions of some events that take place in the story.	Provides basic descriptions of events that take place in the story, although they may not be in any logical sequence.	Describes accurately all main events that take place in the story in the order in which they happen.	Describes accurately all main events that take place in the story in the order in which they happen and includes some details about minor events.	Describes fully and accurately all events—major and minor—that take place in the story in the order in which they happen.

FIGURE 7–7 Rubric for Evaluating Student Comprehension of a Story Through a Retelling

To assess learning outcomes from student involvement in overt instruction and critical framing instructional activities, any of the activities listed in Table 7–1 can be used in addition to the more traditional pen-and-paper tests. To assess discourse knowledge and skills for reading a particular text, for example, students can be asked to choose discourse markers that signal logical connections between sentences and clauses such as cause and effect (e.g., in English, words like *because, due to*), chronological order (e.g., *first, next*), and comparison (e.g., *similarly, likewise*). As a final example, to assess vocabulary knowledge, students can be given a list of words taken from the text and asked to create a semantic web using a framework devised by the teacher. In terms of critical framing activities, the rubric for evaluating a written report, contained in Figure 6–6, is one assessment tool that can be used to evaluate students' learning from critical framing activities for the interpretive mode.

As noted in earlier chapters, designing effective assessment is an evolving process. Each time we assess student learning, we gather significant evidence that can tell us whether and how well the tool measures what we want it to measure. It can also help us decide if what we are doing in our instructional activities is leading to our intended outcomes. We need to use this evidence on a regular basis to carefully and systematically make improvements to our instruction and assessment plans and activities. Such habitual, consistent reflection and action is a hallmark of effective foreign language teaching.

SUMMARY

The purpose of this chapter was to lay out a framework for developing curriculum for the interpretive mode, the second of three modes that comprise the communication goal for foreign language learning. It was also to articulate the means for designing effective instructional activities and assessment tools for use in middle and high school foreign language classrooms. The key concepts and ideas relating to these matters are summarized here.

- The interpretive mode consists of communicative activities accomplished through the reading, listening, or viewing of written, audio, and visual texts. There are two general purposes for engaging in interpretive activities. The first, aesthetic, involves reading, listening, or viewing for pleasure. The second purpose, efferent, involves reading, listening, or viewing in order to seek new information or understanding.
- Several factors influence comprehension including prior topic knowledge, genre familiarity, and past reading experiences. Also shown to influence the development of comprehension skills in the target language are the strategies and skills for decoding and comprehending texts that learners have developed in their first language. The influence of this last factor varies, depending in part on how alike the writing systems of the first and target languages are. The more similar they are, the more likely skills from the first will transfer to the second. Conversely, the greater the degree of difference between the two systems, the more difficult it is to transfer reading skills developed in the first language to developing skills in the target language.
- The concept of listenability has been proposed to capture the degree to which features of "live" aural texts affect the listeners' ability to interpret and remember effectively. A listenable text is characterized by several features including less

complex syntactic constructions, low lexical density and diversity, clear arrangement of information, strategic use of discourse markers, and use of prosody for marking crucial junctures in the aural text.

- In addition to reading and listening skills in the target language, engaging in interpretive activities also involves visual literacy skills. These skills encompass the ability to discriminate and interpret visual objects, images, and symbols.

- The advent of new electronic media has helped to create new kinds of texts, such as the electronic network of the World Wide Web. The Web is constructed as a hypertext, or a text that is linked to several other texts in multiple ways. Unlike more traditional forms of texts, which are inherently linear, hypertext allows students to explore visual, written, and audio texts freely in nonlinear directions, basing their movement between written, video, and audio materials on their own interests. "Reading" such a text requires new kinds of literacy skills for the foreign language learner.

- The first step in designing effective instruction involves setting out the curricular goals and objectives. This entails two related activities. The first is a needs analysis that identifies the interpretive communicative activities in which foreign language learners want or need to become communicatively competent. The second entails identifying the specific communicative components of each of the activities. The selected activities and their components will ultimately form the learning objectives of our instructional activities.

- Once the curricular components have been identified, and curricular goals and objectives articulated, the next step is to create an instructional plan for meeting these goals and objectives. An essential part of the plan involves constructing instructional activities organized around the four types of learning opportunities: situated practice, overt instruction, critical framing, and transformed practice. It also includes providing for multiple and varied opportunities for student participation in these activities.

- A final component of effective pedagogy is the construction of multiple means of assessment including both traditional and alternative tools, which directly match the objectives of the instructional activities. To be fully effective these means of evaluation must be continually analyzed and revised to ensure that they are capturing the full range of interpretive communicative skills and abilities that students are developing in the target language.

Discussion Questions and Activities

1. Make a list of the various kinds of interpretive activities you engage in on a regular basis in English. Do the same for those you engage in using your teaching language. How do they compare? What conclusions can you draw about your interpretive skills and abilities in both languages? What implications are there for you as a teacher of another language?

2. Interview a group of novice foreign language teachers and a group of experienced foreign language teachers—drawing them from either middle or high school

language programs—on the role that reading in their teaching language plays in their lives outside of school. Compare their responses. Write a short report in which you describe your findings, share your reactions to the findings, and speculate on the impact their involvement (or lack of involvement) in reading in their teaching language outside of school might have on their teaching of reading skills in that language to middle and high school students.

3. Examine Figure 7–2. Can you add additional communicative activities to any of the four quadrants? Using the list of activities provided, and those you have added, make a list of the interpretive communicative activities you feel should form part of the curriculum for middle and high school students. Provide reasons for your choices.

4. Examine Table 7–1. Can you add additional instructional activities to each of the four learning opportunities? Choose one instructional activity from one of the learning opportunities to gather additional information on. Prepare to present what you have learned about the activity to your classmates. Give examples of how they might use it in their own language classrooms.

5. Divide into small groups by teaching language. Together, choose one interpretive communicative activity from one of the four quadrants and do the following:

- Identify some of the elements of each of the five components of communicative competence to be learned in the target language.
- Create two instructional activities based on two different kinds of learning opportunities (be sure to identify the learning opportunity and participation structure for each).
- Create an assessment measure for evaluating student learning in one of the two instructional activities.

6. Evaluate the rubric found in Figure 7–7 for assessing student comprehension of a narrative. Can you think of other criteria that should be added? If possible, ask a group of middle or high school teachers to try using the rubric to assess their students' comprehension of a narrative and to provide feedback on its usefulness. Using their feedback, how can you improve the rubric?

TEACHER RESEARCH PROJECTS

A. Student Use of Strategies.

The purpose of this project is to help students develop, reflect on, and improve their use of strategies for language learning.

Pose a Problem

We know that making students aware of the strategies they use for learning helps them become active agents in their own learning. The problem this project addresses is how to help students articulate and reflect on the strategies they use to develop their reading abilities in the target language.

Identify Sources and Gather Information

Have students keep a reading journal for a specified period of time, say one marking period. Provide them with a set of reading assignments to be completed at home that can include, for example, newspaper and magazine articles, comic strips, short stories, and information texts in the target language. In the journal, ask them to keep an account of the reading they do and note the strategies they used to complete each assignment using the self-assessment list provided in Figure 7–8 or one that you have constructed.

Analyze

Three or four times over the duration of the project, ask the students to share the strategies they used. Each time, make a list of those strategies the students found most useful. At the end of the time period, compare lists to discover whether there were any changes.

Reflect and Revise

Together with the students, reflect on the development of their strategy use. How helpful was it to keep a checklist of strategies? Were they able to learn new strategies from their peers? Did they find that their reading became easier over time? Why or why not? As a teacher, given what you have learned from this project, how might you revise your own instructional practices?

Disseminate Information

Consider presenting your experiences to the local chapter of your state professional organization for foreign language education. You may want to involve the students in the pres-

---

Self-Assessment of Reading Strategies

For each reading assignment, check those strategies you used to help you in your reading:

1. I looked up unfamiliar words in the dictionary.

2. I asked someone for help.

3. I guessed the meaning of words I did not understand.

4. I used what I know about the topic to try to figure out the meaning.

5. I took notes.

6. I skipped over what I could not understand.

7. Other _____.

FIGURE 7–8   Self-Assessment of Reading Strategies

entation as well, since they can provide a more personal perspective on the benefits of such a project for other students.

B. Observations on a Day in the Life of a Student.

The purpose of this project is to help teachers become more familiar with the schooling experiences of their students so that they can design activities that foster community building in the foreign language classroom.

Pose a Problem

We know that the more familiar we are with our students, the easier it is to create a sense of community and belonging in our classrooms. Unfortunately, we often know little beyond the information that students share with us in our classrooms. This project provides the opportunity to become better acquainted with our students and the lives they have outside of our particular foreign language classrooms. Use questions such as the following to guide your investigation: What is it like to be a student in this school? What are some of the day-to-day tensions and concerns with which they must deal? How do they perceive their role as students?

Identify Sources and Gather Information

If you are a preservice teacher, ask a teacher who is currently teaching for his or her help with this project. If you are currently a teacher, choose a time during the day that you are able to leave your classroom. It can be during recess, lunchtime, or your free period. Decide on the number of free periods you will need to gather information. You may decide to gather data once a week, say, for a period of one month. Alternatively, you may decide to spend one period a day for a full week.

Data can be collected through nonparticipant observations and open-ended interviews with students. In your observations, walk around the school and note the following: who is in the halls during and between classes; the noise level at these times; how the students are dressed; and whether they appear relaxed and happy or angry and tense. Be sure to base these assessments on concrete actions and behaviors. Of course, make any additional observations you feel are relevant.

Ask four or five students for permission to interview them. Make sure that they know your purpose for interviewng them and that the interviews are informal. Ask them questions such as the following:

- What are the students in this school like?
- What do they like/dislike about the school?
- Do they identify with particular groups or cliques of students?
- How do they characterize these groups?
- What tensions or conflicts must they deal with on a daily basis?

Add other questions as they pertain to your interests. After each observation period and interview, summarize your notes.

Analyze

Examine your notes for particular patterns. Based on the patterns you found, how would you describe the student body of your school? How would you describe their perceptions about school? Are there contrasting views?

Reflect and Revise

What conclusions can you draw about the schooling experiences of your students? What have you learned from your experience? How might you integrate your findings into your classroom practices?

Disseminate Information

Share your findings and conclusions with the students in your classes. How valid do they think they are? What suggestions do they have for incorporating the information into the curriculum? Can they suggest ways to enhance a sense of community in the classroom?

ADDITIONAL READINGS

Christensen, B. (1990). Teenage novels of adventure as a source of authentic material. *Foreign Language Annals, 23*(6), 531–537.

Daniels, H. (1994). *Literature circles: Voice and choice in the student-centered classroom.* York, ME: Stenhouse.

Davis, J. H., & Lyman-Hager, M. A. (1997). Computers and L2 reading: Student performance, student attitudes. *Foreign Language Annals, 30,* 58–72.

Krashen, S. (1991). *The power of reading.* Englewood, CO: Libraries Unlimited.

McQuillan, J., & Tse, L. (1998). What's the story? Using the narrative approach in beginning language programs. *TESOL Journal, 7*(4), 18–23.

Samuels, S. J. (1997). The method of repeated readings. *The Reading Teacher, 50,* 376–381.

Thompson, L. (1997). *Foreign language assessment in grades K–8: An annotated bibliography of assessment instruments.* Washington, DC: Center for Applied Linguistics and Delta Systems.

Weir, C. J., & Urquhart, A. H. (1998). *Reading in a second language: Process, product, and practice.* New York: Longman.

INTERNET RESOURCES

http://www.lingnet.org/home.htm　　The Linguist's Network (LINGNET)

This Web site is maintained by the Defense Language Institute. Although it was created to support military linguists, it is also available to the general public. The LINGNET provides authentic materials and links to foreign language Web sites that support at least 86 different languages. The language links lead to a plethora of sources on cultural, geographic, political, and social information about countries where the languages are spoken.

http://wmbr.mit.edu/stations/   The MIT List of Radio Stations on the Internet

This site provides links to 9,000 radio stations around the world including the United States, Canada, and other countries of North America, Africa, Asia, Europe, the Middle East, South America, and Oceania/Australia.

http://babel.uoregon.edu/yamada/news.html   Language-Related News Groups

This site is maintained by the Yamada Language Center at the University of Oregon. It provides a directory of language-related USENET news groups. These groups provide virtual spaces for interested parties to obtain information and exchange messages about various news-related subjects. News list pages are available for a multitude of languages including Chinese, Esperanto, French, German, Italian, Spanish, and Vietnamese, to name just a few.

http://www.searchengineshowdown.com/   Search Engine Showdown: The User's Guide to Web Searching

This comprehensive Web site provides information on everything one needs to know in order to search the World Wide Web. Here teachers and students can learn about the differences among all the search engines, subject directories, and multisearch engines. In addition, suggestions are given for how to search the Web and when to use which tool. Links are provided to other search engine books, articles, and resources.

http://members.aol.com/maestro12/web/wadir.html   Internet Activities for Foreign Language Classes

This site provides information on how to write Web-based activities for the foreign language classroom, the kinds of strategies students need to navigate the Web, and forms for evaluating Web lessons. It also includes a link to the following site.

http://members.aol.com/maestro12/web/toplinks.html   480 Favorite Teacher Web Pages

This site provides links to an incredible variety of information sources on such topics as geography, foods, sports, music, literature, museums, artists, leisure, history, holidays/ celebrations, and weather for three languages: French, Spanish, and German.

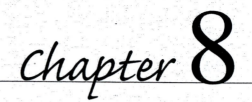

Chapter 8

The Presentational Mode

Preview Questions

Before you begin reading this chapter, spend a few moments reflecting on the kinds of presentational activities you participate in on a daily basis in English and in your teaching language.

- What are the purposes for which you compose?
- Do they vary according to whether you are composing in English or your teaching language?
- How have electronic media and resources such as the computer and Internet access affected the way you compose?
- Do you think your activities as a writer will influence your teaching of writing? If yes, how so? If no, why not?

Key Words and Concepts

Presentational mode
- Transactional purpose
- Expressive purpose
- Cognitive aspects of writing
- Social aspects of writing

Designing instruction
- Target language community activities
- Classroom community activities
- Technological resources
- Analysis of communicative components
- Communicative activities
- Instructional activities
- Learning opportunities
- Participation structures

Designing assessment

Overview

Traditionally, writing in foreign language classrooms has been treated as transcribed speech. The teaching of writing has often taken a transmission approach, which emphasizes writing as a technical skill and focuses on mastery of component skills and structures that are divorced from context or meaning (Haneda & Wells, 2000). In addition, as with oral language development, writing instruction assumed a single standard of language use and correctness. In so doing, it ignored the fact that language varies across situations, writers, and contexts, and that it changes with time.

A sociocultural perspective on writing and development offers a more complex view. According to Vygotsky (1978, 1986) and others (e.g., Barton, 1994; Clay & Cazden, 1990; Haneda & Wells, 2000; John-Steiner, Panofsky, & Smith, 1994; Lee & Smagorinsky, 2000; Scribner & Cole, 1981; Zebroski, 1994), writing is more than speech that is written down. Rather, it is an activity that brings speech to conscious awareness in that in writing one must represent consciously and explicitly features of speech such as emotion and attitude that are produced in speech with little awareness. Nor is writing an independent, decontextualized activity that one learns structural piece by structural piece. Rather, it is inherently linked to its contexts of use and, more generally, to the discourse communities of which the writer is or aspires to be a member. Thus, from this perspective, writing is both an individual, cognitive act as well as a social, conventional act. It is this understanding of writing that underlies the third mode of the communication goal, the presentational mode.

The purpose of this chapter is to present an overview of the presentational communication mode. After first defining the mode and summarizing current research, a framework for designing curriculum, instruction, and assessment is presented. Similar to the discussions of the other two modes, presented in Chapters 6 and 7, the guidelines presented here for designing curricular goals and objectives, and creating instructional activities and assessment tools, draw upon many of the ideas discussed throughout the text.

THE PRESENTATIONAL MODE

The **presentational mode** comprises communicative activities that involve the creation of oral, written, or multimodal texts through which we display what we know, integrate new knowledge with existing knowledge, create new structures of meaning, and explore what we do not know. Our involvement in these activities helps us to make sense of our world and of others and ourselves as participants within it.

There are two general purposes for engaging in presentational activities: *transactional* and *expressive*. In activities with a **transactional** purpose we write or present in order to inform, share knowledge that others will find useful and relevant, solve problems, or explore new topics. We can describe our experiences, physical objects, places, people, or events. We can narrate a story or recount an event. We can demonstrate our understanding of how something works or provide instructions on how to do something. We can explain some phenomenon by providing empirical evidence or logical explanations. Finally, we can attempt to persuade an audience or reader to rethink or recast an idea or understanding, or to consider an alternative (O'Hair, Friedrich, Wienmann, & Wienmann, 1995). Examples of presentational activities with a transactional purpose include giving an oral lecture on a scholarly topic, creating a classroom newsletter, and keeping a daily log of activities.

In presentational activities with an **expressive** purpose we seek to express our opinions and feelings, to make observations and speculative reflections, or to make personal connections with others. Expressive activities are often done for pleasure or entertainment and can include performances of plays, poems, or songs and the creation of personal Web pages, stories, or memory books.

As Britton and his colleagues (Britton, Burgess, Martin, McLeod, & Rosen, 1975) have noted, while these two purposes are different, they are complementary ways of making sense of the world. As with the other communicative modes, the purposes for engaging in presentational activities are not categorical. That is, we can enter into activities for both transactional and expressive purposes. We may choose, for example, to write a narrative in which we both inform the reader of an event and at the same time express our feelings about it. Figure 8–1 illustrates the two-dimensional goal orientation around which presentational activities can be organized.

Although a primary modality for communicating in the presentational mode is writing, representational and expressive forms can also be created through audio and visual texts using a variety of media and a variety of modes like dance, music, and art. However, given that the focus in foreign language learning is on the use of language for meaning-making, the review provided in the next section primarily deals with the act of writing.

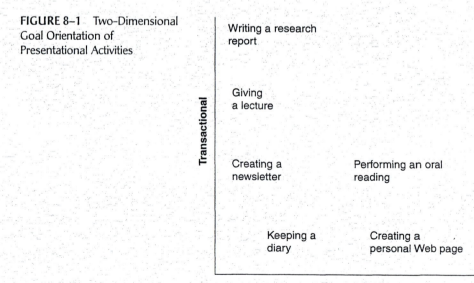

FIGURE 8–1 Two-Dimensional Goal Orientation of Presentational Activities

COGNITIVE ASPECTS OF WRITING

As a psychological tool, writing provides a medium for creating, reflecting on, analyzing, and revising meanings and ideas. Thus, its use promotes the development of deliberate thinking, not only about the topic, but also about the language we use and the mental processes we employ as well (Vygotsky, 1987). In other words, in creating a permanent representation of meaning, writing serves as a base for continued exploration, discussion, and reflection. It is through the process of writing that we come to understand the topic about which we are writing, and the varied ways we can use language to express our ideas.

From this perspective, then, the purpose of writing is not only to display understanding and preserve ideas for later reference. As importantly, writing is a tool for development. Engaging in the process of writing itself facilitates the development of new ideas and experiences and new ways of representing and thinking about these ideas and experiences (Vygotsky, 1987; Wells, 1999).

We learn to write in another language in much the same way that we learn to write in our first, by active involvement in the process of writing. This includes opportunities to write for varied purposes and to varied audiences. Learning to write also involves systematic attention to the specific forms and functions needed in the construction of meaning (Grabe & Kaplan, 1996). As studies on composing have revealed, the process is not linear, but recursive, and involves several interrelated cognitive activities or stages (Flower & Hayes, 1984; Raimes, 1992).

During the **prewriting stage** students, together with the teacher, choose a purpose for writing. It can be to inform others about a particular topic, to compose a song or jingle, or to create a personal Web page. They also choose an audience to whom the final product or presentation will be geared. The audience can be a specific person such as the teacher, another student, or a parent. It can also be a specific group, such as another language class or foreign language club. Students can also write for a more general audience, perhaps orienting their writing to the larger school community or, even more generally, to a "virtual" audience that is part of the World Wide Web.

At this time they also begin generating and organizing their ideas. During this stage the role of the teacher is to help learners connect their purposes for composing to real audiences and to assist them in generating ideas. They do this by helping students brainstorm, talk with experts on a topic, and gather information from reading relevant texts, or from listening to or watching relevant programs.

A second stage of the writing process is **drafting.** During this stage, students begin to craft their product, using writing to help themselves formulate ideas. Initially, the focus is on constructing their ideas, not on forming them accurately and appropriately. The focus of the third stage, **revising,** is on making changes to the writing to improve accuracy and appropriateness. Here, ideas are removed, added, reworked, rearranged, and so on. In addition, students begin to refine the ways their ideas are expressed, revising multiple drafts until the ideas are expressed appropriately and accurately. **Proofreading** is the final stage. This involves checking the mechanics for accurate use of conventions such as spelling, paragraph and sentence structure, punctuation, capitalization, and word choice.

Research investigating the writing strategies of good writers reveals several distinguishing features. No matter what language they choose to write in, good writers plan longer, have more elaborate plans, review on a regular basis, consider the audience when writing, and use cognitive strategies that are specific to the writing task (Durst, 1987; Grabe & Kaplan, 1996).

SOCIAL ASPECTS OF WRITING

While the cognitive aspects of writing are significant, they cannot be divorced from the **social aspects.** All writers write from within a discourse community of readers and writers. Their ideas and ways of expressing the ideas in writing are shaped by these larger social and cultural contexts within which writing occurs. Thus, writing must also be understood as a socially shaped and socially purposeful meaning-making activity (Barton & Hamilton, 1998; Haneda & Wells, 2000; Heath, 1983; Lensmire, 1994; Sperling & Woodlief, 1997).

Research on the literacy activities of different communities has shown that they can vary, in some cases considerably, from community to community. What counts as a valued writing activity and as appropriate conventions for composing, for example, depends not only on the roles writing plays within particular social groups, but also in part on the social identities of the writer and the supposed audience (Rubin, 1995). As these groups differ—and within the groups, as the social identities of the writers and readers differ—so does the value that is placed on literacy activities and the communicative conventions used to engage in them. In other words, what counts as a valued presentational activity and as appropriate choices of words, phrases, and rhetorical structures in realizing that activity will vary according to the sociocultural groups to which the writer and reader belong.

Recent classroom-based research has investigated the links that exist between learners' social contexts and their writing experiences in the classroom (see, for example, Dyson, 2000; Lensmire, 1994; Moll & Dworin, 1996). Findings reveal that learners bring their own varied experiences outside school with them to the classroom. These experiences play a significant role in shaping learners' participation in their classroom writing experiences.

In a study of an elementary-grade writing group, for example, Lensmire (1994) revealed how the children re-created their larger social worlds in their classroom writings. In the stories they wrote, the children described the kinds of social relationships they had established with each other outside the classroom, and used the stories as a way to maintain and, in some cases, subvert these relationships.

As another example, in a study of an elementary classroom community, Dyson (2000) examined the worlds that children created for themselves in their classroom writing experiences. Looking closely at the stories generated in the classroom by two children in particular, Dyson revealed how they appropriated the superhero genre found in popular media to negotiate conflicts and resolutions in their stories. More specifically, she showed how these stories provided a shared context for the two children and their classmates to negotiate their interpersonal relations within the classroom. In this way Dyson brought to light the varied ways in which the complex social and ideological dynamics of the children's lives outside the classroom permeated their writings and relations in school.

It has also been shown that the classroom environment, and more specifically teachers' goals and curricula, the kinds of writing assignments they use, and their beliefs about the role that writing plays in learning, impacts learners' development as writers (Heath, 1993; Sperling & Woodlief, 1997). If the instructional focus, for example, is on accuracy and correctness of surface-level features, then students come to understand and use writing as a basic transcription tool. Conversely, if they are led to use writing as a means for developing and connecting ideas, they develop the requisite skills and abilities for using writing as an activity for both making and discovering meaning.

The kinds of writing that students do in their classrooms, in turn, have been shown to influence the kinds of writers they become outside the classroom. Cazden (1993), for example, revealed how the role of academic writing in the life of one university student was transformed through the student's participation in her classroom writing activities. In discovering what she termed the generative power of language the student found "that through writing one can continually bring new selves into being, each with new responsibilities and difficulties, but also with new possibilities. . . . I write to continually give birth to myself" (pp. 209–210).

A similar transformative role has been claimed for learning to read and write in two languages. In a review of research on biliteracy, Moll (2000) noted that such learning "mediates the intellect not only by providing access to the real world of the community and by offering the expanded possibilities of broader or different experiences of the literate world, but also by creating new worlds that have not existed before" (p. 266).

In an attempt to capture the multiple cognitive and social dimensions of writing, Applebee (in press) has proposed a model that defines writing as a process of participating in social action. In this view, writing is understood as a form of apprenticeship into different contexts. As participants in a particular context, developing writers come to understand what are considered appropriate and accurate uses of language, including structural and rhetorical forms, and strategic processes. They also develop a sense of the underlying issues that make writing in that context interesting and effective. In other words, in developing writing skills, writers develop a repertoire of strategies for composing in particular contexts in addition to a sense of the many different uses that writing can serve. Judging writing development involves evaluating writers' abilities to participate with increasing appropriateness, accuracy, and effectiveness in an ever-expanding range of culturally significant contexts.

This perspective on writing helps us understand the larger, but oftentimes invisible, forces that help shape students' development as writers in foreign language classrooms. These additional forces include the experiences they have with writing both in English and the target language outside the classroom. In addition to what they bring with them to the classroom, our learners' development is shaped by the curricular goals for composing, defined in terms of the presentational activities made available to them, and by the contexts for learning to write that we create for them in our foreign language classroom communities.

GUIDELINES FOR DESIGNING INSTRUCTION AROUND PRESENTATIONAL COMMUNICATIVE ACTIVITIES

Instruction is comprised of "all of the teacher's purposeful activities aimed at producing, stimulating, or facilitating learning by students" (Posner & Rudnitsky, 2001). The primary goal of instruction designed for the presentational mode is to help students, both as individuals and members of social groups, to develop an understanding of the power of language to both convey and create meaning. At the same time, it is to help students learn to use this knowledge to share what they know with others, and, at the same time, to explore new ways of understanding.

Thus, in the instructional environments we create in our classrooms we need to provide multiple opportunities for students to compose oral, written, and visual texts on a variety of topics for a variety of intellectual and practical purposes, and for a variety of audiences. Vygotsky (1978) made this quite clear when he stated that any writing that students engage in "should be meaningful" and "incorporated into a task that is necessary and relevant for life" (p. 118). Also, in creating effective instructional environments, teachers must remember that the knowledge, skills, and abilities required for composing in the target language develop slowly, over time, and require extensive practice. Because the process can sometimes be frustrating and difficult, teachers need to provide enough regular positive feedback to sustain learners' interest and motivation (Grabe & Kaplan, 1996).

Choosing Communicative Activities

The first step in designing instruction around the presentational communication mode is to choose the activities for which students will be expected to develop competence. These activities, along with the selected interpersonal and interpretive communicative activities, comprise the core of the foreign language curriculum. Figure 8–2 lays out some typical presentational communicative activities that can be relevant to middle and high school students. As has been done for the other two communication modes, the activities here are arranged according to the primary purpose for engaging in the activity and the community to which the activities are most appropriately linked.

Quadrants I and II contain *expressive* activities. As stated earlier, in these activities learners compose texts that convey their opinions, feelings, and other kinds of personal meaning through which they and others can come to understand themselves, their own cultures, and those of the target language groups. Quadrant 1 contains expressive activities that are typically associated with communities outside the classroom for whom the target language is the primary code of communication. Quadrant II is comprised of expressive activities realized through the target language that are considered essential to classroom communities of foreign language learners. Located in both quadrants are expressive activities that are typical of both communities.

Quadrants III and IV include *transactional* activities. The purpose of these activities is to convey or share information or knowledge with others, or to explore new ideas and meaning. The transactional activities in Quadrant III are those in which learners are likely to engage with members of target language communities outside the classroom. Quadrant IV contains transactional activities in which learners are likely to engage in their own classroom communities of learners. Similar to activities with an expressive purpose, many transactional activities can be pertinent to both target language and classroom communities and thus they are located in both quadrants.

Many of the activities listed here can involve a wide range of text types. Figure 8–3 contains a short list of different texts typical of presentational communicative activities that are likely to be relevant to middle school and high school students. Competent participation in a wide range of presentational communicative activities using a variety of texts and representing all four quadrants is necessary to full bilingual development.

Target Language Community Activities	Classroom Community Activities
I Writing a eulogy	**II** Creating a bulletin board Creating a comic strip Creating or performing in a play Performing an oral reading Singing/recording/composing a song, jingle, or cheer Creating a poem, short story, or narrative Writing thank-you notes Creating a personal Web page Creating greeting cards Completing crossword puzzle or other word games
EXPRESSIVE	*EXPRESSIVE*
III Writing a resume and cover letter Writing a business letter Keeping a diary Creating a TV or radio commercial	**IV** Writing a composition, essay, or research report Giving an academic lecture Writing an editorial Writing an essay on a current event Keeping a daily journal of activities Creating an information pamphlet or brochure Keeping minutes of a meeting Writing instructions on how to do something Making a formal presentation Conducting a clinic, workshop, or demonstration on how to do something
TRANSACTIONAL	*TRANSACTIONAL*

FIGURE 8–2   Presentational Communicative Activities

Technological Media and Resources for Engaging in Presentational Communicative Activities

Although not as widely accessible as pen and paper, audio and video recording equipment has often been used by students in foreign language classrooms to compose multimedia presentations in the target language. In addition to these more traditional forms of electronic media, the recent inclusion of the Internet, and more specifically the World Wide Web, as classroom instructional resources has expanded the possibilities for composing.

The WWW has been called a revolutionary medium (Bicknell, 1999) in that it allows for the use of not just written text, but graphics, video, and sound as well. Moreover, it provides a significant means for students to develop their navigation skills, connect with others, and establish a real audience to which they can present their electronic creations. In addition to the sources provided on the Web for designing various kinds of presentations, computer-based software programs designed specifically for desktop publishing are available. With the proliferation of such publishing programs, using the computer and other forms of electronic media to create documents should require only a minimum level of

FIGURE 8–3 Abridged List of
Presentational Texts

Annotated lists (of readings, films, videos, purchases, preferences, etc.)
Bulletin boards
Business information letters and reports
Comic strips and cartoons
Daily activity logs
Directions
Editorials
Expository essays
    cause/effect
    classification
    comparison/contrast
    defintion
    description
    persuasion
    problem/solution
    process
Greeting cards
Information brochures or pamphlets
Instructions
Invitations
Memoirs
Newsletters
Plays, dramas, and skits
Poems
Recipes
Research papers
Resumes
Reviews
Songs, jingles, and cheers
Short stories
Time lines and schedules

computational expertise from middle and high school students. Thus, they should be encouraged from the beginning levels of language instruction to incorporate a range of electronic media into their authoring tool kits.

Identifying the Communicative Components

Once it has been decided which activities form the curricular goals for the presentational mode, the next step is to identify the basic components and features of each communicative activity that students need to learn. The components of the various communicative activities selected for inclusion in the foreign language curriculum will form the core of the learning objectives to which the instructional activities are oriented. Following is an example of the kinds of skills, abilities, and knowledge that students need to compose a persuasive essay on an academic topic, using the model of communicative competence proposed by Celce-Murcia et al. (1995) as a framework:

Discourse: Linguistic devices used to make logical connections between phrases, sentences, and paragraphs such as anaphoric reference cues (e.g., use of the pronoun "they" to refer back to the original subject "the farmers" in the following lines: *The farmers had left the village earlier. They used carts and horses to carry their goods.*); the appropriate structuring and ordering of propositional claims to build one's argument of persuasion; and linguistic devices for managing given and new information.

Linguistic: Knowledge of subject-verb agreement, appropriate word order, use of articles, modals, and prepositions, and appropriate use of mechanics (e.g., punctuation, capitalization, paragraph formation, spelling).

Sociocultural: Knowledge of audience variables (e.g, age, gender, social role) that affect the effectiveness of the essay; the stylistic appropriateness (e.g., levels of formality and politeness) for addressing the audience; knowledge of topic parameters (e.g., what counts as taboo claims, adequate evidence, well-supported opinions).

Rhetorical: Knowledge of how to form speech acts conventionally associated with persuasive essays (e.g., introducing main idea, expressing opinions, providing warrants or justification, advising, speculating, encouraging, discouraging, summarizing); knowledge of how to appropriately order the speech acts (e.g., expressing opinion followed by justification).

Strategic: Knowledge of linguistic devices for stimulating interest and motivating the reader to engage in reading the essay; knowledge of visual devices for enhancing written text (e.g., appropriate use of font size, page layout, headings and subheadings, bolded and italicized text).

Creating Instructional Activities

Once the components of the communicative activities have been identified, the next step is to create a set of instructional activities. As discussed in earlier chapters, the purpose of the multiple and varied learning opportunities provided by instructional activities is to help learners develop the various knowledge, skills, and abilities they need to be successful, effective participants in their presentational communicative activities.

Connecting Instructional Activities to Learning Opportunities

The first step in designing effective instructional activities for the presentational communicative mode is to decide on the type of learning opportunity the instructional activity will be. As discussed in earlier chapters, learning involves participation in four kinds of opportunities: situated practice, overt instruction, critical framing, and transformed practice. These opportunities are not meant to represent stages in learning. Rather, they are interrelated in complex ways. As noted by the New London Group, "Elements of each may occur simultaneously, while at different times one or the other will predominate, and all of them are repeatedly revisited at different levels" (New London Group, 2000, p. 32). Table 8–1 provides a list of instructional activities arranged according to the four types of learning opportunities they represent. Each can be used to help students develop the communicative competence they need to be full participating members in their presentational communicative activities.

Situated Practice.   The instructional focus of *situated practice* learning opportunities is on providing meaningful immersion experiences in authentic versions of presentational communicative activities. What makes the experiences meaningful is the provision of an environment in which students feel free to take risks in their composing, and in which they compose for practical understanding and the development of fluency rather than to practice discrete skills.

Situated practice instructional activities, then, involve immersing the learners in the communicative activities for which they are expected to develop full communicative competence. If writing academic research reports is a curricular goal, for example, then the language learners must be given opportunities to engage in composing such reports in contexts that encourage students to explore the possibilities for meaning-making.

The teacher's role in these situated practice activities is to act as a resource and guide, motivating students to become engaged in the activity, and to identify with the purpose and audience. It also involves helping the students locate and sort through material, and try out different linguistic conventions for putting their thoughts into words. Both the teacher's assistance and the experiential learning opportunities themselves will help students form structures of expectations for what counts as competent ways of making meaning in their presentational communicative activities.

As noted in Table 8–1 situated practice learning opportunities can include a range of immersion-based instructional activities such as singing, acting in plays or skits, making voice recordings, and other kinds of oral performances. They can also include writing activities such as journal or diary keeping, writing stories from story maps, taking dictation, and copying written texts. More detailed descriptions of two activities are presented in the following sections.

Making Connections.   *Making connections* is an activity in which learners connect an instructional activity for building listening skills (as part of an interpretive communicative activity) to an instructional activity for building composing skills (for engagement in a presentational communicative activity). Here the learners first listen to or watch a particular

TABLE 8–1 *Instructional and Assessment Activities for Presentational Communicative Activities.*

Learning Opportunities	Activities
Situated Practice	Acting in plays and skits Copying Drafting Free writing (expository essays, informational guides, poems, stories, advertisements, etc.) Oral presentations Parallel writing Performances Voice recordings
Overt Instruction	Choral drill Information gap activity Passage diagramming Pattern analysis and practice (grammar, mechanics, discourse markers, vocabulary, rhetorical structures and functions, pronunciation, prosody [for voice recordings], etc.) Peer review Proofreading Reformulating sections of text Revising Semantic Webs Sentence combining Strategy checklists Word games and puzzles
Critical Framing	Genre and text type comparison Inquiry-based analysis of language use (according to, e.g., social identity, type of text, purpose) Interviews with writers Self-assessment of skills, strategy use, and attitudes Survey of attitudes toward writing
Transformed Practice	Audio, video, and writing diaries Collages Creating a hypertext Creative performances Designing bulletin boards Dramatic monologues Free writing Improvisations Inventions Model building Multimedia showcase Rewriting story endings Script writing Song, jingle, and cheer writing Speeches Writing journals

program that they and the teacher have selected. They can choose, for example, a televised or videotaped program, or a radio news broadcast. After listening to or watching the program the teacher leads the students in creating a story map that features key concepts, ideas, and words and phrases. The teacher then helps the students in arranging the concepts and ideas in some kind of logical order.

Next, using the map as a guide, students—individually, in pairs, or in small groups—write their account of the program. The intent of this activity is to give students the opportunity to compose freely, without the constraints of having to attend to accurate form production. Once the texts have been completed, learners can share them with their classmates, comparing and commenting on the varied ways they each constructed the program in their writing.

The completed texts can also be used as a resource in overt instruction and critical framing activities. For example, selected words and phrases from their accounts can be made into word games or crossword puzzles. Alternatively, selected structures can be used to form the basis for pattern drill and practice. Finally, the texts can be revised and edited in peer review groups.

In terms of critical framing, students can be asked to use the information in the story web to write different kinds of texts, for example, narratives, expository texts, poems, jingles, and so on. They can then compare their written texts, analyzing them, for example, for their choice of words, kinds of language patterns used, and ways the information is arranged. Conclusions about connections between genres and writing can then be drawn.

Language Experience Approach.   The *language experience approach* (Krashen & Terrell, 1983; Rigg, 1987) is an activity that immerses learners in reading and writing experiences. The description here will primarily focus on its use as a writing activity, although it can be equally effective as a situated practice activity for the interpretive communicative mode. The instructional activity begins with the teacher and students choosing the purpose for writing, a topic, and the audience to whom the writing is oriented. It may be, for example, a narrative based on some event experienced by the class that will eventually be published in the class newsletter, or a letter requesting information, or a story based on a set of pictures that will become part of the students' portfolios.

Together with the teacher, the students generate ideas on what should be contained in the text and decide on how to organize it. If necessary to facilitate discussion, the teacher can prompt students with questions such as "When did this happen?", "How did you feel about it?", "Do we want to expand on this?", and so on. Once the ideas have been generated, the students then dictate what they want to write to the teacher. The teacher writes exactly what the students say on the blackboard, a large piece of chart paper, or an overhead transparency so that all the students can see what is being written.

During this stage of the activity, the learners' language is not intentionally corrected by the teacher, although the learners may correct themselves or each other as they work together. Formal corrections are made during the revising and editing stages, which are components of overt instruction learning opportunities. It should also be noted that the length of the produced text is not significant, at least at the beginning levels of language learning, since learners may be able to compose only very simple texts, perhaps even just a few short sentences. At this point, what is significant is that they compose something in writing in the target language that is meaningful and relevant to them.

Once the written text is complete, the teacher or one of the students can read it aloud to the class, or they can each make their own copy of the text. The text itself can be used as a framework for several overt instructional activities. For example, it can be made into a cloze activity, a scrambled sentences activity, a dictionary or thesaurus-based activity, a grammatical pattern drill and practice activity, or used in peer review groups for revising and editing.

Overt Instruction.   As noted in the previous chapters, the focus of *overt instruction* is on providing opportunities for students to split apart and analyze the underlying systems and structural components of oral, written, and visual texts, and to practice using them to compose accurate and appropriate texts of their own. They do so through direct instruction by the teacher, with the goal of leading students to "conscious awareness and control over what is being learned" (New London Group, 2000, p. 33). In addition to becoming conscious of and practiced in using the forms and functions needed to engage in their activities, students develop skills in both English and the target language for identifying, talking about, and reflecting on the forms and functions they encounter in their learning. This means, for example, they learn to use words and phrases like *speech acts, subject-verb agreement, modals,* and *number* to refer to and explain the inner workings of their communicative activities.

As noted in Table 8–1 overt instruction learning opportunities can include a range of instructional activities including information gap activities, pattern analysis and practice, choral drill, and creating semantic Webs. Extended examples of two overt instructional activities are presented in the following sections.

Peer Review Groups.   *Peer review groups,* also known as writing groups, feedback groups, and collaborative writing teams, are based on a process approach to writing, which considers revising an integral aspect of writing. A crucial component of revising involves peer feedback. One common means for providing students with such feedback is through peer review groups.

Setting up review groups involves the following steps. First, before beginning the review, the teacher and students must decide whether the feedback is to focus on the content, on form, or on the mechanics such as spelling, punctuation, capitalization, and so on. Once the focus is made clear, students are provided guidelines for the review and placed into pairs or small working groups. Guidelines should include a list of the items on which students will focus their review. They can use the same forms or rubrics—or components of these forms and rubrics—that the teacher will eventually use to assess their papers. An example of such a rubric can be found in Figure 8–4.

At this time students are also given guidelines for participating in the review. These guidelines should specify how long each review should take to ensure that each paper is given adequate attention and how the review is to be conducted (whether, for example, each student writer will read an individual paper aloud to the other group members before the review begins). The guidelines should also specify what counts as appropriate and inappropriate ways to critique in the target language and appropriate and inappropriate ways of listening and responding to each other. Once the peer reviews are complete, students can be asked to revise their papers, using the peer comments as a guide in their revisions.

CRITERIA FOR EVALUATION OF WRITTEN PROJECT

Content

Topic statement is clearly articulated.

1   2   3   4   5

weak (no improvement)   strong (much improvement)

> Comments:

Significance of the topic is clearly articulated.

1   2   3   4   5

weak (no improvement)   strong (much improvement)

> Comments:

Information is clearly stated, meaningful, relevant, and of adequate amount.

1   2   3   4   5

weak (no improvement)   strong (much improvement)

> Comments:

Assertions are adequately supported with facts, examples, evidence, and details.

1   2   3   4   5

weak (no improvement)   strong (much improvement)

> Comments:

Conclusions are stated clearly and are relevant.

1   2   3   4   5

weak (no improvement)   strong (much improvement)

> Comments:

FIGURE 8–4   Rubric for Providing Feedback and Evaluating Student Writing

Organization

An introduction opens the paper and is clearly stated.

| 1 | 2 | 3 | 4 | 5 |

weak (no improvement)   strong (much improvement)

Comments:

The paper closes with clearly stated conclusions.

| 1 | 2 | 3 | 4 | 5 |

weak (no improvement)   strong (much improvement)

Comments:

Ideas are logically connected throughout the paper.

| 1 | 2 | 3 | 4 | 5 |

weak (no improvement)   strong (much improvement)

Comments:

Discourse transition words are used appropriately and accurately to connect sentences and paragraphs.

| 1 | 2 | 3 | 4 | 5 |

weak (no improvement)   strong (much improvement)

Comments:

Format

Grammar choices (e.g., subject–verb agreement, use of articles, modals, prepositions, pronouns, and conjunctions) are appropriate and accurate.

| 1 | 2 | 3 | 4 | 5 |

weak (no improvement)   strong (much improvement)

Comments:

FIGURE 8–4 (continued)

Sentences are complete and well-formed.

1   2   3   4   5

weak (no improvement)   strong (much improvement)

Comments:

Vocabulary choices are appropriate, accurate, and varied.

1   2   3   4   5

weak (no improvement)   strong (much improvement)

Comments:

Mechanics

Formatting (e.g., page length and use of citations and reference list as appropriate) is adequate.

1   2   3   4   5

weak (no improvement)   strong (much improvement)

Comments:

Conventions such as punctuation, capitalization, spelling, parentheses, and paragraph indentation are used appropriately and accurately.

1   2   3   4   5

weak (no improvement)   strong (much improvement)

Comments:

FIGURE 8–4   *(continued)*

Composing Sentences with a Purpose.   The purpose of this activity is to provide practice for learners in writing sentences with different rhetorical functions such as defining, reporting, inferring, predicting, persuading, opining, evaluating, directly and indirectly quoting, summarizing, concluding, and so on. The particular functions selected should be those identified as components of rhetorical competence for the particular communicative activity that is the object of instructional attention.

So, for example, if the communicative activity is writing a report on a particular topic, students will likely need to know how to compose definitions, summarize, paraphrase, and draw conclusions. To practice writing definitions, they can be provided with a list of words identified as components of linguistic competence for the communicative activity, and asked to produce clear and concise definitions. They can then compare their definitions to those written by their classmates, and together identify the features considered essential to composing clear definitions.

In terms of summarizing, this function requires students to ascertain the main ideas of a text and express them in their own words. Practicing writing summary statements provides students with practice in searching for meaning and communicating that meaning in writing. Here, students can be asked to write summary statements of a report with which they are familiar, and to share their statements with each other for comment and review.

The goal of paraphrasing, another rhetorical function, is for students to restate essential information given in a text using new words. Students can be provided with a series of statements and asked to rewrite them using their own words. As a final example, to practice drawing conclusions, students can be given a list of observations, either created by the teacher or the students themselves, and asked to write a set of conclusions based on the observations.

The teacher's role in this activity is to provide students with models of what is considered clear and appropriate constructions of the different functions and to assist them in writing their own. This may involve helping them locate information in dictionaries and other information sources, brainstorm words, phrases, and structures that can be used in their writing, and analyze and revise their work and the work of their peers.

Critical Framing. As noted in earlier chapters, the purpose of *critical framing* instructional activities is to help students situate their communicative activities in their larger historical, cultural, and social contexts. From such study students can develop an idea of recurrent patterns in the ways these activities are used, by whom, and for what purposes. They can also get a sense of how words are used to refer to or portray people, places, and events, and how these words may vary according to the author's social identities, the purpose of the text, or the larger contexts in which the activity is embedded. Through their participation in critical framing activities, students gain personal and theoretical distance from what they are learning, and learn to analyze its value and usefulness in light of the larger social and cultural purposes it serves. Table 8–1 lists several critical framing activities that can be used in classrooms. Descriptions of two activities are provided in the following sections.

Genre Comparison. The aim of *genre comparison* is to help students explore the multiple links between the purpose for writing and language use, and on a more general level, to consider the different ways that a topic can be represented. Here students are provided with, or asked to gather themselves, different genres of writing on the same topic, say, for example, on a particular sport. Texts about the sport can be gathered from newspapers and popular magazines including sports, news, and entertainment, and from communities where the target language is spoken. Articles can also come from pertinent Web sites and other sources found through searches of the Internet, and from more traditional venues like encyclopedias or information texts. The list found in Figure 8–3 can help in choosing different kinds of texts.

To make the analysis systematic, it would help to create a framework that asks students to identify particular items, such as vocabulary words and main ideas, in their analyses. Once students have completed their analyses of each of the texts, they can compare the use of language across texts. Venn diagrams can be helpful for making such comparisons. They consist of two overlapping circles. In the space where the circles overlap students note the similarities between two texts. In the spaces that do not overlap students note the unique characteristics of each text. Their findings can serve as a springboard for discussion on how different purposes for meaning-making lead to different uses of language.

Writing from Different Perspectives.   This activity is an outgrowth of the preceding one. Here, students are asked to write on the same topic from different perspectives. Using a brief passage on a particular topic from a familiar text, students are asked to rewrite it as it would appear in a variety of text types. These could include, for example, a popular magazine article, a newspaper editorial, an advertisement, an instructional pamphlet, and a textbook. With their classmates they can discuss the kinds of changes they made and the reasons for making them. They can also consider questions such as "How do your changes compare with those of your classmates?", "How did the audience and purpose of the text affect the use of language?", and "What conclusions can you draw about language use and purpose?"

Transformed Practice.   Sometimes, the knowledge gained from critical framing activities can engender feelings of alienation or indifference on the part of the students (Cazden, 2000). Becoming aware of how their language choice is constrained by social forces that are beyond their control, for example, may leave students feeling that they can do nothing to make a difference. This is where *transformed practice* comes in. Transformed practice provides opportunities for students to build on, indeed, to transform, the knowledge they gain from critical framing activities. Using the act of writing and other forms of meaning-making to propose alternative ways of understanding a particular phenomenon or event becomes a way to take action that is personally meaningful.

Wells (1999) has noted that it is through such action that new ideas are brought into ongoing dialogue and made available to others for critique and further development. In addition, transformed practice activities provide students with the chance to explore unfamiliar territory and to use their developing knowledge, skills, and abilities to create, innovate, or invent new ways of communicating with others.

The role of the teacher here is to act as facilitator and coach, aiding students in thinking through and expressing their ideas, helping them locate resources, and in other ways providing an environment that encourages them to take risks. In addition, teachers need to help students find outlets for their work. Their creations or innovations can be displayed in classrooms, school libraries, or in other community-based institutions outside school. Students can publish a class newsletter, create group portfolios, and share their materials with students in other foreign language programs in other geographical locations. The availability of the Web makes it possible for students to extend their reach well beyond their own classroom communities. Table 8–1 contains several suggestions for transformed practice activities. Descriptions of two activities are provided in the following sections.

Improvisations.　The purpose of this activity is to provide opportunities for students to try out their developing communicative skills by creating new forms of oral performance. The instructional activity can be done by students in pairs, small groups, or the whole group. The intent is for a student or group of students to suggest a presentational communicative activity on which another student or group of students must elaborate. The goal is not for the students to perform the activity in expected, conventional ways. Rather, it is to take the activity in unprecedented or unexpected directions. As with other transformed practice activities, improvisations allow students to try out different voices, invent new ways to use language, and transform familiar goals into new ones for self-expression.

Free Composing.　*Free composing* is similar to sustained silent reading, a transformed practice activity for the interpretive mode, except that the free time provided for both students and teachers is for writing or composing texts on topics using means that they have chosen based on their own interests. Free composing provides students with opportunities to apply their presentational skills and knowledge in creating or constructing texts that are personally meaningful to them. They can write poetry, short stories, or expository texts. They can design brochures or newsletters. They can keep a diary or author song lyrics. The only guideline is that the target language must be used as the primary code of communication.

In free composing, the role of the teacher is to provide students with access to a wide variety of composing materials and means, including both traditional pen and paper and the newer electronic technologies. It also involves engaging in the activity as an equal participant. This means that at the same time that the students are involved in their projects, the teacher needs to be working on his or her own project. The teacher may keep a daily diary, write letters to friends, or work on a hypertext project using the computer. Similar to expectations for the students, the only guideline for the teacher is that he or she use the target language as the primary code in composing. By engaging in the activity along with students, the teacher acts as a role model, thus demonstrating to the students the value of free composing.

It should be pointed out that the activities of free composing and improvisation, or, indeed, any transformed practice activity for any of the three communication modes, should never be used as a reward to students who finish their other class work. Approaching transformed practice activities in this way misunderstands the instructional purpose of transformed practice. Such learning opportunities do not simply occur in addition to more traditional instructional activities. Rather, they are instructional activities in their own right. Thus, using class time on a regular basis to engage in student-defined and student-directed instructional activities is as important as using class time for other more traditional teacher-directed activities.

Choosing a Particular Participation Structure

After deciding on the kind of learning opportunity the instructional activity will be, the next decision to make concerns student participation in the activity. Will the activity be geared to individual students, pairs, small groups, or to the whole group? Alternatively, will the activity be part of a learning center where learners either by themselves or with others can engage in the activity on their own? In some cases, the participation structures are defined by the instructional activity itself. Peer review activities, for example, imply that there will be at least two students working together.

As pointed out in earlier chapters, no one participation structure is more valuable or useful than another. Each has its merits. What is important is to provide learners with a variety of different kinds of opportunities for participating in their instructional activities. Figure 8–5 summarizes the various components needed for designing effective instructional activities. It can be used to devise activities for all three communication modes: the interpersonal, the interpretive, and the presentational.

Designing an Instructional Activity

Communicative Activity: _____ Theme or Topic: _____

A. Focus of instructional activity: Identify specific knowledge, skills, and abilities

Discourse	
Linguistic	
Sociocultural	
Actional/Rhetorical	
Strategic	

B. Learning opportunity: Identify particular kind of opportunity
   Situated practice
   Overt instruction
   Critical framing
   Transformed practice

C. Participation structure: Choose a structure for organizing student participation
   Whole group   Pair
   Small group or team   Individual
   Learning center

D. Materials and resources: Identify those that will be integral to accomplishing the instructional activity
   Texts
   Videos
   Television programs
   Internet
   Realia
   Other

FIGURE 8–5   Blueprint for Designing Instructional Activities

DESIGNING ASSESSMENT

The final essential component of effective instruction for the presentational mode is *assessment*. As pointed out in earlier chapters, the traditional approach to assessment in foreign language learning has relied on the use of short-answer, multiple-choice, and other discrete-point tests. While these can be helpful, particularly in assessing student learning resulting from their participation in overt instructional activities, they are quite limited in their usefulness for measuring other kinds of learning. For this, other forms of assessment are needed.

Oral, written, and multimedia presentations or projects created by students are evaluated most usefully using either holistic or analytic rubrics. Holistic rubrics use multiple criteria to produce an overall score for a product, demonstration, or performance. Analytical rubrics are more specific. They isolate the specific elements or components of a product, demonstration, or performance, and articulate criteria for evaluating and scoring each feature. As noted in Chapter 5, although analytical rubrics require more time to create, they provide more detailed information than holistic rubrics do, and thus, are more likely to be of greater value to both students and teachers.

See Figure 5–4 for an example of an analytic rubric that can be used to assess learners' performance in an oral academic presentation. Figure 8–4 is an example of an analytic rubric that can be used to evaluate students' performance on written reports. In addition to providing students with copies of the rubrics before they are used to assess their performances, teachers should provide the students with models of what they consider exemplary oral and written performances. In this way, students will have a clear idea of what is expected of them.

In addition to teacher assessment of student learning, students need to develop skills for reflecting on and assessing their own learning including the means and materials they use in their learning. Figure 8–6 is an example of a rubric that students can use to evaluate their learning. The statements contained in the rubric ask students to consider how effectively they approach an instructional task. In addition to helping them develop skills for reflecting on and monitoring their own learning, self-assessment gives students the language they need to be able to talk about the process. Consequently, students become more fully invested in their own roles as language learners.

A final example of an assessment rubric that can be used for presentational communicative activities can be found in Figure 8–7. This rubric differs from the others in that its focus is not on the learner but on the materials that learners use to gather information for use in their own presentational activities. Learning to evaluate materials is especially important given the proliferation of information on the Internet. In order to develop into knowledgeable consumers of such materials, learners need skills for judging their worthiness. Students may want to use this rubric as a base for developing additional rubrics to assess other kinds of materials. It should be noted that the rubric can also be used to assess Internet resources for use in interpretive communicative activities.

No matter what kinds of assessment tools are used in the foreign language classroom, the key to effective assessment involves making sure that the tools are directly linked to instruction. To ensure that the tools adequately measure what we intend them to measure, we

---

Learning Self-Assessment Tool

I understand the task and apply effort toward meeting the goal of the activity on a consistent basis.

1   2   3   4   5

weak (no improvement)   strong (much improvement)

I understand the key concepts and communicative skills needed to engage in the activity and can use them effectively.

1   2   3   4   5

weak (no improvement)   strong (much improvement)

I connect new understanding to what I already know and can apply my new knowledge to figure out underlying patterns or rules and to solve problems.

1   2   3   4   5

weak (no improvement)   strong (much improvement)

I monitor my own learning process, and can see changes in my knowledge, skills, and abilities.

1   2   3   4   5

weak (no improvement)   strong (much improvement

FIGURE 8–6   Sample of Tool for Self-Assessment of Learning

must evaluate them on a regular basis. Figure 8–8 contains a list of some questions that can be used to assess the value, dependability, and trustworthiness of the different means we use for evaluating student learning in all three communication modes.

SUMMARY

This chapter dealt with designing curriculum, instruction, and assessment based on the third mode of the communication goal for foreign language learning, the presentational mode. Following is a summary of the key concepts and ideas that were discussed in the chapter.

■ The presentational mode consists of activities that involve the creation of oral, written, or multimedia texts through which we display what we know, integrate new knowledge with existing knowledge, create new structures of meaning, and explore what we do not know.

■ We engage in presentational communicative activities for two general purposes. The first purpose, transactional, involves writing or composing to inform, share knowledge that others will find useful and relevant, solve problems, or explore new topics. In activities with an expressive purpose we seek to express our opinions and feelings, to make observations and speculative reflections, or to make personal connections with others.

Questions to Evaluate Usefulness of Internet Resources

Purpose

What is the purpose of the material?

Who is the intended audience of the site or document?

Source

What is the title and who is the author?

What are the author's credentials?

Where does the content come from (e.g., another source, the author's own work, etc.)?

Is there a sponsor of the document or site? If so, does the sponsorship bias the information in any way?

When was the document or site last updated?

Content

What kind of content does the document or site contain (e.g., opinions, facts, history, statistics, stories, definitions, examples, etc.)?

How comprehensive is the material?

How accurate is the material?

Are links to other sources provided? If so, are they relevant and appropriate?

Style

How well organized is the information?

How visually easy is it to read?

How accessible is the writing style?

How easy is it to navigate the document or site?

FIGURE 8–7   Evaluating Internet Resources to Be Used in Presentational Activities

Evaluating the Quality of Assessment Tools

1. Does the tool articulate clearly the specific aspects of student behavior that will be judged?

2. Are the criteria for judging the specific aspects of students' behavior clearly noted?

3. Are there descriptors for the expected behaviors?

4. Are the students familiar with the assessment tool?

5. Are the scoring criteria clearly articulated?

6. Are the goals of the assessment tool linked directly to my instructional goals?

7. Can the students use what they learn from this assessment to improve their learning?

8. Can I use what I learn from this assessment about student learning to improve my teaching?

FIGURE 8–8   Questions for Evaluating the Quality of Assessment Tools

- From a sociocultural perspective, writing is both a cognitively and socially complex activity. In the process of composing, writers reflect on, analyze, and revise their representations of meaning. In addition, they use the process to help them think about and explore new ideas and meanings. The process, however, is not divorced from the contexts in which it occurs. On a broader level, individuals' constructions of meaning and the forms and strategies they use in the process of composing are shaped by the larger social and cultural contexts within which they write. Thus, the process of writing can also be viewed as a means for negotiating one's place within these contexts.

- The increased use of computers and the Internet and other electronic media and resources in presentational communicative activities both in and outside the classroom requires students to add technological knowledge, skills, and abilities to their communicative repertoire for composing in the target language. They need to develop skills for working with the computer, for searching for and evaluating sources of information found on the Internet, and for using authoring tools to integrate written texts, graphics, and both audio and video material into their presentations.

- As was discussed for the other two communication modes, creating effective learning environments for the presentational communication mode entails several steps. The first involves specifying the curricular content. This is done by first selecting the presentational communicative activities in which students are expected to develop competence, and second, identifying the essential components of the activities that they will be expected to master.

- After determining what is to be learned, the next step is to create an instructional plan for facilitating student learning. Part of the plan calls for designing instructional activities that engage students in four different learning opportunities and providing various opportunities for student participation.

- A last piece to designing effective pedagogy requires the design and use of multiple assessment tools to evaluate student learning resulting from their instructional activities. It also requires the use of tools that can help teachers evaluate their own effectiveness as teachers, and on another level, the program's effectiveness in leading students to develop a range of communicative knowledge, skills, and abilities in the target language that suit their academic, social, and personal needs.

DISCUSSION QUESTIONS AND ACTIVITIES

1. Make a list of the ways in which you used writing in English and in the target language this past week. Compare the activities across both languages and draw some conclusions about your writing habits. In which writing activities do you feel most competent? Why? Compare your list with those of your classmates. How different or similar are they? What implications can you draw for how you might approach the teaching of writing in your own classroom?

2. In what types of composing activities do you regularly make use of a computer? Of other electronic media? Does your use vary according to the language you are

composing in (English versus your teaching language)? Has your use of them changed your writing habits at all in either language? How might your use (or lack of use) of such media for composing in the target language affect your teaching of composing skills in your classroom?

3. Examine the list of presentational communicative activities provided in Figure 8–2. How relevant are these to middle and high school students? Can you add others? Survey a group of middle or high school students about their choices of activities. In what kinds of activities would they like to become communicatively competent target language users? Survey a group of teachers of middle or high school students about their choices of activities for their students. What kinds of presentational communicative activities do they feel should form part of the curriculum for the students they teach? Compare their responses with those of the students. Prepare a report in which you summarize your findings and reflect on the implications of your findings for designing curriculum.

4. Have you been involved in peer review of your own writing in the target language? What elements of the process worked best for you? Why? What implications can you draw for using peer review in your own classroom?

5. Examine Figure 8–2. Can you add additional communicative activities to any of the four quadrants? Using the list of activities provided here, and those you have added, make a list of the presentational communicative activities you feel should form part of the curriculum for middle and high school students. Provide reasons for your choices.

6. Divide into small groups by teaching language. Together, choose one presentational communicative activity from one of the four quadrants and do the following. When the activities are completed, share them with your classmates for feedback.

   ■ Identify some of the elements of each of the five components of communicative competence to be learned in the target language.

   ■ Create two instructional activities based on two different kinds of learning opportunities (be sure to identify the learning opportunity and participation structure for each).

   ■ Create an assessment measure for evaluating student learning in one of the two instructional activities.

7. Look at the questions found in Figure 8–8. Can you add other questions that can be used to assess the quality of assessment tools used in the foreign language classroom?

TEACHER RESEARCH PROJECTS

A. Students' Funds of Knowledge.

This project is based on the work done by Luis Moll and his associates on students' funds of knowledge. Their work is based on the premise that students' home communities are rich reservoirs of information that can be of great value to teachers in transforming the content of their curriculum (see, for example, Gonzalez, Moll, Floyd-Tenery, Rivera, Rendon,

Gonzales, & Amanti, 1993; Moll, Amanti, Neff, & Gonzalez, 1992). The goal of the funds of knowledge project is to help teachers become familiar with students' lives outside school and to use their new knowledge to transform their instructional practices.

Pose a Problem

The students in your classes come to school already possessing valuable cultural knowledge upon which you can build to create a more meaningful curriculum and classroom environment. Some students may come from communities that are similar to yours, while others may differ significantly. To uncover some of the knowledge and skills your students already possess, engage students in the creation of a document that portrays their home communities in ways that are meaningful to them. If you do not yet have your own classroom, see if you can pair with someone who does.

Identify Sources and Gather Information

Explain your project to your students and elicit their help in gathering information on their local communities. This research project could easily be integrated with a curriculum project in which the target language is used. Have the students create portfolios in which they include written, visual, graphic, audio, video, and other kinds of materials that they feel best represent their home communities.

Analyze

Together with students, compare the information contained in the portfolios. How similar or different are they? What do they tell you about the needs, interests, and abilities of your students?

Reflect and Revise

Summarize and arrange the wealth of information provided by the student portfolios into particular funds of knowledge and reflect on how you might incorporate them into the curriculum.

Disseminate Information

Displaying the student-created portfolios in a prominent place in your school will allow them to be appreciated by the larger school community. You might also ask your students to present their portfolios to other foreign language classes, or organize an event for the larger community where the students can present their work.

B. Teaching Journal.

In this project the teacher keeps a record of experiences, reflections, and interpretations of her daily classroom practices to gain insight into her teaching practices. Preservice teachers who are student teaching might find this a particularly beneficial project to engage in during the student teaching practicum.

Pose a Problem

To gain some insight into your teaching practices, you might ask yourself the following questions: What are my perspectives on teaching? What events are significant to me and why are they significant? How can I use what I learn to improve upon my day-to-day teaching?

Identify Sources and Gather Information

Maintain a daily or weekly personal reflection journal for a designated period of time. To ensure that you gather enough data to be useful, you should consider maintaining the journal for no less than a month. Although they can be time-consuming, journals provide a written account of your experiences and thoughts on which you can reflect. The following is a sample format for keeping a journal:

Date of lesson or day of teaching:

Sequence of events: Briefly describe the events of the lesson, or the teaching day. This allows you to keep track of what transpires.

Significant episodes: Choose one or two events that are significant to you in some way. Describe them in detail, taking care to be as descriptive as possible. Note what was said and by whom and how you felt at that time.

Analyze

Once the episodes are sufficiently described, the next step is to analyze them in terms of their significance to you. Perhaps they validated a particular idea you had, or perhaps they caused you to rethink some of your ideas. Include a detailed description of your feelings about these events. Try responding to such questions as: How did you feel as you were going through them? How do you feel now as you write about them? What questions have your experiences answered? What questions do your experiences raise?

Reflect and Revise

After the specified time period for maintaining the journal has ended, reread your entries with the following in mind: Are there patterns to the significant episodes? Do they highlight your successes or your failures or are they a mix? Has your ability to analyze the significance of your episodes developed? How so? What conclusions about your own teaching can you draw? Given what you have learned, how might you change your teaching practices?

Disseminate Information

Share what you have learned about your own teaching and about the use of journals for enhancing self-reflections and professional growth with your peers. You might consider posting your reflections to an electronic chat room or listserv serving foreign language education, or giving a report on your experiences at an annual meeting of a local or state professional organization devoted to teaching.

ADDITIONAL READINGS

Biber, D. (1988). *Variation across speech and writing.* Cambridge: Cambridge University Press.

Connor, U. (1995). *Contrastive rhetoric: Cross-cultural aspects of second language writing.* Cambridge: Cambridge University Press.

Dyson, A. H. (1993). *Social worlds of children learning to write in an urban primary school.* New York: Teachers College Press.

Gee, J. P. (1996). *Social linguistics and literacies: Ideology in discourses* (2nd ed.). Bristol, PA: Taylor & Francis.

Olson, D. (1994). *The world on paper.* Cambridge: Cambridge University Press.

Warschauer, M. (1999). *Electronic literacies: Language, culture, and power in online education.* Mahwah, NJ: Lawrence Erlbaum.

Warschauer, M., & Kern, R. (Eds.). (2000). *Network-based language teaching: Concepts and practice.* New York: Cambridge University Press.

Wells, G., & Chang-Wells, G. K. (1992). *Constructing knowledge together: Classrooms as centers of inquiry and literacy.* Portsmouth, NH: Heinemann.

INTERNET RESOURCES

http://www.northernwebs.com/bc/   Beginner's Central

This site is a great source of information for beginners. It shows how to locate and sort through the overwhelming amount of information found on the Internet. It is a useful resource for both students and teachers.

www.thinkquest.org   ThinkQuest®

ThinkQuest, a philanthropic initiative created by Advanced Network & Services, is an educational initiative whose aim is to advance learning through the use of computer and networking technology. Each ThinkQuest program encourages participants to create high-quality, content-rich educational Web sites that are then made available to others via the ThinkQuest Web server. ThinkQuest has several programs in which participants can compete for awards by creating an innovative Web-based educational tool. The Web site has links to award-winning projects, some of which are for foreign language learning. Following is the address for one project for foreign language learners, aged 12 to 19, which was created by students of German:

http://www.thinkquest.org/php/lib/site sum.php3?lib id=1762&team id=26231

http://web.bu.edu/mfeldman/Students/

This is a site of Web units created by Michael Feldman for use by ESL and EFL students. However, they can easily be adapted for other languages. Each unit contains instructions for the students, instructions for the teacher, links to sites related to the theme of the unit, and question sets, activities, and quizzes for the student to do.

http://polyglot.lss.wisc.edu/lss/lang/teach.html   Teaching with the Web

This Web site is a compilation of ideas for using WWW resources as a language teaching tool. It also offers links to other sites on language pedagogy.

http://www.languagebox.com   Language Box

This site offers links to information on language learning, multimedia, translation tools, maps, culture, contemporary world issues, and more. Information on different languages can be found in one of the links—the learning zone. The dictionary zone links to 17 different language dictionaries.

http://www.encyclopedia.com   The Online Encyclopedia

This is the site of the Internet's free encyclopedia. More than 14,000 articles from the *Concise Columbia Electronic Encyclopedia,* Third Edition have been assembled to provide free, quick, and useful information on almost any topic. It is a useful resource for gathering information for use in class presentational projects.

http://www.facstaff.bucknell.edu/rbeard/grammar.html

This Web site contains grammars and dictionaries for more than 100 languages. It includes all types of grammars: reference grammars, language lessons, and historical grammars. All are free except where otherwise indicated. Each grammar or language lesson entry is linked to dictionaries, fonts, and additional language-learning resources.

A few Web sites offer free art that can be clipped by students (and teachers, of course) for use in Web-based projects. Web addresses of three sites are provided as follows:

Caboodles of clip art   **http://www.caboodles.com/**
Clip-art.com   **http://www.clip-art.com/main.html**
Animation library   **http://www.animationlibrary.com/**

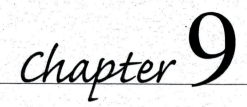

Chapter 9

Professional Development

Preview Questions

Before you begin reading this chapter, spend a few moments considering the following questions:

- Have you ever been involved in professional development activities outside the university classroom? Based on your experiences what do you think are some conditions for effective professional development?
- What are some professional activities and experiences that you feel are important for foreign language teachers to engage in on a regular basis? Why do you think they are important?
- Do you belong to any professional organizations? What are the advantages of belonging? Are there any disadvantages? If so, what are they? If you do not belong to any professional organizations, why not? What could you do to find out about organizations that may be of interest to you?
- Do you belong to any professional electronic listservs or subscribe to any professional journals? If so, how helpful do you think they are in keeping you informed about the field of language teaching?

Key Words and Concepts

Professional development
Possibilities for professional development
    Professional development centers
    Mentoring
    Professional organizations
    Electronic networks

Overview

The main purpose of this methods text was to present a comprehensive approach to designing curriculum, instruction, and assessment for foreign language programs in middle schools and high schools that is based on a sociocultural understanding of language and learning. From reading the preceding chapters you have learned, for example, about the socioculturally constituted nature of language. When we use language, whether it is our first or second language, we simultaneously create our individual social identities, our interpersonal relationships, and our memberships in various sociocultural groups and communities. You have also come to understand learning as a socially situated, collaborative, and mutually beneficial process of transformation of both academic and social knowledge and skills.

Based on this perspective of language and learning, a theoretical framework for designing foreign language pedagogy organized around the National Foreign Language Standards was presented, and in several chapters key ideas and concepts for creating communities of foreign language learners in your classroom were discussed. You also learned that an important component of developing effective instructional environments involves continued reflection on issues and concerns related to your specific contexts of teaching.

There is no doubt that your expertise in foreign language pedagogy and your understanding of your role as a foreign language teacher have grown significantly from the many readings, activities, and experiences you have encountered as a member in your classroom community of foreign language teachers. Once you leave this course and enter or return to a middle or high school foreign language classroom, however, your learning does not come to an end. Rather, the development of teacher expertise is a lifelong process. From a sociocultural perspective on pedagogy, continued development is as essential to creating effective communities of learners as all the other components presented in this text. In fact, research has shown that sustaining effective learning communities requires teachers' regular engagement in professional development activities (Rueda, 1998; Sprinthall, Reiman, & Thies-Sprinthall, 1996). In other words, no matter how many years they have been in the classroom, teachers need to participate regularly in collaborative support programs and other kinds of professional communities.

Professional development for foreign language teachers is especially important for at least three reasons. First, the demographic composition of most communities across the United States is continually changing as individuals from different sociocultural groups move to and from different geographical areas. This movement is reflected in the cultural, linguistic, and academic diversity that constitutes most populations in middle schools and high schools. This dynamic mosaic of learners requires foreign language teachers to work with students whose needs, educational experiences, and first language skills are likely to be quite varied, even within the same classroom. To sustain effective instructional environments in such varied classrooms, teachers need to keep themselves informed of current pedagogical theories and research concerned with heterogeneous classrooms.

A second reason why professional development is so important for foreign language teachers has to do with the National Foreign Language Standards. As discussed in earlier chapters, in order to create effective contexts of learning, teachers require a high level of communicative competence in the target language. They need to be able to use the language to meet diverse communicative needs, in multiple contexts, for social, academic, and professional purposes. They also need to keep abreast of ever-changing social, political, and economic realities of the regions where the language they teach is spoken. This requires regular teacher involvement in target language activities outside the classroom.

Finally, the technological transformation of means for communicating requires teachers to continue to develop their own technological skills and knowledge. They not only need to know how to use the different technologies for communicating in the target language, but they also need to know how to use them to transform the conditions for learning in their classrooms.

The purpose of this last chapter is to present an overview of the many professional development activities and resources available to teachers. In addition to a discussion on the nature of professional development and its importance to teacher growth, the chapter includes a discussion of some means by which foreign language teachers can sustain professional growth and collegial support.

PROFESSIONAL DEVELOPMENT

Professional development is a broad, comprehensive term that refers to activities and experiences geared to supporting the lifelong development of teacher expertise. According to Rueda (1998), a sociocultural model of effective professional development is characterized by several features. First, a coherent plan for professional development is fully integrated into school policies. It is considered an essential component of the school community, and thus, funds and other resources are made available on a regular basis for professional development initiatives.

Second, effective professional development is based on the premise that it is a social process that is best facilitated through joint activity among all school community members. Thus, rather than taking the form of information transmitted from the top level of administration to teachers, the focus is on collaborative activity in which teachers and other school staff, both novices and experts, work together.

Third, a related feature of effective professional development from a sociocultural perspective locates learning in the experiences and skills of participants. This means that professional development activities and joint problem-solving tasks focus on authentic issues and problems arising from teachers' daily lives. That is, they are not based on issues and concerns deemed important by individuals outside the schooling community. Rather, the issues of interest emerge from the local concerns and needs of teachers in a particular schooling context. Moreover, the activities themselves are designed and directed by teachers, incorporate the best principles of adult learning, and involve shared decision making.

Fourth, professional development is incorporated into the normal working day of teachers. Because it is recognized as an essential aspect of teachers' professional lives, teachers are given adequate time and resources to engage in activities. At the same time, engaging in professional development activities is voluntary. That is, for professional development to be effective, teachers cannot be coerced into participating. Rather, they must have choice and control over the kinds of activities they participate in. Finally, effective professional development takes place in a schooling environment that encourages risktaking, change, and innovation among faculty and staff.

POSSIBILITIES FOR PROFESSIONAL DEVELOPMENT

A traditional means by which teachers participate in professional development activities is through the pursuit of advanced degrees at institutions of higher education. Since many teachers continue to work while they pursue advanced degrees, most university programs for teachers provide the course work they need during the late afternoon or evenings and in summer sessions. Teachers who already have advanced degrees often opt to continue their studies by matriculating as nondegree students in their local universities. This allows them to take a course or two to update particular skills and knowledge areas as they see fit.

In addition to their regular academic programs, universities often sponsor summer institutes for teachers. Tedick and Tishcer (1996), for example, report on a summer language immersion and pedagogy program organized by the University of Minnesota for Spanish, French, and German teachers. Teachers who attended the first summer session reported that as a result of their participation they felt a renewed commitment to professional development.

In addition to courses and programs offered by colleges and universities, there are at least four additional means by which teachers can take part in professional development activities: professional development centers, mentoring programs, professional organizations, and professional electronic networks. Each is briefly described in the following sections.

Professional Development Centers

Professional development centers are usually formed as partnerships or unions among several school districts. They give priority to those concerns identified as important by the districts and state boards of education. They join forces to reduce the cost of providing materials and resources to individual schools. Costs of maintaining a center are usually spread out among the participating schools.

Professional development centers are like university programs in that they provide access to current research and initiatives and practical information. They also provide access to resources and services that teachers might not otherwise be able to obtain on their own. Typically, centers can help in producing instructional materials. They can also provide skill training, access to information systems, and resources to help schools meet state and federal requirements.

Professional development centers can benefit foreign language teachers by helping them form networks and partnerships with other foreign language teachers across schools. Such networks provide opportunities for teachers to share their expertise and ideas with other teachers, exchange information and materials, collaborate on curricula, and, more generally, to sustain ongoing dialogue with their colleagues.

Mentoring

A second means of supporting professional development is through mentoring programs. **Mentoring** is the process by which practicing members of the profession who are considered experts in their teaching field share their expertise with others through structured activities. Mentoring is usually a component of preservice field experiences. As part of their preservice foreign language education programs, students who aspire to be teachers are typically assigned to cooperating teachers. Cooperating teachers are full-time teachers of foreign languages who serve as mentors to the student teachers. These experiences last anywhere from several weeks to several months and are considered a "rite of passage" (Head, 1992, p. 101) into the teaching profession. The role of the cooperating teacher is to apprentice the student teacher into the role of teacher.

Research on this form of mentoring has shown it to be very beneficial to the professional development of student teachers (Davis & Hall, 1998; Hall & Davis, 1995; Kalekin-Fishman & Kornfeld, 1991; Shannon & Meath-Lang, 1992). In addition to providing students with feedback on their teaching, mentoring relationships with cooperating teachers were found to provide opportunities for both groups to form lasting collegial relationships. The student teachers reported that these relationships helped sustain them through the more difficult aspects of their teaching practicum.

More recently, the teaching profession has recognized the importance of continuing mentoring relationships beyond the preservice stage. Mentoring programs to help beginning teachers, veteran teachers in new assignments, and teachers in need of remedial aid are being established in schools across the country. Typically, in-service mentoring programs establish a one-to-one relationship between a mentor teacher and another teacher. Mentor teachers and teachers being mentored are usually released from some teaching duties during the school day to work with their partners.

Effective mentors of both preservice and in-service teachers are distinguished by the following characteristics: In terms of interpersonal skills and abilities, effective mentors offer criticism and critiques in positive and productive ways. They are able to articulate effective instructional strategies, are good listeners, and know how to ask questions that promote reflection and understanding. They are approachable and easily establish rapport with others. In addition, effective mentors have strong intercultural communicative skills and thus work well with individuals from different cultures and groups.

In terms of professional knowledge, effective mentors are considered outstanding teachers with strong foundations in content knowledge, pedagogical content knowledge, and pedagogical knowledge. Moreover, they enjoy new challenges, are confident in their abilities, and are highly involved in the profession through membership in organizations and teacher networks. More generally, effective mentors model a strong commitment to the teaching profession and to lifelong learning.

Professional Organizations

A third means for sustaining professional development of educators is through membership in **professional organizations.** There are several professional organizations devoted to education in general, and foreign language education in particular, at the local, state, regional, and national levels. Typically these organizations have annual meetings that include presentations by peer teachers, lectures by guest speakers, workshops, and displays by publishing companies of recently published books, videos, computer software, and other resources. Some professional organizations publish newsletters and journals for the members. They also offer study and travel abroad programs, summer institutes, and seminars. The following sections list just a few of the many organizations pertinent to foreign language education.

ACTFL: American Council on the Teaching of Foreign Languages (http://www.actfl.org)

This is a national organization dedicated to the improvement and expansion of the teaching and learning of all languages at all levels of instruction. ACTFL is an individual membership organization of more than 7,000 foreign language educators and administrators from elementary through graduate education as well as government and industry.

AAAL: American Association for Applied Linguistics (http://www.aaal.org)

Founded in 1977, the American Association for Applied Linguistics (AAAL) is a professional organization of scholars who are interested in the multidisciplinary field of applied linguistics. AAAL members are involved in a variety of language-related concerns including language education, acquisition and loss, bilingualism, discourse analysis, literacy, rhetoric and stylistics, language for special purposes, psycholinguistics, second and foreign language pedagogy, language assessment, and language policy and planning.

AATSP: American Association of Teachers of Spanish and Portuguese (http://www.aatsp.org)

The AATSP was founded in 1917 and since that time has promoted the study and teaching of Hispanic, Luso-Brazilian, and other related languages, literatures, and cultures at all levels.

AATG: American Association of Teachers of German (http://www.aatg.org)

AATG is the only national individual membership organization dedicated to the advancement and improvement of the language, literature, and culture of German-speaking countries. It has more than 6,500 members, and is for teachers of German at all levels of instruction and all those interested in the teaching of German.

AATF: American Association of Teachers of French (http://aatf.utsa.edu)

AATF was founded in 1927 and is the largest national association of French teachers in the world with nearly 10,000 members. Members are French teachers at all levels of instruction. Approximately three fourths of the members teach at the secondary school level and one fourth at the postsecondary level.

AERA: The American Educational Research Association (http://www.area.net)

AERA is an international professional organization whose primary goal is to advance educational research and its practical application. It has more than 22,000 members from a broad range of disciplines including education, psychology, statistics, sociology, history, economics, philosophy, anthropology, and political science.

CALICO: The Computer Assisted Language Instruction Consortium (http://www.calico.org)

CALICO serves a membership involved in both education and high technology. It has an emphasis on modern language teaching and learning, but reaches out to all areas that employ the languages of the world to instruct and to learn. CALICO is a recognized international clearinghouse and leader in computer-assisted learning and instruction.

IRA: International Reading Association (http://www.ira.org)

The International Reading Association seeks to promote high levels of literacy in first and second languages by improving the quality of reading instruction through studying the reading processes and teaching techniques. The IRA serves as a clearinghouse for the dissemination of reading research through conferences, journals, and other publications.

MLA: Modern Language Association (http://www.mla.org)

Founded in 1883, the MLA is devoted to the study and teaching of language and literature. MLA hosts an annual convention and other meetings, works with related organizations, sustains one of the finest publishing programs in the humanities, and provides programs serving English and foreign language teachers.

SIETAR: The International Society for Intercultural Education, Training, and Research (http://www.sietarinternational.org/)

SIETAR is an international professional association comprised of consultants, trainers, educators, researchers, and other professionals from a wide range of disciplines who share a common interest in international and intercultural relations.

As mentioned previously, many professional organizations offer their members subscriptions to professional journals either as part of the membership fees or at a reduced rate. The aim of professional periodicals is to provide up-to-date comprehensive reviews, reports of research projects, and descriptions of innovative methods and techniques for teaching. Figure 9–1 contains brief descriptions of just a few of the many journals that may be of interest to foreign language teachers.

In addition to offering journal subscriptions, professional organizations usually sponsor annual conferences. As an example, annual language teaching conferences are sponsored by different regional affiliates of ACTFL. Figure 9–2 or page 237 includes the names and Web site addresses of these conferences.

Applied Linguistics is published four times a year. It publishes work in such areas as first and second language learning and teaching, bilingualism and bilingual education, discourse analysis, translation, language testing, language teaching methodology, language planning, the study of interlanguages, stylistics, and lexicography.
Website: http://www3.oup.co.uk/jnls/list/applij/

The *Canadian Modern Language Review* publishes articles on all aspects of language learning and teaching. Article topics range from ESL to French immersion to international languages and to native languages.
Website: http://www.utpress.utoronto.ca/journal/cmlr.htm

Computer Assisted Language Learning is an international journal concerned with all matters associated with the use of computers in language learning (L1 and L2). It provides a forum to discuss the discoveries in the field and to exchange experience and information about existing techniques.
Website: http://www.swets.nl/sps/journals/call.html

Educational Researcher (ER) is published nine times per year and is received by all members of AERA. It contains scholarly articles of general significance to educational research and development.
Website: http://www.aera.net/pubs/er/

Foreign Language Annals is published four times a year and received by members of ACTFL. The journal contains articles on teaching, administration, and research in the areas of curriculum design and development; instructional methods, materials, and techniques; issues in research and research methodology; and testing and evaluation.
Website: http://www.actfl.org/htdocs/pubs/subscribe.htm

French Review is the official journal of the American Association of Teachers of French. The *Review* publishes articles and reviews on French and francophone literature, cinema, society and culture, linguistics, technology, and pedagogy six times a year.
Website: http://www.montana.edu/wwwaatf/french_review/

The *German Quarterly* and *Die Unterrichtspraxis* are produced by AATG. In four issues per year, the *German Quarterly* contains literary and philological scholarship. *Die Unterrichtspraxis* is published twice per year and contains articles on classroom strategies, research, practical hints, and techniques.
Website: http://www.aatg.org/publications/publications.htm

Harvard Educational Review is a scholarly journal of opinion and research in the field of education. Its mission is to provide an interdisciplinary forum for discussion and debate about education's most vital issues.
Website: http://hugse1.harvard.edu/~hepg/online.html

Hispania is published four times a year and is received by members of AATSP. It publishes articles on Hispanic or Luso-Brazilian literature, language, linguistics, and pedagogy having to do with Spanish and Portuguese.
Website: http://www.georgetown.edu/publications/hispania/

FIGURE 9-1   Journals Relevant to Foreign Language Education

International Journal of Bilingualism focuses on bilingualism from a cognitive science perspective. Some areas covered include bilingual language competence and bilingual language acquisition in children and adults.
Website: http://www.kingstonpress.com/ijb-online.htm

Journal of Second Language Writing appears three times a year. Areas of interest include L2 writers' composing processes; features of L2 writers' texts; assessment and evaluation of L2 writing; and contexts (cultural, social, political, situational) for L2 writing.
Website: http://icdweb.cc.purdue.edu/~silvat/jslw/index.html

Language Learning is published four times a year and is dedicated to the understanding of language learning. It is concerned with issues such as child, second, and foreign language acquisition, language education, bilingualism, and literacy.
Website: http://www.blackwellpublishers.co.uk/Static/online.htm

Language Learning & Technology is published twice a year and only on the Web. It seeks to disseminate research to foreign and second language educators on issues related to technology and language education.
Website: http://llt.msu.edu/

Linguistics and Education is an international journal that publishes original research and commentary on all aspects of the use of language in educational institutions and practices.
Website: http://academic.brooklyn.cuny.edu/education/jlemke/L-and-E.htm

The *Modern Language Journal* is published four times per year. It is devoted to concerns with the learning and teaching of foreign and second languages. It publishes research studies, editorials, reports, book reviews, and professional news and announcements pertaining to modern languages including teaching English as a second language.
Website: http://polyglot.lss.wisc.edu/mlj/index.html

Spanish Applied Linguistics is a journal devoted to theory and research on the acquisition and use of Spanish as a nonnative and bilingual language. SAL is published twice a year by the Department of Spanish, Italian, and Portuguese of the University of Illinois at Urbana–Champaign.
Website: http://www.lang.uiuc.edu/sip/dept/sal/

Studies in Second Language Acquisition, published four times a year, is devoted to the scientific discussion of issues in second and foreign language acquisition of any language.
Website: http://www.indiana.edu/~ssla/

FIGURE 9-1   Journals Relevant to Foreign Language Education (*continued*)

Professional Electronic Networks

In addition to using professional development centers, being mentored and mentoring other teachers, joining organizations, and attending their annual meetings, teachers can stay current by forming **electronic networks** with other foreign language teachers. Increased

The Northeast Conference on the Teaching of Foreign Languages; http://www/dickinson.edu/nectfl

The Southern Conference on Language Teaching; http://www.valdosta.edu/scolt/

The Southwest Conference on Language Teaching;
http://www.learnalanguage.org/swcolt/

The Central States Conference on Language Teaching;
http://www.centralstates.cc/

FIGURE 9-2 Annual Conferences on Foreign Language Teaching

worldwide access to electronic network capabilities such as the Internet has changed the ways in which teachers can stay in touch with current practices in the field and communicate and connect with others. They can now gain entry to a myriad of research and teaching sites, connect with colleagues around the country, and both present and respond to innovations almost as quickly as they are developed.

One easy way to establish professional ties with teachers from outside local schooling communities is through participation in electronic chat rooms, bulletin boards, and listservs designed specifically for teachers. A few of the many listservs relevant to foreign language teaching are contained in Figure 9–3. Readers are directed to <http://babel.uoregon.edu/yamada/lists.html> for a list of all electronic listservs.

CALICO-L: This discussion list is an open forum of the Computer Assisted Language Instruction Consortium. The purpose of the list is to discuss topics relating to the development, distribution, and implementation of language-learning courseware. To subscribe send the message <subscribe calico-l> to the address: majordomo@calico.org. Once subscribed, you may send your comments to the group at: calico-l@calico.org.

FL-TEACH: Topics on this electronic list include foreign language teaching methods, school to college articulation, training of student teachers, classroom activities, curriculum, and syllabus design. To subscribe send mail to: LISTSERV@listserv.acsu.buffalo.edu with the message <SUBSCRIBE FLTEACH firstname lastname> for example: SUBSCRIBE FLTEACH Snow White.

FLAC-L: Foreign Language Across the Curriculum List. To subscribe send mail to LISTSERV@BROWNVM.BITNET with a message consisting of one line: <SUBSCRIBE listname your name>.

SCT-L2L: Sociocultural Theory and Second Language Learning List. Topics include theoretical and practical concerns with second and foreign language learning. To subscribe send mail to: Majordomo@coe.uga.edu with the message <subscribe listname your name>.

FIGURE 9-3 Electronic Listservs for Foreign Language Teachers

Summary

The following is a summary of some of the more significant ideas presented in this chapter.

- Maintaining active involvement in the teaching profession is essential to the continued development of teacher expertise in foreign language.
- The following features characterize effective professional development. It is based on a coherent plan that is fully integrated into school policies; it is considered a social process, facilitated through joint activity; it is located in the experiences and skills of participants, with issues of interest emerging from the local concerns and needs of teachers in a particular schooling context; teachers play an active role in designing professional development activities; the activities are incorporated into the normal working day of teachers; and it is supported by a schooling community that encourages risktaking, change, and innovation.
- There are several ways by which teachers can continue to develop their expertise and sustain lifelong involvement in communities of scholars. These include pursuing advanced degrees in institutions of higher education, participating in professional development centers, mentoring and being mentored by other teachers, and becoming members of professional organizations. Professional development can also be sustained through the formation of professional networks with other foreign language teachers through electronic means such as bulletin boards and professional chat rooms.

Discussion Questions and Activities

1. With a partner, find out what you can about a professional development center. It can be one that your local school district is affiliated with or one from another area with which you are familiar. Find out about the programs they offer, the resources and materials they make available to teachers, and other means by which they support professional development. Prepare a report on the center to present to your classmates.
2. Using the list of professional organizations contained in this chapter, conduct a search of the Web sites of two organizations of your choosing. Prepare a two-page report for each site that includes a description of the organization, benefits of membership, a list of resources and/or interesting information, and anything else you feel would be helpful. Share your findings with your classmates.
3. Develop an annotated list of three journals that you feel are pertinent to foreign language learning. Use the list found in Figure 9–1 as a starting point, but feel free to add other journals to the list. Survey the topics of the articles published over the last 5 years in each of the journals. Can you detect any trends?
4. Interview three or four teachers who are currently teaching a foreign language in middle schools or high schools on their involvement in professional organizations. Do they regularly attend meetings? If so, what are some positive outcomes arising

from their membership? If they do not participate in professional organizations, what do they feel are some obstacles that prevent them from doing so? What implications can you draw for the role that professional organizations play in teacher development?

5. Have you ever been mentored by another teacher? If so, describe the situation and summarize what you feel were some of the advantages and disadvantages of such a relationship. Based on your experiences what do you think are some of the more essential qualities of an effective teacher mentor?

TEACHER RESEARCH PROJECTS

A. Discovering Community Beliefs about Foreign Language Education.

In addition to knowledge and skills for effective classroom teaching and learning, teachers need to develop knowledge of their larger schooling communities within which their particular schools are situated. This includes becoming familiar with the home communities of the students, and the perspectives and attitudes of parents, administrators, community service providers, and other groups who have a stake in what happens at their local schools. This knowledge can help teachers create more effective communities of learners in their classrooms and at the same time build community-wide support for their programs. The purpose of this particular research project is to uncover the beliefs and attitudes toward foreign language learning held by members of the community.

Pose a Problem

Since, as voters, members of your communities have some control over decisions made about foreign language programs, understanding their perspectives can better help you build and sustain support for your program. Most community members have had their own experiences as learners of a foreign language. Their perspectives on the value of foreign language study depend in part on these experiences. To understand their perspectives, then, it would be useful to explore their experiences and the meanings and attitudes about language learning they have drawn from them.

Identify Sources and Gather Information

Identify and interview five or so members from the larger schooling community about their experiences with and attitudes toward foreign language learning. You might choose members of the school board or local chamber of commerce, school or district administrators, local politicians, or parents of your students. It is suggested that the interviews be semi-structured and audio- or videotaped. Questions can include the following: What were your experiences as a foreign language learner? What language(s) have you studied? What were your classes like? Can you relate a story about a memorable experience as a language learner? How do you feel about your language learning experiences in general? Have they affected your life in any way, positively or negatively? How important do you think it is for students these days to study another language? What can teachers do to improve foreign language instruction in their classes?

Analyze

Each taped interview should be fully transcribed. Once completed, read each transcript several times noting common themes and topical patterns across the interviews. Summarize your findings.

Reflect and Revise

In your opinion, which findings are most significant? Why? Were you surprised by any of your findings? What questions have these findings answered? What additional questions have they raised? How can you use what you have learned to improve your program?

Disseminate Information

Share your findings with your colleagues and together discuss ways you can build on the findings to enhance community support of foreign language education as well as your own instructional practices in your classroom communities.

B. Professional Development Needs Analysis.

The purpose of this project is to uncover the professional needs of a group of teachers with whom you are familiar. If you are not yet working in a school, you may want to find out about the needs of preservice teachers. If you are currently teaching, use this project to explore the professional needs of your colleagues.

Pose a Problem

Begin by deciding on the particular group of teachers you wish to focus on. You can choose middle or high school teachers and preservice or in-service teachers. If you do this project as a small-group activity, you might wish to work with all four groups (preservice middle school teachers, preservice high school teachers, in-service middle school teachers, and in-service high school teachers) and then compare their needs. Use the following questions to help guide your research: What do teachers perceive to be their greatest needs in terms of professional development? How do their needs compare across groups? What are some ways to address their needs?

Identify Sources and Gather Information

Once you have identified a group of foreign language teachers you are interested in you need to decide on the number of teachers from whom you will gather information. Once this has been decided, invite individual teachers to participate. Remind them that their participation is voluntary, and their identities will be kept confidential. Since personal identities are not important to the project, you may decide to omit any identifying information on the questionnaire other than asking teachers to identify the grade level they teach, or, in the case of preservice teachers, the grade level they aspire to teach.

One easy way to collect information on perceived professional needs is through the use of surveys. To prepare a survey, construct a list of possible professional development needs or use the one provided in the following box. Ask the participants to identify their needs by checking all those that apply. To get an idea of their importance, you may decide to ask teachers to choose and rank-order five of their most significant needs.

As part of my professional development, I would like regular opportunities to (check all that apply):

_____ Further develop my target language competence
_____ Further develop my target culture knowledge
_____ Spend time during the school day in self-reflection
_____ Examine newly published instructional materials
_____ Work with other colleagues on action research projects
_____ Experiment with innovative instructional technologies
_____ Receive help with classroom management
_____ Attend professional organizational meetings and conferences
_____ Work with parents and other members of the community on developing curriculum
_____ Other (please explain)

Analyze

Once you have collected the completed surveys, compute the average number of times each need is checked. You can also compile a list of needs provided by the participants in the "other" category and compute the average number of times each is mentioned. If you have collected information from different groups, create a graph comparing their needs.

Reflect and Revise

After completing the analysis, ask yourself the following questions: What needs do the groups of teachers perceive to be most important? How do the needs of one group of teachers compare with those of other groups? What are some ways that these needs can be met?

Disseminate Information

Your findings will likely be of great interest to the teachers who participated. If it is a group from one school or a school district they may be able to use the findings to plan for future school-based professional development activities.

ADDITIONAL READINGS

Collay, M., Dunlap, D., Enloe, W., & Gagnon, W. (1998). *Learning circles: Creating conditions for professional development.* Thousand Oaks, CA: Corwin Press.

Daniels, H. (1999). The missing link in school reform: Professional development. North Central Regional Educational Laboratory, http://www.ncrel.org/mands/docs/7-10.htm.

Green, S. (1996). The professional development of modern language teachers. *Language Learning Journal, 14,* 75–79.

Hall, J. K. (2000). A proposal for the governance of pre-K–12 teacher preparation. *ADFL Bulletin, 31*(2), 64–66.

Lafayette, R. C. (Ed.). (1996). *National standards: A catalyst for reform.* Lincolnwood, IL: National Textbook Company.

Lange, D. (1991). Implications of recent reports on teacher education reform for departments of foreign languages and literatures. *ADFL Bulletin, 23*(1), 28–34.

Moon, J. (1999). *Reflection in learning and professional development.* London: Kogan Page.

Richards, J., & Lockhart, C. (1994). *Reflective teaching in second language classrooms.* Cambridge: Cambridge University Press.

INTERNET RESOURCES

http://www.mentors.net/LibraryFiles/OneDistModel.html   The Mentoring Leadership and Resource Network (MLRN)

MLRN is an affiliate of the Association for Supervision and Curriculum Development. It was started by a few educators and over the last several years has grown to become an international initiative. The site provides a variety of links to resources and materials on teacher mentoring and induction.

http://www.woodrow.org/teachers/   Leadership Program for Teachers (LPT)

The Woodrow Wilson National Fellowship Foundation (WWNFF) is an independent not-for-profit organization whose aim is to sponsor excellence in education. One of its three primary concerns is the development of teachers as intellectual leaders. LPT has been an important part of the foundation's educational efforts since 1982. The site provides links to several professional development programs for teachers.

http://www.lightspan.com/   LightSpan

This is a site of an education portal providing links to a variety of educational resources and programs. In particular it has several links to programs, research tools, and resources geared specifically to the professional development of teachers including guides on using the Internet in teaching, dates and information on upcoming conferences and workshops, and articles on professional development.

http://edsitement.neh.gov/   EDSITEment

Sponsored by the National Endowment for the Humanities (NEH), EDSITEment contains a variety of links to other Web sites and references to resources available through government, not-for-profit, and commercial entities. In addition to a variety of learning activities the site includes links to funding opportunities for teachers and schools.

http://knowledgeloom.org/   Knowledge Loom

This is the site of the Knowledge Loom, a development of the Northeast Regional Educational Laboratory (LAB) at Brown University with funding from the U.S. Department of Education. The LAB's goals are to improve teaching and learning, advance school improvement, and develop alliances with educational and policymaking communities. This site links educators to research on best practices, online events and discussions, educational products and services, and other organizations.

http://www.nhsa.net/index.html   National High School Association

This is the Web site of the National High School Association (NHSA), an organization committed to facilitating improvement in high school student learning and educational practices. The purpose of the organization is to provide opportunities for professional growth and dialogue among high school educators and other advocates of quality education including students, parents, community members, policymakers, and postsecondary educators.

Appendix

National Standards for Foreign Language Learning

COMMUNICATION: Communicate in Languages Other Than English

Standard 1.1: Students engage in conversations, provide and obtain information, express feelings and emotions, and exchange opinions.

Standard 1.2: Students understand and interpret written and spoken language on a variety of topics.

Standard 1.3: Students present information, concepts, and ideas to an audience of listeners or readers on a variety of topics.

CULTURES: Gain Knowledge and Understanding of Other Cultures

Standard 2.1: Students demonstrate an understanding of the relationship between the practices and perspectives of the culture studied.

Standard 2.2: Students demonstrate an understanding of the relationship between the products and perspectives of the culture studied.

CONNECTIONS: Connect with Other Disciplines and Acquire Information

Standard 3.1: Students reinforce and further their knowledge of other disciplines through the foreign language.

Standard 3.2: Students acquire information and recognize the distinctive viewpoints that are only available through the foreign language and its cultures.

COMPARISONS: Develop Insight into the Nature of Language and Culture

Standard 4.1: Students demonstrate understanding of the nature of language through comparisons of the language studied and their own.

Standard 4.2: Students demonstrate understanding of the concept of culture through comparisons of the cultures studied and their own.

Source: National Standards in Foreign Language Education Project. (1996). *Standards for foreign language learning: Preparing for the 21st century* (p. 9). Yonkers, NY: ACTFL.

COMMUNITIES: Participate in Multilingual Communities at Home and Around the World

Standard 5.1: Students use the language both within and beyond the school setting.

Standard 5.2: Students show evidence of becoming lifelong learners by using the language for personal enjoyment and enrichment.

References

Aebersold, J. A., & Field, M. L. (1997). *From reading to reading teacher: Issues and strategies for second language classrooms.* Cambridge: Cambridge University Press.

Alderson, J. C. (1984). Reading in a foreign language: A reading problem or a language problem? In J. C. Alderson & A. H. Urquhart (Eds.), *Reading in a foreign language* (pp. 1–24). London: Longman.

Aljaafreh, A., & Lantolf, J. P. (1994). Negative feedback as regulation and second language learning in the zone of proximal development. *Modern Language Journal, 78*(4), 465–483.

American Council on the Teaching of Foreign Languages. (1986). *Proficiency guidelines.* Yonkers, NY: ACTFL.

American Council on the Teaching of Foreign Languages. (1998). *ACTFL performance guidelines for K–12 learners.* Yonkers, NY: ACTFL.

Anderson, V., & Roit, M. (1996). Linking reading comprehension instruction to language development for language-minority students. *The Elementary School Journal, 96*(3), 295–309.

Anton, M., & DiCamilla, F. (1998). Socio-cognitive functions of L1 collaborative interaction in the L2 classroom. *Canadian Modern Language Review, 54*(3), 314–342.

Apple, M. (1992). The text and cultural politics. *Educational Researcher, 21*(7), 4–11.

Applebee, A. N. (in press). Alternative models of writing development. In R. Indrisano & J. R. Squire (Eds.), *Writing: Research/theory/practice.* Newark, DE: International Reading Association.

Bachman, L. (1988). Problems in examining the validity of the ACTFL oral proficiency interview. *Studies in Second Language Acquisition, 10*(2), 149–164.

Bachman, L. (1990). *Fundamental considerations in language testing.* Oxford: Oxford University Press.

Baker, C. (1992). Description and analysis in classroom talk and interaction. *Journal of Classroom Interaction, 27*(2), 9–14.

Bakhtin, M. M. (1981). *The dialogic imagination* (C. Emerson & M. Holquist, Trans.). Austin, TX: University of Texas Press.

Bakhtin, M. M. (1986). *"Speech genres" and other essays* (M. Holquist & C. Emerson, Eds., V. McGee, Trans.). Austin, TX: University of Texas Press.

Bandura, A. (1977). *Social learning theory.* Englewood Cliffs, NJ: Prentice Hall.

Bangert-Drowns, R., & Swan, K. (1997). *Electronic texts and literacy for the 21st century.* Washington, DC: U.S. Department of Education, Office of Educational Research and Improvement, Educational Resources Information Center.

Barnes, D. (1992). *From communication to curriculum.* Portsmouth, NH: Boynton/Cook.

Barnhardt, S., Kevorkian, J., & Delett, J. (1998). *Portfolio assessment in the foreign language classroom.* Washington, DC: National Capital Resource Center.

Barnwell, D. (1989). Proficiency and the native speaker. *ADFL Bulletin, 20*(2), 42–46.

Barton, D. (1994). *Literacy: An introduction to the ecology of written language.* London: Blackwell.

Barton, D., & Hamilton, M. (Eds.). (1998). *Local literacies: Reading and writing in one community.* London: Routledge.

Barton, D., & Ivanic, R. (Eds.). (1991). Writing in the community. *Written communication annual, Vol. 6.* Newbury Park, CA: Sage Publications.

Becker, J. (1975). *The phrasal lexicon.* Bolt Bernall & Newman Report #3081. AI Report #28.

Berk, L. E., & Garvin, R. A. (1984). Development of private speech among low-income Appalachian children. *Developmental Psychology, 20,* 271–286.

Berman, R., & Slobin, D. (1994). *Relating events in narratives: A crosslinguistic developmental study.* Hillsdale, NJ: Lawrence Erlbaum.

Bernhardt, E. (1991). *Reading development in a second language.* Norwood, NJ: Ablex.

Bialystok, E. (1991). Metalinguistic dimensions of bilingual language proficiency. In E. Bialystok (Ed.), *Language processing in bilingual children* (pp. 113–140). Cambridge: Cambridge University Press.

Bicknell, J. (1999). Promoting writing and computer literacy skills through student-authored web pages. *TESOL Journal, 8*(1), 20–26.

Bloom, B. S. (Ed.). (1984). *Taxonomy of educational objectives: The classification of educational goals.* White Plains, NY: Longman.

Bodrova, E., & Leong, D. J. (1996). *Tools of the mind: The Vygotskian approach to early childhood education.* Englewood Cliffs, NJ: Merrill.

Bouton, L. F. (1994). Conversational implicature in the second language: Learned slowly when not deliberately taught. *Journal of Pragmatics, 22,* 157–167.

Bowers, C. A., & Flinders, D. (1990). *Responsive teaching: An ecological approach to classroom patterns of language, culture, and thought.* New York: Teachers College Press.

Boyd, M., & Maloof, V. (2000). How teachers can build upon student-proposed intertextual links to facilitate student talk in the ESL classroom. In J. K. Hall & L. S. Verplaetse (Eds.), *Second and foreign language learning through classroom interaction* (pp. 163–182). Mahwah, NJ: Lawrence Erlbaum.

Breiner-Sanders, K., Lowe, P., Miles, J., & Swender, E. (2000). ACTFL proficiency guidelines—speaking: Revised 1999. *Foreign Language Annals, 33*(1), 13–18.

Britton, J., Burgess, T., Martin, N., McLeod, A., & Rosen, H. (1975). *The development of writing ability (11–18).* London: Macmillan.

Brooks, F. B., & Donato, R. (1994). Vygotskyan approaches to understanding foreign language learner discourse during communicative tasks. *Hispania, 77,* 262–274.

Brown, A., Ash, D., Rutherford, M., Nakagawa, K., Gordon, A., & Campione, J. (1993). Distributed expertise in the classroom. In G. Salomon (Ed.), *Distributed cognitions: Psychological and educational considerations* (pp. 188–228). Cambridge: Cambridge University Press.

Brown, A., & Campione, J. (1994). Guided discovery in a community of learners. In K. McGilly (Ed.), *Classroom lessons: Integrating cognitive theory and classroom practice.* Cambridge, MA: MIT Press.

Brown, J. D. (1995). *The elements of language curriculum.* Boston: Heinle and Heinle.

Bruner, J. (1986). *Actual minds, possible worlds.* Cambridge, MA: Harvard University Press.

Bruner, J. (1990). *Acts of meaning.* Cambridge, MA: Harvard University Press.

Byram, M. (1989). *Cultural studies in foreign language education.* Clevedon, England: Multilingual Matters.

Byram, M. (1997). *Teaching and assessing intercultural communicative competence.* Clevedon, England: Multilingual Matters.

Byram, M., & Morgan, C. (1994). *Teaching-and-learning language-and-culture.* Clevedon, England: Multilingual Matters.

Byram, M., & Zarate, G. (1997). *The sociocultural and intercultural dimensions of language learning and teaching.* Strasbourg, France: Council of Europe.

Cabello, B., & Terrell, R. (1994). Making students feel like family: How teachers create warm and caring classroom climates. *Journal of Classroom Interaction, 29*(1), 17–23.

Calero-Breckheimer, A., & Goetz, E. T. (1993). Reading strategies of biliterate children for English and Spanish tests. *Reading Psychology, 14,* 177–204.

Canale, M. (1983). From communicative competence to communicative language pedagogy. In J. Richards & R. W. Schmidt (Eds.), *Language and communication* (pp. 2–27). New York: Longman.

Canale, M., & Swain, M. (1980). Theoretical bases of communicative approaches to second language teaching and testing. *Applied Linguistics, 1*(1), 1–47.

Carlsen, W. S. (1992). Closing down the conversation: Discouraging student talk on unfamiliar science content. *Journal of Classroom Interaction, 27*(2), 15–21.

Carrell, P., Devine, J., & Eskey, D. E. (Eds.). (1988). *Interactive approaches to second language reading.* Cambridge: Cambridge University Press.

Carrell, P., & Eisterhold, J. C. (1983). Schema theory and ESL reading pedagogy. *TESOL Quarterly, 17*(4), 553–574.

Carter, K. (1990). Teacher's knowledge and learning to teach. In W. R. Houston (Ed.), *Handbook of research on teacher education.* New York: MacMillan.

Cazden, C. (1988). *Classroom discourse.* Portsmouth, NH: Heinemann.

Cazden, C. (1993). Vygotsky, Hymes and Bakhtin: From word to utterance. In E. Forman, N. Minick, & C. A. Stone (Eds.), *Contexts for learning: Sociocultural dynamics in children's development* (pp. 197–212). New York: Oxford University Press.

Cazden, C. (2000). Taking cultural differences into account. In B. Cope & M. Kalantzis (Eds.), *Multilit-*

eracies: Literacy learning and the design of social futures (pp. 249–266). London: Routledge.

Celce-Murcia, M. (1991). Grammar pedagogy in second and foreign language teaching. *TESOL Quarterly, 25,* 459–480.

Celce-Murcia, M., Zoltan, D., & Thurrell, S. (1995). Communicative competence: A pedagogically motivated model with content specification. *Issues in Applied Linguistics, 6*(2), 5–35.

Cenoz, J., & Genesee, F. (1998). Psycholinguistic perspectives on multilingualism and multilingual education. In J. Cenoz & F. Genesee (Eds.), *Beyond bilingualism* (pp. 16–31). Clevedon, England: Multi-lingual Matters.

Chamot, A. U., & O'Malley, J. M. (1994). *The CALLA handbook: How to implement the cognitive academic language learning approach.* White Plains, NY: Addison Wesley Longman.

Chang-Wells, G. L. M., & Wells, G. (1993). Dynamics of discourse: Literacy and the construction of knowledge. In E. A. Forman, N. Minick, & C. A. Stone (Eds.), *Contexts for learning: Sociocultural dynamics in children's development* (pp. 58–90). New York: Oxford University Press.

Chastain, K. (1989). The ACTFL proficiency guidelines: A selected sample of opinions. *ADFL Bulletin, 20*(2), 47–51.

Chen, Q., & Donin, J. (1997). Discourse processing of first and second language biology texts: Effects of language proficiency and domain-specific knowledge. *Modern Language Journal, 81*(2), 209–227.

Cho, K.-S., & Krashen, S. (1994). Acquisition of vocabulary from the Sweet Valley Kids series: Adult ESL acquisition. *Journal of Reading, 37,* 662–667.

Chomsky, N. (1957). *Syntactic structures.* The Hague, Netherlands: Mouton.

Chomsky, N. (1965). *Aspects of the theory of syntax.* Cambridge, MA: MIT Press.

Chomsky, N. (1966). *Topics in the theory of generative grammar.* The Hague, Netherlands: Mouton.

Clark, H. (1996). *Using language.* Cambridge: Cambridge University Press.

Clark, J. L., & Clifford, R. T. (1988). The FSI/ILR/ACTFL proficiency scales and testing techniques: Development, current status, and needed research. *Studies in Second Language Acquisition, 10*(2), 129–147.

Clay, M. M., & Cazden, C. B. (1990). A Vygotskian interpretation of Reading Recovery. In L. C. Moll

(Ed.), *Vygotsky and education: Instructional implications of sociohistorical psychology* (pp. 206–222). New York: Cambridge University Press.

Cohen, E. (1994). *Designing groupwork: Strategies for heterogeneous classrooms* (2nd ed.). New York: Teachers College Press.

Consolo, D. (2000). Teachers' action and student oral participation in classroom interaction. In J. K. Hall & L. S. Verplaetse (Eds.), *Second and foreign language learning through classroom interaction* (pp. 91–108). Mahwah, NJ: Lawrence Erlbaum.

Cook, G. (1997). Language play, language learning. *ELT Journal, 51*(3), 224–231.

Cook, V. (1992). Evidence for multicompetence. *Language Learning, 42*(4), 557–591.

Cook, V. (1995). Multi-competence and the learning of many languages. *Language, Culture and Curriculum, 8,* 93–98.

Cook, V. (1996). Competence and multi-competence. In G. Brown, K. Malmkjaer, & J. Williams (Eds.), *Performance and competence in second language acquisition* (pp. 57–69). Cambridge: Cambridge University Press.

Cook, V. (1999a). Going beyond the native speaker in language teaching. *TESOL Quarterly, 33*(2), 185–209.

Cook, V. (1999b, March). *Transfer from L2 to L1.* Paper presented at the AAAL 1999 Conference, Stamford, CT.

Cook, V. (in press). Using the first language in the classroom. *Canadian Modern Language Review, 57.*

Cooper, P. J., & Simonds, C. (1998). *Communication for the classroom teacher* (6th ed.). Boston: Allyn & Bacon.

Cope, B., & Kalantzis, M. (Eds.). (2000). *Multiliteracies: Literacy learning and the design of social futures.* London: Routledge.

Crookes, G., & Gass, S. (Eds.). (1993a). *Tasks and language learning: Integrating theory and practice.* Clevedon, UK: Multilingual Matters.

Crookes, G., & Gass, S. (Eds.). (1993b). *Tasks in a pedagogical context: Integrating theory and practice.* Clevedon, UK: Multilingual Matters.

Cummins, J. (1979). Linguistic interdependence and the educational development of bilingual children. *Review of Educational Research, 49,* 222–251.

Davis, J., & Hall, J. K. (1998). The student teaching practicum: The perceived importance of collaborative relationships. *The ESPecialist, 19*(1), 91–121.

Detterman, D., & Sternberg, R. (Eds.). (1993). *Transfer on trial: Intelligence, cognition and instruction.* Norwood: Ablex.

Diaz, R. M. (1985). Bilingual cognitive development: Addressing three gaps in current research. *Child Development, 56,* 1376–1388.

Diaz, R. M. (1992). Methodological concerns in private speech. In L. E. Berk & R. M. Diaz (Eds.), *Private speech: From social interaction to self-regulation* (pp. 55–81). Hillsdale, NJ: Lawrence Erlbaum.

DiCamilla, F., & Anton, M. (1997). Repetition in the collaborative discourse of L2 learners: A Vygotskian perspective. *Canadian Modern Language Review, 53,* 609–633.

Dien, T. (1998). Language and literacy in Vietnamese American communities. In B. Perez (Ed.), *Sociocultural contexts of language and literacy* (pp. 123–162). Mahwah, NJ: Lawrence Erlbaum.

Donato, R. (1994). Collective scaffolding in second language learning. In J. Lantolf & G. Appel (Eds.), *Vygotskian approaches to second language research* (pp. 33–56). Norwood, NJ: Ablex.

Donato, R., & Lantolf, J. P. (1990). The dialogic origins of L2 monitoring. *Pragmatics and Language Learning, 1,* 83–98.

Donato, R., & McCormick, D. (1994). A sociocultural perspective on language learning strategies: The role of mediation. *Modern Language Journal, 78*(4), 453–464.

Doughty, C., & Williams, J. (1998). Pedagogical choices in focus on form. In C. Doughty & J. Williams (Eds.), *Focus on form in classroom second language acquisition* (pp. 197–261). Cambridge: Cambridge University Press.

Duff, P. (2000). Repetition in foreign language classroom interaction. In J. K. Hall & L. S. Verplaetse (Eds.), *Second and foreign language learning through classroom interaction* (pp. 109–138). Mahwah, NJ: Lawrence Erlbaum.

Dunn, W. E., & Lantolf, J. P. (1998). Vygotsky's zone of proximal development and Krashen's "I+1": Incommensurable constructs, incommensurable theories. *Language Learning, 48*(3), 411–442.

Duranti, A. (1997). *Linguistic anthropology.* Cambridge: Cambridge University Press.

Durgunoglu, A., Nagy, W. E., & Hancin-Bhatt, B. J. (1993). Cross-language transfer of phonological awareness. *Journal of Educational Psychology, 85,* 453–465.

Durst, R. K. (1987). Cognitive and linguistic demands of analytic writing. *Research in the Teaching of English, 21*(4), 347–376.

Dyson, A. H. (2000). Linking writing and community development through the children's forum. In C. Lee & P. Smagorinsky (Eds.), *Vygotskian perspectives on literacy research* (pp. 127–149). Cambridge: Cambridge University Press.

Edelsky, C. (1996). *With literacy and justice for all: Rethinking the social in language and education* (2nd ed.). New York: Falmer Press.

Eder, D. (1982). Differences in communicative styles across ability groups. In L. C. Wilkinson (Ed.), *Communicating in the classroom* (pp. 245–264). New York: Academic Press.

Edwards, A. D., & Westgate, D. P. G. (1994). *Investigating classroom talk.* London: Falmer Press.

Elley, W. (1991). Acquiring literacy in a second language: The effect of book-based programs. *Language Learning, 41*(3), 375–411.

Elley, W., & Mangubhai, F. (1983). The impact of reading on second language learning. *Reading Research Quarterly, 19,* 53–67.

Ellis, R. (1992). *Second language acquisition and language pedagogy.* Clevedon, UK: Multilingual Matters.

Erickson, E., & Shultz, J. (1982). *The counselor as gatekeeper: Social interaction in interviews.* New York: Academic Press.

Fielding, L. G., & Pearson, P. D. (1994). Reading comprehension: What works. *Educational Leadership, 51*(5), 62–68.

Firth, A., & Wagner, J. (1997). On discourse, communication, and (some) fundamental concepts in SLA research. *Modern Language Journal, 81*(3), 277–300.

Fischer, K., Bullock, D., Rotenberg, E., & Raya, P. (1993). The dynamics of competence: How context contributes directly to skill. In R. Wozniak & K. Fischer (Eds.), *Development in context: Acting and thinking in specific environments* (pp. 93–117). Hillsdale, NJ: Lawrence Erlbaum.

Fisher, S. (1991). A discourse of the social: Medical talk/power talk/oppositional talk? *Discourse & Society, 2*(2), 157–182.

Fitzgerald, J. (1995). English-as-a-second-language learners' cognitive reading processes: A review of research in the United States. *Review of Educational Research, 65*(2), 145–190.

Flower, J., & Hayes, J. (1984). Images, plans and prose: The representation of meaning in writing. *Written Communication, 1,* 120–160.

Foley, K. (1993). Talking journals. *TESOL Journal, 3*(1), 37–38.

Forman, E. A. (1996). Learning mathematics as participation in classroom practice: Implications of sociocultural theory for educational reform. In L. Steffe, P. Nesher, P. Cobb, G. A. Goldin, & B. Greer (Eds.), *Theories of mathematical learning* (pp. 115–130). Hillsdale, NJ: Erlbaum.

Foster, M. (1989). "It's cooking now": A performance analysis of the speech events of a Black teacher in an urban community college. *Language in Society, 18,* 1–29.

Fotos, S. (1994). Integrating grammar instruction and communicative language use through grammar consciousness-raising tasks. *TESOL Quarterly, 28* (2), 323–351.

Fradd, S. H., & McGee, P. L. (1994). *Instructional assessment: An integrative approach to evaluating student performance.* Reading, MA: Addison-Wesley Publishing Company.

Gass, S. M. (1997). *Input, interaction, and the second language learner.* Mahwah, NJ: Lawrence Erlbaum.

Gass, S. M., & Varonis, E. M. (1985). Variation in native speaker speech modification to non-native speakers. *Studies in Second Language Acquisition, 7,* 37–58.

Gee, J. (1996). *Social linguistics and literacies: Ideologies in discourses* (2nd ed.). London: Taylor & Francis.

Genesee, F., Nicoladis, E., & Paradis, J. (1995). Language differentiation in early bilingual development. *Journal of Child Language, 22,* 611–631.

Giles, H., Coupland, J., & Coupland, N. (Eds.). (1991). *Contexts of accommodation: Developments in applied sociolinguistics.* Cambridge: Cambridge University Press.

Giles, H., Mulac, A., Bradac, J., & Johnson, P. (1987). Speech accommodation theory: The first decade and beyond. In M. McLauglin (Ed.), *Communication yearbook, Vol. 10* (pp. 13–48). Beverly Hills, CA: Sage.

Godwin-Jones, B. (2000). Emerging technologies: Speech technologies for language learning. *Language Learning and Technology, 3*(2), 6–9.

Goldenberg, C. (1991). *Instructional conversations and their classroom application.* Washington, DC: The National Center for Research on Cultural Diversity and Second Language Learning.

Gonzalez, N., Moll, L., Floyd-Tenery, M., Rivera, A., Rendon, P., Gonzalez, R., & Amanti, C. (1993). *Teacher research on funds of knowledge: Learning from households* (Educational Practice Report No. 6). Santa Cruz, CA and Washington, DC: National Center for Research on Cultural Diversity and Second Language Learning.

Goodwin, G., & Goodwin, M. H. (1992). Assessments and the construction of context. In A. Duranti & C. Goodwin (Eds.), *Rethinking context: Language as an interactive phenomenon* (pp. 147–189). Cambridge: Cambridge University Press.

Grabe, W. (1991). Current developments in second language reading research. *TESOL Quarterly, 25,* 375–406.

Grabe, W., & Kaplan, R. (1996). *Theory and practice of writing.* New York: Longman.

Graesser, A. C., Person, N. K., & Magliano, J. P. (1995). Collaborative dialogue patterns in naturalistic one-on-one tutoring. *Applied Cognitive Psychology, 9,* 359–387.

Green, J., & Dixon, C. (1993). Introduction to "Talking knowledge into being: Discursive and social practices in classrooms." *Linguistics and Education, 5*(3–4), 231–239.

Grosse, C. (1993). The foreign language methods course. *Modern Language Journal, 77*(3), 303–312.

Grossman, P. (1990). *The making of a teacher: Teacher knowledge and teacher education.* New York: Teachers College Press.

Gumperz, J. (1981). The linguistic bases of communicative competence. In D. Tannen (Ed.), *Analyzing discourse: Text and talk* (pp. 323–334). Washington, DC: Georgetown University Press.

Gumperz, J. (Ed.). (1982). *Language and social identity.* Cambridge: Cambridge University Press.

Gutierrez, K. (1994). How talk, context, and script shape contexts for learning: A cross-case comparison of journal sharing. *Linguistics and Education, 5,* 335–365.

Gutierrez, K. (1995). Unpackaging academic discourse. *Discourse Processes, 19,* 21–37.

Gutierrez, K., Larson, J., & Kreuter, B. (1995). Cultural tensions in the scripted classroom: The value of the subjugated perspective. *Urban Education, 29,* 410–442.

Hadley, A. O. (1993). *Teaching language in context: Proficiency-oriented instruction* (2nd ed.). Boston: Heinle and Heinle.

Hall, J. K. (1993). Oye oye lo que ustedes no saben: Creativity, social power and politics in the oral practice of Chismeando. *Journal of Linguistic Anthropology, 3*(3), 75–98.

Hall, J. K. (1995). (Re)creating our world with words: A sociohistorical perspective of face-to-face interaction. *Applied Linguistics, 16*(2), 206–232.

Hall, J. K. (1997). A consideration of SLA as a theory of practice. *Modern Language Journal, 81*(3), 301–306.

Hall, J. K. (1998). Differential teacher attention to student utterances: The construction of different opportunities for learning in the IRF. *Linguistics and Education, 9*(3), 287–311.

Hall, J. K. (1999). The communication standards. In J. Phillips & R. Terry (Eds.), *Foreign language standards: Linking research, theories, and practices* (pp. 15–56). Lincolnwood, IL: National Textbook Company.

Hall, J. K., & Davis, J. (1995). What we know about relationships that develop between cooperating and student teachers. *Foreign Language Annals, 28,* 32–48.

Hall, S. (1996). Introduction: Who needs identity? In S. Hall & P. de Gay (Eds.), *Questions of cultural identity* (pp. 1–17). London: Sage.

Halliday, M., & Hasan, R. (1976). *Cohesion in English.* New York: Longman.

Hamayan, E. (1995). Approaches to alternative assessment. *Annual Review of Applied Linguistics, 15,* 212–226.

Hammadou, J. (1991). Interrelationships among prior knowledge, inference, and language proficiency in foreign language reading. *The Modern Language Journal, 75*(1), 27–38.

Haneda, M., & Wells, G. (2000). Writing in knowledge-building communities. *Research in the Teaching of English, 34,* 430–457.

Harkness, S., Super, C. M., & Keefer, C. H. (1992). Learning to be an American parent: How cultural models gain directive force. In R. G. D'Andrade & C. Strauss (Eds.), *Human motives and cultural models.* New York: Cambridge University Press.

Haviland, J. B. (1977). *Gossip, reputation and knowledge in Zinacantan.* Chicago: University of Chicago Press.

Head, F. A. (1992). Student teaching as initiation into the teaching profession. *Anthropology and Education Quarterly, 23:* 89–107.

Heath, S. (1983). *Ways with words: Language, life and work in communities and classrooms.* Cambridge: Cambridge University Press.

Heath, S. B. (1993). Inner city life through drama: Imagining the language classroom. *TESOL Quarterly, 27,* 177–192.

Herron, C., Cole, S., Corrie, C., & Dubreil, S. (1999). The effectiveness of a video-based curriculum on teaching culture. *Modern Language Journal, 83*(4), 518–533.

Howatt, A. (1984). *A history of English language teaching.* Oxford: Oxford University Press.

Hymes, D. (1964). Formal discussion of a conference paper. In U. Bellugi & R. Brown (Eds.), *The acquisition of language* (pp. 107–112). Lafayette, IL: Child Development Publications.

Hymes, D. (1972a). Models of the interaction of language and social life. In J. J. Gumperz & D. Hymes (Eds.), *Directions in sociolinguistics: The ethnography of communication* (pp. 35–71). New York: Holt, Rinehart & Winston.

Hymes, D. (1972b). On communicative competence. In J. B. Pride & J. Holmes (Eds.), *Sociolinguistics.* Baltimore, MD: Penguin.

Jiménez, R. J., García, G. E., & Pearson, P. D. (1995). The reading skills of bilingual Latina/o students who are successful English readers. *Reading Research Quarterly, 31*(1), 90–114.

John-Steiner, V., & Meehan, T. (2000). Creativity and collaboration. In C. Lee & P. Smagorinksy (Eds.), *Vygotskian perspectives on literacy research.* Cambridge: Cambridge University Press.

John-Steiner, V., Panofsky, C. P., & Smith, L. W. (1994). *Sociocultural approaches to language and literacy: An interactionist perspective* (pp. 31–50). New York: Cambridge University Press.

Johnstone, B. (Ed.). (1994). *Repetition in discourse* (Vols. 1–2). Norwood, NJ: Ablex.

Kalekin-Fishman, D., & Kornfeld, G. (1991). Construing roles: Co-operating teachers and student teachers in TEFL: An Israeli study. *Journal of Education for Teaching, 17,* 151–163.

Katriel, T. (1987). Bexibudim!: Ritualized sharing among Israeli children. *Language in Society, 16,* 305–320.

Kellough, R. D., & Kellough, N. G. (1999). *High school teaching: A guide to methods and resources.* Upper Saddle River, NJ: Merrill/Prentice Hall.

Kieffer, R. D., & Faust, M. A. (1994). Portfolio process and teacher change: Elementary, secondary, and university teachers reflect upon their initial experiences with portfolio assessment. In C. Kinzer & D. Leu (Eds.), *Multidimensional aspects of literary research, theory and practice.* Washington, DC: National Reading Conference.

Kim, D., & Hall, J. K. (2000). *The role of an interactive book reading program in the development of L2 pragmatic competence.* Unpublished manuscript.

Kinginger, C. (2000). Learning the pragmatics of solidarity in the networked foreign language classroom. In J. K. Hall & L. S. Verplaetse (Eds.), *Second and foreign language learning through classroom interaction* (pp. 23–46). Mahwah, NJ: Lawrence Erlbaum.

Knutson, E. K. (1997). Reading with a purpose: Communicative reading tasks for the foreign language classroom. *Foreign Language Annals, 30*(1), 49–57.

Koda, K. (1988). Cognitive process in second language reading: Transfer of L1 reading skills and strategies. *Second Language Research, 4*(2), 133–156.

Koda, K. (1989). The effects of transferred vocabulary knowledge on the development of L2 reading proficiency. *Foreign Language Annals, 22*(6), 529–540.

Kowal, M., & Swain, M. (1994). Using collaborative language production tasks to promote students' language awareness. *Language Awareness, 3*(2), 73–93.

Kramsch, C. (1993). *Context and culture in language teaching.* Oxford: Oxford University Press.

Kramsch, C. (1998). The privilege of the intercultural speaker. In M. Byram & M. Fleming (Eds.), *Language learning in intercultural perspective* (pp. 16–31). Cambridge: Cambridge University Press.

Krashen, S. (1982). *Principles and practice in second language acquisition.* Oxford, England: Pergamon.

Krashen, S. (1985). *The input hypothesis: Issues and implications.* Oxford, England: Pergamon.

Krashen, S. (1995). Free voluntary reading: Linguistic and affective arguments and some new applications. In F. Richman, D. Highland, P. Lee, J. Mileham, & R. Weber (Eds.), *Second language acquisition and pedagogy* (pp. 187–202). Mahwah, NJ: Lawrence Erlbaum.

Krashen, S. D., & Terrell, T. D. (1983). *The natural approach.* Hayward, CA: Alemany Press.

Lamoureux, E. L. (1988/89). Rhetoric and conversation in service encounters. *Research in Language and Social Interaction, 22,* 93–114.

Lantolf, J. P. (1997). The function of language play in the acquisition of L2 Spanish. In W. R. Glass & A. T.

Perez-Leroux (Eds.), *Contemporary perspectives on the acquisition of Spanish.* Somerville, MA: Cascadilla Press.

Lantolf, J. P., & Frawley, W. (1985). Oral proficiency testing: A critical analysis. *Modern Language Journal, 69*(4), 337–345.

Larsen-Freeman, D. (2000). An attitude of inquiry: TESOL as a science. *The Journal of the Imagination in Language Learning, 5,* 18–21.

Lave, J., & Wenger, E. (1991). *Situated learning: Legitimate peripheral participation.* New York: Cambridge University Press.

Lee, C. D. (1995). A culturally based cognitive apprenticeship: Teaching African American high school students skills in literary interpretation. *Reading Research Quarterly, 30,* 608–630.

Lee, C., & Smagorinsky, P. (2000). Introduction: Constructing meaning through collaborative inquiry. In C. Lee & P. Smagorinsky (Eds.), *Vygotskian perspectives on literacy research* (pp. 1–18). Cambridge: Cambridge University Press.

Lemke, J. (1988). Genres, semantics, and classroom education. *Linguistics and Education, 1*(1), 81–89.

Lensmire, T. J. (1994). *When children write: Critical revisions of the writing workshop.* New York: Teachers College Press.

Leontiev, A. A. (1981). *Psychology and the language learning process.* Oxford: Pergamon.

Leontiev, A. N. (1981). *Problems of the development of the mind.* Moscow: Progress Publishers.

Lerner, G. (1994). Responsive list construction: A conversational resource for accomplishing multifaceted social action. *Journal of Language and Social Psychology, 13*(1), 20–33.

Levy, E., & Nelson, K. (1994). Words in discourse: A dialectical approach to the acquisition of meaning and use. *Journal of Child Language, 21,* 367–389.

Light, P., & Butterworth, G. (Eds.). (1993). *Context and cognition: Ways of learning and knowing.* Hillsdale, NJ: Lawrence Erlbaum.

Lightbown, P. M., & Spada, N. (1990). Focus-on-form and corrective feedback in communicative language teaching: Effects on second language learning. *Studies in Second Language Acquisition, 12,* 429–448.

LoCastro, V. (1996). The acquisition of pragmatic competence by Japanese learners of English. In T. Fujimura, Y. Kato, M. Ahmed, & M. Leoung (Eds.), *Proceedings of the 7th Conference on Second*

Language Research in Japan (pp. 115–134). Nigata, Japan: International University of Japan.

Long, M. (1981). Input, interaction, and second language acquisition. In H. Winitz (Ed.), *Native language and foreign language acquisition* (pp. 259–278). New York: Annals of the New York Academy of Sciences.

Long, M. H. (1983). Native speaker/non native speaker conversation and the negotiation of comprehensible input. *Applied Linguistics, 4,* 126–141.

Long, M., & Robinson, P. (1998). Focus on form, theory, research and practice. In C. Doughty & J. Williams (Eds.), *Focus on form in classroom second language acquisition* (pp. 15–41). Cambridge: Cambridge University Press.

Lotan, R. (1997). Complex instruction: An overview. In E. Cohen & R. Lotan (Eds.), *Working for equity in heterogeneous classrooms* (pp. 15–30). New York: Teachers College Press.

Luke, A. (1988). *Literacy, textbooks, and ideology.* Philadelphia, PA: Falmer Press.

Luke, C. (2000). Cyber-schooling and technological change. In B. Cope & M. Kalantzis (Eds.), *Multiliteracies: Literacy learning and the design of social futures* (pp. 69–91). London: Routledge.

Lyster, R. (1994). The effect of functional-analytic teaching on aspects of French immersion students' sociolinguistic competence. *Applied Linguistics, 15*(3), 263–287.

Lyster, R. (1998). Recasts, repetition, and ambiguity in L2 classroom discourse. *Studies in Second Language Acquisition, 20,* 51–81.

Lyster, R., & Ranta, L. (1997). Corrective feedback and learner uptake: Negotiation of form in communicative classrooms. *Studies in Second Language Acquisition, 19,* 37–66.

Mackey, A., & Philp, J. (1998). Conversational interaction and second language development. Recasts, responses, and red herrings? *Modern Language Journal, 82*(3), 338–356.

Mandelbaum, J., & Pomerantz, A. (1991). What drives social action? In K. Tracy (Ed.), *Understanding face-to-face interaction* (pp. 151–166). Hillsdale, NJ: Lawrence Erlbaum.

McCafferty, S. G. (1994). Adult second language learners' use of private speech: A review of studies. *Modern Language Journal, 78*(4), 421–436.

McCarty, T., & Watahomigie, L. (1998). Language and literacy in American Indian and Alaska native communities. In B. Perez (Ed.), *Sociocultural contexts of language and literacy* (pp. 69–98). Mahwah, NJ: Lawrence Erlbaum.

McCormick, D., & Donato, R. (2000). Teacher questions as scaffolded assistance in an ESL classroom. In J. K. Hall & L. S. Verplaetse (Eds.), *Second and foreign language learning through classroom interaction* (pp. 183–201). Mahwah, NJ: Lawrence Erlbaum.

McHoul, A. (1990). The organization of repair in classroom talk. *Language in Society, 19,* 349–377.

Mehan, H. (1979). *Learning lessons.* Cambridge, MA: Harvard University Press.

Miramontes, O., Nadeau, A., & Commins, N. (1997). *Restructuring schools for linguistic diversity.* New York: Teachers College Press.

Moerman, M. (1988). *Talking culture: Ethnography and conversation analysis.* Philadelphia: University of Pennsylvania Press.

Moll, L. (1990). Introduction. In L. Moll (Ed.), *Vygotsky and education: Instructional implications and applications of sociohistorical psychology* (pp. 1–27). Cambridge: Cambridge University Press.

Moll, L. (2000) Inspired by Vygotsky: Ethnographic experiments in education. In C. Lee & P. Smagorinsky (Eds.), *Vygotskian perspectives on literacy research* (pp. 256–268). Cambridge: Cambridge University Press.

Moll, L., Amanti, C., Neff, D., & Gonzalez, N. (1992). Funds of knowledge for teaching: Using a qualitative approach to connect homes and classrooms. *Theory Into Practice, 31*(2), 132–141.

Moll, L., & Dworin, J. (1996). Biliteracy in classrooms: Social dynamics and cultural possibilities. In D. Hicks (Eds.), *Child discourse and social learning* (pp. 221–246). New York: Cambridge University Press.

Morson, G. S., & Emerson, C. (Eds.). (1989). *Rethinking Bakhtin: Extensions and challenges.* Evanston, IL: Northwestern University Press.

Murison-Bowie, S. (1993). TESOL Technology: Imposition or opportunity? *TESOL Journal, 3*(1), 6–8.

Nation, R., & McLaughlin, B. (1986). Novices and experts: An information processing approach to the 'good language learner' problem. *Applied Psycholinguistics, 7,* 41–56.

National Middle School Association. (1995). *This we believe: Developmentally responsive middle level schools.* Columbus, OH: National Middle School Association.

National Standards in Foreign Language Education Project. (1996). *Standards for foreign language learning: Preparing for the 21st century.* Yonkers, NY: ACTFL.

Nayak, R., Hasen, N., Krueger, M., & McLaughlin, B. (1989). Language-learning strategies in monolingual and multilingual adults. *Language Learning, 40,* 221–244.

Nellen, T. (2000). Using the web for high school student-writers. In S. Gruber (Ed.), *Weaving a virtual web: Practical approaches to new information technologies* (pp. 211–240). Urbana, IL: National Council of Teachers of English.

New London Group. (1996). A pedagogy of multiliteracies: Designing social futures. *Harvard Educational Review, 66,* 60–92.

New London Group. (2000). A pedagogy of multiliteracies: Designing social futures. In B. Cope & M. Kalantzis (Eds.), *Multiliteracies: Literacy learning and the design of social futures* (pp. 9–38). London: Routledge.

Newman, F., & Holzman, L. (1993). *Lev Vygotsky: Revolutionary scientist.* London: Routledge.

Nicoladis, E., & Genesee, F. (1996). A longitudinal study of pragmatic differentiation in young bilingual children. *Language Learning, 46,* 439–464.

Nicoladis, E., & Genesee, F. (1998). Parental discourse and codemixing in bilingual children. *The International Journal of Bilingualism, 2*(1), 85–99.

Ninio, A., & Snow, C. (1996). *Pragmatic development.* Boulder, CO: Westview.

Nystrand, M. (1997). *Opening dialogue.* New York: Teachers College Press.

Ochs, E. (1988). *Culture and language development.* Cambridge: Cambridge University Press.

O'Hair, D., Friedrich, G., Wienmann, J., & Wienmann, M. (1995). *Competent communication.* New York: St. Martin's Press.

Ohta, A. S. (1995). Applying sociocultural theory to an analysis of learner discourse: Learner-learner collaborative interaction in the zone of proximal development. *Issues in Applied Linguistics, 6*(2), 93–121.

Ohta, A. S. (1997). The development of pragmatic competence in learner-learner classroom interaction. *Pragmatics and Language Learning, 8,* 223–242.

Ohta, A. S. (2000). Re-thinking recasts: A learner-centered examination of corrective feedback in the Japanese language classroom. In J. K. Hall & L. S. Verplaetse (Eds.), *Second and foreign language*

learning through classroom interaction (pp. 47–72). Mahwah, NJ: Lawrence Erlbaum.

O'Malley, J. M., & Pierce, L. V. (1996). *Authentic assessment for English language learners: Practical approaches for teachers.* New York: Addison-Wesley.

Oxford, R. (1990). *Language learning strategies.* New York: Newbury House.

Palincsar, A. S., & Brown, A. L. (1984). Reciprocal teaching of comprehension-fostering and comprehension-monitoring activities. *Cognition and Instruction, 2,* 117–175.

Panel on Educational Technology. (1997). *Report to the President on the Use of Technology to Strengthen K–12 Education in the United States.* Washington, DC: President's Committee of Advisors on Science and Technology.

Panese, M. (1996). Calling in: Prosody and conversation in radio talk. *Pragmatics, 6*(1), 19–87.

Patthey-Chavez, G. G., Clare, L., & Gallimore, R. (1995). *Creating a community of scholarship with instructional conversations in a transitional bilingual classroom.* Washington, DC: The National Center for Research on Cultural Diversity and Second Language Learning.

Pearson, B. Z., Fernandez, S. C., & Oller, D. K. (1993). Lexical development in bilingual infants and toddlers: Comparison to monolingual norms. *Language Learning, 43*(1), 93–120.

Peralta-Nash, C., & Dutch, J. (2000). Literature circles: Creating an environment for choice. *Primary Voices K–6, 8*(4), 29–37.

Peters, A., & Boggs, S. (1986). Interactional routines as cultural influences upon language acquisition. In B. Schieffelin & E. Ochs (Eds.), *Language socialization across cultures* (pp. 80–96). New York: Cambridge University Press.

Phillips, J. (1999). Introduction: Standards for world languages – on a firm foundation. In J. Phillips & R. Terry (Eds.), *Foreign language standards: Linking research, theories, and practices* (pp. 1–14). Lincolnwood, IL: National Textbook Company.

Phillipsen, G. (1975). Speaking like a man in Teamsterville: Cultural patterns of role enactment in an urban neighborhood. *Quarterly Journal of Speech, 61,* 13–22.

Pianta, R. (1992). Conceptual and methodological issues in research on relationships between children and nonparental adults. In R. Pianta (Ed.), *Beyond the parent: The role of other adults in children's lives* (pp. 121–129). San Francisco: Jossey-Bass.

Pica, T. (1988). Interlanguage adjustments as an outcome of NS-NNS negotiated interaction. *Language Learning, 38*(1), 45–73.

Pica, T. (1994). Research on negotiation: What does it reveal about second-language learning conditions, processes, and outcomes? *Language Learning, 44*(3), 493–527.

Pica, T., Kanagy, R., & Falodun, J. (1993). Choosing and using communication tasks for second language teaching and research. In G. Crookes & S. Gass (Eds.), *Tasks and language learning: Integrating theory and practice* (pp. 1–34). Clevedon, UK: Multilingual Matters.

Pine, J. (1994a). The language of primary caregivers. In C. Gallaway & B. Richards (Eds.), *Input and interaction in language acquisition* (pp. 15–37). Cambridge: Cambridge University Press.

Pine, J. (1994b). Environmental correlates of variation in lexical style: Interactional style and the structure of input. *Applied Psycholinguistics, 15,* 355–370.

Poole, D. (1992). Language socialization in the second language classroom. *Language Learning, 42*(4), 593–616.

Posner, G., & Rudnitsky, A. (2001). *Course design: A guide to curriculum development for teachers.* New York: Longman.

Psathas, G. (Ed.). (1990). *Interaction competence: Studies in ethnomethodology and conversation analysis.* Washington, DC: University Press of America.

Purves, A., Rogers, T., & Soter, A. (1995). *How porcupines make love III: Readers, texts, cultures in the response-based literature classroom.* New York: Longman.

Raimes, A. (1992). *Exploring through writing: A process approach to ESL composition.* New York: St. Martin's Press.

Ramirez, A. (1995). *Creating contexts for second language acquisition: Theory and methods.* New York: Longman.

Rampton, B. (1995). *Crossing: Language and ethnicity among adolescents.* London: Longman.

Ravitch, D. (1995). *National standards in American education: A citizen's guide.* Washington, DC: Brookings Institution Press.

Reddy, M. J. (1979). The conduit metaphor: A case of frame conflict in our language about language. In A. Ortony (Ed.), *Metaphor and thought.* Cambridge: Cambridge University Press.

Rennie, J. (1998). Current trends in foreign language assessment. *The ERIC Review: K–12 Foreign Language Education, 6,* 1.

Rigg, P. (1987). The Language Experience Approach: Reading naturally. In P. Rigg & V. Allen (Eds.), *When they all don't speak English.* Urbana, IL: NCTE.

Rogoff, B., Matusov, E., & White, C. (1996). Models of teaching and learning: Participation in a community of learners. In D. R. Olson & N. Torrance (Eds.), *The handbook of education and human development* (pp. 388–414). Oxford, UK: Blackwell.

Romney, J. C., Romney, D. M., & Braun, C. (1988). The effects of reading aloud in French to immersion children in second language acquisition. *The Canadian Modern Language Review, 45,* 530–538.

Rosenblatt, L. (1938/1995). *Literature as exploration.* New York: Modern Language Association.

Rothlein, L., & Meinbach, A. (1991). *The literature connection.* Glenview, IL: Scott Foresman.

Rubin, D. (1993). Listenability = oral-based discourse + considerateness. In A. Wolvin and C. G. Coakley (Eds.), *Perspectives on listening.* Norwood, NJ: Ablex.

Rubin, D. (1995). Introduction: Composing social identity. In D. Rubin (Ed.), *Composing social identity in written language* (pp. 1–30). Hillsdale, NJ: Lawrence Erlbaum.

Rubin, D., Hafer, T., & Arata, K. (2000). Reading and listening to oral-based versus literate-based discourse. *Communication Education, 49*(2), 1–24.

Rueda, R. (1998). *Standards for professional development: A sociocultural perspective* (Research Brief No. 2). Santa Cruz, CA: University of California, Center for Research on Education, Diversity and Second Language Learning.

Rueda, R., Goldenberg, C., & Gallimore, R. (1992). *Rating instructional conversations: A guide* (Educational Practice Report No. 4). Santa Cruz, CA and Washington, DC: National Center for Research on Cultural Diversity and Second Language Learning.

Rymes, B., & Pash, D. (2001). Questioning identity: The case of one second language learner. *Anthropology and Education Quarterly.*

Sanders, R. (1987). *Cognitive foundations of calculated speech.* Albany, NY: SUNY Press.

Sanders, R. (1992). Conversation, computation and the human factor. *Human Communication Research, 18*(4), 623–636.

Sarangi, S. (1994). Intercultural or not? Beyond celebration of cultural differences in miscommunication analysis. *Pragmatics, 4*(3), 409–427.

Sasaki, M., & Hirose, K. (1996). Explanatory variables for EFL students' expository writing. *Language Learning, 46*(1), 137–174.

Schegloff, E. (1982). Discourse as an interactional achievement: Some uses of "uh huh" and other things that come between sentences. In D. Tannen (Ed.), *Analyzing discourse: Text and talk* (pp. 71–93). Washington, DC: Georgetown University Press.

Schmidt, R. (1994). Deconstructing consciousness in search of useful definitions for Applied Linguistics. *AILA Review, 11,* 11–26.

Scholes, R. (1989). *Protocols of reading.* New Haven, CT: Yale University Press.

Scribner, S., & Cole, M. (1981). *The psychology of literacy.* Cambridge, MA: Harvard University Press.

Shannon, N. B., & Meath-Lang, B. (1992). Collaborative language teaching: A co-investigation. In D. Nunan (Ed.), *Collaborative language learning and teaching* (pp. 120–140). New York: Cambridge University Press.

Sherzer, J. (1983). *Kuna ways of speaking.* Austin, TX: University of Texas Press.

Shotter, J. (1996). Living in a Wittgensteinian world: Beyond theory to a poetics of practices. *Journal for the Theory of Social Behaviour, 26*(3), 292–311.

Shulman, L. (1987). Knowledge and teaching: Foundations of the new reform. *Harvard Educational Review, 57,* 114–135.

Sims-Holt, G. (1972). Stylin' outta the black pulpit. In T. Kochman (Ed.), *Rappin' and stylin' out.* Urbana, IL: University of Illinois Press.

Smagorinsky, P., & Fly, P. (1993). The social environment of the classroom: A Vygotskyan perspective on small group process. *Communication Education, 42*(2), 159–171.

Snow, C. (1989). Understanding social interaction and language acquisition: Sentences are not enough. In M. Bornstein & J. Bruner (Eds.), *Interaction in human development* (pp. 83–103). Hillsdale, NJ: Lawrence Erlbaum.

Snow, C. (1994, March). *Learning to read a second time: Influence of L1 and L2 oral proficiency.* Plenary given at AAAL Annual Conference, Baltimore, MD.

Snow, C., Cancino, H., de Temple, J., & Schley, S (1991). Giving formal definitions: A linguistic or metalinguistic skill? In E. Bialystok (Ed.), *Language processing in bilingual children* (pp. 90–112). Cambridge: Cambridge University Press.

Solokov, J., & Snow, C. (1994). The changing role of negative evidence in theories of language development. In C. Gallaway & B. Richards (Eds.), *Input and interaction in language acquisition* (pp. 38–55). Cambridge: Cambridge University Press.

Spada, N., & Lightbown, P. (1993). Instruction and the development of questions in L2 classrooms. *Studies in Second Language Acquisition, 15*(2), 205–224.

Sperling, M., & Woodlief, L. (1997). Two classrooms, two writing communities: Urban and suburban tenth-graders learning to write. *Research in the Teaching of English, 31*(2), 205–239.

Sprinthall, N. A., Reiman, A. J., & Thies-Sprinthall, L. (1996). Teacher professional development. In J. Sikula (Ed.), *Handbook of research on teacher education* (2nd ed., pp. 666–703). New York: Macmillan.

Stanovich, K. (1980). Toward an interactive-compensatory model of individual differences in the development of reading fluency. *Reading Research Quarterly, 1,* 32–71.

Stansfield, C. W., & Kenyon, D. (1996). Simulated oral proficiency interviews: An update. *ERIC Digest.* Washington, DC: ERIC Clearinghouse on Languages and Linguistics (Report No. EDOFL 9606).

Sternberg, R. J., & Horvath, J. A. (1995). A prototype view of expert teaching. *Educational Researcher, 24*(6), 9–17.

Stone, A., & Forman, E. (1988). Cognitive development in language-learning disabled adolescents: A study of problem-solving performance in an isolation-of-variables task. *Learning Disabilities Research, 3*(2), 107–114.

Sullivan, P. (2000). Spoken artistry: Performance in a foreign language classroom. In J. K. Hall & L. S. Verplaetse (Eds.), *Second and foreign language learning through classroom interaction* (pp. 73–90). Mahwah, NJ: Lawrence Erlbaum.

Swaffar, J., & Vlatten, A. (1997). A sequential model for video viewing in the foreign language curriculum. *Modern Language Journal, 81*(2), 175–188.

Swain, M. (1995, March). *Collaborative dialogue: Its contribution to second language learning.* Paper presented at the American Association of Applied Linguistics Conference, Long Beach, CA.

Swain, M., & Lapkin, S. (1996). Interaction and second language learning: Two adolescent French immersion students working together. *Modern Language Journal, 82*(3) pp. 292–311.

Swan, K. (1999). *Nonprint media and technology literacy standards for K–12 teaching and learning* (Report Series No. 12013). Albany, N.Y.: National Research Center on English Learning and Achievement.

Tajfel, H. (1981). *Human groups and social categories: Studies in social psychology.* Cambridge: Cambridge University Press.

Tajfel, H. (Ed.). (1982). *Social identity and intergroup relations.* Cambridge: Cambridge University Press.

Takahashi, E., Austin, T, & Morimoto, Y. (2000). Social interaction and language development in a FLES classroom. In J. K Hall & L. S. Verplaetse (Eds.), *Second and foreign language learning through classroom interaction* (pp. 139–159). Mahwah, NJ: Lawrence Erlbaum.

Tannen, D. (1989). *Talking voices: Repetition, dialogue and imagery in conversational discourse.* Cambridge: Cambridge University Press.

Tedick, D. J., & Tischer, C. A. (1996). Combining immersion experiences and pedagogy for language teachers: Lessons learned and changes implemented. *Foreign Language Annals, 29*(3), 415–427.

Tharp, R., & Gallimore, R. (1988). *Rousing minds to life: Teaching, learning and schooling in social context.* Cambridge: Cambridge University Press.

Tharp, R. G., & Gallimore, R. (1991). *The instructional conversation: Teaching and learning in social activity.* Washington, DC: National Center for Research on Cultural Diversity and Second Language Learning.

Tomasello, M. (1999). *The cultural origins of human mind.* Cambridge: Harvard University Press.

Tomasello, M., Conti-Ramsden, G., & Ewert, B. (1990). Young children's conversations with their mothers and fathers: Differences in breakdown and repair. *Journal of Child Language, 17*, 115–130.

Tomasello, M., Kruger, A. C., & Ratner, H. H. (1993). Cultural learning. *Behavioral and Brain Sciences, 16,* 495–552.

Toohey, K. (1998). "Breaking them up, taking them away": ESL students in Grade 1. *TESOL Quarterly, 32*(1), 61–84.

Torres-Guzman, M. (1998). Language, culture and literacy in Puerto Rican communities. In B. Perez (Ed.), *Sociocultural contexts of language and literacy* (pp. 99–122). Mahwah, NJ: Lawrence Erlbaum.

Tulviste, P. (1991). *The cultural-historical development of thinking.* New York: Nova Science Publishers.

Tunnell, M., & Jacobs, J. (2000). *Children's literature, briefly.* Upper Saddle River, NJ: Merrill/Prentice Hall.

Tyler, A., & Davis, C. (1990). Cross-linguistic communication missteps. *Text, 10*(4), 385–411.

Valdes, G. (1998). The construct of the near-native speaker in the foreign language profession: Perspectives on ideologies about language. *ADFL Bulletin, 29*(3), 4–8.

van der Veer, R., & Valsiner, I. (1994). The problem of the environment. In R. van der Veer & I. Valsiner (Eds.), *The Vygotsky reader* (pp. 338–354). Oxford: Blackwell.

van Ek, J. A. (1986). Objectives for foreign language learning. *Scope, 1.* Strasbourg, France: Council of Europe.

van Lier, L. (1996). *Interaction in the language classroom: Awareness, autonomy and authenticity.* New York: Longman.

Van Patten, B., & Cadierno, T. (1993). Explicit instruction and input processing. *Studies in Second Language Acquisition, 15,* 225–241.

Verplaetse, L. S. (2000). Mr. Wonder-ful: Portrait of a dialogic teacher. In J. K. Hall & L. S. Verplaetse (Eds.), *Second and foreign language learning through classroom interaction* (pp. 221–242). Mahwah, NJ: Lawrence Erlbaum.

Vygotsky, L. S. (1978). *Mind in society: The development of higher psychological process.* Cambridge, MA: Harvard University Press.

Vygotsky, L. S. (1981). The genesis of higher mental functions. In J. V. Wertsch (Ed. and Trans.), *The concept of activity in Soviet psychology.* Armonk, NY: M.E. Sharpe.

Vygotsky, L. S. (1986). *Thought and language.* Cambridge, MA: MIT Press.

Vygotsky, L. S. (1987). Thinking and speech. In R. W. Reiber and A. S. Carton (Eds.) (N. Minick, Trans.), *The collected works of L. S. Vygotsky, Vol. 1: Problems of general psychology.* New York: Plenum.

Vygotsky, L. S., & Luria, A. (1994). Tool and symbol in child development. In R. van der Veer & J. Valsiner (Eds.), *The Vygotsky reader.* Oxford: Blackwell.

Walz, J. (1998). Personalizing foreign language instruction with world wide web home pages. In D. Alley & P. Heusinkveld (Eds.), *Dimension* (pp. 57–72). Valdosta, GA: SCOLT Publications.

Warren, B., & Rosebery, A. S. (1996). "This question is just too, too easy!": Students' perspectives on accountability in science. In L. Schauble & R. Glaser (Eds.), *Innovations in learning environments for education* (pp. 97–125). Mahwah, NJ: Erlbaum.

Warschauer, M. (2000, March). *Technology and literacy in the 21st century.* Paper presented at TESOL 2000, Vancouver, BC.

Weber, R.-M. (1991). Literacy in the U.S. *Annual Review of Applied Linguistics, 12,* 172–189.

Wells, G. (1993). Reevaluating the IRF sequence: A proposal for the articulation of theories of activity and discourse for the analysis of teaching and learning in the classroom. *Linguistics and Education, 5,* 1–17.

Wells, G. (1996). Using the tool-kit of discourse in the activity of learning and teaching. *Mind, Culture, and Activity, 3*(2), 1–22.

Wells, G. (1999). *Dialogic inquiry: Toward a sociocultural practice and theory of education.* Cambridge: Cambridge University Press.

Wertsch, J. V. (1991). *Voices of the mind: A sociocultural approach to mediated action.* Cambridge, MA: Harvard University Press.

Wertsch, J. V. (1994). Mediated action in sociocultural studies. *Mind, Culture, and Activity, 1,* 202–208.

Wertsch, J., & Tulviste, P. (1992). L. S. Vygotsky and contemporary developmental psychology. *Developmental Psychology, 28*(4), 548–557.

Weyers, J. (1999). The effect of authentic video on communicative competence. *Modern Language Journal, 83*(3), 339–349.

Whitley, M. S. (1993). Communicative language teaching: An incomplete revolution. *Foreign Language Annals, 26*(2), 137–154.

Wiggins, G. (1993). Assessment: Authenticity, context, and validity. *Phi Delta Kappan, 75*(3), 200–214.

Wiggins, G. (1998). *Educative assessment: Designing assessments to inform and improve student performance.* San Francisco, CA: Jossey-Bass.

Winter, R. (1996). Some principles and procedures for the conduct of action research. In O. Zuber-Skerritt (Ed.), *New directions in action research* (pp. 14–27). London: Falmer Press.

Wittgenstein, L. (1966). *Lectures and conversations on aesthetics, psychology, and religious belief.* C. Barrett (Ed.). Oxford: Blackwell.

Wong-Fillmore, L., Ammon, P., McLaughlin, B., & Ammon, M. S. (1985). *Final report for learning English through bilingual instruction.* Berkeley, CA: University of California at Berkeley.

Wood, D., Bruner, J., & Ross, G. (1976). The role of tutoring in problem-solving. *Journal of Child Psychology and Psychiatry and Applied Disciplines, 17,* 89–100.

Wortham, S. (1992). Participant examples and classroom interaction. *Linguistics and Education, 4,* 195–218.

Wray, A. (1992). *The focusing hypothesis: The theory of left hemisphere lateralised language re-examined.* Amsterdam: John Benjamins.

Wu, H.-F., de Temple, J., Herman, J., & Snow, C. (1994). "L'animal qui fait oink!oink!": Bilingual children's oral and written picture descriptions in English and French under varying conditions. *Discourse Processes, 18,* 141–164.

Zebroski, J. T. (1994). *Thinking through theory: Vygotskian perspectives on the teaching of writing.* Portsmouth, NH: Heinemann.

Author Index

Aebersold, J.A., 171, 175
Alderson, J.C., 171, 172
Aljaafreh, A., 33
Ammon, M.S., 37
Ammon, P., 37
Anderson, V., 179, 182
Anton, M., 33, 35, 94, 95
Apple, M., 113
Applebee, A.N., 203
Arata, K., 169
Ash, D., 48
Austin, T., 28, 84, 93

Bachman, L., 13, 119
Baker, C., 78
Bakhtin, M.M., 3
Bandura, A., 85
Bangert-Drowns, R., 177
Barnes, D., 80, 81
Barnhardt, S., 116, 117, 118, 119
Barnwell, D., 119
Barton, D., 5, 199, 202
Becker, J., 3
Berk, L.E., 34
Berman, R., 26, 27
Bernhardt, E., 169, 171
Bialystok, E., 17
Bicknell, J., 206
Bloom, B., 88
Bloom, S., 56
Bodrova, E., 118
Boggs, S., 26
Bouton, L.F., 54
Bowers, C.A., 45
Boyd, M., 35, 86
Bradac, J., 141
Braun, C., 179
Breiner-Sanders, K., 119
Britton, J., 200
Brooks, F.B., 94, 95
Brown, A., 48
Brown, A.L., 85
Brown, J.D., 108

Bruner, J., 26, 31, 37
Bullock, D., 51
Burgess, T., 200
Butterworth, G., 87
Byram, M., 18

Cabello, B., 48
Calero-Breckheimer, A., 172
Campione, J., 48
Canale, M., 12, 13
Cancino, H., 26
Carlsen, W.S., 48
Carrell, P., 169, 171
Carter, K., 49
Cazden, C., 80, 81
Cazden, C.B., 78, 79, 199, 203, 216
Celce-Murcia, M., 14, 15, 16, 56, 120, 121, 146, 159,
     178, 207
Cenoz, J., 17
Chamot, A.U., 93
Chang-Wells, G.L.M., 78
Chen, Q., 171
Cho, K.-S., 179, 185
Chomsky, N., 12, 25, 55
Clare, L., 83
Clark, H., 138
Clark, J.L., 115
Clay, M.M., 199
Clifford, R.T., 115
Cohen, E., 57
Cole, M., 199
Cole, S., 173
Commins, N., 172
Conti-Ramsden, G., 26
Cook, G., 37
Cook, V., 17, 18, 94, 95
Cooper, P.J., 96
Cope, B., 48
Corrie, C., 173
Coupland, J., 141
Coupland, N., 141
Crookes, G., 92
Cummins, J., 17

Davis, C., 10
Davis, J., 232
de Temple, J., 26, 28
Delett, J., 116, 117, 118, 119
Detterman, D., 87
Devine, J., 169, 171
Diaz, R.M., 17, 34
DiCamilla, F., 33, 35, 94, 95
Dien, T., 10
Dixon, C., 48
Donato, R., 33, 39, 91, 92, 93, 94, 95
Donin, J., 171
Doughty, C., 91
Dubreil, S., 173
Duff, P., 35, 36
Dunn, W.E., 91
Duranti, A., 7
Durgunoglu, A., 172
Durst, R.K., 202
Dutch, J., 181
Dworin, J., 202
Dyson, A.H., 202

Edelsky, C., 79
Eder, D., 79
Edwards, A.D., 78
Eisterhold, J.C., 169, 171
Elley, W., 179
Emerson, C., 3
Erickson, E., 10
Eskey, D.E., 169, 171
Ewert, B., 26

Falodun, J., 91
Faust, M.A., 117
Field, M.L., 171, 175
Fielding, L.G., 179
Firth, A., 17, 91
Fischer, K., 51
Fisher, S., 10
Fitzgerald, J., 172
Flinders, D., 45
Flower, J., 201
Fly, P., 45, 48, 78, 79
Foley, K., 149
Forman, E.A., 51, 83, 87
Foster, M., 10
Fradd, S.H., 113
Frawley, W., 119
Friedrich, G., 200

Gallimore, R., 83, 171
García, G.E., 171, 172
Garvin, R.A., 34
Gass, S.M., 91, 92
Gee, J., 4, 5
Genesee, F., 17, 94
Giles, H., 141
Godwin-Jones, B., 145
Goetz, E.T., 172
Goldenberg, C., 83, 88
Goodwin, G., 138, 140
Goodwin, M.H., 138, 140
Gordon, A., 48
Grabe, W., 169, 172, 201, 202, 204
Graesser, A.C., 56
Green, J., 48
Grosse, C., 113
Grossman, P., 49
Gumperz, J., 3, 9, 10
Gutierrez, K., 45, 48, 78, 79, 81, 82, 83

Hadley, A.O., 115, 136
Hafer, T., 169
Hall, J.K., 4, 11, 25, 79, 81, 82, 91, 97, 149, 169, 232
Halliday, M., 35
Hamayan, E., 116
Hamilton, M., 5, 202
Hammadou, J., 169, 171
Hancin-Bhatt, B.J., 172
Haneda, M., 169, 199, 202
Harkness, S., 6
Hasan, R., 35
Hasen, N., 17
Haviland, J.B., 10
Hayes, J., 201
Head, F.A., 232
Heath, S.B., 10, 171, 202, 203
Herman, J., 28
Herron, C., 173
Hirose, K., 172
Holzman, L., 34
Horvath, J.A., 49, 50, 107, 111
Howatt, A., 94
Hymes, Dell, 3, 9, 11, 12, 17

Ivanic, R., 5

Jacobs, J., 179, 181, 185
Jiménez, R.J., 171, 172
John-Steiner, V., 55, 199

Johnson, P., 141
Johnstone, B., 35

Kalantzis, M., 48
Kalekin-Fishman, D., 232
Kanagy, R., 91
Kaplan, R., 201, 202, 204
Katriel, T., 10
Keefer, C.H., 6
Kellough, N.G., 90, 91
Kellough, R.D., 90, 91
Kenyon, D., 116
Kevorkian, J., 116, 117, 118, 119
Kieffer, M.A., 117
Kim, D., 149
Kinginger, C., 28
Knutson, E.K., 171
Koda, K., 172
Kornfeld, G., 232
Kowal, M., 92
Kramsch, C., 3, 17
Krashen, S., 25, 55, 56, 91, 92, 94, 179, 181,
    185, 210
Kreuter, B., 48, 78
Krueger, M., 17
Kruger, A.C., 35

Lamoureux, E.L., 10
Lantolf, J.P., 33, 34, 91, 119
Lapkin, S., 33
Larsen-Freeman, D., 64
Larson, J., 48, 78
Lave, J., 30, 39, 51
Lee, C., 33, 48, 83, 199
Lemke, J., 45
Lensmire, T.J., 48, 202
Leong, D.J., 118
Leontiev, A.A., 19, 38
Leontiev, A.N., 25, 26
Lerner, G., 138
Levy, E., 26
Light, P., 87
Lightbown, P.M., 86
LoCastro, V., 54
Long, M., 91
Lotan, R., 57
Lowe, P., 119
Luke, A., 113
Luke, C., 145
Lyster, R., 54, 86

Mackey, A., 86
Magliano, J.P., 56
Maloof, V., 35, 86
Mandelbaum, J., 139
Mangubhai, F., 179
Martin, N., 200
Matusov, E., 46
McCafferty, S.G., 34
McCarty, T., 10
McCormick, D., 33, 91, 93
McGee, 113
McHoul, A., 80
McLaughlin, B., 17, 37
McLeod, A., 200
Meath-Lang, B., 232
Meehan, T., 55
Mehan, H., 80
Meinbach, A., 185
Miles, J., 119
Miramontes, D., 172
Moerman, M., 10
Moll, L., 31, 45, 202, 203
Morgan, C., 18
Morimoto, Y., 28, 84, 93
Morson, G.S., 3
Mulac, A., 141
Murison-Bowie, S., 61

Nadeau, A., 172
Nagy, W.E., 172
Nakagawa, K., 48
Nation, R., 17
Nayak, R., 17
Nellen, T., 118
Nelson, K., 26
Newman, F., 34
Nicoladis, E., 17, 94
Ninio, A., 26
Nystrand, M., 48, 78, 80, 82, 83, 96

O'Hair, D., 200
O'Malley, J.M., 93, 116, 117
Ohta, A.S., 33, 86, 94
Oxford, R., 93

Palincsar, A.S., 85
Panese, M., 10
Panofsky, C.P., 199
Paradis, J., 94
Pash, D., 89

Patthey-Chavez, G.G., 83
Pearson, P.D., 171, 172, 179
Peralta-Nash, C., 181
Person, N.K., 56
Peters, A., 26
Phillips, J., 25, 58
Phillipsen, G., 5
Philp, J., 86
Pianta, R., 49
Pica, T., 91, 92
Pierce, L.V., 116, 117
Pine, J., 26, 27
Pomerantz, A., 139
Poole, D., 79
Posner, G., 203
Purves, A., 174
Pyathas, G., 138

Raimes, A., 201
Ramirez, A., 136
Rampton, B., 11
Ranta, L., 86
Ratner, H.H., 35
Ravitch, D., 58
Raya, P., 51
Reddy, M.J., 2
Reiman, A.J., 229
Rennie, J., 115, 116
Rigg, P., 210
Robinson, P., 91
Rogers, T., 174
Rogoff, B., 46
Roit, M., 179, 182
Romney, D.M., 179
Romney, J.C., 179
Rosebery, A., 83
Rosen, H., 200
Rosenblatt, L., 169
Ross, G., 31
Rotenberg, E., 51
Rothlein, L., 185
Rubin, D., 169, 172, 173, 202
Rudnitsky, A., 203
Rueda, R., 83, 229, 230
Rutherford, M., 48
Rymes, B., 89

Sanders, R., 138, 140
Sarangi, S., 11

Sasaki, M., 172
Schegloff, E., 138
Schley, S., 26
Schmidt, R., 87, 92
Scholes, R., 169
Scribner, S., 199
Shannon, N.B., 232
Sherzer, J., 10
Shotter, J., 30
Shulman, L., 49
Shultz, J., 10
Simonds, C., 96
Sims-Holt, G., 10
Slobin, D., 26, 27
Smagorinsky, P., 33, 45, 48, 78, 79, 199
Smith, L.W., 199
Snow, C., 26, 28, 172
Sokolov, J., 26
Soter, A., 174
Spada, N., 86
Sperling, M., 79, 202, 203
Sprinthall, N.A., 229
Stanovich, K., 172
Stansfield, C.W., 116
Sternberg, R., 49, 50, 87, 107, 111
Stone, A., 87
Sullivan, P., 35, 37
Super, C.M., 6
Swaffar, J., 173
Swain, M., 12, 13, 33, 92
Swan, K., 61, 177
Swender, E., 119

Tajfel, H., 4
Takahashi, E., 28, 84, 93
Tannen, D., 35
Tedick, D.J., 231
Terrell, R., 48, 94, 210
Terrell, T., 55, 56
Tharp, R., 83, 171
Thies-Sprinthall, L., 229
Thurrell, S., 14
Tischer, C.A., 231
Tomasello, M., 26, 27, 29, 35
Toohey, K., 48
Torres-Guzman, M., 10
Tulviste, P., 25
Tunnell, M., 179, 181, 185

Tyler, A., 10

Valdes, G., 17
Valsiner, I., 29
van der Veer, R., 29
van Ek, J.A., 13
van Lier, L., 33, 83
Varonis, E.M., 91
Verplaetse, L.S., 35, 85, 96
Vlatten, A., 173
Vygotsky, L.S., 25, 26, 29, 30, 31, 34, 35, 37, 83, 118,
    199, 201, 204

Wagner, J., 17, 91
Walz, J., 113
Warren, B., 83
Warschauer, M., 61, 177
Watahomigie, L., 10
Weber, R.-M., 169
Wells, G., 30, 31, 33, 39, 46, 48, 78, 82, 83, 169, 186,
    199, 201, 202, 216
Wenger, E., 30, 39, 51

Wertsch, J., 25, 27, 29, 30, 92
Westgate, D.P.G., 78
Weyers, J., 179
White, C., 46
Wienmann, J., 200
Wienmann, M., 200
Wiggins, G., 85, 116
Williams, J., 91
Winter, R., 64
Wittgenstein, L., 2
Wong-Fillmore, L., 37
Wood, D., 31
Woodlief, L., 79, 202, 203
Wortham, S., 48
Wray, A., 7
Wu, H., 28

Zarate, G., 18
Zebroski, J.T., 199
Zoltan, D., 14

Subject Index

AAAL (American Association for Applied Linguistics), 233

AATF (American Association of Teachers of French), 233

AATG (American Association of Teachers of German), 233

AATSP (American Association of Teachers of Spanish and Portuguese), 233

Accommodate, 141

Accommodation, 141–142

Achievement strategies, 16

Acquisition, process of, 26

ACTFL (American Council on the Teaching of Foreign Languages), 115, 119, 233, 234

ACTFL Performance Standards, 121

ACTFL Proficiency Guidelines, 120

Action words for teacher questions, 89

Actional competence, 14, 15

Actional skills for e-mail, 146

Activity analysis, 152

Acts in SPEAKING model, 9

Adjacency pairs, 14

Advanced degrees for professional development, 231

AERA (American Educational Research Association), 234

Aesthetic activities, 169–170

Aesthetic communicative activities, 174

Affective dimension of intercultural communicative competence, 18

Affective dimensions of learning, 96–98

Alternative assessment, 116–117

American Association for Applied Linguistics (AAAL), 233

American Association of Teachers of French (AATF), 233

American Association of Teachers of German (AATG), 233

American Association of Teachers of Spanish and Portuguese (AATSP), 233

American Council on the Teaching of Foreign Languages (ACTFL), 115, 119, 233, 234

American Educational Research Association (AERA), 234

Analysis domain, 89

Analytical rubrics, 122, 219

Analyzing data, 68

Anaphoric reference cues, 207

Application domain, 89

Assessment, 113

   demonstrations as, 116

   designing, 155–160, 187–191, 219–220

   dimensions of, 113–118

   peer, 117

   projects and exhibitions as, 116

   purposes of, 113

   sources of data for, 113–118, 121

   student, 117

   student journals as, 116

   teacher observations as, 116

   traditional means for foreign language classroom, 115–116

Assessment tools

   designing effective, 118–125

   steps for designing, 121–125

Assessment validity, 118

Asynchronous communication, 145

Asynchronous interaction, 143

Asynchronous media, 145

Audio–lingual methods of grammar teaching, 55

Authentic assessment, 116

Avoidance strategies, 16

Back channel cues, 96

Backchannel, 15

Basic skills, 61

Behavioral dimension of intercultural communicative competence, 18

Bilateral convergence, 141

Bilinguals, 17

Bloom's taxonomy of cognitive abilities, 108

Bloom's taxonomy of cognitive objectives, 88–89

Book flooding programs, 179

CALICO (Computer Assisted Language Instruction Consortium), 234

California Achievement Test, 114

Caregiver–child conversation, 27
Celce-Murcia et al. model of communicative competence, 159, 178, 207
Chapter tests, 155
Chat room, 145
Chomsky's theory of language, 25
Clarification requests, 86
Classroom communities, 142
Classroom discourse, 78–88
    typical patterns of, 80–83
Cognitive aspects of writing, 201–202
Cognitive complexities, 138–142
Cognitive dimension of intercultural communicative competence, 18
Cognitive strategies, 93
Collaborative writing teams, 211
Communication, 2–9
    study of, 9–11
Communication Goal, 25
Communication goal for learning languages, 19
Communication goals, 58
    designing curricular activities around, 59–60
Communication modes, 58
Communication Standard, 16
Communications strategies domain, 120
Communicative ability, van Ek's model of, 13
Communicative activities, 7, 147, 174–177
    choosing, 142–145, 204–207
    everyday, 10
Communicative competence, 11–16
    Canale and Swain's early model of, 12
    framework for curriculum design and evaluation, 12
    model of, 13
Communicative components, 146
    identifying the, 146, 177–178, 207
Communicative event, 9
    formal, 10
Communicative language ability, Bachman's model of, 13
Communicative roles, 4
Communities, goals for, 58
Communities of learners, 45–50
    contextual characteristics of effective, 48
    definition of, 45–46
    goals of, 45–46
    teacher role in constructing, 49
Comparisons, goals for, 58
Composing sentences, 214–215
Comprehensibility domain, 120
Comprehension domain, 88, 120

Computer Assisted Language Instruction Consortium (CALICO), 234
Computer-mediated communication, 28
Connections, goals for, 58
Connector, 181
Consciousness-raising tasks, 53
Construction skills, 61
Content knowledge of teachers, 49
Content standards for foreign language learning, 57–59
Content validity of assessment tool, 118
Context-based classroom interaction, 93
Contextualization cues, 10, 11
Contingency managing, 86–87
Conventional meanings, 7, 8
Conventions, dissolution of, 11
Corrective feedback, 85–86
Course syllabus, 109
Creativity in communication, 7–9
Criterion-based tests, 155
Criterion-referenced tests, 114
    scoring criteria for, 122
Critical framing, 51, 54, 55, 151–152, 154, 159, 215–216
    assessing learning outcomes from, 191
    instructional activities, 183–184
Critical literacies, 61
Cultural awareness domain, 120
Cultural factors, 16
Cultures, goals for, 58

Daily lessons, 110
Daily planning, 108
Data
    analyzing, 68
    disseminating, 69
    reflecting on, 68–69
    revising, 68–69
    sources of, 65–68
Data for assessments, sources of, 121
Definite articles, 53
Demonstrations as assessment, 116
Descriptive statements, 66
Designing assessment, 155–160, 187–191, 219–220
Designing instruction for interpersonal communicative activities, 142
Development, nature of, 25
Diagnostic assessment, 113
Dictionary use in overt instruction, 150

Direct teaching, 87
Discourse competence, 12, 14–15
Discourse conventions, 53–54
Discourse skills, 178, 207
    for e-mail, 146
Discrete-point grammar and vocabulary tests, 155
Discussion leader, 181
Divergence, 141
Documents, official, 67
Drafting stage of writing, 201
Dyadic interactions, 139

Efferent communicative activities, 174
Efferent interpretive activities, 170–171
Electronic mail, 145
Electronic networks, 236–237
Emoticons, 146
Ends in SPEAKING model, 9
Ethnography of speaking, 9, 10, 11
Evaluation domain, 89
Evaluation norms and standards, 119–125
Evaluative statements, 67
Explaining, 87
Explicit correction, 86
Expressive communicative activities, 204
Expressive purpose, 199, 200

Face validity of assessment tool, 119
Father–child interaction, 27, 28
Feedback groups, 211
Feeding back, 85–86
Field notes, 66
First language development, 26–27, 28
First language skills, 171–172
Focus-on-form instruction, 53
Foreign language classroom,
    means for assessment in, 115–116
    studies of, 28
Foreign language learners, communities of, 46
Foreign language learning
    organizing instruction for effective, 50–59
    private speech in, 34
Form-focused instructional talk, 91–92
Form-function process of language acquisition, 27
Formal communicative events, 10
Formative assessment, 113
Formative portfolio, 117
Free composing, 217
Free reading, 185

Genre comparison, 215–216
Genre familiarity, 171
Genre in SPEAKING model, 9
Goals, 108
Grade equivalent score, 114
Grades, 125
Grading, 125–126
Grammar teaching, role of, 55–56
Grammar-translation methods, 55
Grammatical choices, 3, 6
Grammatical components of communicative
        competence, 12
Grammatical knowledge, 13

High school students, characteristics of, 46–47
High schools, focus of, 46
Holistic rubrics, 122, 219
Humor, 8–9
    use of, 96–97
Hypertext, 177

Illocutionary knowledge, 13
Imitation, 34–36
Improvisations, 217
    as transformed practice, 153
In-service mentoring programs, 232
Indefinite articles, 53
Individual instruction, 56
Information, disseminating, 69
Information Literacy Standards for Student Learning, 61
Information maps, 183
Initiation–Response–Evaluation (IRE), 80–83
Input, 91
Input enhancement, 53, 91–92
Input-oriented research, 91
Instruction, 203
Instructional activities, 147, 178
    connecting learning opportunities to, 147–153,
        178–186, 208–217
    creating, 146–155, 178–187, 207–218
Instructional conversations (IC), 83–88
Instructional objectives, 108
    benefits in language classrooms, 108
Instructional plans, preparing, 109–113
Instrumentalities in SPEAKING model, 9
Intellectual characteristics of middle and high school
        students, 47
Interaction, 138
    cognitive and social underpinnings of, 138–142

Interactional activities, 137, 142
Interactional strategies, 16
Interactive means for community, 96–98
Interactive process of language acquisition, 27
Intercultural communicative competence, 18, 19
Intercultural communicators, 18
Interdisciplinary teams, 46
Intermediate level learners, 120
International Reading Association (IRA), 234
International Society for Intercultural Education,
        Training and Research (SIETAR), 234
Internet, 177, 205
Internet Relay Chat (IRC), 145
Interpersonal activities
    familiarity with, 138–139
    past experiences in, 138–139
Interpersonal communication mode, 109
Interpersonal communicative activities
    designing instruction around, 142–155
    media resources for, 143–145
    technological resources for, 143–145
Interpersonal mode, 136–137
    of communication, 19, 58
Interpretation strategies, 16
Interpretive communication mode, 109
Interpretive communicative activities
    designing instruction around, 174–187
    technological media and resources for, 177
Interpretive mode, 169–171
    designing assessment for, 187–191
    of communication, 19, 58
Interviews, 65–66
Intonation, 3, 10
Iowa Test of Basic Skills, 114
IRA (International Reading Association), 234

Journal sharing,
    responsive, 82–83
    responsive/collaborative, 82–83
Journals, personal reflection, 67

Key in SPEAKING model, 9
Knowledge domain, 88

L1, 95
    role in classroom of, 94–96
L2, role in classroom of, 94–96
Language code, 10

Language competence, 13
Language control domain, 120
Language experience approach, 210
Language functions, Celce-Murcia's key areas of, 15
Language logs, 150
Language play, 37
Learning center, 57
Learning environments created by teachers, 49
Learning opportunities, 147
    designing, 51–56
Learning strategies, 92
Lesson planning, components of, 110–112
    role of textbooks in, 113
Lexical choices, 3, 6
Lexical forms, choice, 10
Linguistic anthropology, 9, 10
Linguistic competence, 12, 14, 15
Linguistic forms, 6
Linguistic means for community, 96–98
Linguistic resources, 3–4, 7, 8, 9, 11
    conventional meanings in, 7–9
    knowledge of, 49
Linguistic skills, 178, 207
    for e-mail, 146
Listenability, 172–173
Listener feedback cues, 15
Literate activities, 10
Literature circles, 181
    self-assessment by students in, 189
    teacher assessment in, 189
Literature review, 67
Logs, 67
Long-range planning, 107

Making connections, 208, 210
Meaning making, 34
Meaning-making resources, 29
Media resources for interpersonal communicative
        activities, 143–145
Mediational means, 29–30
    learning new, 30
Mentoring programs, 232
Metacognitive strategies, 92
Metalinguistic feedback, 86
Middle school students, characteristics of, 46–47
Middle schools,
    features of exemplary, 46–47
    focus of, 46

Miscommunication, 10–11
Mismatched cultural styles, 11
MLA (Modern Language Association), 234
Modeling, 84–85
Modern Language Association (MLA), 234
Monolinguals, 17, 18
Morphology, 15
Mother–child interaction, 27, 28
MUD Object-Oriented (MOO), 145
Multi-User Dimension (MUD), 145
Multicompetence, 16–18
Multiparty interactions, 139

*National Educational Technology Standards for
    Students*, 61
National Foreign Language Communities Standard, 55
*National Foreign Language Comparisons and Cultures
    Standards*, 54
National Foreign Language Content Standards, 50
National Foreign Language Standards, 109, 115
National Standards for Foreign Language Learning, 2,
    245–246
Natural Approach, 55, 56
Nature of development, 25
Needs analysis, 142
Negotiated interaction, 53, 92
Negotiation-oriented research, 91
Netique, 146
New London Group, 50, 51, 54, 55, 208
Noninterventionist approach to language teaching, 56
Nonverbal communicative factors, 16
Norm-referenced tests, 114
Norms for evaluation, 119–125
Norms in SPEAKING model, 9
Novice learners, 120

Official documents, 67
Open interviews, 66
Open questionnaires, 66
OPI, 115, 155
Oral Proficiency Interview (OPI), 115, 155
Orthography, 15
Output by students, 92
Output-oriented research, 91
Overt instruction, 51, 52–54, 55, 150–151, 152, 154,
    155, 181–183, 184, 211–215
    assessing learning outcomes from, 191
Overt teaching, 87

Panel on Educational Technology, 61
Paralanguage, 10
Paralinguistic features, 3
Paralinguistic resources, 11
Paraphrasing, 215
Participant observation, 66–67
Participant observer, 66
Participants in SPEAKING model, 9
Participation structure, 153–154
    choosing a, 186–187, 217–218
    for learning, 56–57
Past experiences in interpersonal activities, 138
Past experiences with reading, 171
Pausing, 3
Pedigogical content knowledge of teachers, 49
Pedigogical knowledge, 50
Peer assessments, 117
Peer review groups, 211
Peer tutoring, 56
Percentile score, 114
Performance-based measures for interpretive mode,
    187–188
Performance-based rubrics, 159
Performance-based standards, 115, 119
Personal reflection journals, 67
Phonology, 15
Physical characteristics of middle and high school
    students, 47
Pitch, 10
Planning for instruction, 107–108
Play in communicative development, 36–38
Portfolio, 117
Portfolio assessment, 117–118
Pragmatic knowledge, 13
Pre-advanced learners, 120
Predicting, 183–184
Prefixes, 53
Presentational communication mode, 109
Presentational communicative activities, 204
    assessment rubric for, 219, 220
    designing instruction around, 203–218
    technological media and resources for, 205–207
Presentational mode, 199–200
Presentational mode of communication, 19, 58
Preservice field experiences, 232
Prewriting stage, 201
Principles for learning additional languages, 38
Prior topic knowledge, 171

Private speech, 34

Probing questions, 90

Professional development, 230–231
  advanced degrees for, 231
  possibilities for, 231–237

Professional development centers, 231

Professional electronic networks, 236–237

Professional organizations, 232–234

Projects and exhibitions as assessment, 116

Proofreading, 201

Prosodic cues, 10

Prosodic features, 3

Prosodic pattern, 8

Psychological characteristics of middle and high school
    students, 47

Psychological nature, 26

Questioning by teacher, 87

Questionnaires, 66

Rating scale for assessment, 123

Reader's Theatre, 185–186, 187

Recasts, 35, 86, 96

Reciprocal Teaching, 85

Records of performance, 67

Reformulations, 96

Relevant identities in interactions, 139–140

Repartee, 37

Repetition, 34–36, 86, 96
  ineffective, 36

Research process, steps in, 64–69
  guidelines for, 69

Resources for teaching, 113

Responsive/collaborative journal sharing, 82–83

Responsive journal sharing, 82–83

Revising stage of writing, 201

Rhetorical competence, 14, 15

Rhetorical skills, 178, 207

Rhetorical structures, 3, 6, 53

Role play, 36

Role playing, 148–149

Scaffolding, 31–33, 83, 93
  specific strategies for, 31–33

Scholastic Aptitude Test (SAT), 114

Scoring rubrics, 122

Second language classrooms, studies of, 28

Second language learning, private speech in, 34

Second language skills, 171–172

Semantic webbing activity, 182–183

Semistructured interviews, 66

Semistructured questionnaires, 66

Shared reading, 179, 181, 186
  self-assessment by students in, 179, 181, 189
  teacher assessment in, 189

SIETAR (International Society for Intercultural
    Education, Training, and Research), 234

Simulated Oral Proficiency Interview (SOPI), 116

Situated practice, 51–52, 55, 147–150, 208–211
  instructional activities, 179–181

Situation in SPEAKING model, 9

Social aspects of writing, 202–203

Social characteristics of middle and high school
    students, 47

Social contextual factors, 16

Social identities, 4–7, 139–140
  conventional meanings in, 7–9
  dissolution of, 11

Social nature of development, 26

Socioaffective strategies, 93

Sociocultural competence, 14, 15–16

Sociocultural model of effective professional
    development, 230–231

Sociocultural perspective on language learning, 25–38

Sociocultural skills, 178, 207
  for e-mail, 146

Sociolinguistic components of communicative
    competence, 12

Sociolinguistic knowledge, 13

Sociolinguistic markers, 53

SOPI, 155

Sound play, 37

SPEAKING model, 9

Speech act pattern analysis, 151–152

Speech act sets, 53

Speech acts, 3, 15, 53

Standardized tests, 114

Standards-based assessment, 115

Standards-based instruction, 119

Standards for evaluation, 119–125

Standards for the English Language Arts, 61

Stanine score, 114

Story puzzles, 182

Strategic competence, 13, 14, 16

Strategic components of communicative competence, 12

Strategic skills, 178, 207
  for e-mail, 146

Strategy instruction, 93

Stress, 3, 10
Structured interviews, 65–66
Structured questionnaires, 66
Student advisory groups, 46–47
Student assessments, 117
Student journals as assessment, 116
Student self-assessment tools, 159
Student–student relationships, developing effective, 50
Stylistic appropriateness factors, 16
Suffixes, 53
Summarizing, 215
Summative assessment, 113
Summative portfolio, 117–118
Sustained Silent Reading (SSR), 185, 187, 217
Syllabus, 109
Synchronous interaction, 143, 144
Synchronous media, 145
Syntactic form, 8
  use of, 10
Synthesis domain, 89
Systematic intervention activities, 53
Systemically valid assessment tool, 118–119

Talking journals, 149–150, 153
Target language communities, 142
Task structuring, 87–88
Teacher, role of the, 48–50
Teacher expertise, 50
Teacher-made tests, 114, 155
Teacher observations as assessment, 116
Teacher questions, 88–91
Teacher research, 64
  process of, 64–69
Teacher–student relationships, developing effective, 50
Team learning, 57
Technological media for presentational communicative
    activities, 205–207
Technological resources for interpersonal communicative
    activities, 143–145
Technological resources for presentational
    communicative activities, 205–207
Technology, integrating in foreign language curriculum,
    60–63
Technology and Literate Thinking Research Strand of the
    National Research Center on English Learning
    and Achievement, 61
  technology standards of, 61, 62–63

Tempo, 3
Tests, 67
Text analysis, 184
Textbooks, 113
Textual knowledge, 13
Time-gaining strategies, 16
Topical choices, 3
Traditional assessment, 114
Transactional activities, 136, 140, 142
Transactional communicative activities, 204
Transactional purpose, 199–200
Transformative role of writing, 203
Transformed practice, 51, 54–55, 152–153, 216–217
  instructional activities, 184–186
Turn-taking patterns, 3, 10, 14
Two-dimensional goal-oriented continuum, 137

Unilateral convergence, 141
Unit, developing a, 109
Unit planning, 107–108, 109

van Ek's model of communicative ability, 13
Venn diagrams, 216
Verb inflections, 53
Verbal dueling, 37
Visual literacy, 173
Vocabulary, 15
Vocabulary domain, 120
Vygotsky's genetic law of development, 26
Vygotsky's theory of learning, 25

Web page, personal, 201
Webfolio, 118
Whole–group instruction, 56
Word coinage, 37
Word finder, 181
World Wide Web, 113, 145, 177, 201, 205, 206
  skills needed for, 177
Writing
  cognitive aspects of, 201–202
  from different perspectives, 216
  social aspects of, 202–203
Writing groups, 211

Zone of proximal development (ZPD), 30–31, 34,
    35, 83